D0385850

# IN THE FIELD

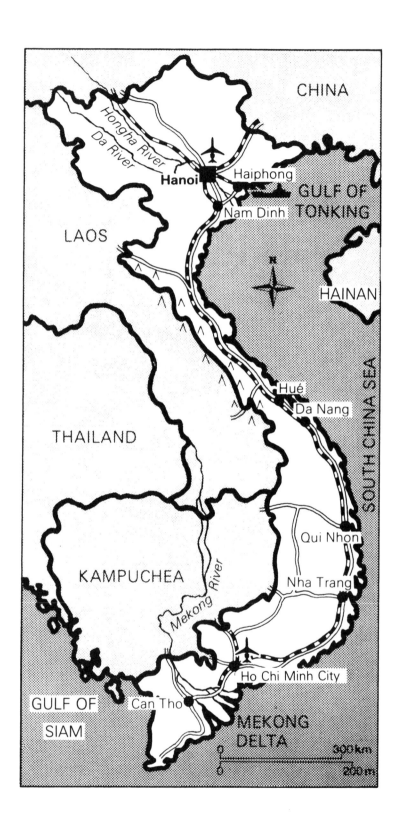

CHINA

Hongha River

Da River

Hanoi

Haiphong

GULF OF
TONKING

Nam Dinh

LAOS

HAINAN

THAILAND

Hué

Da Nang

SOUTH CHINA SEA

Qui Nhon

KAMPUCHEA

Mekong River

Nha Trang

Ho Chi Minh City

GULF OF
SIAM

Can Tho

MEKONG
DELTA

300 km

200 m

# IN THE FIELD

## THE LANGUAGE OF
## THE VIETNAM WAR

**Linda Reinberg, Ph.D.**

Facts On File
*New York • Oxford*

**In the Field**

Copyright © 1991 by Linda Reinberg, Ph.D.

All rights reserved. No part of this book may be reproduced or utilized in any form or by any means, electronic or mechanical, including photocopying, recording, or by any information storage or retrieval systems, without permission in writing from the publisher. For information contact:

Facts On File, Inc.
460 Park Avenue South
New York NY 10016
USA

Facts On File Limited
Collins Street
Oxford OX4 1XJ
United Kingdom

**Library of Congress Cataloging-in-Publication Data**
Reinberg, Linda.
   In the field: the language of the Vietnam War / [Linda Reinberg].
      p.  cm.
   Includes bibliographical references and index.
   ISBN 0-8160-2214-3 (alk. paper)
   1. Soldiers—United States—Language (New words, slang, etc.)
—Dictionaries.  2. Vietnamese Conflict, 1961-1975—Language (New
words, slang, etc.)—Dictionaries.  3. United States— History,
Military—20th century—Dictionaries.  4. Military art and science-
-United States—Dictionaries.  5. English language—United States-
-Slang—Dictionaries.  6. Americanisms—Dictionaries.  I. Title.
PE3727.S7R4   1990
427—dc20                                              90-41550

A British CIP catalogue record for this book is available from the British Library.

Facts On File books are available at special discounts when purchased in bulk quantities for businesses, associations, institutions or sales promotions. Please call our Special Sales Department in New York at 212/683–2244 (dial 800/322–8755 except in NY, AK or HI) or in Oxford at 865/728399.

Jacket design by Donald West
Composition by Facts On File
Manufactured by Maple-Vail Manufacturing Group

Printed in the United States of America

10 9 8 7 6 5 4 3 2 1

This book is printed on acid-free paper.

# FOREWORD

Since the resurgence of interest in the Vietnam War began, hundreds of novels and nonfiction books have been written. Still, there are holes in the literature that require filling. *In the Field* is a quick and handy reference to the myriad terms and many languages we spoke in Vietnam. I keep poking around in it, finding new and interesting tidbits.

I say languages because if one has spent time talking with Vietnam combat vets, as Linda Reinberg has, he or she will notice that grunts and gunbunnies, doorgunners and LRPs, have vocabularies different from each other, and very different from those spoken by REMFs. Marines communicated differently than paratroopers; advisors next door could sound a world apart. The author has gotten just about every term associated with the war down on paper, and defined each succinctly and accurately. Slang is particularly well represented, but bureaucratic jargon, hardware, acronyms and geography are all here too.

*In the Field* may well become recognized as the standard reference to our bewildering and imaginative languages. It will be indispensable to writers, vets, students and others and is an important contribution to our understanding of this long and divisive conflict.

John M. Del Vecchio
Author of *The Thirteenth Valley* and
*For the Sake of All Living Things*

To Alan, my husband and best friend.
To our daughters Debbie, Susan, Julie, and Melissa.

With special thanks to Steve M.

To the fifty-eight thousand,
and to all who served our country
during the Vietnam War.

And in memory of John W.

# AUTHOR'S NOTE

"I haven't been called a 91-bedpan for 20 years!" a former medic said to me on the phone when he was making a first appointment.

"Wow, I haven't heard of an I & I since 1968," said a member of one of my rap groups.

"My job was . . . what was that word for a parachute rigger?" a vet asked me during a session.

I wrote this book because I wanted the colorful language and terms that servicemen and women used during the Vietnam War to be remembered. Vietnam War fiction and nonfiction contain vocabulary and terminology special to that time and place. These words, phrases, slang expressions, acronyms and nicknames should not become extinct.

I limited the entries in this book to those for which I found at least two sources: either two written sources, one written and one oral source (from a vet), or two oral sources (from two vets). I soon learned that there were differences in terms used depending on the year of service, the branch of the military and the location within Vietnam. One could be an FNG, a fenugie, a newby, a twink, a greenseed, a cherry boy, or other terms, all meaning that one was new in-country. One could fire an elephant gun, a thumper, a burp gun, or a blooker, and it would in all cases be an M–79 grenade launcher. One could swallow a Monday pill, a CP pill, a horse pill or Commander Orange, and it would be the same antimalaria tablet. There were well over a dozen ways to say that someone got killed. Spelling of specific terms and the use of hyphens and spaces were variable as well. Until May 1990 *Time* used Viet Nam, while *Newsweek* referred to Vietnam. Cross-references to similar terms are indicated by small capital letters.

Like most projects of this kind, it became larger than expected. A few of the entry words are not associated solely with the Vietnam War, but I included some words and phrases if they were used or heard at all in Vietnam, and would be useful to those interested in this subject.

I am the sole author of this volume, and I take full responsibility for it, including its errors. I would welcome hearing from vets with additions and corrections. Please write to me at:

> 1771 Post Road East
> Suite 209
> Westport, CT 06880

> Linda Reinberg, Ph.D.
> Westport, Connecticut

# IN THE FIELD

# A

**A Shau Valley** a harsh and uninhabited area in THUA TIEN PROVINCE near the border of Laos. It was a main entry to the HO CHI MINH TRAIL and a North Vietnamese Army base in 1966. A number of U.S. and South Vietnamese operations were carried out there in attempts to dislodge the NVA throughout 1968 and 1969, and many bloody battles ensued. The area, however, remained a Communist stronghold in South Vietnam during most of the war.

**AA** 1. abbr. for Air-to-Air weapon. 2. abbr. for Antiaircraft Artillery. 3. abbr. for Airman Apprentice.

**AAA** abbr. for Anti-Aircraft Artillery, also called the Triple A.

**Aardvark** nickname for the F–111, General Dynamic's swing-wing attack aircraft. It was also nicknamed the Edsel and the TFX.

**abn** abbr. for airborne.

**aboard** marine or navy term for on a base or on a ship.

**abort** to cancel or stop a mission or flight for any reason other than enemy action.

**Abrams, Creighton W.** chief of staff, U.S. Army 1972–1974. Prior to that, he was deputy commander, Military Assistance Command, Vietnam (MACV), 1967–1969, and commander, MACV, 1969–1972. Abrams nickname was Honest Abe.

**AC** 1. abbr. for Acting Commander. 2. abbr. for Army Corps. 3. abbr. for Air Corps.

**A/C** abbr. for Aircraft Commander (also spelled AC).

**ACAV** abbr. for Armored Cavalry Assault Vehicle, an M-113 ARMORED PERSONNEL CARRIER. It was modified for use in Vietnam and was usually armed with FLAMETHROWERS and mounted machine guns. It was also called Big Boy, Dragon Lady and Zippo. Pronounced "á cav."

**Accelerated Pacification Campaign** the plan begun in November 1968 by the Government of Vietnam and the United States under William COLBY for increasing government control of 1,200 previously contested or VIET CONG-dominated hamlets. REGIONAL FORCES and POPULAR FORCES were used for this program, which was to be carried out within three months but was not successful in destroying the Viet Cong power in the villages.

**acceleration maneuver** aerial term for a low-speed YO-YO maneuver.

**ace** 1. a pilot who has downed five enemy aircraft; an unofficial but generally understood term in aerial warfare. 2. Marine slang for killing or being killed.

**ace of spades** a card that was the symbol of death to the Vietnamese people and was placed on enemy dead to frighten them. United States playing card manufacturers sent packages of the ace of spades to the troops in Vietnam to be used just for this purpose.

**acft** abbr. for aircraft.

1

**Acheson, Dean**   one of the WISE OLD MEN, a group of American academicians, statesmen, and military experts who advised President Lyndon Johnson about the Vietnam War.

**ACLU**   abbr. for American Civil Liberties Union. An organization founded in 1920 to defend the civil rights of all U.S. Citizens. The ALCU was involved in many court cases during the Vietnam War of war protesters, the right of people to gather and other constitutional issues.

**ACM**   abbr. for Air Combat Maneuvering, or dogfighting. Also called ACT for Air Combat Tactics.

**AC–119K**   the Fairchild Stinger transport aircraft and gunship.

**acoubuoy**   a sensor activated by noise; often buried with only its antenna exposed above ground.

**ACOUSID**   abbr. for Air Dropped SEISMIC INTRUSION DEVICE.

**acoustic sensors**   remote control devices used by U.S. troops to pick up voices and movements. Dropped from aircraft, these sensors drifted by parachute, catching in trees near enemy trails and base areas.

**ACP**   abbr. for Automatic Colt Pistol.

**ACR**   abbr. for Armored Cavalry Regiment, referring to tanks and ARMORED PERSONNEL CARRIERS as well as INFANTRYMEN.

**Acting Jack**   slang for the acting NCO (noncommissioned officer). These were usually privates first class who were needed as sergeants and were temporarily given that rank, but continued to draw the paychecks of PFCs.

**ACTIV**   abbr. for U.S. Army Concept Team in Vietnam. These teams evaluated communication and other problems of army units in the field and worked out solutions with the assistance of modern technology.

**activate**   putting a unit on the active list and making it available for quick organization by the assignment of personnel.

**ACTOV**   abbr. for the Accelerated Turnover Plan. This plan involved reducing U.S. troops in South Vietnam and gradually turning the war over to the Vietnamese.

**actual**   the unit commander. This term distinguished the commander from the radioman when call signs were used.

**AD**   1. abbr. for Air Division. 2. abbr. for Accidental Discharge. 3. abbr. for Active Duty.

**ADA**   abbr. for Americans for Democratic Action. This liberal organization—one of whose founders was Hubert Humphrey—lobbied against the war in Vietnam.

**ADF**   abbr. for Automatic Direction Finder, a receiver that can detect signal strength and give bearings to transmitters.

**adjutant**   a staff officer who takes care of all official correspondence with the exception of combat orders.

**admin**   abbr. for administration.

**Admino**   abbr. for Administrative Officer.

**ADSID**   abbr. for Air-Delivered SEISMIC INTRUDER detection. This device consisted of a microphone and a transmitter; it was dropped into questionable areas to sense sounds of motion and wire them back.

***adv***    abbr. for advanced.

***Advanced Individual Training***
eight weeks of advanced training after basic training, usually referred to as AIT, in any one of several specialties, such as medic, dog handler, or mechanic. It is sometimes confused with Advanced Infantry Training, a special training for infantrymen.

***aerorifle platoon***    a platoon of 44 to 50 enlisted men and one officer joined as a light airmobile infantry group and sent on missions by helicopter as assault teams. Part of an AIR CAVALRY troop the platoon was called a BLUE TEAM.

***aeroscout platoon***    an observation unit of the AIR CAVALRY called a WHITE TEAM.

***AFB***    abbr. for Air Force Base.

***AFBRVN***    abbr. for Air Force Base Republic of Vietnam, where U.S. Air Force facilities were housed.

***AFC***    1. abbr. for Airman First Class. 2. abbr. for AIR FORCE CROSS.

***AFFE***    abbr. for Army Forces, Far East, including U.S. troops in Vietnam.

***AFHQ***    abbr. for Air Force Headquarters.

***A–5***    the Vigilante, a fast-strike aircraft, used by the U.S. mainly as a two-seat tactical reconnaissance aircraft. This aircraft introduced numerous new technological devices, including the capacity to eject a nuclear bomb.

***AFM***    abbr. for Air Force Manual.

***AFN***    abbr. for Allied Forces Network, the radio station run by the U.S.

military, playing songs currently popular in THE WORLD for the troops in Vietnam.

***A–4***    the Douglas SKYHAWK, a single-seat, light attack jet bomber used on U.S. Navy carriers and with land-based U.S. Marine attack squadrons. Also called Scooter, Tinkertoy, and Heinemann's Hotrod.

***AFPAC***    abbr. for Army Forces in the Pacific, including U.S. troops in Vietnam.

***AFQT***    abbr. for Armed Forces Qualification Test. This test was given to all volunteers and draftees who were classified into five categories according to test scores. A special remedial program was set up for minorities so that they could be accepted into the military despite lower scores. See PROJECT 100,000.

***AFSC***    abbr. for American Friends Service Committee, a private Quaker organization that had several service projects in Vietnam during the war. This organization is still involved with such projects as supplying medicines and other needed items to orphanages in Vietnam. 2. abbr. for Air Force Specialty Code, a numerical code for assigned jobs in the air force, the equivalent of NEC (Navy) and MOS (army and marines).

***afterburner***    the mechanism used to provide jet aircraft with added power needed during take-off or ascents. Extra fuel is put into the afterburner, the temperature rises, and the jet's speed increases.

***AFUS***    abbr. for Air Force of the United States.

***AFVN***    abbr. for Armed Force Vietnam Network, the U.S. Armed Forces radio and television network in Vietnam broadcast from Saigon, delivering music and news to military personnel.

**AGCT**    abbr. for Army General Classification Test, an examination given to recruits to place them into specialties.

**Agency, The**    nickname for the CENTRAL INTELLIGENCE AGENCY.

**Agent Orange**    one of several defoliants that were designated by the color stripe on the container, as Agent White, Agent Purple, and so forth. Defoliants were used by the U.S. military to destroy enemy cover and to prevent the enemy from growing needed crops. Agent Orange is a mixture of 2,4–D, 2,4,5–T, and dioxin; more than 11 million gallons were sprayed between 1965 and 1970. Agent Orange is believed to cause many types of illnesses to those directly exposed to it or indirectly exposed through the food chain or drinking water. Chloracne, a severe skin condition, as well as certain cancers and neurological conditions, and other diseases are associated with Agent Orange exposure. It is also believed to cause miscarriages in the wives of men exposed, as well as infant deaths and birth disorders in their children. There is documentation of 65,000 children with birth defects fathered by servicemen exposed to Agent Orange. A lengthy and complex lawsuit against the manufacturers of Agent Orange was settled in 1984 with a $180 million award. Final plans for disbursement of the funds were made in 1989.

**AgitProp**    abbr. for Agitation Propaganda, a Communist term meaning revolutionary agitation and propaganda of ideological indoctrination.

These techniques were most used during the early stages of the war.

**AGL**    abbr. for Above Ground Level.

**AGM**    abbr. for Air-to-Ground Missile.

**Agnew, Spiro**    Vice-President of the United States from 1969 to 1973 under President Richard Nixon. Agnew resigned in 1973 in the midst of a financial scandal. He strongly opposed the antiwar groups.

**AGO**    abbr. for Adjutant General's Office.

**agrovilles**    resettlements of South Vietnamese. The purpose was to protect Vietnamese peasants from the Viet Cong. Many new communities were built under this program, though the peasants were reluctant to leave their homelands. The program resulted in resentment against the government of Ngo Dinh Diem, which abandoned the agroville program in 1961.

**A-Gunner**    abbr. for Assistant Gunner.

**AH–1**    the Bell single-rotor, armed helicopter. See COBRA.

**AHQ**    abbr. for Army (or Air) Headquarters.

**AID**    abbr. for Agency for International Development. This U.S. agency administered economic aid to countries around the world, including South Vietnam. Also referred to as USAID for United States Agency for International Development.

**aileron**    aerial term for wing surface used to control the rolling of an aircraft.

**aim-dot**    aerial term for an electronic dot appearing on a radar scope when radar has located a target and is locked on. It is also called DOT and STEERING DOT.

**AIM–4D** the Falcon air-to-air missile.

**aiming error** aerial term for the deviation of the actual aim point from the desired aim point.

**AIM–9** the Sidewinder air-to-air missile.

**AIM–7** the Sparrow air-to-air missile.

**air** slang for air power, usually meaning fighter-bombers.

**air abort** the cancellation of an aircraft mission for any reason other than enemy action, at any time from takeoff to mission completion.

**Air America** at one time a private airline, later funded by the CIA and linked to the U.S. State Department. Based in Taiwan, Air America rented its services in Vietnam and was often used for secret operations throughout Asia. After the PARIS PEACE ACCORDS, Air America helicopters were used to protect air transportation of the International Commission of Control and Supervision (ICCS).

**air burst** an explosive device (artillery, mine, or grenade) set to detonate before touching the ground. Thus, it enhanced the killing radius of the SHRAPNEL.

**Air Cavalry** often called simply the Air Cav, these were helicopter-borne infantry assault teams and helicopter gunship assault teams. Blue teams, white teams, and red teams referred to aerorifle (assault teams) platoon units, observation platoon units, and armed helicopter platoon units.

**Air Force Cross** see DISTINGUISHED FLYING CROSS.

**Air Mattress** nickname for the Third Brigade of the 82d Airborne Division. See ALL AMERICAN.

**Air Medal** an award in the name of the president of the United States for single acts of merit or heroism or meritorious service while participating in aerial flight. Awards following the first are indicated by bronze numerals. The Air Medal ranks just below the Meritorious Service Medal.

**air mobile** an infantry unit having its own squadron of helicopters or unrestricted access to them.

**air support** military term for bombing.

**Air Vietnam** the airline of South Vietnam. It was used by the South Vietnamese and the U.S. military and operated throughout the war and after.

**airboat** a shallow draft watercraft used on the inland waterways of Vietnam. With a crew of two and up to five soldiers plus their gear, they could move at 40 knots. These airboats were designed after those used in the Florida Everglades.

**airborne** 1. soldiers who are qualified as parachutists. 2. any personnel or piece of equipment dropped by parachute. Also called AIRMOBILE.

**airborne command center** the U.S. Air Force aircraft which controlled large ground or air operations.

**airborne platform** a square support with adjustable legs on which a HOWITZER could be placed when the ground was too wet to support it.

**aircraft**  helicopters or fixed-wing planes.

**aircrew**  a full complement of air officers and airmen who operated an aircraft. Aircrew was often shortened to crew.

**airmobile**  personnel or equipment delivered by helicopter; also referred to as airborne.

**airops**  abbr. for air operations.

**airstrike**  bombing attacks by planes.

**air-to-ground**  gunnery, or bombing from aircraft against surface targets; also called air-to-mud.

**air-to-mud**  slang for gunnery, or bombing from aircraft against surface targets; also called air-to-ground.

**AIT**  abbr. for ADVANCED INDIVIDUAL TRAINING.

**AJ**  abbr. for ACTING JACK.

**AK**  short for AK–47

**AK/SKS**  Soviet-built automatic and semiautomatic rifles, used by the North Vietnamese and Viet Cong, respectively, during the Vietnam War.

**AK–50**  a later version of the AK–47. Some AK–50s had triangular bayonets mounted on them, which inflicted sucking wounds that were very difficult to close.

**AK–47**  the standard infantry piece of the North Vietnamese and Viet Cong soldier, the Kalashnikov assault rifle. A fully automatic 7.62 mm assault rifle of Soviet design, it was the basic individual weapon of the Communist forces during the Vietnam War. It was named after its Russian inventor

and was thought to be a highly effective and reliable weapon.

**Albatross**  nickname for the HU–16 Grumman amphibian plane.

**Alcatraz**  a particularly high-security prisoner of war camp near Hanoi in North Vietnam. Especially troublesome U.S. military prisoners were held there.

**Alcoholics Anonymous**  nickname for the 82nd Airborne Division. See ALL AMERICAN.

**ALICE**  abbr. for All-purpose Lightweight Individual Carrying Equipment, the standard Marine field pack.

**All-African**  nickname for the 82nd Airborne Division. See ALL AMERICAN.

**All-Afro**  nickname for the 82nd Airborne Division. See ALL AMERICAN.

**ALL AMERICAN**  most common nickname of the 82nd Airborne Division, taken from the two As on its shoulder patch, signifying All American. Other nicknames were All-African, All-Afro, Air Mattress, Alcoholics Anonymous, Almost Airborne, and Eighty Deuce. Some nicknames were derived from beliefs that there was racial imbalance within the division, and that there were many heavy drinkers. Others may have stemmed from envy toward a proud and tough unit.

**Alliance of National, Democratic, and Peace Forces**  South Vietnamese opposition front organization established under the auspices of the NATIONAL LIBERATION FRONT in 1968. This was an effort by the Communists to include non-Communist, nationalist forces in a collaboration against the South Vietnamese administration.

**allies** those who fought on the side of the United States and South Vietnam. The United States had the assistance of the armies of several other countries: South Korean combat troops included the TIGER DIVISION, Blue Dragon Brigade, White Horse Infantry Division, Capital Division, and Ninth Infantry Brigade. Australia was represented by the First Battalion, Royal Australian Regiment, First Australian Task Force, and a Special Air Service Squadron. Bangkok participated with the Royal Thai Army Volunteer Force, and the Philippines sent a construction battalion.

**alligator clip** the quick-release toggle fastener that attached the IBS DOUGHNUT rope to another craft. It was also called a gator clip.

**ALMAR 65** an order of the U.S. Marine Corps commandant in 1969 to reduce racial tension and discrimination. Black Power salutes and Afro haircuts became acceptable.

**Almost Airborne** sarcastic nickname for the 82nd Airborne Division. See ALL AMERICAN.

**Aloha Airlines** the name of an aviation unit that was part of the 25th Infantry Division, stationed at CU CHI. This unit, nicknamed the 25th Wolfhounds, adopted this name to show their appreciation for the time they spent in Hawaii.

**alpha** the military phonetic for the letter A.

**Alpha Bravo** phonetic alphabetization for ambush.

**Alpha Sierra** phonetic alphabetization for air support.

**Alpha Strike** a preplanned bombing mission against given targets in North Vietnam. These were usually large missions, using all of a carrier's offensive aircraft.

**ALQ-51** a broadband ECM deception system.

**ALQ-71** a noise jamming ECM pod.

**ambl** abbr. for AIRMOBILE.

**ambulatory** those wounded in action who were able to walk, also referred to as ROUTINE DUSTOFFS.

**ambush** a surprise attack.

**ambush academy** slang for coursework on jungle warfare or unconventional warfare.

**Ambush Alley** part of Highway Route 9 near Khe Sanh nicknamed by U.S. soldiers because of numerous and treacherous Viet Cong ambushes.

**AMEMB** abbr. for American Embassy.

**Ameri** slang for AMERICAL Division.

**Americal** name for the 23d Infantry Division, disbanded and deactivated in November 1971 because of its poor performance generally. The 23d was the only named division in the U.S. Army. It was formed from a group sent to New Caledonia at the beginning of World War II, and the name is a combination of American and New Caledonia. The Americal Division was also called Americalley, Amerikill, Atrocical, and other insulting nicknames because of its role in the massacre of civilians at MY LAI.

**Americalley**  insulting nickname for the AMERICAL Division, used after the MY LAI INCIDENT.

**American Legion**  a service organization of honorably discharged United States veterans.

**Amerikill**  insulting nickname for the AMERICAL Division, called that because of the MY LAI INCIDENT.

**ammo**  abbr. for ammunition.

**ammo dump**  a safe place where live or spent ammunition was stored.

**ammo humper**  slang for INFANTRYMAN.

**AMTRAC, AMPHTRAC**  an amphibious tractor mounted with machine guns and able to cross water barriers.

**AmVets**  a service organization of American veterans who served in the U.S. military after 1940.

**An Giang**  one of the 44 provinces of South Vietnam, located in IV CORPS.

**An Loc**  capital of Binh Long Province.

**An Long**  a village of the Tam Chim District on the banks of the Mekong River. It is noted for a large stone fortress left there from the French colonial era.

**An Quang**  the militant arm of organized BUDDHISTS in South Vietnam.

**An Xuyen**  one of the 44 provinces of South Vietnam, located in IV CORPS.

**ANC**  abbr. for Army Nurse Corps.

**anchor**  nickname for aerial refueling tracks.

**ANDPF**  abbr. for the Alliance of National, Democratic, and Peace Forces, which was a South Vietnamese opposition group trying to gain support from the populace. This group and the NATIONAL LIBERATION FRONT combined as the Provisional Revolutionary Government. See PRG.

**angel**  1. affectionate nickname for the American nurse. 2. slang for a helicopter that hovered near a carrier to pick up pilots who had crashed.

**angel track**  nickname for Armored Personnel Carrier used as an aid station.

**Angel's Wing**  area shaped like an angel's wing in southern Vietnam near the Cambodian border.

**angels**  term for altitude in thousands of feet. Thus, "angels two zero" is 20,000 feet.

**angle-off**  aerial term for the angle between the longitudinal axis of a defender and the line of sight of an attacker.

**ANGLICO**  abbr. for Air and Naval Gunfire Liaison Company, an organization of marine and navy personnel. They were qualified to control naval gunfire and to choose air support for units other than U.S. Marines. They also supported U.S. airborne units, Rangers, and allied foreign forces.

**ANGRY–109**  slang for the AN–109 radio used by SPECIAL FORCES units for long-range communication.

**anh (chi, em) khỏe không?**  Vietnamese for "How are you?" Often answered *Không duoc khoe,* meaning good or well. Also spelled *anh (chi, em) chỏe không?*

**anh (chi, em) tên gì?**  Vietnamese for "What is your name?"

**animal, the** slang for the device that detonated 12 to 20 CLAYMORE mines at the same time. It was also called the monster.

**Animals, The** a rock group that sang one of the troops' favorite songs, "We've Gotta Get Out of This Place."

**AN/MRC–34** the standard VHF radio with a flyswatter-shaped antenna.

**Annam** name of the former protectorate that was part of French Indochina. Its area was roughly that of the Central Highlands and Central Lowlands in Vietnam, between Cochin China and Tonkin.

**Annamite Mountains** a large mountain chain in South Vietnam.

**antipersonnel weapon** official euphemism for a weapon that kills people.

**AN–TVS–2** a STARLIGHT SCOPE.

**AO** 1. abbr. for AREA OF OPERATIONS. 2. abbr. for Aerial Observer, the lookout who watches the ground from a helicopter.

**ao baba** the traditional dress of Vietnamese peasants. It resembled pajamas and was usually black.

**ao dai** the traditional dress of Vietnamese women consisting of trousers and a long tunic split all the way up the sides.

**AOBC** abbr. for Armored Officers' Basic Course, a nine-week course for Army Officers at Fort Knox, Kentucky.

**AOC** 1. abbr. for Aviation Officer Candidate. 2. abbr. for Air Operations Center.

**AOD** abbr. for administrative officer on duty.

**A–1E** the Douglas Skyraider, a propeller-driven, single-engine attack aircraft (also known as the AD–5), used mainly for ground support. Its nicknames were Spad and Sandy.

**AP** 1. abbr. for Armor-Piercing Ammunition; also called AP rounds. 2. abbr. for Armor-Piercing. 3. abbr. for Ambush Patrol, a squad or platoon-sized patrol whose main assignment is to attack enemy forces who enter their KILL ZONE, and attack from a hidden position. 4. abbr. for Air Police. 5. abbr. for Anti-personnel.

**áp** Vietnamese for hamlet.

**Ap Bac** site of the South Vietnamese Army's first major defeat in a battle with the Viet Cong in January 1962.

**Ap Bia Mountain** hill 937 was known for the fierce battles in which the U.S. Army, Marines, and the South Vietnamese Army fought against the North Vietnamese Army in May 1969. The 10-day battle resulted in heavy casualties for both sides. No real objectives were met. Although U.S. troops "captured" the hill, it was soon abandoned and the North Vietnamese recaptured the hill the following month. This battle became known as Hamburger Hill because of the level of bloodshed, and because the conflict became known as the "meat-grinder."

**Ap Doi Moi** Vietnamese for "New Life Hamlet." See STRATEGIC HAMLET PROGRAM.

**Ap Moi Hamlet Program** see STRATEGIC HAMLET PROGRAM.

**AP rounds**  abbr. for Armor-Piercing ammunition, sometimes shortened to AP.

**ấp tan sin**  Vietnamese for a secure HAMLET.

**APB**  abbr. for armored patrol boat.

**APC**  see ARMORED PERSONNEL CARRIER.

**APD**  abbr. for Airborne Personnel Detector. See PEOPLE-SNIFFER.

**APH–5**  abbr. for the helmet worn by GUNSHIP pilots and crewmen.

**APO**  abbr. for Army and Air Force Post Office in San Francisco for overseas mail to Vietnam.

**apparatus**  a generally used term for the Communist political organization.

**apron**  the part of an airport where planes are parked. Also called a ramp.

**APU**  abbr. for Auxiliary Power Unit, an outside source of power used to start aircraft engines.

**ARA**  1. abbr. for Aerial Rocket Artillery, a term for helicopter gunships. 2. abbr. for Australian Regular Army.

**Arc**  RECONNAISSANCE nickname for an electronically controlled B–52 bomb strike.

**Arc Light**  code for U.S. B–52 bombing operations over North Vietnam during the Southeast Asia War. The bombs shook the earth as far as 10 miles away from target area.

**Arc Light Strike**  see ARC LIGHT.

**ARCOM**  abbr. for the ARMY COMMENDATION MEDAL. It was also abbreviated as ArCOM.

**area of burst**  the area immediately affected by an explosion.

**area of operations**  the area involved in war actions and the administration of those actions. The place where military operations are conducted as part of an assigned mission.

**area target**  a target covering a large area, such as an airport.

**area warfare**  warfare essentially based on the destruction of the enemy, with no front or line between the opposing forces.

**areca**  the BETEL NUTS chewed by many Vietnamese.

**Arizona Territory**  nickname for an inexact area southwest of DA NANG. This region was known for sudden ambushes by the Viet Cong.

**ARM**  abbr. for the Anti-Radiation Missile developed to destroy enemy radar sites.

**Arm**  abbr. for Armored.

**Armed Forces Expeditionary Medal**  see  VIETNAM SERVICE MEDAL.

**Armed Forces Honor Medal**  see VIETNAM SERVICE AWARDS.

**armed reconnaissance**  1. mission flown where it was expected that pilots would locate and bomb enemy targets. 2. a euphemism for bombing.

**armor piercing ammunition**  ammo that penetrates armor (tanks, etc.)

**armored personnel carrier**  a tracked vehicle used to transport troops and supplies. They were frequently armed with .50 caliber machine guns and FLAMETHROWERS. Usually referred to as APCs, their nicknames included track and B–40 MAGNET.

**armored units** tanks, armored personnel carriers, and other tracked and armed vehicles.

**armpit sauce** slang for NUOC MAM, the prevalent Vietnamese sauce, made from fermented fish.

**Army Achievement Medal** an award for outstanding achievement and superior performance of duty given to enlisted men and officers of the grade of major or under.

**army banjo** slang for ENTRENCH-ING TOOL.

**Army Commendation Medal** award for outstanding performance in combat or noncombat, awarded in the name of the Secretary of Defense for acts of valor of lesser degree than that required for the Bronze Star. This medal was also called the Navy, Air Force, and Coast Guard Commenda-tion Medal. It ranks just below the Joint Service Commendation Medal.

**army green** the uniform author-ized for year-round wear for officers, warrant officers, and enlisted person-nel during the Vietnam War.

**army regulations** rules of the U.S. Army to control the activities and conduct of those in the military.

**army shade 107** the color of many items issued to soldiers, olive (or drab) green.

**ARP** 1. abbr. for an AERORIFLE PLA-TOON, also called a BLUE TEAM. 2. abbr. for Airborne Rifle Platoon, a small group which set up ambushes and conducted reconnaissance opera-tions.

**ARPA** abbr. for Advanced Research Projects Agency, which was part of the Department of Defense. It sponsored and carried out research and studies on all types of COUNTERINSURGENCY.

**ARPAC** abbr. for Army of the Pa-cific, including U.S. troops in Viet-nam.

**ARSID** abbr. for Artillery-Deliv-ered SID (SEISMIC INTRUSION DEVICE).

**Article 15** a frequently used non-judicial punishment, given by an offi-cer to an enlisted man for minor infractions.

**ARTIE/ARTY** slang for ARTILLERY.

**artillery** this unit used gunpowder weapons too large to be hand carried. The weapons are classified as light (up to 120mm), medium (121–160mm), and heavy (160mm). Artillery is often called the "king of battle," the origin perhaps stemming from the game of chess.

**artillery raid** jungle warfare in-volving CHINOOK helicopters lifting a battery of field ARTILLERY into enemy territory. The battery would fire at tar-gets located by air recon and air intel-ligence. The Chinooks then would move the battery to other positions, continuing to bewilder the enemy.

**artilleryman** member of an AR-TILLERY unit. Slang for artillerymen includes fuse lighter, cannon cocker, redlegs, gun ape, and gun bunny.

**Arvin** slang for an individual South Vietnamese soldier.

**ARVN** abbr. for the regular forces of the Army of the Republic of Vietnam, including airborne and ranger units. Referred to as the South Vietnam Army and the Army of Saigon, ARVN was also nicknamed Marvin Arvin and was not altogether respected by the U.S. troops. Pronounced "ar vin."

**ARVN attitude**  derogatory slang for a cowardly personality.

**ASAP**  abbr. for As Soon As Possible.

**ASE circle**  abbr. for the aerial term *Allowable Steering Error circle* on a radar display, provided by the fire control computer.

**ASEAN**  abbr. for the Association of Southeast Asian Nations. Established in 1967, this economic and political group was made up of Thailand, Malaysia, Indonesia, the Philippines, and Singapore. ASEAN attempted to encourage cooperation among these countries. This organization sidestepped military unity of any type; since 1975, they have been involved with security affairs.

**A–7**  the Corsair II, Ling-Tempo-Vought's light attack aircraft used by the Navy and the Air Force; also known as SLUF (short little ugly feller). Originally developed for the Navy, this single-seat attack aircraft was capable of high speed and able to carry large payloads of rockets, bombs, and cannons.

**A72**  a navy or marine 72 hour pass, the equivalent to the army's three-day pass.

**ASH**  abbr. for Assault Support Helicopter.

**ash and trash**  slang for a single helicopter carrying out a mission of flying supplies, cargo, troops, or mail. Also called ass and trash.

**Asian Cuba**  slang expression referring to Vietnam.

**Asian two-step**  slang for a krait (snake) found in the Vietnam jungle. This snake's venom is supposedly so strong that a person bitten can barely take two steps before dying. It was also called the one-step, the seven-step, and so forth.

**A–6/A6–A**  Grumman's Intruder was the most advanced twin-jet, all-weather strike aircraft in the world when it entered combat in 1965. Able to carry up to thirty 500-pound bombs, it was second only to the B–52 in ORD-NANCE capacity. The two- man crew included a pilot and a bombardier/navigator.

**asking for 6 and going airborne**  slang phrase for using the ROTATION travel allowance of six cents a mile to fly home.

**ASN**  abbr. for Army Serial (or Service) Number. In 1969 this number assigned to all servicemen and women was replaced by social security numbers.

**ASP**  1. abbr. for Ammunition Storage Point. 2. abbr. for Ammunition Supply Point.

**ASPB**  abbr. for Assault Support Patrol Boat; also known as a MONITOR.

**assets**  available helicopter and other aircraft support.

**AT**  abbr. for Antitank, referring to certain types of weapons.

**AT–3 Sagger**  a Russian antitank rocket used by North Vietnamese troops.

**ATC**  1. abbr. for Armored Troop Carrier. 2. abbr. for Air Traffic Control.

**ATC (H)** abbr. for Armored Troop Carrier (Helicopter).

**A-team** the basic 10- or 12-man team of U.S. SPECIAL FORCES. A-teams frequently led irregular military units not responsible to the Vietnamese military command.

**A–3** the Douglas Skywarrior, a large subsonic twin-engine aircraft designed for heavy attack in addition to refueling and recon. This carrier-based bomber was used only in the early days of the Vietnam War.

**A–37** an American-made jet plane used as a fighter-bomber by the Saigon air force. A heavier version called the Dragonfly was put into use in 1967.

**Atoll** an infrared heat-seeking air-to-air missile fired by Soviet-built fighters, used by North Vietnamese soldiers. It was similar to the U.S. Sidewinder.

**Atrocical** insulting nickname for the AMERICAL Division, called that because of the MY LAI INCIDENT.

**attach** to place units or personnel in an organization as a temporary assignment.

**attack aircraft** a multiweapon plane for destroying targets on the ground. It could also deliver air-to-ground ORDNANCE.

**Audie Murphied** slang for what happens when a formerly scared GI learns to love combat and becomes a gung-ho warrior. Audie Murphy was a highly decorated and respected hero of World War II.

**auger in** military pilot's term for crash.

**AUS** abbr. for Army of the United States.

**auto-getem** slang for automatic weapons fire.

**autonomous cities** South Vietnam was divided into 44 provinces and 11 autonomous cities. These cities are the capital city of Saigon, Cam Ranh, Can Tho, Dalat, Danang, Hue, My Tho, Nha Trang, Qui Nhon, Rach Gia, and Vung Tau.

**autorotation** aerial term for the free rotation of rotor blades without engine power, used for an unpowered descent. This is usually an emergency procedure.

**auto-track** automatic tracking in which a power-driven mechanism acts as a correctional or compensating device to keep a radar beam aimed at a target.

**autovon** abbr. for automatic voice network. This direct dial phone system connected U.S. military bases all over the world, including Vietnam.

**auxiliary weapons** lethal weapons carried and used by tankers though not actually mounted on vehicles. An example is the M-3 grease gun, a 30-shot, .45 caliber submachine gun.

**aviation cadet** a person in training to become an air force officer pilot.

**AVLB** abbr. for Armored Vehicle Launch Bridge, a bridge constructed as troops advanced. Able to hold up to 60 tons, it could extend over as much as 60 feet of water.

**avn** abbr. for aviation.

**AW** abbr. for Automatic Weapons, referring to those that could fire multiple rounds without having to be re-loaded.

**AWACS** abbr. for Airborne Warning And Control System. This U.S. surveillance, command, control, and communications system could operate in all weather and had the capability to participate in long-range surveillance.

**AWCC** abbr. for Air Warning Control Center, used to warn aircraft of artillery or mortar fire.

**AWL** abbr. for Absent With Leave, meaning that a serviceman or woman was given permission to be absent for an assignment.

**AWLS** abbr. for All Weather Landing System.

**AWOL** abbr. for Absent Without Official Leave, meaning to leave a post or position without permission. Consequences of going AWOL ranged from its being overlooked or ignored to being given an ARTICLE 15 or a COURT-MARTIAL.

**AWOL Bag** slang for an overnight bag.

**azimuth** a bearing or magnetic direction from North, given in degrees.

# B

**BA** abbr. for BASE AREA.

**bà** Vietnamese for Mrs. or lady.

**Ba Me Ba** a beer brewed in Saigon. Its trademark was 33 (Ba Muoi Ba in Vietnamese). It was also spelled Bameba and Ba Muoi Ba.

**ba si dế** Vietnamese for home-made whiskey made from rice.

**Ba Xuyen** one of the 44 provinces of South Vietnam, located in IV CORPS.

**baby hero** slang for a brave person.

**baby 007** slang for an Army Criminal Investigation Division agent working undercover in a unit to find drug users.

**baby shit** slang for mustard.

**baby-san** slang for Vietnamese child.

**Bac Bo** Viet Cong term for North Vietnam.

**Bac Lieu** one of the 44 provinces of South Vietnam, located in IV CORPS.

**Bac Lieu City** capital of Bac Lieu Province.

**Bach Mai Hospital** the hospital in North Vietnam presumed to have been bombed by the United States during the CHRISTMAS BOMBING in 1972.

**back** the individual occupying the back or rear seat of an F–4 aircraft. He was also called the guy in back.

**Back Porch** code for a communication system in Vietnam linked by cables and antennas with U.S. forces in Thailand. This $240 million tropospheric communication network was built through the U.S. Department of Defense.

**back time** slang for rear-area duty or off the line.

**back-scratching** slang for disposing of hostiles who have climbed onto a tank. This was usually done by firing light weapons at the turret.

**bác-sĩ** Vietnamese for doctor. Bác-si also referred to American army medics and navy and marine corpsmen.

**Bad Conduct Discharge** not an honorable discharge, but not as damaging as an undesirable or a dishonorable discharge. Given for such reasons as drug use or trouble making. Nicknamed the big chicken dinner.

**bad news** slang for the modified bulldozer tank, the M–48 Patton.

**bad paper** slang for any discharge except honorable.

**Bad-Ass Billy** nickname for General William R. Bond of the 199th Light Infantry Brigade, because of his reputation for being tough.

**badges** pin-on devices given for proficiency or experience in marksmanship or other military skills.

**bagged and tagged** slang for the procedure of processing dead soldiers.

**Bahnar** a MONTAGNARD tribe living mainly in Pleiku, Binh Dinh and Kontum provinces.

**Bailey bridge** a standard Army military bridge constructed with pre-fabricated steel panels.

**ball** see MEATBALL.

**ballgame** 1. slang for a firefight or a contact with the enemy. 2. slang for an operation.

**ballistic** something unguided, as in a missile which follows a ballistic trajectory when thrust is terminated.

**bamboo** a grass in Vietnam that grew as tall as a tree.

**bamboo telegraph** slang for word-of-mouth communication. This term was applied to both friendly and enemy sides, especially in rural regions.

**bamboo viper** a highly venomous snake in Vietnam; also called the two step because it was believed that after having been bitten, one could take only two steps before dying. Also called a one-step, seven-step, and so forth.

**bamboo whip** a spiked Viet Cong booby trap. A piece of bamboo with spikes attached was bent and wedged into place. When a trip wire was released, the whip would sweep across a trail, maiming and killing all in its path.

**bắn** Vietnamese for shooting.

**Ban Long Secret Zone** a heavily forested area near the My Tho River in South Vietnam. It was called a secret zone because of the many enemy bases and VIET CONG activity there.

**Ban Me Thuot** capital of Darlac Province. This Central Highlands town was the first target of the North Vietnamese Final Offensive. See EASTERTIDE OFFENSIVE.

**banana clip** an ammo magazine; a curved clip holding 30 rounds of ammunition.

**Band-Aid** nickname for a MEDIC, taken from the medic's MOS, 91 B.

**bandit** radio code for an aircraft identified as hostile. Over North Vietnam, bandits were color-coded: red was a MiG–17, white was a MiG–19, and blue a MiG–21.

**bandolier** device worn by GIs over their shoulders and across their chests with loops or small pockets in which cartridges or extra M–16 magazines were stored.

**Bangalore Torpedoes** the torpedoes that the North Vietnamese used to cut through the wire of FIRE SUPPORT BASES and for exploding mines. The TNT-loaded pipe had a long fuse, to give the enemy time to leave quickly after lighting it. It was named for the city of Bangalore, India, where similar devices had been used.

**Bang-clap** slang for Bangkok, Thailand, an R & R location known for its willing females during the Vietnam War.

**Banish Beach** code name for Hercules (C–130) operations during which fuel drums were dropped to start fires, depriving the Viet Cong of their forest sanctuaries.

**Bank of America** an American bank which opened a branch in Saigon to serve Americans.

**bank shot** shooting a delayed exploding shell to cause a ricochet.

**Bao Cao** a Vietnamese phrase shouted by American POWs when they needed an English-speaking guard to request medical assistance or for other needs.

***báo chí*** Vietnamese for press or news media, a common Vietnamese expression to describe journalists.

***Bao Loc*** capital of Lam Dong Province.

***bao nhiêu*** Vietnamese for "How much?" or "How many?"

**BAR** abbr. for BROWNING AUTOMATIC RIFLE.

***BAR belt*** an ammunition belt and pouch originally meant to hold five BROWNING AUTOMATIC RIFLE magazines. Later MOBILE STRIKE FORCE units used them to hold M–16 magazines.

***Barbara*** code for the SON TAY PRISON model built by the CIA. This prison near Hanoi was the object of an Army-Air Force raid on November 21, 1970, to rescue American POWs thought to be there. The SON TAY PRISON was found to be empty, but the operation raised prisoners' morale when they learned of it and caused considerable concern to the North Vietnamese.

**BARCAP** abbr. for Barrier Combat Air Patrol. This usually referred to two fighters positioned between threatened aircraft and an aircraft carrier and was often used to protect naval vessels in the area.

***barracks*** army term for shared living space, where enlisted men were housed.

***barrage fire*** artillery fire designed to fill a volume of area rather than aimed at a given target.

***barrel roll*** code for U.S. bombing missions of the HO CHI MINH TRAIL in Laos, beginning in 1964.

***base area*** 1. an area of territory having installations and defensive fortifications. 2. MACV name for an area used by the North Vietnamese as a base camp. These areas ordinarily contained supply depots, fortifications, hospitals, and training areas.

***base camp*** 1. the rear area. 2. a resupply base for field units and a location for headquarters units, artillery batteries, and air fields. 3. a semipermanent home for tactical organizations. 4. a brigade or division headquarters. 5. administrative and logistical camp for a unit, usually semipermanent and containing a unit's support elements (mess hall, supply, etc.).

***baseball*** a baseball-shaped FRAG GRENADE, about 2 1/2 inches in diameter.

***basic*** short for basic training, a recruit's first duty in the United States after enlistment or recruitment.

***basket heads*** derogatory slang for Vietnamese peasants wearing straw hats.

***basketball*** refers to illumination-dropping aircraft mission, capable of lighting approximately a square mile of terrain.

***Bassac River*** French name for the Hau Giang River in the southern part of South Vietnam.

***Batangan Peninsula*** an entrenched and heavy VIET CONG stronghold on the coast about 12 kilometers north of Quang Ngai City in South Vietnam.

**bats**  slang for the 106mm M40A1 recoilless rifle.

**battalion**  a military unit composed of a headquarters and two or more companies, batteries, or similar units, usually under the command of a major or lieutenant colonel. About 400 to 600 men made up a battalion.

**battalion days in the field**  the number of days that a BATTALION was patrolling in the field, used in measuring that battalion's effectiveness.

**battery**  in the U.S. Marine Corps and in the U.S. Army, this is a COMPANY-sized unit of artillery, about 100 officers and enlisted men.

**Battle for the Highlands**  the ferocious battle in the CENTRAL HIGHLANDS from June to December 1967. See DAK TO.

**Battle of Bunker's Bunker**  the VIET CONG attack on the U.S. Embassy grounds in Saigon, while Ellsworth Bunker was ambassador, during the TET OFFENSIVE in 1968.

**Battle of Cam Ne**  see CAM NE.

**Battle of Dak To**  see DAK TO.

**Battle of 55 Days**  see DIEN BIEN PHU.

**Battle of the Thanh Hoa Bridge**  see BRIDGE AT THANH HOA.

**Battle of the Ia Drang Valley**  the first major U.S. engagement with the North Vietnamese Army. In October and November 1965 U.S. troops first encountered MAIN FORCE VC units. The North Vietnamese withdrew, leaving heavy casualties on both sides. President Lyndon Johnson gave the First Cavalry Division the PRESI-DENTIAL UNIT CITATION, the first to be awarded during the Vietnam War.

**Battle of Xuan Loc**  See XUAN LOC.

**battle star**  a small metal star on CAMPAIGN ribbons denoting participation in a battle in that particular theater.

**battle-sight zeroing**  the process of adjusting a weapon's sights so that the weapon would hit the object it was aimed at when fired.

**bẫy**  Vietnamese for trap.

**bẫy nổ**  Vietnamese for booby trap.

**bayonet**  a long knife attached to the muzzle of a rifle to be used in close combat.

**bazooka**  early nickname for the shoulder-fired rocket launcher.

**BC**  abbr. for BODY COUNT, meaning a tally of enemy dead.

**BCD**  abbr. for BAD CONDUCT DISCHARGE.

**BCT**  abbr. for Basic Combat Training (boot camp).

**BDA**  1. abbr. for Bomb Damage Assessment, conducted at the end of each flight to estimate damage caused by a strike. The BDA included the number of people killed, number of buildings and vehicles destroyed, and so forth. 2. abbr. for Battle Damage Assessment, a similar evaluation.

**Bde**  abbr. for brigade.

**BDU**  abbr. for Battle Dress Uniform, the camouflage uniform worn in the field.

**be nice**  a slang expression used by GIs when startled or when provoked.

**beanies**   slang for SPECIAL FORCES.

**beans**   slang for any meal.

**beans and baby dicks**   slang for C-RATION hot dogs and beans.

**beans and motherfuckers** slang for unpopular C-RATION lima beans and ham.

**bear huntin' with a switch** phrase for an understaffed and lightly armed RECONNAISSANCE patrol.

**beast**   derogatory nickname for the white soldier, used by blacks and Hispanics in Vietnam.

**beaten zone**   1. the ground area struck by automatic weapon or artillery projectile fire. 2. where most of the bullets hit when a machine gun is fired.

**beaucoup** (pronounced "boo coo") French word meaning many or plenty, used often by Vietnamese, Cambodians, and Americans during the war.

**bedpan commando**   slang for an enlisted man of the Medical Corps, a medic.

**beef and shrapnel**   slang for C-RATION beef and potatoes.

**beehive rounds**   an explosive artillery shell that delivered thousands of small projectiles or metal darts resembling nails with fins rather than conventional SHRAPNEL. The first combat use of beehive rounds was by U.S. troops in late 1966.

**beehiving it**   slang for leaving quickly or getting out because of imminent danger.

**been there medal**   slang for the VIETNAM CAMPAIGN SERVICE MEDAL.

**beer can house**   slang for the houses that Vietnamese constructed by flattening and fastening together empty beer cans.

**Beer 33**   a brand of Vietnamese beer.

**Beginning of Morning Nautical Twilight**   naval term for the period of early morning when it is just becoming light.

**being interviewed for the morning papers**   slang for morning roll call.

**Bel Air**   ironic slang for a section of the HANOI HILTON prison camp.

**believer**   slang for a dead soldier, especially a dead enemy soldier.

**bell**   the U.S. Navy's system of telling time aboard ship. At 8:30 a.m. or p.m., a bell is rung once, with one bell added every half hour. When eight bells are reached, the cycle begins again. Four, eight, and twelve o'clock are thus marked by eight bells. Each four-hour cycle establishes a WATCH.

**Bell Telephone Hour**   slang for the interrogation and/or torture of Viet Cong suspects by applying electricity from field telephones to the genitals or breasts as part of the interrogation.

**below**   Marine term for downstairs.

**Below The Zone**   an unexpectedly early promotion.

**Ben Cat**   a village just north of SAIGON, one of a series of STRATEGIC HAMLETS.

**Ben Hai**   the river that flowed through the DEMILITARIZED ZONE, separating North and South Vietnam along the 17th parallel.

**Ben Het**  A U.S. fortification and Special Forces support camp close to the Cambodian border. A North Vietnamese attack on the camp in May 1969 developed into a 55-day siege. The North Vietnamese amphibious tank PT-76 was pitted against U.S. armor. The North Vietnamese then withdrew.

**Ben Suc**  a Viet Cong village in the IRON TRIANGLE north of Saigon. A major target for operation CEDAR FALLS, after the village was assaulted and secured by the U.S. Army, it was destroyed and abandoned.

**Ben Tre**  a tiny village in the MEKONG DELTA region of South Vietnam destroyed by U.S. airpower during the TET OFFENSIVE in 1968. An unidentified U.S. major was quoted as saying, "It became necessary to destroy the village in order to save it."

**bends and motherfuckers**  slang for the squat-thrust drill exercise.

**bennies**  slang for benefits. In the field, that meant a warm shower, hot food, and a cot instead of a sleeping bag.

**Benning School for Boys**  slang for Officers Candidate School at Fort Benning, Georgia.

**BENT**  abbr. for Beginning of Evening Nautical Twilight, a naval term for getting dark.

**Bent Whore**  slang for the city of Bien Hoa in South Vietnam.

**BEQ**  abbr. for Bachelor Enlisted Quarters, where single enlisted men were housed, on U.S. bases.

**berm**  1. a parapet or built-up area around a fortification or buildings on the perimeter line. 2. a rise in the ground, such as a dike. 3. the perimeter itself.

**berm line**  a built-up foliated area used to divide wet places.

**Bertrand Russell War Crimes Tribunal**  a tribunal initiated by Bertrand Russell, the writer and philosopher. Two sessions were held in 1967, and evidence was heard from many well-known scientists and legal experts. Many investigators reported U.S. war crimes in North and South Vietnam. Many U.S. Vietnam veterans gave evidence as well, and the tribunal drew the conclusion that serious war crimes had been committed. This was an unofficial group that met in Stockholm, and grew out of an antiwar parade in New York City in 1965. David Dellinger, one of the CHICAGO SEVEN, participated as a judge at the tribunal.

**betel nut**  a type of palm seed grown in Southeast Asia which was rolled in leaves and chewed by Vietnamese, staining the teeth after years of use. It is an opiate, also known as areca.

**Betty Crocker**  sarcastic slang for a Saigon warrior, one who is safe behind a desk.

**BFA**  abbr. for Blank Firing Apparatus, a metal device attached to a rifle to prevent accidental burns when shooting blanks.

**B–57**  the Martin straight-wing, two-seat bomber, Camberra. Used as a bomber in the early part of the Vietnam War, it was soon retired because of its age and lack of high speed.

**B–52**  U.S. Air Force high-altitude superbomber, the Boeing Stratofortress, an eight-engine, swept-wing, heavy jet bomber. The B–52 could carry up to ninety-six 500-pound bombs. It was nicknamed Buff and the Flying Battle Cruiser. Seven and a half million tons of bombs were dropped on Indochina by B–52s during the Vietnam War. 2. nickname for a large marijuana cigarette. 3. nickname for a church key, or can opener.

**B–5 Front**    the Communist military command working in South Vietnam in the two provinces farthest to the north.

**B–40/B–41**    1. shoulder-fired, rocket-propelled GRENADE LAUNCHER carried by VIET CONG and North Vietnamese. Similar to the American 3.5-inch rocket launcher, it was used for antitank and antipersonnel targets. The B–41 was a newer version 2. the rockets fired from the B–40.

**B–40 Magnet**    slang for the AR-MORED PERSONNEL CARRIER, thought to be easy prey for the B–40.

**B–4 Bag**    a gray canvas bag carried by a paratrooper to hold his parachute after a jump. It was also used by air force personnel to hold gear.

**bhat**    a Vietnamese money unit.

**bic**    used by GIs meaning to comprehend, from the Vietnamese word *biet*, meaning to understand.

**bicycle mine**    a booby trap in which an explosive hidden in the frame of a bicycle and connected to a firing device in the headlamps went off after a preset time interval.

**Bien Hoa**    one of the 44 provinces of South Vietnam, located in III CORPS, headquarters of III Corps Tactical Zone.

**Bien Hoa City**    capital of Bien Hoa Province, where a large air force base was located.

**Bien Hoa incident**    on November 1, 1964, the Viet Cong mortared the South Vietnam air base at Bien Hoa. Four American servicemen were killed, 72 were wounded, and 28 American aircraft were destroyed.

**big belly program**    a 1965 program which modified 80 B–52 planes to carry very large bombs inside the plane as well as additional ORDNANCE.

**big boy**    1. slang for tank, especially the armored cavalry assault vehicle armed with FLAMETHROWERS and mounted machine guns. Other nicknames were Dragon Lady and Zippo. 2. slang for ARTILLERY.

**big chicken dinner**    slang for BAD CONDUCT DISCHARGE.

**big dad**    slang for senior drill instructor.

**Big Dead One**    derogatory take off on Big Red One, the nickname of the First Infantry Division after years of heavy casualties and poor morale.

**Big Eye**    USAF airborne EC–121 early warning radar aircraft used from April 1965 to March 1967, when it became known as COLLEGE EYE.

**big orange pill**    slang for the antimalarial CHLOROQUINE-PRIMAQUINE tablet taken once a week in Vietnam.

**big pond**    slang for the Pacific Ocean.

**big PX**    Vietnamese nickname for America.

**big PX in the sky**    slang for death, as in "going to the big PX in the sky."

**big R** ROTATION home. Compare with Little R, for R & R.

**Big Red One** the nickname for the First Infantry Division, because of the red number 1 on its patch.

**big shotgun** slang for a 106mm recoilless rifle.

**big stuff** slang for ARTILLERY fire.

**Big–20** slang for a 20-year army career.

**bị mất-tích ồ chiến-trường** Vietnamese for missing in action.

**bingo** pilot term for out of gas or almost empty fuel tanks.

**Binh Dinh** one of the 44 provinces in South Vietnam, located in II CORPS. The Vietnamese words *binh dinh* mean pacified.

**Binh Duong** one of the 44 provinces of South Vietnam, located in III CORPS.

**Binh Long** one of the 44 provinces of South Vietnam, located in III CORPS.

**Binh Thuan** one of the 44 provinces of South Vietnam, located in II CORPS.

**Binh Tran** a North Vietnamese logistical unit which defended and maintained part of the HO CHI MINH TRAIL.

**Binh Tuy** one of the 44 provinces of South Vietnam, located in III CORPS.

**Binh Van** Communist political action among the North Vietnamese military.

**Binh Xuyen** the organized crime syndicate that controlled much of the Vietnamese underworld and SAIGON police until ousted by President Ngo Dinh Diem's forces in 1955. These were the Vietnamese gangs who controlled Saigon's drug trade and other activities. Many of these gang members fled to the Mekong Delta area in the southern part of South Vietnam and became part of the Viet Cong guerrilla force.

**binoctal** barbiturate sold as headache medicine in Vietnam.

**bird** slang for any aircraft, though usually referring to helicopters.

**bird colonel** slang for a full colonel, referring to the eagle on the insignia. Slang for a lieutenant colonel was light colonel.

**bird corporal** slang for a SPECIALIST FOURTH CLASS.

**birddog** 1. a light, fixed-wing observation plane, especially Cessna's O–1, a single-engine spotter plane. 2. any light observation aircraft. 3. slang for a FORWARD AIR CONTROLLER.

**bird dog, to** to work hard at something hoping to be able to cope with it.

**birdbath** nickname for the area in a motor pool where vehicles and tanks were washed, called that because it resembled a birdbath.

**bird-shit** slang for paratroopers.

**birdwatching** slang for girl watching.

**biscuit** slang for C-RATIONS.

**biscuit bitches** derogatory term for Red Cross women, though they were usually called the more affectionate DONUT DOLLIES.

**BIT** abbr. for Built-In Test, a series of fault-checking routines used in electronic systems.

**bị thương** Vietnamese for wounded.

**black** term meaning clandestine.

**black belt** slang for senior drill instructor, called that because of the black leather belt he wore.

**black crow** an ignition detector that could locate static from a gasoline internal combustion engine within an area of 10 miles. This was used for locating and destroying enemy convoys.

**black death** Viet Cong slang for the Americans' M–16 rifle.

**black flights** AIR AMERICA and other commercial transport airlines operated by the CIA. Pilots flew these unmarked planes on secret missions.

**black hats** nickname for PATH-FINDERS. Pathfinder teams were dropped behind enemy lines to establish LANDING ZONES.

**Black Hawks** slang for U.S. Navy HUEY assault helicopters that supported SEALS and patrols in the ME-KONG DELTA. They were called that because they were painted black.

**Black Horse** nickname and call sign for the U.S. Army's 11th Armored Cavalry Regiment, called that because of its shoulder patch of a rearing black horse in front of a white and red shield.

**Black Luigi** nickname for Lucien CONEIN, the U.S. Army major and CIA agent involved with the generals who overthrew President NGO DINH DIEM.

**black magic** nickname for the M–16 rifle.

**black radio station** a Special Operations Group established psycho-logical radio operation that pretended to be located in North Vietnam, but was actually located in South Vietnam. The point was to confuse the enemy.

**black shoe** slang for a navy officer who is not an aviator. At one time, only aviators wore brown shoes with the khaki uniforms.

**Black Virgin Mountain** a mountain called Nut Ba Den by the Vietnamese in WAR ZONE C south of Saigon. A holy place to those of the Buddhist faith, it was controlled by the South Vietnamese.

**black widow** slang for an M–16 rifle with a night scope attached.

**Blackbird** nickname for Lockheed's SR–71.

**blackbird** the unmarked C–123 and C–130 SOG aircraft, called that because they carried no insignia.

**Blackburn, Paul R** commander of the Seventh Fleet, March to October 1965.

**Black Horse Regiment** nickname for the 11th Armored Cavalry Division because of the black horse on its insignia.

**Blackjack mission** slang for MOBILE GUERRILLA FORCES operations. See MOBILE STRIKE FORCE.

**bladder** a heavy, collapsible drum for petroleum, oil, lubricant or water.

**bladder bird** a C–123 or C–130 aircraft equipped with a rubberized drum and 350-gallon-per-minute pumps. It was also called cow or flying cow.

**bladder boat** an inflatable non-self-propelled watercraft.

**blade time**  available helicopter support. Units were assigned a certain amount of blade time for COMMAND AND CONTROL and for logistical support.

**Blanket Division**  nickname for the First Cavalry Division because of the large size of the unit's shoulder patch.

**blanket party**  slang for hazing or punishment by shipmates, who wrapped up their victim in a blanket so that he could not identify them.

**blast**  slang for a parachute jump.

**Blind Bat**  infrared-equipped AC–130 aircraft used by the United States forces in Vietnam.

**blind blast**  a parachute INSERT at night without friendly forces in contact at the DROP ZONE, a very difficult and dangerous parachute operation.

**blind fire**  spraying an area thoroughly with machine-gun fire.

**blip**  a spot of light on a radar scope which represents the relative position of a reflecting object, such as an aircraft; also called a pip.

**blister bandit**  slang for recruits whose blisters excuse them from strenuous chores.

**blivet**  a large rubberized, collapsible drum, holding water or fuel.

**blocs**  the individual tread sections of a tank.

**blood**  slang for black soldier.

**blood chit**  slang for the piece of white nylon with an American flag that pilots carried, identifying the bearer as an American citizen who spoke only English. A message, translated into several languages, requested assistance in getting food, shelter, and protection and promised a reward from the American government. A serial number was printed on it for later identification.

**blood stripe**  the additional stripe awarded when someone was promoted to take the place of someone badly wounded or killed in the field.

**blood trail**  a trail of blood left on the ground by an escaping person who has been wounded.

**Bloody One**  nickname for the First Infantry Division, because of the red number 1 on its unit patch. Also known as the Big Red One and the Big Dead One.

**blooker**  slang for the M–79 grenade launcher.

**blooper**  1. slang for a bad round. 2. slang for the M–79 grenade launcher. Also spelled bluper and blooker.

**blooper balls**  slang for the ammunition for the M–79 grenade launcher.

**blouse**  marine term for uniform jacket.

**blousing garter**  marine term for elastic retaining bands for trouser cuffs.

**blow and go**  the venting of air while equipped with a breathing apparatus, when one is outside of a submerged submarine before a vertical ascent. This maneuver prevents ruptured lungs or embolisms.

**blow bath**  slang for a sauna, steam bath, massage, and then intercourse and/or fellatio. Also called steam and cream and steam job.

**blow smoke** slang for trying to confuse or do a snow job on someone.

**blow the rag** to launch one's reserve parachute because the main parachute did not work.

**Blow Torch, The** nickname for ROBERT KOMER of the CIA, called that because of his aggressive style toward PACIFICATION.

**blow Zs** slang for sleep.

**blown away** slang for killed.

**Blue Chip** code for the Seventh Air Force Headquarters at TAN SON NHUT airfield.

**Blue Dragon** nickname of a South Korean Marine unit.

**blue feature** any body of water on a map; called that because of the color used to designate water on maps.

**Blue Jay** see KEYSTONE.

**blue line** stream or river on a map.

**blue line sweep** slang for an operation involving checking out a stream or river.

**Blue Max** 1. nickname for First Air Cavalry Division gunships. 2. slang for the congressional MEDAL OF HONOR, called that because of its blue background.

**Blue Spaders** nickname for the First Battalion, 26th Infantry, because of the Blue Spade on the unit's insignia.

**Blue Team** nickname for an AERO-RIFLE PLATOON with UH–1 transport helicopters. A red team has two UH–1 armed helicopters, and a white team is made up of OH–13 scouts.

**blue ticket** slang for a discharge from the service under SECTION 8.

**Blue Water Navy** ships offshore of Vietnam, as differentiated from BROWN WATER NAVY, on the inland waters of Vietnam.

**blues** 1. nickname for an AIRMO-BILE company. 2. a reaction platoon or an individual in an airmobile company. 3. slang for marine dress blue formal uniforms.

**Blues, The** an aerorifle platoon.

**bluper** nickname for an M–79 grenade launcher.

**BMNT** abbr. for Beginning of Morning Nautical Twilight or Before Morning Nautical Twilight.

**B/N** abbr. for Bombardier/Navigator, a crewman who functions as both bombadier and navigator on an aircraft.

**Bn** abbr. for BATTALION.

**bộ binh** Vietnamese for infantry.

**bộ chỉ huy** Vietnamese for headquarters.

**Bô Dôi** signifies "soldiers of the Liberation Army," regular uniformed North Vietnamese soldiers.

**bộ-dội nuồć ban** Vietnamese for friendly troops.

**Bodes** slang for Cambodians.

**body bag** the plastic bag used to retrieve and transport American dead from the field. Each bag had a zipper and carrying handles.

**body count** a MACV term for the number of enemy killed, wounded, or captured during an operation. It was used by Saigon and Washington as a means of measuring the progress of the war, or success in a mission. Along with Secretary of Defense ROBERT MC-

NAMARA, General William Westmoreland created the body count criteria. The North Vietnamese Army reportedly lost over 900,000 soldiers.

**bogey** radio code for an approaching aircraft not yet identified as friend or foe, and usually assumed to be hostile until proven otherwise.

**bogies** two or more unidentified aircraft.

**Bohlen, Charles** one of the WISE OLD MEN, a group of Americans who advised President Lyndon Johnson about the Vietnam War.

**bolter** failure to engage the arresting cable while landing on an aircraft carrier, usually due to failure to lower the arresting hook.

**bomb damage assessment** recording the results of a strike estimate at the end of a flight. The bomb damage assessment contained the number of people killed, the number of buildings and trucks destroyed, and so forth.

**bombardier** 1. the person who released bombs to a target. 2. a crew member on an aircraft who oversaw bombsights.

**bombing limitation** the 1967 order from President Lyndon Johnson to restrict the bombing of North Vietnam to the panhandle area south of the 20th parallel. He ordered the beginning of the peace talks at the same time.

**B–1 Unit** peanut butter and crackers that came with C-RATION.

**booby-trap** a hidden device, usually explosive, used to kill or maim enemy soldiers. The Viet Cong used many types of booby-traps against American troops. A coconut shell, for example, could be filled with gunpowder, or traps could be made by burying a cartridge with the primer against a nail with the top of the bullet protruding. A heavy footstep would set it off and fire a bullet through a victim's foot. For other booby traps, see PUNJI STAKE, MALAY WHIP, MALAYSIAN SLING, OVERHEAD GRENADE, BICYCLE MINE, CARTRIDGE TRAP, and SPIKE PIT.

**boo-coo** perversion of the French word BEAUCOUP (many), passed down to Americans by the Vietnamese, who learned it from the French.

**boom-boom** 1. term used by the Vietnamese prostitutes in selling their product. 2. slang for sex.

**boom-boom girl** slang for whore.

**boom-boom house** slang for a whorehouse.

**boondocks** slang for the jungle or remote area away from base camp or village. See BOONIES.

**boondockers** marine slang for boots.

**boonie hat** a soft floppy jungle hat with a brim all around it, plus air-holes. It was colored olive drab or with camouflage markings.

**boonie rat** slang for INFANTRYMAN.

**boonies** slang for the jungle, the field, or the bush; any place the INFANTRY operated that was not a FIREBASE, BASE CAMP, or VILLE.

**boot** slang for an inexperienced and innocent soldier just out of BOOT CAMP.

**Boot Brown Bar** marine slang for a new and raw second lieutenant (brown bar).

**boot camp**    stateside basic training in the U.S. Navy or Marines Corps.

**boot it**    slang meaning to make an extended patrol on foot.

**Bootstrap Program**    a program in which the military paid for an enlisted person's education to prepare for officer candidacy.

**BOQ**    abbr. for Bachelor Officer Quarters, living quarters for unmarried officers.

**boss**    marine slang for a senior drill instructor.

**bottle baby**    marine slang for an alcoholic.

**bought the farm**    slang for being killed.

**bought the ranch**    slang for being killed.

**Bouncing Betty**    a land mine that when triggered, bounced waist-high and sprayed SHRAPNEL. Designed to kill and disable, this antipersonnel mine was first used in World War II and its use continued in Vietnam. When detonated, it exploded up to six feet into the air before releasing its steel balls.

**bowl**    slang for pipe used for smoking dope.

**brass**    1. an officer. 2. brass fittings of various types.

**brass band**    slang for a reaction force sent to help a small team in combat with a larger force.

**brass monkey**    an interagency radio term asking for help.

**brave**    Army designation for the infantryman, probably from his 11–B (eleven bravo) MOS designation.

**brave bull**    C–97 plane fitted with infrared equipment for RECONNAISSANCE missions in Southeast Asia in 1963.

**bravo**    1. the military phonetic for the letter B. 2. slang for infantryman, from the B in 11B, the MOS designation of the infantryman.

**break**    aerial term for a maneuver or command to initiate a maximum turn to avoid an attacking aircraft or to defeat a tracking missile; considered an emergency measure.

**break tape**    slang meaning to fire one's weapon.

**break x**    aerial term for minimum range indication for missile launch. An X appeared on a radar scope at minimum range.

**breakfast**    see MENU.

**breaking contact**    disengaging from contact with the enemy.

**breaking squelch**    breaking up the natural static of radios by pushing down the transmit bar of a second radio set on the same frequency to reduce the static on the first radio.

**Bren Gun**    a silencer-equipped submachine gun, the MK–II British Sten Gun, used mainly by SPECIAL FORCES.

**Briarpatch, The**    nickname for the Hoa Lo Prison, a North Vietnamese prisoner-of-war camp near Hanoi for American and South Vietnamese troops. See HANOI HILTON.

**Bridge at Thanh Hoa**    a North Vietnamese bridge which appeared immune to all attempts of U.S. forces to destroy it. This bridge crossed the Song Ma River, just south of Hanoi. Hundreds of unsuccessful attacks were carried out between 1965 and 1968. In May 1972, the bridge went down after being hit with 15 LASER-GUIDED bombs. The bridge was known to the Vietnamese as Hàm Rồng, or Dragon's Jaw.

**bridge trap**    a booby trap in which the center of a bridge was almost severed and then covered over so that when a person crossed the bridge, it gave way and propelled him downward onto spikes.

**brief**    preflight or premission intelligence and planning session.

**briefback**    a detailed discussion of an intended mission.

**brig**    slang for military jail.

**Brig**    abbr. for BRIGADIER GENERAL (also abbreviated BG).

**brigade**    1. in Vietnam, army BATTALIONS were grouped into brigades, each commanded by a colonel. INFANTRY brigades were separate and were usually commanded by a BRIGADIER GENERAL. Three army brigades made up a DIVISION. 2. a tactical and administrative military unit composed of headquarters and one or more BATTALIONS of INFANTRY or ARMORED UNITS, with other supporting units.

**brigadier general**    the lowest grade of general. The symbol for this rank is one star.

**brightlight team**    code for small groups of armed men who rescued other teams in trouble, a SOG operation.

**brightwork**    marine term for brass or other shiny metal.

**bring up the rear**    slang for the last man in a patrol, the tail.

**bringing red leg**    slang for ARTILLERY fire.

**bringing smoke**    1. out-going ARTILLERY fire. 2. to punish or attack or harshly reprimand. 3. to shoot someone.

**Brinks Hotel**    a hotel in Saigon billeting U.S. officers. It was bombed by the Viet Cong on Christmas Eve 1964, killing two Americans and injuring many Americans and Vietnamese.

**bro**    slang for a black soldier or soul brother. The term was occasionally used to refer to men from the same unit.

**broken down**    taken apart or disassembled.

**Bronco**    North American's OV–10 twin-engine COUNTERINSURGENCY aircraft, built for the Marine Corps. The air force and the marines used this plane for FORWARD AIR CONTROL missions. Equipped with ROCKETS and MINIGUNS, it was often used as a spotter aircraft.

**Bronze Star**    U.S. military decoration awarded for heroic or meritorious service not involving aerial flights. Heroism is shown by a V on the ribbon, and the Bronze Star is given for actions of a lesser merit than required for a SILVER STAR. Subsequent awards are shown by an OAK LEAF (a star for the U.S. Marine Corps and Navy) worn on the ribbon. The Bronze Star ranks just below the Soldier's or Airman's Medal and the Navy and Marine Corps medal.

**brother**    slang for a black soldier or soul brother.

**brown bar**    slang for a second lieutenant, denoting the single brass bar of the rank. In the field, officers wore camouflaged rank which was often brown or black instead of brass. Sometimes called a butter bar.

**brown bomber** slang for a large brown laxative pill given out by MEDICS in Vietnam.

**Brown Cradle** nickname for EB–66C aircraft equipped with ECM equipment used for jamming enemy fire control radar.

**brown derby** slang for a hot meal flown out to the field.

**brown nosing** slang for kissing up to a superior.

**Brown Water Navy** the U.S. Navy units assigned to the inland boat patrols of the MEKONG RIVER DELTA, the U.S. Allied RIVERINE FORCES. See also BLUE WATER NAVY.

**Browning Automatic Rifle** a .30 caliber magazine-fed, gas-operated, automatic rifle. It could fire 350 rounds per minute and was somewhat awkward to handle. Used by U.S. troops during World War II and the Korean Conflict, it was replaced by the M–16 during the Vietnam War. Abbreviated BAR.

**Browning M–35** automatic pistol, a 9mm weapon preferred by SPECIAL FORCES.

**Browning M–2** a .50-caliber machine gun manufactured by Browning.

**Bru** a MONTAGNARD TRIBE living mainly in QUANG TRI Province.

**bs** 1. abbr. for border surveillance 2. abbr. for bull shit, also referred to as bull-shitting or b-sing.

**B–66/EB–66** the air force version of the A–3 Skywarrior, used in the early days of the war for ELECTRONICS INTELLIGENCE and ECM.

**B-Team** a SPECIAL FORCES unit acting as headquarters for three or more A-TEAMS.

**B–2 unit** crackers and jelly or cheese that came with C-RATIONS.

**BTZ** abbr. for Below The Zone, referring to someone who unexpectedly receives an early promotion.

**bubble** 1. nickname for the two-man OH–13 SIOUX observation helicopter, manufactured by Bell and used by the army. It was called that because of the transparent plastic cover which enclosed the pilot. 2. slang for a MUST (Medical Unit, Self-Contained, Transportable).

**bubble top** slang for the Bell OH–13 observation helicopter.

**bubbler** 1. a scuba diver using an open-circuit breathing device. 2. an air tank.

**bubbles** see MUST.

**buck sergeant** slang for the lowest grade of sergeant (E-5).

**buckle** slang meaning to fight.

**buckle for your dust** phrase meaning to fight hard and win the respect of your buddies.

**Buddha grass** slang for marijuana.

**Buddha zone** 1. slang for death. 2. slang for heaven.

**Buddhism** the main organized religion in Vietnam.

**Buddhist barbecue** slang for Buddhist monks who set themselves on fire to protest the war. Buddhists demonstrated against the war and several Buddhist monks immolated themselves. This led to criticism of Ngo Dinh Diem's government and was part of the reason for its downfall.

**Buddhist priest**  expression used in Vietnam for mild surprise or annoyance.

**buddy operations**  see BUDDY SYSTEM.

**buddy system**  1. putting South Vietnamese troops under U.S. command for training; also called buddy operations. 2. term used when a new U.S. soldier was teamed up with an experienced soldier.

**BUFE**  abbr. for Big Ugly Fucking Elephants, also termed buffie. These multicolored ceramic elephants were sold to soldiers in Vietnam as souvenirs.

**BUFF**  abbr. for Big Ugly Fat Fellow (or Big Ugly Fat Fucker), the nickname for the B–52 Stratofortress.

**Buffalo**  DeHavilland's CV–7, which could carry up to 40 combat-ready troops.

**Buffie**  see BUFE.

**bug juice**  1. slang for KOOL-AID, which soldiers in Vietnam drank in great quantity. 2. slang for the government-provided insecticide, which was usually not effective.

**bug ship**  slang for HUEYS spraying pesticides on villages.

**Bugsmasher**  nickname for the Sneeb, a twin Beech plane used by the U.S. Navy and the Marine Corps and called the C–45 by the U.S. Air Force.

**Buis, Dale R.**  an American adviser in Vietnam, killed in Vietnam on July 8, 1959 by Viet Cong while watching a movie in a mess hall in Bien Hoa. His is the first name inscribed on the Vietnam Veterans Memorial.

**bulkhead**  naval and marine term meaning wall.

**bullboat**  small round boat used by Vietnamese fishermen.

**bullet shot**  the buildup of SAC B–52 forces in the Western Pacific starting in February 1972.

**bullet stabber**  slang for a loader, a beginner's position for a new man on a TRACK.

**Bullpup**  nickname for the 250-pound missile carried by U.S. jets.

**bullseye**  a reference point in North Vietnam.

**bullshit bombers**  1. slang for psychological warfare units. 2. slang for HUEYS dropping leaflets for psychological purposes.

**bummer**  slang for a bad occurrence.

**Bundy, McGeorge**  special assistant to the president for national security affairs, 1961–1966.

**bunk**  bed; marines usually called a bunk a rack.

**bunker**  a fighting position with an overhead cover to protect from enemy fire. Made of concrete and sandbags, they were used by both sides during the war.

**Bunker, Ellsworth**  ambassador to South Vietnam, 1967–1973.

**Burke, Arleigh**  chief of naval operations, 1955–1961.

**burner**  slang for jet engine's afterburner.

**burning shitters**  the least favorite job in Vietnam, involving pouring diesel fuel into collected human feces from latrines and setting fire to it, stirring often. "Willie the shit-burner" was a PAPA-SAN who sometimes took on the job.

**burp** slang for a Marine, often used by infantrymen.

**burp-gun** M–79 grenade launcher.

**Burrows, Larry** a photographer for *Life* who died in a helicopter accident on February 10, 1971, with other combat photographers over Laos. He was one of more than 50 journalists and photographers who died in the Vietnam War.

**burst** explosion. The area of burst is the area immediately affected by the explosion.

**burst interval** the time between bursts of explosions.

**bursting fart** nickname for the marine gunner's insignia.

**Buse, Henry, W.** commander of the Fleet Marine Force, 1968–1970.

**bush** 1. anywhere outside a base where a firefight is a possibility. 2. the BOONDOCKS, the BOONIES, or simply, the FIELD. 3. short form of AMBUSH.

**Bushmaster** 1. any special unit proficient in jungle operations such as GREEN BERETS, LRRPS, or sniper patrols. 2. a bushmaster operation was a patrol carried out by a company or a platoon. 3. a large, deadly snake found in Vietnam.

**bust caps, to** marine slang for rapidly firing one's rifle.

**buster** aerial term for full power or using 100 percent of engine power without the AFTERBURNER.

**busting caps** marine slang for firing a weapon, especially rapidly firing the M–16. This term may have been derived from paper percussion caps used in toy guns. Also called rock and roll.

**bustle rack** armored units' slang for the pipe framework in which supplies such as food and beer were stored, usually attached to the backs of turrets on tanks.

**Butcher Brigade** derogatory nickname given the 11th Infantry Brigade of the AMERICAL Division after Lt. William CALLEY's actions at MY LAI became known.

**butt plates** 1. GRUNT slang for riflemen. 2. marine term for INFANTRY.

**butter bar** slang for second lieutenant, after the single brass bar of the rank.

**butterfly** 1. patrolling in frequently changing patterns, often practiced when patrolling through unfamiliar and possibly hostile territory. 2. often used by Vietnamese bargirls, meaning to give sexual favors. 3. to leave someone.

**butt-fucked** slang for attacked from the rear.

**button bomblets** a GRAVEL mine set up with an aspirin-sized fuse which when triggered by the enemy would blow off toes and feet.

**button up** to shut and lock all tank hatches.

**buy the farm** slang meaning to die.

**buy the ranch** slang meaning to die.

**BX** abbr. for Base Exchange, the store on base.

# C

**c's**   see C-RATIONS.

**C & C**   abbr. for COMMAND AND CONTROL.

**C & C Ship**   abbr. for COMMAND AND CONTROL helicopter, used for RECONNAISSANCE or for unit commanders.

**C & E**   abbr. for Clothing and Equipment.

**C & GSC**   abbr. for the U.S. Army's Command and General Staff in Ft. Leavenworth, Kansas. It is often referred to simply as Leavenworth.

**C & S**   abbr. for CORDON AND SEARCH, a tactic used to seal off a village so that it could be searched.

**C Spt**   abbr. for Combat Support.

**CA**   1. abbr. for Combat Assault, referring to taking troopers into a HOT LANDING ZONE. 2. abbr. for Combined Action. 3. abbr. for Civil Affairs.

**Ca Mau Peninsula**   VIET CONG base in the Delta area.

**CAB**   abbr. for Combat Aviation Battalion.

**CABOOM**   abbr. for Clark Air Base Officers' Open Mess, a U.S. air base in the Philippines.

**CAC**   1. abbr. for Corps Aviation Company. 2. abbr. for Combined Action Company.

**cạc-bin**   Vietnamese for carbine.

**caca dow**   Vietnamese slang for threatening violence.

**cach mang**   Vietnamese for revolution.

**cache**   hidden enemy supplies.

**cadence**   the rhythmic chants used to keep marchers in step; also referred to as Jody calls.

**cadre**   1. a dependable, indoctrinated Communist party member or small group trained in some type of management specialty. The cadre was assigned individually or in groups to various organizations within or outside the North Vietnamese government. The cadre was considered a basic North Vietnamese Army Unit. It was called *can bo* in Vietnamese. 2. headquarters personnel.

**CAG**   1. abbr. for Combined Action Groups, pacification teams organized by U.S. Marines. CAGs contained a South Vietnamese Popular Forces battalion and a U.S. Marine Company. 2. abbr. for Carrier Air Group commander.

**cảhn sát**   Vietnamese for policeman.

**call fire**   a request for fire on a target in response to an appeal from a unit.

**call sign**   a coded combination of letters, words, or numbers used to identify a person, unit, or activity and keep in communication.

**Calley Hall**   army slang for the Officers Candidate School at Fort Benning, Georgia. Lt. William

CALLEY was a graduate of Infantry OCS at Fort Benning.

**Calley, William**  Lt. Calley, a platoon leader in the AMERICAL Division, was court-martialed and found guilty of the murder of Vietnamese citizens at MY LAI in March 1968. He was sentenced to life imprisonment but after review, his sentence was reduced to 10 years. He was released on parole in 1974 and dishonorably discharged.

**Cam Ne**  site of the deliberate burning of a Vietnamese HOOTCH by U.S. troops. CBS news cameras filmed, and later broadcast on American television, scenes of GIs setting fires with cigarette lighters.

**cam nhông**  Vietnamese for truck.

**cám ởn**  Vietnamese for thank you.

**Cam Pha**  a major North Vietnamese port which was mined, immobilizing shipping. Cam Pha was 35 miles from the Chinese border.

**Cam Ranh**  one of the 11 AUTONOMOUS CITIES of South Vietnam. Cam Ranh is Vietnamese for sweet stream.

**Cam Ranh Bay**  a large seaport and an IN-COUNTRY R & R location in Khanh Hoa Province, south of the city of NHA TRANG in II CORPS. A large U.S. air force base was located here.

**Camberra**  see B–57.

**Cambodian Incursion**  a large-scale invasion into Cambodia from April 29 to June 29, 1970. See INCURSION.

**Cambodian Red**  nickname for local marijuana.

**cami**  short for camouflage. The utility uniform of jungle fatigues worn in the field consisted of a cap, shirt (blouse), and pants. Also spelled cammies.

**cammies**  see CAMI.

**camouflage**  to disguise troops, uniforms, or equipment, by changing their appearance. The purpose of camouflage is to hide from the enemy.

**Camp Alpha**  the outprocessing center near Saigon.

**Camp Carroll**  a USMC combat base in I CORPS named in honor of a U.S. Marine captain killed in action in 1966.

**Camp Davis**  a camp inside TAN SON NHUT Airport, used by the Americans. After the PARIS PEACE ACCORD, it became the headquarters of the PRG delegation in SAIGON. It was named for specialist-4 James Davis, the first American soldier to be killed in Vietnam.

**Camp Enari**  a camp near Pleiku, at the foot of Dragon Mountain, the home base of the Fourth Infantry Division. It was named after First Lieutenant Mark N. Enari who had saved the lives of at least five other men.

**Camp Faith**  a North Vietnamese POW camp near Hanoi, holding U.S. servicemen.

**Camp Holloway**  an installation near PLEIKU, named for Chief Warrant Officer Charles E. Holloway, who was killed when the helicopter he piloted went down on his first flight in Vietnam.

**Camp Hope**  nickname for the SON TAY PRISON, a POW camp near Hanoi.

**Camp Radcliff**  the home of the First Cavalry Division, named for Major Donald Radcliff who had been killed as he piloted his helicopter. This camp was nicknamed "The Golf Course" because of the low-cut, smooth grass on its helicopter landing area.

**Camp Unity** a POW camp near Hanoi. The resistance of some prisoners there earned them the name "Hell's Angels."

**campaign** a connected series of military operations which form a specific phase of a war. The 17 authorized campaigns of the Vietnam War, categorized by the U.S. military, are listed individually in this volume.

**campaign medal** medal awarded for participation or service in a battle, campaign, or war. Also called service medal.

**Cam Son Secret Zone** an area 30 KILOMETERS west of Dong Tam, a major U.S. port in the southern part of South Vietnam. It was called that because of intense VIET CONG activity at the enemy base near there.

**Can Bo** Vietnamese for Communist party members or small, trained groups. These political CADRE of the National Liberation Front were assigned to organizations within or outside the North Vietnamese government.

**căn cước** Vietnamese for identification card.

**Can Do, Madame Nhu** slang expression of GIs for something they were willing or able to do.

**canh tạc** Vietnamese for air strike.

**Can Lanh** capital of KIEN PHONG Province.

**Can Lao Party** the powerful semisecret political party of the government headed by Ngo Dinh Nhu, President NGO DINH DIEM's brother. This party infiltrated the entire administrative, intelligence, and defense structure of South Vietnam.

**can of worms** slang for C-RATION spaghetti.

**can opener** slang for a bulldozer tank.

**Can Tho** capital of PHONG DINH Province, one of the 11 AUTONOMOUS CITIES of South Vietnam, and headquarters for IV Corps Tactical Zone.

**Candlestick** code for FLARE-dropping operations.

**Candy Machine** code for the periodic use of F–102s in South Vietnam for air defense duty near TAN SON NHUT and DA NANG.

**canister rounds** short-range antipersonnel projectiles, loaded with submissiles such as FLECHETTES or steel balls. The casing was designed to open just beyond the muzzle of the weapon, dispersing the submissiles. Canister rounds in the M–79 grenade launcher were 40mm.

**canistered bomblet unit** see CBU.

**cannibalize** slang for using parts of a piece of equipment or a vehicle to repair another one.

**cannon cocker** slang for ARTILLERYMAN.

**Canoe U** slang for the U.S. Naval Academy.

**canopy** the overhead foliage in the jungle, usually described as double or triple, as "We have a triple canopy."

**cans and vans** slang for enemy tanks and trucks in a convoy, called in as a target.

**cao boi** Vietnamese slang for cowboy, the motorcycle-riding gangs of criminals in Saigon.

**Cao Dai** a religious and political sect formed in the 1920s by a group of South Vietnamese intellectuals who combined the three major religions of Vietnam (Buddhism, Confucianism, and Christianity) with the worship of Vietnamese and Eastern heroes. Many of these men were recruited by the U.S. SPECIAL FORCES for the Civilian Irregular Defense Groups, CIDG. The Cao Dai had a strength of more than 1.5 million followers, many of them living and practicing near TAY NINH.

**Cao Lanh** capital of KIEN PHONG Province.

**CAP** abbr. for Combined Action Platoon. These American marine and South Vietnamese militia units were set up to safeguard designated villages. The CAPs were usually made up of 15-man marine squads and three squads of Popular Forces working together. 2. abbr. for Combat Air Patrol, an aircraft patrol provided over an area, combat zone, or air defense area to intercept and demolish aircraft before they could reach their target and before they could provide cover for strike aircraft. 3. abbr. for Civil Action Program which worked with Vietnamese civilians in various ways in an attempt to improve their lives.

**Cap St. Jacques** the French name for the Vietnam city of VUNG TAU, an IN-COUNTRY R & R spot for GIs during the war.

**CAP/Strike** aircraft with a primary COMBAT AIR PATROL role, and a secondary strike role.

**CAP team** abbr. for COMBINED ACTION PLATOON team.

**Capital Division** South Korea's combat troops, also called the Tiger Division, who fought on the American side during the war.

**Capital Military Zone** SAIGON and its adjacent region. Also called Capital Military District.

**capping** slang for shooting.

**Capt** abbr. for captain.

**captain's mast** naval term for the process in which a commanding officer administers the lowest disciplinary action or punishment; also used to dispense awards and commendations. The U.S. Marine Corps terms this procedure OFFICE HOURS; the army's term is ON THE CARPET.

**CAR** abbr. for COMBAT ACTION RIBBON, the Marines' decoration for action under enemy fire in a combat zone. See also CIB.

**car wash** slang for the place where a GI could go for a haircut, shave, shower, steam bath, and massage, carefully given by Vietnamese ladies.

**Caravelle** the largest hotel in SAIGON, on TU DO STREET. It contained 135 air-conditioned rooms, extravagantly decorated with glass and Italian marble.

**carbine** a short-barreled, lightweight automatic or semiautomatic rifle.

**Card, The** a U.S. transport ship sunk by the Viet Cong in 1964.

*Cardinal* see KEYSTONE.

*CARDIV* naval designation for Carrier Division.

*CARE* abbr. for Cooperative American Remittances to Europe, which sent food and clothing to those in need.

*Care package* slang for a package from home containing food and other needed items; named after CARE supplies.

*Caribou* DeHavilland's small transport plane, the main cargo transport utilized in the early days of the Vietnam War. Used by the army until 1966; it was then used by the air force as well.

*CAR–15* the Colt Automatic Rifle, a carbine rifle.

*carry on* phrase meaning to continue as before.

*cartridge* shell casing for bullets.

*cartridge belt* the belt that holds AMMO pouches and canteens, first-aid equipment, and other gear.

*cartridge trap* a booby trap activated when a soldier stepped on, a bamboo slat or a shotgun shell. When stepped on, the cartridge beneath the slat pressed down on the firing pin, causing the shell inside to go off through the soldier's foot.

*cartwheel* aerial term for an enemy defensive formation in which two or more aircraft circle on a horizontal plane while covering each other's rear area against attack. Also called a wheel or wagon wheel.

*CAS* 1. abbr. for Controlled American Service, which was a euphemism for the CIA. 2. abbr. for Covert Action branch, the SAIGON office of the CIA.

3. abbr. for Chief of Air Staff. 4. abbr. for Close Air Support, the weapons delivery which was in direct support of ground troops. 5. abbr. for Calibrated Air Speed, the airspeed data that reflected both instrument error and sensor error.

*Case-Church Amendment* the amendment passed by the U.S. Senate in June 1973 banning the use of future funds for U.S. combat activities in Indochina without the specific authorization of Congress.

*Casey* the KC–130 four-engined troop aircraft. This aircraft was used for many U.S. Marine Corps parachute operations. It had long-distance capability and could carry a substantial load, including 64 fully equipped paratroopers.

*cash* slang for a hidden supply (from cache).

*CAS-Team* abbr. for Controlled American Sources Teams which were groups of American-trained Vietnamese agents placed in North Vietnam to perform intelligence and sabotage missions.

*casual* a military person waiting for an assignment or transportation.

*casual company* a group of men waiting for reassignment, transfer, or discharge.

*casualty* a person lost to an organization. Battle casualties include dead, wounded, or missing. Nonbattle casualties include sick or injured-not-in-combat, or missing-not-in-combat.

*cat* nickname for the Caterpillar tractor.

**CAT**  abbr. for Civil Air Transport, a Taiwan-based, American-owned private airline used in Vietnam.

**cat shot**  a jet being catapulted off an aircraft carrier.

**catch a hit**  marine slang meaning to be told off or chewed out.

**Caterpillar**  1. slang for a noncombative convoy on a reasonably secure road. 2. a brand of tractor and other heavy equipment.

**Caterpillar Club**  nickname for a group of fliers who had made parachute jumps which saved their lives.

**cầu tiêu**  Vietnamese for latrine.

**CAV**  abbr. for Cavalry.

**Cav of the Cav**  slang for the elite First Squadron of the Ninth U.S. Cavalry.

**Cayuse**  a utility and observation helicopter manufactured by Hughes and used by the army.

**Cbt**  abbr. for Combat.

**CBU**  abbr. for Canistered (Cluster) Bomblet Unit. Any of a variety of air-deliverable weapons that contained and dispensed a larger number of smaller bomblets. The CBU–55 was nicknamed the earthquake bomb.

**CBW**  abbr. for Chemical and Biological Warfare.

**CC**  abbr. for Company Commander.

**CCC**  abbr. for COMMAND AND CONTROL CENTRAL, the Kontum-based MACV–SOG field command set up in 1968 to control unconventional warfare in the central area of South Vietnam. CCC was renamed TASK FORCE 2 in 1971.

**CCK**  abbr. for Ching Chuan Kang, an air base in Taiwan.

**CCM**  abbr. for counter-countermeasures.

**CCN**  abbr. for COMMAND AND CONTROL NORTH, the Danang-based MACV–SOG field command set up in 1968 to manage and control unconventional warfare in the northern area of South Vietnam. CCN was renamed TASK FORCE 1 in 1971.

**CCS**  1. abbr. for COMMAND AND CONTROL SOUTH, the Ban Me Thuot-based MACV–SOG field command set up in 1968 to control unconventional warfare in the southern area of South Vietnam. CCS was renamed TASK FORCE 3 in 1971. 2. abbr. for Combined Chiefs of Staff.

**CCT**  abbr. for COMMAND AND CONTROL Team.

**CE**  1. abbr. for Combat Emergency. 2. abbr. for Corps of Engineers (U.S. Army).

**CEC**  abbr. for Civil Engineering Corps.

**Cedar Falls**  a U.S. Army operation to rid the IRON TRIANGLE of Viet Cong. The village of Ben Suc was evacuated and then abandoned. There were heavy casualties on both sides.

**ceiling**  1. the height of the lowest surface of a cloud layer. 2. the maximum height an aircraft can fly.

**cell**  a cellular unit of airborne military aircraft, bombers, or tankers. These individually organized cells or teams could operate independently of one another or together.

**centerline tank**  aerial term for a fuel tank carried externally on the centerline of an aircraft.

**Central Highlands**  the highlands area in Vietnam in the western part of II CORPS, populated mainly by MONTAGNARD tribes.

**Central Intelligence Agency**  in the 1960s, the CIA tried to destroy the Viet Cong infrastructure and was involved in the PHOENIX PROGRAM. When the CIA began monitoring antiwar critics in the United States, there was a strong, negative public reaction. In 1974 Congress enacted legal restrictions on the CIA, permitting only intelligence operations outside the United States. William Colby, at one time the director of the Phoenix program, directed the CIA from 1973 to 1976.

**Cercle Sportif**  a private club in Saigon used by Vietnamese and foreigners, including U.S. service personnel, especially in the early days of the war.

**C–47**  the Douglas DC–3 Skytrain, also known as Puff the Magic Dragon. Equipped with MINIGUNS, it was used for nighttime close air support and for the dropping of FLARES.

**C4**  abbr. for the white plastic explosive carried by military personnel in one-pound bars. It burned like Sterno when lit and was used to heat C-RATIONS and for detonating.

**CG**  1. abbr. for Commanding General. 2. abbr. for Civil Guard.

**CGUSARV**  abbr. for Commanding General, U.S. Army, Vietnam.

**CH**  abbr. for CHINOOK, a large U.S. helicopter.

**chaff**  a reflector made of narrow metal strips or metalized fiberglass to create misleading signals on radarscopes.

**chaff corridor**  the innumerable pieces of silver foil spread out in an effort to disrupt surface-to-air missile radar.

**chain of command**  the hierarchy of military authority. In the military one must go systematically through the chain of command to get help or make a complaint.

**chairborne commando**  derogatory slang for clerks or office personnel.

**chairborne rangers**  derogatory slang for clerks or office personnel.

**Chairman, Joint Chiefs of Staff**  the senior officer of the U.S. Armed Services and the person who transmitted the commands of the president and the secretary of defense. The chairmen of the Joint Chiefs of Staff during the Vietnam War were Air Force General Nathan F. Twining, 1957–1960; Army General Lyman L. Lemnitzer, 1960–1961; Army General Maxwell Taylor, 1961–1964; Army General Earle G. Wheeler, 1964–1970; Admiral Thomas H. Moorer, 1970–1974; and Air Force General George S. Brown, 1974–1978.

**chalk**  a helicopter's position in line; for example, the third ship is called Chalk Three. Also spelled chock.

**Cham**  an Indian ethnic tribe living mainly in THUA THIEN Province.

**chấm dứt (or hết)**  Vietnamese for the end.

**Chams** a group of poor Vietnamese in the south-central part of the country. About 35,000 of them lived in modest villages quite apart from the mainstream of Vietnamese life.

**chancre mechanic** slang for an enlisted man of the Medical Corps, a medic or corpsman.

**Chandelle** pilot's term for a maximum performance climbing turn in which speed is converted to altitude while the direction is being reversed.

**changing tune** slang for retreating.

**chào** Vietnamese for hello or goodbye, depending on the context.

**Chaos** code for an operation involving the CIA and its actions against the antiwar movement. Despite CIA rules, this operation monitored antiwar critics.

**chaplain** a clergyman in the military. Holding an officer's rank, he was responsible for the religious welfare of military personnel.

**Chapman, Leonard** commandant of the U.S. Marine Corps, 1968–1972.

**chaptered out** to be involuntarily separated from the service. A chapter 10 army discharge was given instead of a court-martial. This discharge is usually an undesirable discharge.

**Charge of Quarters** an officer placed in charge of a unit headquarters, usually at night.

**Charles** nickname for the enemy. See GOOK.

**Charlie** 1. the military phonetic for the letter C. 2. short for Victor Charlie, meaning the VIET CONG, or the enemy. See GOOK.

**Charlie Alpha** military phonetic alphabetization for Combat Assault. The official name for these maneuvers was air assault, using helicopters to bring troops in to battle.

**Charlie Bird** slang for a helicopter used by a tactical commander to COMMAND AND CONTROL.

**Charlie Charlie** see CHARLIE BIRD.

**Charlie Cong** marine slang for VIET CONG.

**Charlie four** see C4.

**Charlie Mike** term for Continue the Mission.

**Charlie rats** slang for Army C-RATIONS (c-rats).

**Charlie Ridge** a generic term for any location in Vietnam.

**Charlie Tango** phonetic alphabetization for Control Tower, from military phonetics.

**Chas** nickname for Charlie, the enemy. See GOOK.

**Chase Manhattan Bank** an American bank which opened a branch in SAIGON to serve Americans.

**chatter** multiple communications on the same radio frequency, often used to refer to communications of little interest to the listener.

**Chau Doc** one of the 44 provinces of South Vietnam, located in IV CORPS.

**Chau Doc City** capital of CHAU DOC Province.

**che**   a sweet Vietnamese soup made from peas and rice, with water and sugar added.

**cheap charlie**   slang for a stingy or cheap person, often applied to GIs who were frugal with their money in bars.

**check your six**   aerial term for a warning to a pilot to look behind him for hostile aircraft. Configured as a clock, twelve o'clock is straight ahead, three o'clock directly to the right, and six o'clock directly behind.

**checkerboard sweep**   a technique where a specific area is divided into blocks and searched. Ground and other missions are arranged to deny the enemy an escape or way out.

**checkerboarding**   tactical term for an infantry sweep of a map area divided into blocks; each block is searched by a group of men.

**checking the dictionary**   slang for confirming ambiguous orders or directions.

**checkmate**   a security roadblock.

**checkpoint**   1. the point where units would call their bases to inform them that they had reached a specific area. 2. a spot where MILITARY POLICE or others check passing cars and personnel.

**Cheeseburger**   slang for the U.S. DAISY-CUTTER jungle-clearing bomb.

**che-kho**   a variety of Vietnamese tea made from dried tea leaves.

**chem**   abbr. for chemical.

**che-man**   a variety of Vietnamese tea made from roasted tea leaves.

**che-nu**   a variety of Vietnamese tea made from dried flower buds.

**Cheo Reo**   capital of PHU BON Province.

**cherry**   slang for a new troop; used to suggest youth, inexperience, and virginity. See also FNG.

**cherry boy**   see CHERRY and FNG.

**cherry juice**   slang for hydraulic fluid.

**chev**   slang for combat engineer vehicle.

**CH–54**   the Tarhe, the largest of the American helicopters. This double-engined aircraft built by Sikorsky was used mainly for heavy cargo. It was called the Skycrane and Flying Crane.

**CH–53**   Sikorsky's Sea Stallion, a heavy aircraft used by the marines and navy for transporting men and materiel. It was powered by two shaft-turbine engines.

**CH–45**   the Boeing twin-turbine, tandem-rotor helicopter; also called Sneeb and Bugsmasher.

**CH–47**   a Chinook helicopter, a large and frequently used aircraft in Vietnam; also called Shithook and Hook.

**CH–46**   the Boeing Sea Knight. This twin-turbine, tandem-rotor medium helicopter was used mainly for transport by the marines. It was able to move as much as 4,000 pounds of men and materiel at once.

**Chi bo**   Vietnamese for the lowest LAO DONG party organization, similar to a chapter. The larger chi bo were divided into cells, called tiêu tò.

**Chic**  RECONNAISSANCE nickname for the UH–1E HUEY helicopter.

**Chicago Seven**  the defendants in a conspiracy trial, who were indicted for crossing state lines with the purpose of rioting during the 1968 Democratic Convention in Chicago. The seven participants were Rennie Davis, Dave Dellinger, John Froines, Tom Hayden, Abbie Hoffman, Jerry Rubin, and Lee Weiner. Bobby Seale was often included in this group, then called the Chicago Eight.

**Chickasaw**  a utility helicopter manufactured by Sikorsky; used by the U.S. Army and the Vietnam Air Force.

**chicken corporal**  slang for a SPECIALIST FOURTH CLASS.

**chickenhawk**  slang for someone who is undecided whether to be a chicken (dove) or hawk.

**chickenplate**  slang for the ceramic armor that helicopter crews wore to cover their chest and groin areas.

**Chicom**  1. abbr. for Chinese Communist, also spelled Chi-Com. 2. weapons manufactured in China.

**Chicom Grenade**  a homemade weapon made from Coca-Cola cans filled with plastique or TNT, rocks and nails. These grenades were particularly destructive.

**Chicom Mine**  a Chinese Communist mine, frequently made from plastic.

**Chief of Naval Operations**  the senior officer of the United States Navy. During the Vietnam War, the chiefs of naval operations were Admiral Arleigh Burke, 1959–1960; Admiral George Anderson, 1961–1963; Admiral David McDonald, 1963–

1965; Admiral Thomas Moorer, 1965–1970; Admiral Elmo Zumwalt, 1970–1974; and Admiral James Holloway, 1974–1975.

**Chief of Staff, U.S. Air Force**  the senior officer of the U.S. Air Force. During the Vietnam War, the chiefs of staff were General Thomas White, 1959–1961; General Curtis LeMay, 1961–1965; General John McConnell, 1965–1968; General John Ryan, 1968–1973; General George S. Brown, 1974; and General David Jones, 1974–1975.

**Chief of Staff, U.S. Army**  the senior officer of the U.S. Army. During the Vietnam War, the chiefs of staff were General Maxwell Taylor, 1959; General Lyman Lemnitzer, 1959–1960; General George Decker, 1960–1962; General Earle Wheeler, 1962–1964; General Harold Johnson, 1964–1968; General William Westmoreland, 1968–1972; General Creighton Abrams, 1972–1974; and General Fred Weyand, 1974–1975.

**chiến sĩ**  Vietnamese for soldier.

**chiến thuật du kích**  Vietnamese for guerrilla warfare.

**chiến-xa**  Vietnamese for tank.

**Chieu Hoi**  the open arms program promising fair treatment to enemy soldiers who voluntarily stopped fighting. This amnesty program, beginning in early 1963 and continuing until 1973, enabled VC to defect with safety to the South Vietnamese government side and about 200,000 did so. Many of these Chieu Hois acted as scouts for U.S. units and were called Kit Carson Scouts. Pronounced "choo hoy."

**Chin Chin, Ho Chi Minh**  a toast given by bargirls in Vietnam.

**Chin Luan** a daily newspaper in SAIGON.

**China Beach** a recreational facility, an IN-COUNTRY R & R spot. Infantry were given one day mini-R & R here.

**China Lobby** a group of influential and conservative American politicians, journalists, and businessmen who supported the regime of Chiang Kai-shek and the Chinese Nationalists against Mao Tse-tung and the Communists during the 1960s and early 70s.

**ChiNats** abbr. for Chinese Nationalists.

**Chinese** more than 1 million Chinese lived in Vietnam, mainly in the Cholon district of SAIGON, and in other large cities.

**Chinh Huan** North Vietnamese indoctrination sessions for all Communist party members.

**Chinook** the CH–47, a large, twin-rotor Boeing helicopter used primarily for carrying cargo or large groups of soldiers on nontactical movements. Basically a supply and transport helicopter, it was used by the U.S. Army and by the Vietnam Air Force. Nicknamed Shithook, Hook, and FLYING OSCAR.

**chit** 1. a paper indicating approval of a serviceman's request. 2. a receipt.

**CHJCS** abbr. for Chairman of the Joint Chiefs of Staff.

**chloracne** medical term for a rash characterized by boils, itching, and redness; caused by exposure to the toxic chemical DIOXIN. Many Vietnam veterans are still suffering from its effects.

**chlorobenzamalononitrile** chemical name for CS gas.

**chloroquine-primaquine** a tablet given weekly to U.S. servicemen to help prevent malaria. It was often called the Monday pill, as it was usually dispensed on Mondays. Other nicknames were horse pill, elephant pill, CP pill, Big Orange pill and Commander Orange, because of its color, a yellowish orange.

**CHMAAG** abbr. for Chief, Military Assistance Advisory Group.

**CHNAVADVGRU** abbr. for Chief, Naval Advisory Group.

**chock** the number of aircraft in a flight; for example, Chock Two is the second and Chock Five is the fifth. Also spelled chalk.

**Chocktaw** a transport helicopter manufactured by Sikorsky and used by the U.S. Marines and the Vietnam Air Force.

**chocolate bunnies** slang for Vietnamese prostitutes who charged black GIs less than white GIs and frequently did not charge the black GIs at all.

**chogie** slang meaning to move out quickly. A term from the Korean war, it was used in Vietnam by U.S. soldiers who had served in Korea. Also phrased as "cut a chogie."

**Cholon** the Chinese quarter of Saigon. At one time it was a separate city from SAIGON and was inhabited almost exclusively by Chinese.

**Cholon PX** a very large PX similar to a department store in Cholon, a restricted part of SAIGON.

**chông**  Vietnamese for mountain pass.

**chống chiến xa**  Vietnamese for antitank.

**chop-chop**  1. Vietnamese slang for food. 2. slang meaning to hurry up, or to move a little faster.

**chopped rag**  slang for a parachute altered by cutting out of some of its panels.

**chopper**  slang for helicopter.

**CHOPS**  abbr. for Chief of Operations.

**chow**  slang for food.

**chow down**  slang for eating a meal.

**CHO**  1. abbr. for Company Headquarters. 2. abbr. for Corps Headquarters.

**Chrau**  a MONTAGNARD tribe living mainly in TUYEN DUC Province.

**Christmas bombing**  sarcastic nickname for the bombing of Hanoi and Haiphong in December 1972 as part of Operation LINEBACKER II.

**Christmas truce**  a halt to the bombing of North Vietnam in 1972, during Operation Linebacker II. This period of restricted air attacks led to the cease-fire of January 23, 1973.

**chrome dome**  marine slang for the aluminum-painted fiber helmet worn during HOT/SOP to protect the head from the sun.

**chron**  abbr. for Chronology.

**CH–37**  Sikorsky's Deuce, a twin-engined assault heavy transport helicopter with the capacity to carry three crew members in addition to 36 passengers.

**CH–3**  a Sikorsky twin-turbine, single rotor helicopter, the Jolly Green Giant.

**Chu Hoi**  Vietnamese for I surrender. See CHIEU HOI.

**Chu Lai**  a town on the coast of the South China Sea in QUANG TRI Province in I CORPS where a major Marine Corps base was located.

**Chủ Lực**  the elite MAIN FORCE of the North Vietnamese Army.

**Chủ Lực Quân**  Vietnamese for regular forces.

**Chuck**  1. a term used by black marines to identify white soldiers. 2. often derogatory term referring to the enemy. See GOOK.

**chunker**  slang for the M–79 grenade launcher. Also spelled clunker.

**Chuong Thien**  one of the 44 provinces of South Vietnam, located in IV CORPS.

**churning butter**  slang for having sex.

**CI**  1. abbr. for counterinsurgency. 2. abbr. for counterintelligence.

**CI Team**  abbr. for Counterintelligence Team.

**CIA**  abbr. for U.S. CENTRAL INTELLIGENCE AGENCY.

**CIB**  abbr. for the Combat Infantry badge, an army award limited to the infantry, for being under fire in a combat zone. It was worn on both fatigues and dress uniforms. See also CAR (Combat Action Ribbon).

**CIC**  1. abbr. for Combat Information Center. 2. abbr. for Commander In Chief. 3. abbr. for Counterintelligence Corps.

**CID** abbr. for the Criminal Investigation Division of the U.S. Army.

**CIDG** (pronounced: "Sidgee") abbr. for Civilian Irregular Defense Groups. These ethnic minorities moved from remote areas to train with U.S. SPECIAL FORCES for village defense or commando operations.

**CINC** abbr. for Commander in Chief.

**CIP** abbr. for Counterinsurgency Plan.

**circle jerk** slang for activity with no purpose.

**City, The** slang for the complex south of SNUOL in Cambodia where a very large cache was found by U.S. soldiers in 1970.

**Civic action** a combination of MEDCAPS, DENTCAPS, and other civil affairs projects of U.S. military for pacification programs in South Vietnam.

**civilization** fond nickname for the United States of America.

**clacker** a small hand-held firing mechanism with a squeeze handle used to set off CLAYMORE mines. It made a clacking sound when used.

**CLAK** abbr. for CLANDESTINE KILL.

**Clandestine Kill** A recon term for silent killing, usually by a two-man team and often by use of the hands or a knife. This type of assasination technique is not legal by U.S. military standards and was used only when necessary.

**clap checker** slang for enlisted men of the Medical Corps, MEDICS.

**Claymore** an ANTIPERSONNEL mine used by U.S. troops; when detonated it propelled many small steel cubes in a 60-degree fan-shaped pattern. Its maximum distance was about 100 meters and the lethal range was about 50 meters. Claymores were inscribed "Front toward Enemy." The VC also used a similar type of claymore mine, a DH–5.

**clean sheets** slang for sleeping on an actual bed or cot, as opposed to in the field.

**clear and hold** a military tactic where U.S. troops captured and attempted to hold a specific area.

**clear and secure** a military mission to find and capture or destroy all enemy forces within a specified area and then prevent the enemy from reentering that area.

**clearance** 1. clearing an area of the enemy. 2. permission to engage the enemy in a specific area.

**clerks and jerks** slang for office and support personnel.

**click** slang for KILOMETER. Also spelled klik and klick.

**Clifford, Clark** secretary of defense, 1968–1969.

**clip** an AMMO magazine.

**clock positions** aerial term for calls relative to things outside an aircraft. These are made as if the nose of the aircraft were twelve o'clock, the tail at six o'clock, the right wing three o'clock, and the left wing at nine o'clock.

**close** aerial term meaning to decrease separation between aircraft.

**close air support** the use of planes and helicopters to fire on enemy units close to FRIENDLIES.

**cloud nine** slang for a feeling of elation, most often felt just before R & R or ROTATION.

**cloverleaf** a formation used in search operations that allowed a rapid search of a large area. The subordinate elements moved out from a central area and spiraled back to the starting point. It was used when advancing into unknown and possibly hostile enemy territory.

**CLP** a type of oil used to clean rifles; it cleans, lubricates, and penetrates.

**Clubs and messes scandal** slang for the 1969 bribery/kickback/smuggling operation operative among U.S. Army personnel in Vietnam and on European bases.

**clunker** slang for the M-79 grenade launcher. Also spelled chunker.

**cluster bomb** a bomb used as an ANTIPERSONNEL weapon. It held hundreds of pellets that burst outward to maim and kill.

**cluster fuck** slang for grunts who gather closely together in small groups.

**cluster belt** term for the ammunition CARTRIDGE BELT that marines wore in Vietnam.

**Clyde** slang for enemy troops.

**CM** abbr. for Court-Martial.

**CMD** abbr. for Capital Military District, referring to the Saigon environs. Also called Capital Military Zone.

**CMH** 1. abbr. for CONGRESSIONAL MEDAL OF HONOR. Two hundred and thirty-eight Medals of Honor were awarded during the Vietnam War. 2. abbr. for casket with metal handles, a phrase grunts used as "don't want no CMH."

**CN** abbr. for tear gas. CN stands for chloroacetophenone, a toxic solid material used as a solution in making tear gas.

**CO** 1. abbr. for Conscientious Objector. 2. abbr. for Commanding Officer.

**Cô** Vietnamese for an unmarried woman. It is used as a title, like Miss.

**cô cong** Vietnamese for female Viet Cong soldier.

**cố vấn** from the Vietnamese word *co van my,* which means American advisor, an American assigned to Vietnamese military units or to political divisions within the country to help direct and train Vietnamese military and civilian officials.

**Coast Guard** the smallest branch of the U.S. military. Coast Guard personnel did their part in Vietnam mainly by plying its internal waterways. It was called the Freshwater Navy because it operated inland. The Coast Guard became a part of the Department of Transportation on April 1, 1967; formerly it had been a part of the Department of the Treasury.

**Cobra** the AH–1G small Bell attack helicopter. It was also known as a GUNSHIP, armed with GRENADE LAUNCHERS, ROCKETS, and MACHINE GUNS. Cobras were supplied to the Army of Vietnam and the American forces and were used by the U.S. Army, Navy, and Marines. The Cobra's nickname was Red Bird.

**COC** abbr. for Combat Operation Center.

**Cochinchina** the former French name for the southernmost part of Vietnam and the richest, most fertile part of the country. The MEKONG DELTA is located here, and the area is known as Vietnam's rice bowl. Some of this area was formerly a part of Cambodia.

**Cockbang** slang for Bangkok, Thailand, a popular R & R location.

**cocksuckers** slang for LEECHES.

**coconut mine** a booby trap in which a hollowed-out coconut was filled with black powder and buried in the ground. When someone walked by, a trip wire triggered an explosion.

**coconut monk** nickname given by the Americans to Dao Dua, a Vietnamese Buddhist monk who vowed not to speak until Vietnam was at peace.

**COD** 1. abbr. for Close Order Drill. 2. abbr. for Carrier Onboard Delivery aircraft, usually bringing mail to an aircraft carrier or serving as a ship-to-shore shuttle.

**code of conduct** military instructions for U.S. soldiers taken prisoner. The code discussed surrender; trying to escape; refusal to accept favors from the enemy; refusal to aid the enemy or to make disloyal statements; and the refusal to give any information other than name, rank, serial number, and date of birth.

**Codel** abbr. for Congressional Delegation.

**COFRAM** abbr. for Controlled Fragmentation Munition, an antipersonnel artillery projectile loaded with small bomblets. This powerful weapon was surrounded by secrecy and could be used only with special permission. Its nickname was Firecracker.

**cohabitation license** the license U.S. soldiers could buy for $1.00, was good for one year, and gave a soldier the legal right to cohabit with a part-time wife without police interference. In Vietnam a soldier could have as many "wives" as he could afford.

**COIN** abbr. for Counterinsurgency.

**Col** abbr. for Colonel.

**Colby, William** chief of Far East Division, CIA, from 1962 to 1967, director of CORDS, 1968–1971, and director of the CIA, 1973–1976.

**cold** descriptive word for no fire. See also HOT.

**cold hole** slang for an empty tunnel, clear of the enemy.

**Cold LZ** abbr. for Cold LANDING ZONE, meaning there was no fire in the Landing Zone and that it was a relatively safe place to land. See also HOT LANDING ZONE.

**COLD/SOP** abbr. for Cold Standard Operation Procedures. These rules were in effect from October 15 to April 15, when certain precautions against the heat were not necessary. See also HOT/SOP.

**collectivization** the grouping together of Vietnamese laborers and poor farmers to cultivate state-owned land.

**College Eye** USAF EC–121 airborne early warning and airborne navigational assistance. Its radio call sign was Disco.

**colors**  1. ceremony of raising or lowering the flag. 2. slang for LSD.

**Colt**  the company that manufactured the M–16 rifle.

**Colt Commando**  slang for the 5.56 submachine gun, also known as CAR–15.

**com rats**  short for commuted rations, the subsistence payment for those who did not eat in mess halls.

**Com Z**  just forward of the combat zone where communications, supplies, and other support for field forces were established.

**Combat Action Ribbon**  the U.S. Marine Corps decoration for action under enemy fire in a combat zone. See also COMBAT INFANTRY BADGE.

**Combat Air Patrol**  an aircraft patrol over an area, combat zone, or air defense which could intercept and demolish aircraft before they could reach their target and before they could provide cover for strike aircraft.

**combat emplacement evacuator**  military term for a shovel or ENTRENCHING TOOL.

**combat engineers**  units that went in ahead of combat troops to prepare landing zones, roads, and so forth. See also CONSTRUCTION ENGINEER.

**Combat Infantry Badge**  a U.S. Army award limited to the infantry for being under fire in a combat zone. It is worn on both fatigues and dress uniforms. See also COMBAT ACTION RIBBON.

**Combat Medic Badge**  a decoration awarded to Army medical personnel who performed medical duties in direct support of infantry units or Spe-cial Forces detachments under fire in combat. Personnel in navy, marine, and air force medical departments who performed medical duties under fire were also eligible.

**combat pay**  combat pay in Vietnam was $65 per month and was first issued to troops in April 1965, retroactive to January 1965.

**combat professor**  slang for American military advisors in Vietnam.

**combat sky spot**  a radar-controlled air strike. A ground station system was used to accurately drop bombs up to 100 miles away.

**combat spread**  aerial term for a loose formation which allowed each flight member maximum vision.

**combat tracker teams**  a team of five men and one scout dog who searched out the Viet Cong and the North Vietnamese Army.

**combat tree**  an electronic system on U.S. fighter planes making it possible to identify enemy aircraft from the Identification Friend or Foe (IFF) signals.

**Combined Action Platoon**  joint American Marine and South Vietnamese militia units set up to safeguard designated villages. The combined action platoons were usually made up of 15-man marine squads and three squads of POPULAR FORCES working together.

**Combined Action Program**  the marine-initiated pacification technique which integrated a marine rifle squad with a South Vietnamese Popular Force platoon for purposes of hamlet and village security.

**Comfy Bridle**   code for a U.S. Air Force secure communications network in South Vietnam.

**comics**   slang for topographic maps, also called funny papers.

**comm**   short for communications.

**Command and Control**   the aircraft in which a commander circles a battle area to direct a firefight. Also called Charlie Charlie and Charlie Bird.

**Command and Control North**   the MACV–SOG field command and forward operating base set up in 1968 to manage and control unconventional warfare. Command and Control North was based in Danang.

**Command and Control Central**   the MACV–SOG field command and forward operating base set up in 1968 to manage and control unconventional warfare. Command and Control Central was based in Kontum.

**Command and Control South**   the MACV–SOG field command and forward operating base set up in 1968 to manage and control unconventional warfare in South Vietnam. Command and Control South was based in Ban Me Thuot.

**command bird**   a unit commander in an aircraft which circled an area of ENGAGEMENT to watch and oversee his troops. Also called C & C or Command and Control.

**Commandant, U.S. Marine Corps**   the senior officer of the U.S. Marine Corps. During the Vietnam War, the commandants were General Randolph Pate, 1959–1960; General David Shoup, 1960–1964; General Wallace Greene, 1964–1968; General

Leonard Chapman, 1968–1972; General Robert Cushman, 1972–1975.

**Commander Orange**   slang for the CHLOROQUINE PRIMAQUINE (CP pill) antimalaria tablets taken weekly by U.S. personnel in Vietnam to protect against malaria.

**Commando Hunt**   code term used after 1968 to describe operations designed to destroy the HO CHI MINH TRAIL. U.S. Air Force, Marines, and Naval aircraft worked together in this attempt.

**Commando Vault**   a 15,000 pound concussion superbomb.

**commbird**   nickname for an airborne communications link.

**Commendation Medal**   see ARMY COMMENDATION MEDAL.

**Commendation Ribbon**   a ribbon and medallion decoration awarded to military personnel who displayed meritorious achievement.

**COMMIKE**   a microphone which could be switched off and on by remote control in an aircraft above. This device was attached to ACOUSID and ADSID sensors.

**commissioned officer**   an officer ranking as a second lieutenant or higher in the U.S. Army, Air Force, or Marine Corps, or as an ensign or higher in the U.S. Navy or Coast Guard.

**commo**   short for communications, communication wire, signal capacity, or communications personnel or equipment.

**commo bunker**   a bunker containing vital communications equipment.

**commo check**   slang for a radio check.

**commo wire** short for communications wire.

**Communist party of Vietnam** established in 1929, it was later called Viet Nam Doc Lap Dong Minh Hoi, or League for the Independence of Vietnam, or Viet Minh. The Viet Minh became proficient in guerrilla warfare. During the very early 1960s, the term *Viet Cong* replaced Viet Minh as the term used outside of North Vietnam for Vietnamese Communists.

**company** a military unit usually consisting of a headquarters and two or more platoons under the command of a captain.

**company lift** the number of helicopters in flight.

**Company, The** slang for the CIA.

**company uniform** the UHF radio frequency on which a company communicated. These were often changed to bewilder the enemy. Also called team uniform.

**Composite Marine Aircraft Group** an aircraft group made up of both helicopters and fixed-wing aircraft.

**composition CS** a tear gas used to smoke out Viet Cong concealed in tunnels.

**compound** a fortified military installation.

**compressor stall** the failure of the compressor in a jet engine.

**compromised** forewarning that the enemy has learned a unit's call sign code or password.

**con dao** Vietnamese for knife.

**Con Son** prison on the island called POULO CONDOR, which was known for its TIGER CAGES used as cells.

**Con Thien** a group of three hills in QUANG TRI Province near the Demilitarized Zone. There were many fierce battles here, near the border of North Vietnam. Also known as the Hill of Angels.

**concentrated fire** the fire from the batteries of two or more ships aimed at a given target.

**concertina wire** coiled barbed wire used as an obstacle, to impede the progress of ground troops and to protect perimeters.

**concussion grenade** a grenade filled with TNT. When detonated, it sent out shock waves rather than shrapnel.

**condition CAP** standing by for sudden takeoff if it becomes necessary.

**condolence award** slang for the compensation paid to the family of a dead North Vietnamese soldier. This compensation was thought to be equal to about U.S. $50.

**coolies** slang for Vietnamese civilian workers.

**C–1** the C–1A Trader. This was the standard COD aircraft during the Vietnam War, bringing mail to carriers and acting as a shuttle to carriers. This aircraft was a variant of the S–2 Tracker, a twin-engined, propeller-driven, antisubmarine aircraft. The C–1 delivered mail, people, and spare parts.

**C–119** the Convair-twin-boom cargo plane equipped with miniguns and flares for night missions. It was nicknamed the flying box car.

**C–141**   An American Air Force transport plane, the Starlifter. One of the largest planes of its type in the world, it was used as an intercontinental jet transport.

**C–117**   the Hummer aircraft. This stretched version of the C–47 was used by the marines for transport and flare missions.

**C–117D**   the Douglas Skytrain. This twin-engine, transport aircraft first became operational for the marines in 1943.

**C–130**   an air force medium cargo plane, Lockheed's Hercules was also known as Herky Bird. It was a medium transport used by the U.S. Air Force for supply and by the Marine Corps for supply and air refueling. The Herky Bird was a very well- respected aircraft.

**C–123**   a small cargo plane, the Caribou. Designed to operate out of small airstrips, it was used as a workhorse plane. Also called Provider.

**conex**   large corrugated metal packing crate about six feet in length often used as shelter on fire bases and to transport heavy equipment. Also spelled connex.

**conflict**   because the Vietnam War was not a declared war, it was and is referred to by the government as the Vietnam Conflict or Vietnam Era.

**công binh**   Vietnamese for engineer.

**cộng sản**   Vietnamese for Communist.

**Congressional Medal of Honor**   the highest award, given for bravery above and beyond the call of duty.

There were 238 Medals of Honor awarded during the Vietnam War.

**Congrint**   abbr. for Congressional Interest, a message from a congressperson in response to his or her being contacted by a relative or friend of a combatant.

**Conien, Lucien**   a U.S. Army major and CIA agent who was involved with the generals who overthrew NGO DINH DIEM. Born in France and raised in the United States, he fought in the French Army at the beginning of World War II and later joined the Office of Strategic Services, which became the CIA. He was, in 1963, the liaison to the South Vietnamese generals who were attempting to overthrow Ngo Dinh Diem. Conien left Vietnam after the coup. His nickname was Black Luigi.

**conn**   the person responsible for controlling a ship's movements.

**connex**   See CONEX.

**Connie**   see CONSTELLATION.

**conscientious objector**   a SELECTIVE SERVICE category used to avoid military service, usually on religious grounds. Most young men who qualified for this classification were required to serve for two years in low-paying community service jobs, usually away from their home areas.

**const**   short for construction.

**Constant Guard**   the emergency use of U.S. Air Force aircraft which responded to the invasion of North Vietnam into South Vietnam in March 1972.

**Constellation**   1. Lockheed's EC–121, a military version of Lockheed's piston-driven airliner. This was used for airborne COMMAND

AND CONTROL of fighter aircraft over the North and in Laos. 2. U.S. Navy carrier, serving in Vietnam. Often called by its nickname, Connie, it was the object of the antiwar protest slogan "Keep Connie Home" when it was deployed for its sixth tour in October 1971.

**construction engineer** u n i t s which built ports, airfields, and base camps. Later in the war (after 1967) they built roads, hospitals, and bridges as well. Also see COMBAT ENGINEERS.

**contact** enemy engagement, including firing on or being fired on by the enemy.

**containment** American foreign policy after World War II. This focused on the use of political, diplomatic, and military tactics to keep Communism from spreading.

**Continental** a modern hotel on TU DO STREET in SAIGON. During the war, it had 95 rooms of which 65 were air-conditioned.

**Continental Air Service** a privately owned airline which operated alongside AIR AMERICA and worked for the benefit of the CIA.

**Continental Shelf** nickname for the outdoor sidewalk cafe of the Hotel CONTINENTAL in Saigon.

**Control Commission** the group who signed the PARIS PEACE ACCORDS and agreed to supervise the terms of the cease-fire. This commission was not very effective. See ICCS.

**CONUS** abbr. for Continental United States.

**convoy** a traveling line of trucks or tanks.

**Convoy of Tears** nickname for the evacuation of PLEIKU by South Vietnamese civilians in March 1975.

**Cookie Division** slang for the Ninth Infantry Division, called that due to the octofoil design of its shoulder insignia. Also called Psychedelic Cookie.

**cool** the use of a gas for cooling the heat-seeker head of the AIM–4D air-to-air missile in preparation for firing.

**Cooper-Church Amendment** an amendment adopted by the Senate that prohibited spending, without Congress's approval, funds for keeping United States troops in Cambodia, or for otherwise supporting Cambodia after June 1970.

**cordon and search** an operation in which an area is first sealed by a military force and then searched.

**CORDS** a U.S. agency that attempted to put under a single command many resources from the military, the State Department, the Central Intelligence Agency and other agencies for purposes of pacification. It was established in 1967. By 1969, CORDS was pursuing pacification goals in South Vietnam. After 1969, the pacification efforts continued by the United States were actually considering how to get out of Vietnam. CORDS encouraged the PHUONG HOANG program in attempting to neutralize the Viet Cong infrastructure.

**Coronado** code for a series of vital RIVERINE FORCE operations.

**corps** two or more divisions, responsible for the defense of a MILITARY REGION.

**Corps I** (pronounced "eye core") area of South Vietnam nearest the Demilitarized Zone.

**Corps II** area of South Vietnam near the CENTRAL HIGHLANDS.

**Corps III** area of South Vietnam near the IRON TRIANGLE.

**Corps IV** area of South Vietnam near the MEKONG DELTA.

**Corps Tactical Zone** see MILITARY REGION.

**corpsman** navy medical personnel or medic.

**corpsman up** marine call in the field for a medic.

**corridor six thirteen** a route that was the supply line which paralleled the HO CHI MINH TRAIL, following along the Truong Son Mountains in South Vietnam. This route was also known as the Truong Son Corridor.

**Corsair II** Ling-Temco-Vought's A–7 single-seat attack aircraft, also known as SLUF (Short Little Ugly Feller). See A–7.

**COS** abbr. for Chief of Staff.

**cosmoline** an oily, protective substance used to prevent rust when storing items such as rifles.

**COMUSMACV** abbr. for Commander, U.S. Military Assistance Command, Vietnam.

**COSSAC** abbr. for Chief of Staff to the Supreme Allied Commander.

**COSVN** abbr. for Central Office for South Vietnam. This was the Communist headquarters of the North Vietnamese and the Viet Cong in South Vietnam. It was located in TAY NINH province near the Cambodian border.

**counter** an air mission over North Vietnam.

**counterfire** fire meant to destroy enemy weapons.

**counterguerrilla warfare** operations by armed forces using nonmilitary government forces against insurgents.

**counterinsurgency** U.S. military phrase for counterrevolution or operations against nonregular or guerrilla forces.

**counterintelligence** intelligence activity used to destroy the effectiveness of foreign enemy intelligence activities. Counterintelligence protects against espionage, subversion, and various types of sabotage.

**countermeasure pod** a radar-jamming device.

**country team** the staff and personnel of an American embassy assigned to a particular country, especially as applied to the United States ambassador to South Vietnam and the commander of Military Assistance Command, Vietnam (MACV).

**County Fair** a form of CORDON AND SEARCH or the seek and destroy mission in which American and South Vietnamese troops surrounded a village as South Vietnamese police searched for arms, guerrillas, and political infrastructure. Meanwhile, the villagers were provided entertainment and welfare and other services. Country Fair was a marine program to return security to rural areas. The army version of this activity was called hamlet festival.

**court-martial** legal proceedings in the armed forces. The court is made up of military personnel to try charges of offenses against military law.

**cover** 1. the protection given to a surface area or force, or the aircraft used to provide the protection. 2. marine term for hat.

**covering fire** fire used to shield troops when they are in range of enemy small arms.

**Cow** slang for an aircraft, usually a C–123 or C–130 equipped with rubberized drums and large pumps. They were also called flying cow and bladder bird.

**cowboy** slang for a Vietnamese gangster or thief, or someone not to be trusted. Rebellious American soldiers were called cowboys by some Vietnamese.

**Cowboy, The** nickname for NGUYEN CAO KY.

**COWIN** abbr. for Conduct of the War in Vietnam, which was the title of an official report by the army deputy chief of staff of the military in 1971.

**coxswain flat** naval designation for the spot where the driver (coxswain) stands when steering a ship or boat.

**coz** short for COSMOLINE.

**CP** abbr. for Command Post. Units of platoon size or larger established command posts or field headquarters to coordinate the activities of the unit from a central point.

**CP Pills** the yellowish-orange anti-malaria pill, taken from CHLOROQUINE-PRIMAQUINE, its chemical name.

**CPO** 1. abbr. for Chief Petty Officer, a navy NCO. 2. abbr. for Civilian Personnel Office.

**Cpt** abbr. for Captain.

**CPX** abbr. for Command Post Exercise.

**CQ** see CHARGE OF QUARTERS.

**CR** abbr. for credit, referring to aerial victory credit, or downing an enemy aircraft.

**crachin** a constant drizzle of rain with foggy, poor visibility. From the French word for spit.

**CRAF** abbr. for Civil Reserve Air Fleet.

**crank time** the starting up of a helicopter.

**c-rations** the standard meals eaten in the bush. C-rations came in cartons containing 12 different meals, complete with instant coffee and three cigarettes.

**c-rats** see C-RATIONS.

**CRB** abbr. for CAM RANH BAY.

**Credible Chase** code for the plan to use short takeoff and landing aircraft as mini GUNSHIPS.

**CREEP** abbr. for Committee to Re-elect the President, active during the 1968 election. Their activities led to the Watergate Scandal and the 1974 resignation of President Richard Nixon.

**crib** tying down equipment on the exterior deck of a submarine.

**CRID** abbr. for the Republic of Korea Capital Infantry Division, nicknamed the TIGER DIVISION.

**Crimp** abbr. for the Consolidated Improvement and Modernization Program.

**CRIP** abbr. for Combat Recon Intelligence Platoon. These were U.S. and South Vietnamese troops working for the district chief to collect intelligence from civilians.

**crispy critters** slang for burned bodies, especially those burned by NAPALM.

**CRITIC** abbr. for Critical Intelligence Message.

**crocodile, to** slang meaning to kill.

**crop denial** a U.S. program to prevent the enemy from growing food, especially rice. Chemical DEFOLIANTS were used to reach this goal.

**Crossbar Hotel** slang for jail.

**cross-turn** aerial term for a rapid simultaneous 180 degree change of heading by the members of a flight or an element, in which half of the unit turns toward the other half.

**crotch rot** generic term for a tropical disease covering many different infections of the genital area; also called gunge.

**Crotch, The** affectionate slang for the marines, used mainly by marines.

**CROW** abbr. for Counter Recoil Operated Weapon.

**Crow's Foot** see EAGLE'S CLAW.

**CRP** 1. abbr. for Combat Reconnaissance Platoon. 2. abbr. for Control and Reporting Post. 3. abbr. for CORPS.

**cruise** 1. naval and marine term for a tour of duty. 2. naval designation for enlisted period or a shipboard deploy-ment. 3. air force formation involving a parade formation with very close-quarter maneuvers. This formation was never made in a hostile area.

**cruise and kill** light scout team work used along with a NIGHT HAWK to seek and destroy the enemy.

**crunch cap** slang for the BOONIE HAT, so-called because it could be crunched up and put into a pack or a pocket.

**crunchies** slang for INFANTRYMAN.

**Crusader** see F–8.

**Crusaders** nickname for the 523d Tactical Fighter Squadron.

**Crusher** short for the LETOURNEAU TREE CRUSHER.

**CS** 1. a riot control gas agent from a CS grenade, used to clear out enemy tunnels. 2. a nonlethal tear gas.

**CS/CN grenade** the M–7 tear gas grenade used to clear bomb shelters and tunnels.

**CS gas** see CS.

**CSA** abbr. for Chief of Staff, Army.

**CSM** 1. abbr. for Combat Sergeant Major. 2. abbr. for Company Sergeant Major.

**CSMO** abbr. for Close-Station March Order, meaning preparation to move equipment.

**CT** abbr. for COUNTRY TEAM.

**C³** short for Command, Control, and Communication, also referred to as C-cubed. Slang for COMMAND AND CONTROL.

**CTU** abbr. for Commander Task Unit.

**C–2** Grumman Greyhound, a navy cargo transport airplane.

**CTZ** abbr. for Corps Tactical Zone, the principal military and political territorial subdivision of the Republic of South Vietnam; divisions were numbered I through IV, from north to south.

**Cu Chi** a town near Saigon. The area around Cu Chi was known for its extensive system of enemy TUNNELS.

**Cu Chi National Guard** nickname of the 25th Infantry Division, called that because the division headquarters and most of the troops were stationed there during the war. The 25th Infantry Division was also known as Tropic Lightning because of its insignia.

**Cu Loc Prison** a North Vietnamese prison known as THE ZOO.

**Cua** a MONTAGNARD tribe living mainly in QUANG NGIA and QUANG NAM provinces.

**CUNT** derogatory abbr. for Civilian Under Naval Training, referring to civilian personnel being trained by the navy for specific jobs.

**cunt cap** slang for the narrow green garrison cap worn by enlisted personnel with khakis or the class Z uniform. It was probably called that because of its shape, resembling a vulva. Also called a piss cutter.

**cuntsville** slang for the United States during the Vietnam War.

**Cushman, Robert E.** commandant of the U.S. Marine Corps, 1972–1975.

**Customer, The** slang used by AIR AMERICA staff referring to the CIA.

**cut a chogie** slang meaning to move out quickly. This phrase is from the Korean War and was used in Vietnam by U.S. soldiers who had served in Korea.

**cut me a hus** marine slang for "do me a favor." Also phrased as "shoot me a hus."

**cut Zs** slang for sleep.

**cut-off** aerial term used for taking the shortest route to intercept an enemy airborne target.

**cứu-cấp** Vietnamese for first aid.

**CV–7** DeHavilland's Buffalo, a larger CV–2 which could carry up to 40 combat-ready troops.

**CV–2** DeHavilland of Canada's CARIBOU, a light transport. It could take off on a very short runway.

**CWO** abbr. for Chief Warrant Officer.

**CYA** abbr. for Cover Your Ass. This was widely scribbled all over army installations in the late 1960s and early 1970s.

**cyclo** a type of motorized rickshaw.

**cyclo boy and cyclo girl** slang for a pimp and his prostitute.

**cyclo may** slang for motorized version of a pedicab.

**cyclo-pousse** slang for pedicab.

# D

**d and the z, the** slang for DE-MILITARIZED ZONE.

**d, the** slang for DEMILITARIZED ZONE.

**dạ** Vietnamese for yes.

**DA** abbr. for Department of the Army.

**dạ, chắc chắn** Vietnamese for yes, certainly.

**dạ không or không** Vietnamese for no.

**Da Nang** a major deep-water port in I CORPS, with a large U.S. air base. Da Nang also was headquarters of I Corps Tactical Zone. Da Nang was known as Tourane by the French.

**Dac Cong** the Viet Cong Special Forces. These were the elite North Vietnamese GUERRILLAS, some of whom were the SAPPERS who broke through the wire to enable the troops behind to assault a camp.

**dại bác** Vietnamese for cannon.

**dại bác lòng ngắn** Vietnamese for howitzer.

**Dai Doan Ket party** the party of Great Solidarity. It was organized in 1954 to unify the noncommunist nationalist organizations in South Vietnam, before NGO DINH DIEM came to full power. The Dai Doan Ket party was the forerunner of the CAN LAO party.

**dại dội** Vietnamese for company.

**Dai Viet Party** this party formed in 1930 as a nonCommunist revolutionary and political organization in Vietnam. By the mid-1960s the Dai Viet party had evolved into several major parties that played key roles in opposing or supporting the other Dai Viet party governments. Since 1975 there has been harsh repression against Dai Viet members, some of whom still engage in resistance to the Communist government.

**daily-daily** slang for antimalaria pills which were taken every day, in addition to the Monday pills (CHLOROQUINE-PRIMAQUINE) which were taken weekly.

**daisy chain** slang for attaching one CLAYMORE to another with DET cord so that firing one set off the others. An endless number of claymores could be attached in this manner.

**daisy cutter** a bomb used in clearing LANDING ZONES; 15,000 pound bombs were used to create LZs in thick jungles, where they exploded about seven feet above the ground.

**dai-uy** Vietnamese word for captain or person in charge or village chief. Pronounced: die-wee.

**Dak Son** site of a MONTAGNARD village where civilians were burned to death by VIET CONG flamethrower teams in December 1967.

**Dak To** a CENTRAL HIGHLANDS town which was the scene of a fierce battle in June, 1967. Fighting continued for nearly six months and the conflict became known as the Battle for the Highlands, resulting in the highest number of American deaths in a single battle during the war. The peak of the battle was November 19–22 for Hill 875, 12 miles southwest of Dak To; 158 members of the 173d Airborne Brigade lost their lives at Hill 875, including 30 who died as a result of the accidental U.S. air strike on U.S. positions on November 19.

**Dalat** one of the 11 AUTONOMOUS CITIES in South Vietnam. It was a resort area in the CENTRAL HIGHLANDS, enjoyed by the elite of South Vietnam.

**dạn** Vietnamese for cartridge.

**dạn dược** Vietnamese for ammunition.

**dân quê** Vietnamese for peasant.

**dạn vạch sáng** Vietnamese for tracer bullet.

**Daniel Boone** code name for secret ground cross-border reconnaissance directed by U.S. Army SPECIAL FORCES in Cambodia. See PROJECT DANIEL BOONE.

**Daniel Boone Squads** slang for the teams of U.S. soldiers and locals who went into Cambodia for purposes of sabotage or to gain intelligence. These were also called Daniel Boone Teams.

**Daniel Boone Team** see DANIEL BOONE SQUADS.

**DAO or U.S. DAO** abbr. for United States Defense Attache Office. This was the office of the American embassy's military attache at TAN SON NHUT Airport in what had formerly been the offices of Military Assistance Command, Vietnam. It was established in SAIGON after the January 1973 cease-fire.

**dap** a soul handshake and greeting, used mainly by nonwhite soldiers. It was often specific to certain units and highly ritualized.

**dapping** ritualized, distinctive handshaking used by many black soldiers.

**Dapsone** an experimental tablet taken daily to prevent malaria. It was used mainly in 1967 through 1969 in combat areas in the Central Highlands to prevent a particular strain of malaria found there.

**dark-green** marine slang for a black, as "he's a dark-green Marine."

**Darlac** one of the 44 provinces of South Vietnam, located in II CORPS.

**DARMA** abbr. for Defense Against Rocket/Mortar Attacks. This refers to defense against preplanned artillery and mortar fire.

**DASC** abbr. for Direct Air Support Center, a subordinate operational part of the marine air control system. It was designed for control and direction of close air support and other direct air support operations.

**dash-13** helicopter maintenance report.

**dau** Vietnamese for pain.

**dầu dạn** Vietnamese for bullet.

**Davis, James** the first American to lose his life in open battle with the Viet Cong on December 22, 1961.

**Davis, Rennie** one of the CHICAGO SEVEN and a former SDS leader.

**DAV** abbr. for Disabled American Veterans, a service organization made up of former servicemen and women who have sustained war-related injuries.

**dawk**   slang for someone who is neither a DOVE nor a HAWK, and yet objected to the war but would not demonstrate against it.

**DC**   an eastern direction, referring to Washington, D.C. as east.

**DCI**   abbr. for Director, Central Intelligence.

**DCM**   abbr. for Distinguished Conduct Medal.

**DCNO**   abbr. for Deputy Chief of Naval Operations.

**DCO**   1. abbr. for Deputy Commander for Operations. 2. abbr. for Deputy Commanding Officer.

**DCPG**   abbr. for Defense Communications Planning Group, a secret and low-profile research organization which reported directly to the secretary of defense. DCPG conceived of "the electronic battlefield" and developed new weapons in its five years of service; these included remote sensing devices, laser-guided weapons, and weapon systems that could decide when to fire.

**DCSOPS**   abbr. for Deputy Chief of Staff for Operations (U.S.), the service operations staff officer of a branch of service at the Washington level.

**DC–3**   American-made Douglas propeller-driven plane used to transport passengers and cargo.

**DD**   abbr. for Dishonorable Discharge.

**deactivate**   to withdraw an active unit, or to withdraw all personnel and the designation of an active or organized unit. Also termed to demobilize or to disband.

**dead man's rounds**   slang for ROUNDS held incorrectly so that the wrong end pointed toward a soldier's body.

**Dead Man's Zone**   slang for the DEMILITARIZED ZONE.

**Dead Marine Zone**   marine slang for the Demilitarized Zone, especially used by those who served in the northernmost part of I CORPS, closest to the DMZ.

**dead space**   an area which could not be watched or protected because of the land's characteristics.

**dead stick**   aerial term for a flight test carried out with engine or engines purposely shut down or otherwise inoperative.

**dead time**   active duty time required if a serviceman was detained in the stockade. He then had to make up that time in the field.

**dead zone**   a radio dead spot, a location where it was impossible to carry out understandable radio communication.

**deadlined**   slang for down for repairs.

**Dean, John Gunther**   regional director, CORDS, 1970–1972 and deputy chief of mission, American Embassy, Laos, 1972–1974.

**Dear John letter**   a letter from a girlfriend at home, saying that she wanted to end the relationship.

**deck**   1. aerial term for a flight altitude just above the ground surface. 2. navy and marine term meaning floor.

**Decker, George**  chief of staff, U.S. Army, 1960–1962.

**deedee**  slang derived from the Vietnamese word *di,* for goodbye, leave, or depart. It was commonly spelled *didi.*

**deep serious**  slang for the worst possible predicament, such as being ambushed or overrun.

**DEFCON**  abbr. for Defensive Contact Artillery Fire. DEFCONs were planned mainly at night by artillery forward observers. The term used later in the war was DEFTAR (for Defensive Target) or Delta Tango.

**Defense Distinguished Service Medal**  award to military staff officers for exceptionally meritorious service with the office of the secretary of defense, joint chiefs of staff, or other joint activities. It ranks just below the Distinguished Service Cross (U.S. Army, Air Force Cross, Navy Cross).

**Defense Meritorious Service Medal**  award to officers who exhibited exceptionally meritorious service with the office of secretary of defense, joint chiefs of staff, or other joint activities, but not to the degree demanded of the Defense Superior Service Medal. It ranks just below a BRONZE STAR Medal (U.S. Army, Air Force, Navy, and Marine Corps).

**Defense Superior Service Medal**  awarded for exceptionally meritorious service in a position of high responsibility with the office of secretary of defense. It ranks just below the DISTINGUISHED SERVICE MEDAL (Army, Air Force, Navy, Marine Corps).

**defense suppression**  a military operation which neutralized or demolished enemy defensive procedures.

**defensive spiral**  in flying, a descending, accelerating dive using high speed and continuous roll action to avoid attack and to gain lateral separation.

**defensive split**  in flying, a controlled separation of the target group into several smaller units, used in an attempt to force interceptors to commit themselves to just one of the members of the target group.

**defensive targets**  see DEFCON.

**defensive turn**  in flying, a defensive move with the purpose of preventing an attacker from reaching a firing position. The intensity of the turn is determined by the ANGLE-OFF, range, and closure of the attacking aircraft.

**deferment**  an exemption from induction into the military. During the Vietnam Era, 16 million of the approximately 27 million men of draft age never served because they were deferred or otherwise disqualified. Until the end of 1971, men could be deferred merely by attending college.

**defoliants**  chemicals used to destroy vegetation to deny the enemy natural cover and to prevent crops from being produced. In Vietnam, a particularly destructive defoliant was the herbicide made up of 2,4–D,2,4,5–T, and dioxin, also known as AGENT ORANGE.

**DefSec**  abbr. for secretary of defense.

**DEFTARS**  Defensive Targets, or Delta Tangoes, formerly called DEFCONS.

**Delaware**  code name for American and South Vietnamese operation in the A SHAU VALLEY in the spring of

1968, undertaken to prevent North Vietnamese Army threats to the city of HUE. Our troops were not successful in keeping the North Vietnamese Army out of the A Shau Valley for any length of time.

**delayed stress syndrome**    early name for POST-TRAUMATIC STRESS DISORDER.

**Dellinger, David**    one of the CHICAGO SEVEN and a leader of the Mobilization Against the War.

**Delta**    1. the military phonetic for the letter D. 2. short for the MEKONG DELTA in IV CORPS. 3. the code name for the U.S. Army's Detachment B–52, Fifth SPECIAL FORCES Group, a reconnaissance group.

**Delta Dagger**    see F–106.

**Delta Dart**    see F–102.

**Delta Delta**    code for DONUT DOLLY, a female Red Cross Volunteer. The term was sometimes used to refer to nurses as well.

**Delta dust**    a variety of marijuana.

**Delta Tango**    abbr. for Defensive Targets. These were formerly called DEFCONS.

**demarcation line**    the line dividing South and North Vietnam. It was near, but not exactly on the 17th parallel.

**demilitarized zone.**    the dividing line between North and South Vietnam, as designated in the Geneva Convention in 1954. It included a 15 mile buffer on both sides. In slang terms, it was also called the DMZ, The D and the Z, Dead Man's Zone, Dead Marine's Zone, The D, and the Ultra Militarized Zone

**demobilize**    withdrawing all personnel from an organized unit and withdrawing the unit's designation. This procedure effectively terminated a unit's existence. Also termed to disband or to deactivate.

**Democratic Republic of Vietnam (DRV)**    the official name of HO CHI MINH'S government, which was known as North Vietnam from 1954 to 1975.

**DENTCAP**    the Dental Civic Action Program in which dentists and their technicians went into outlying areas to pull teeth, perform dental work, and teach oral hygiene to Vietnamese civilians.

**dẹp**    Vietnamese for beautiful.

**deploy**    to relocate forces to a desired area of operation.

**DEPTAR**    abbr. for Department of the Army, which was also known as DOA.

**DepTel**    abbr. for Department of State telegram.

**Deputy CG**    abbr. for Deputy Commanding General. Each U.S. division had two deputies, one for maneuvers and one for supplies.

**DePuy foxhole**    a defensive position. It was named for Major General William DePuy, the commander of the First Infantry Division in Vietnam in 1966, who devised a method of positioning with interlocking defensive fire.

**DEROS**    the Date of Expected Return from Overseas, a military term referring to the fixed length of service in Vietnam; this meant that each serviceman knew the exact date he or she would be released. Twelve months was the usual tour of service for all branches except the marines who served 13 months. The terms *derosed* and *derosing* were also used.

**Desert Inn**   nickname for an area of cells in the Las Vegas section of North Vietnam's Hoa Lo Prison (HANOI HILTON).

**Desota**   code name for U.S. Navy destroyer patrols in the GULF OF TONKIN.

**Desota Missions**   code for covert U.S. Navy operations.

**Desota Patrol**   a naval vessel equipped with electronic gear. These vessels advanced on hostile coastlines in Vietnam seeking intelligence concerning the enemy.

**Dessert**   see MENU.

**destruction fire**   fire dispensed to destroy material objects.

**det**   abbr. for Detachment.

**det cord**   see DETONATING CORD.

**detail**   a work assignment.

**detainee**   euphemism for indigenous personnel taken into custody.

**detonating cord**   cord attached to explosives when attaching CLAYMORES to one another so that one could be fired, setting the others off sequentially.

**deuce**   see CH–37.

**deuce-and-a-half**   a 2 1/2 ton, all-wheel-drive, military transport truck. Also called a Six-Bye Truck or simply SIX-BY.

**deuce-gear**   marine term for ALICE pack, web belt, and other items carried in the field.

**deuce-point**   the second man in line in a patrol.

**Devil's Teeth**   slang for the three-pronged barbs spread by the Viet Cong on roads to cut the tires of U.S. and South Vietnamese vehicles.

**dew**   slang for marijuana.

**Dewey Canyon**   code for a marine operation against the North Vietnamese Army's main force near Laos. Operations Dewey Canyon I and II prepared for the South Vietnamese Army's invasion of Laos in February 1971.

**Dewey Canyon III**   ironic term given to the Vietnam Veterans Against the War's five-day demonstration in Washington, D.C., in April 1971. DEWEY CANYON I and II were U.S. military operations in Vietnam, thus implying that the demonstration was also a battle.

**Dexedrine**   an amphetamine drug (also called speed) used by troops out in the field when they had to do without sleep or had to be especially alert to the enemy.

**DF**   1. abbr. for Direction Finding. 2. abbr. for Defense Support.

**DFC**   see DISTINGUISHED FLYING CROSS.

**DH–5**   a type of Viet Cong CLAYMORE mine.

**DH–10**   a type of Viet Cong CLAYMORE mine.

**DI**   abbr. for DRILL INSTRUCTOR.

**di**   Vietnamese for go.

**Di An**   a small town northeast of SAIGON.

**DI shack**   slang for drill instructor's quarters with a desk and bunk for the DI on duty.

**DIA**   abbr. for Defense Intelligence Agency. The DIA is the intelligence department of the Joint Chiefs of Staff.

**địa đồ**   Vietnamese for map.

**địa phưỡng quân**   Vietnamese for Regional Forces.

**Diamond Shamrock**   one of the chemical companies that manufactured the defoliant, AGENT ORANGE.

**dịch**   (pronounced dick) Vietnamese for enemy and used as slang for enemy dead.

**dicks**   derogatory expression referring to the enemy. See DICH.

**diddy-bopping**   slang for walking carelessly, a dangerous activity in the jungle.

**didi**   slang from the Vietnamese word *di,* meaning to leave or to go. Also spelled deedee.

**didi mau**   Vietnamese for go quickly.

**Diem, Ngo Dinh**   see NGO DINH DIEM.

**Dien Bien**   a brand of strong North Vietnamese cigarettes.

**Dien Bien Phu**   location where the French were defeated in 1954, after 55 days of fighting, ending their rule in Vietnam. Called the Battle of 55 days, this was the last battle of the first war in Vietnam and caused the French to surrender on May 7, 1954. Dien Bien Phu is on the Laotian border, west of Hanoi.

**dime**   slang for the number 10.

**dime-nickel**   nickname for a 105mm HOWITZER.

**ding**   slang for killed.

**ding team**   slang for a scout and sniper team who alternate as spotter and shooter. See KILL TEAM.

**dinger**   slang for a sniper.

**Dinh Tuong**   one of the 44 provinces of South Vietnam, located in IV CORPS.

**dink**   derogatory slang for an Oriental. See GOOK.

**dinky dau**   (also spelled dinky dow) from the Vietnamese diên cau dau meaning to be literally off the wall, or crazy, bad, or no good.

**Dinner**   see MENU.

**dioxin**   the deadly and illness-causing chemical ingredient in the herbicide AGENT ORANGE.

**dip**   short for dipshit, derogatory slang for a Vietnamese. See GOOK.

**Dirty Bird**   a POW camp near Hanoi.

**disband**   to withdraw the designation of an inactive unit, or to withdraw all personnel and the designation of an active or organized unit. This terminates that unit's existence. Also termed to deactivate or demobilize.

**Disco**   radio call sign for College Eye, the EC–121 aircraft which provided airborne navigational assistance and border warnings.

**disengage**   to break off combat with the enemy.

**disengagement**   pulling back troops. Cutting back the U.S. troops to end the Americanization of the Vietnam War after the TET OFFENSIVE was the goal of Secretary of Defense Clark Clifford.

**Disneyland East**  slang for the Pentagon.

**Disneyland Far East**  slang for MACV or USARV headquarters.

**Distinguished Flying Cross**  an award for heroism or extraordinary achievement while participating in aerial flight. The award designated voluntary action above and beyond the call of duty. The second highest award in the U.S. Air Force, it was formerly called the Air Force Cross.

**Distinguished Service Cross (Army)**  the second highest award for bravery, awarded by the U.S. Army for extraordinary heroism while in action against the enemy. Risk of life is presumed to be so unusual that it sets apart the hero's action from the action of his comrades.

**Distinguished Service Cross (Navy)**  award while in service with the U.S. Navy, indicating serving with extraordinary heroism in military operations against an armed enemy. Also called the Navy Cross, it is the navy's second highest award.

**Distinguished Service Medal**  award to a person serving in the Army, Navy, Air Force, or Coast Guard who distinguished himself or herself by exceptionally meritorious service to the government in a duty of great responsibility. It ranks just below the Distinguished Service Cross of the Army, the Navy Cross, and the Air Force Cross.

**district**  a level of South Vietnamese government organization just beneath the level of province.

**District Mobile Company**  t h e major VIET CONG fighting unit in Vietnam. The districts were organized within each PROVINCE. The DMC was authorized to carry out various missions including direct offensive operations, terrorism, and sabotage.

**District Team**  the American personnel assigned at district level to act as advisors to Vietnamese military and civilian officials.

**ditty bag**  small zip bag issued for gear.

**Div**  abbr. for Division.

**Divarty**  1. Division ARTILLERY. 2. usually the division's headquarters.

**dive toss**  an F–4 Phantom computerized bombing device.

**Division**  1. an army or marine unit of 15,000 to 20,000 men, under the command of a general officer. A division is made up of two or three brigades or regiments plus smaller units of artillery, engineers, and other combat support. 2. an air force formation involving a flight made up of two or more SECTIONS that support each other.

**Dixie Station**  cruising area for U.S. Navy carriers in the South China Sea, about 100 miles southeast of CAM RANH BAY. Dixie Station was used for launching strikes in support of allied forces in South Vietnam, Laos, and Cambodia. Compare to YANKEE STATION.

**DKZ–57**  a Soviet-made 57mm. recoilless rifle.

**DKZ–75**  a Soviet-made 75mm. recoilless rifle.

**DMC**  see DISTRICT MOBILE COMPANY.

**DME**  abbr. for Distance Measuring Equipment. This was part of the navy's TACAN system, which supplied pilots with readouts of distance from known points on the ground.

**DMS Boot**  abbr. for Direct Molded-Sole jungle boot, the combat boot worn in Vietnam.

**DMZ**  abbr. for DEMILITARIZED ZONE.

**DNG**  abbr. for DA NANG.

**DNI**  abbr. for Director of Naval Intelligence.

**DO**  1. abbr. for Defense Order. 2. abbr. for Duty Officer.

**D.O.**  abbr. for Director of Operations.

**DOA**  abbr. for Department of the Army. Also called DEPTAR.

**dòan-tàu**  Vietnamese for convoy of ships.

**doàn-xe**  Vietnamese for convoy of vehicles.

**doc**  affectionate and respectful nickname given to MEDICS or corpsmen.

**Doc Lap**  Vietnamese for independence. The Doc Lap Palace was South Vietnamese President NGUYEN VAN THIEU'S residence, and it then became the seat of the Saigon-Gia Dinh Military Administration Committee.

**DOD**  abbr. for Department of Defense. DOD came to refer to the United States's military establishment.

**Dodge City**  1. marine slang for an area 15 kilometers south of DA NANG.

2. a generic nickname for anywhere in Vietnam where there was action.

**dog and pony show**  slang phrase for taking visiting VIPS on a guided tour of a base.

**Dogpatch**  1. nickname for an area of bars and shops near the DA NANG Air Base. 2. Dogpatch was the name of a POW camp northeast of HANOI.

**dog robbers**  slang for rear area personnel. Originally the phrase referred to the general's aides who would "rob the dogs" for the general.

**Dog's Head**  nickname for an area southeast of the FISH HOOK region near the Cambodian border; called that because of its shape.

**dogbone**  nickname for the weapon select panel in the F–4 cockpit; the panel was called that because of its shape.

**dogface**  slang for GRUNT or INFANTRYMAN.

**dogfight**  an aerial clash between opposing fighters, with much complex maneuvering and violent actions on both sides.

**doggie**  marine term for INFANTRYMAN.

**doggie straps**  slang for backpack suspenders.

**dogs**  highly useful in Vietnam for scouting, mine-detection, sentry duty, drug detection, tracking, and checking out tunnels. The dogs were trained at Fort Benning, Georgia, for six months, and had additional training on arrival in Vietnam.

**dogtags**  small metal tags imprinted with the soldier's name, serial number, blood type, and religion. Usually worn around the soldier's neck or laced into boots, they were often worn with one around the neck and one in a boot so that a body could be identified even if dismembered. Soldiers out in the FIELD often taped them together to prevent glare and jangling sounds.

**Dogwood Eight**  radio term used in the 101st Airborne Division for a wounded American soldier.

**Dogwood Six**  radio term used in the 101st Airborne Division for a dead American soldier.

**dojo**  marine slang for Karate School.

**domino theory**  a theory stating that if the United States did not take a stand in South Vietnam, the rest of Southeast Asia would fall to Communism, as in a row of dominoes. This was the rationale for our involvement in Vietnam, according to some American officials, including presidents Harry Truman, Dwight Eisenhower, John Kennedy, and Lyndon Johnson.

**dòn gánh**  Vietnamese for shoulder poles, used for carrying.

**Don Muang**  an air base in Thailand.

**Don, Tran Va**  see TRAN VA DON.

**don't rock the sampan**  a modern version, often heard in Vietnam, of the expression "Don't rock the boat."

**dong**  a unit of North Vietnamese money about equal to an American penny. See also DONG VIET. The dong is now the monetary unit of Vietnam. The dong replaced the South Vietnamese PIASTER and the North Vietnamese dong in 1978. New dong replaced the old in 1985 and are issued in 1, 2, 5, 10, 20, 50, 100, 500, 1,000,

and 5,000 denominations. The bank rate in 1988 was 87 dong to the dollar, but the exchange rate fluctuates from city to city and within cities.

**dong den stick**  marine term for a straight, multisectioned plant used for support when walking.

**Dong Khoi**  the current name for Tu Do Street in Saigon. The French called it Rue Catinet.

**Dong Thap Muoi**  the PLAIN OF REEDS, the swampy open area west of Long An Province.

**Dong Hoi**  a small port in North Vietnam which was heavily mined, immobilizing shipping.

**Dong Nai Valley**  valley formed by the Dong Nai River as it flowed through WAR ZONE D.

**Dong, Pham Van**  see PHAM VAN DONG.

**Dong Tam**  a major port constructed in IV Corps, on once flooded rice land. General William WESTMORELAND named this base, and Americans translated it from Vietnamese as "United Hearts and Minds."

**Dong Thien**  a strategic district within KIEN PHONG Province in the MEKONG RIVER DELTA. It bordered the banks of the Mekong and extended westward across the PLAIN OF REEDS.

**Dồng Tiến**  Vietnamese for Progress Together, a MACV Vietnamization program attempted in 1969. First Infantry soldiers joined with a South Vietnamese division to train ARVN soldiers in various combat operations.

**Dong Viet**  used for both the singular and the plural of the basic unit of currency in North Vietnam. In Hanoi in 1966, the dong was valued at 3.53 to the U.S. dollar.

**donkey sight**  slang for a metal sight on a tank used for quick and approximate pointing but not for precise targetting.

**donut dolly**  nickname for the Red Cross women who handed out coffee and doughnuts. They were well loved and respected by the men in the field.

**donut six**  the chief of Red Cross women. On the radio, six was the customary military number of a commander of any level.

**doobie**  slang for a marijuana cigarette.

**DOOM**  abbr. for DA NANG Officers' Open Mess.

**DOOM Pussy Mission**  slang for night SORTIES flown by B–57 crews over North Vietnam. DOOM Pussy got its name from the Da Nang Officers' Open Mess (DOOM).

**doo-mommie**  slang approximation of the Vietnamese words du ma, meaning literally "fuck your mother." Term used by GIs usually toward the enemy.

**door gunner**  the soldier in a helicopter who fired the M–60 machine gun out the open door.

**dope**  the adjustment of rifle sights taking range and wind into consideration.

**doper**  slang for a pot smoker. Dopers were also called heads.

**DOS**  abbr. for Department of State.

**dot**  aerial term for an electronic dot appearing on the radar scope when the radar was locked on. This gave accurate computed aiming information.

**DOTC**  see TIC.

**double canopy**  thick jungle growth with two layers of tropical foliage. Compare to TRIPLE CANOPY.

**Double Eagle**  code for a marine operation to sweep across the Quang Ngia and Binh Dinh provincial boundaries to capture enemy units retreating from operation MASHER.

**double force**  South Vietnamese units paired with United States units for operations jointly carried out against the enemy.

**double veteran**  a soldier who raped a Vietnamese woman and then killed her.

**double-digit fidget**  slang for having 10 to 99 days left to serve in Vietnam. Also called double-digit midget, and two-digit fidget.

**double-digit midget**  see DOUBLE-DIGIT FIDGET.

**double-time**  running 36-inch steps at the rate of 180 per minute, twice the usual rate.

**doubtful**  indigenous personnel who, after being questioned, could not be classified as either Viet Cong, civil offenders or friendlies.

**Douc Langur**  a monkey native to Vietnam.

**douche**  slang for shower.

**douche bag**  slang for shower kit.

**doughnut**  nickname for the IBS.

**doughnut dolly**  see DONUT DOLLY.

**Douglas Skywarrior**  the A–3 twin-engine aircraft. See A–3.

***Doumer Bridge*** see PAUL DOUMER BRIDGE.

***doves*** slang for Americans who opposed U.S. military intervention in Vietnam.

***DOW*** abbr. for Died Of Wounds.

***Dow Chemical*** one of the chemical companies that manufactured AGENT ORANGE, the deadly and illness-causing DEFOLIANT. Dow was also the only chemical company that manufactured NAPALM.

***downrange*** the area between the shooter and the target.

***downtown*** slang for the Hanoi area.

***downtowner*** derogatory term used by combatants for embassy staff based in Vientiane, the capital of Laos.

***dozer tank*** a command tank that carried 4,000 pounds of bulldozer equipment. It was used for earth moving and for fighting.

***dozer-infantry*** teams of bulldozers, ROME PLOWS, and infantry which worked together to clear the jungle for more effective fighting.

***DR*** abbr. for Delinquency Report. This report was turned in by Military Police for those breaking regulations or military law including minor violations of uniform or traffic rules.

***draft lottery*** in the later years of the war—1969 and after—the draft system was replaced by the lottery. Based on his date of birth, each eligible man was assigned a draft number chosen by lottery. This was viewed as a fairer system than the student DEFERMENT. Until late 1971, however, a student in college was eligible for a deferment because of a loophole in the lottery system.

***drag squad*** slang for the squad left behind a main element to keep up security on the road.

***drag, the*** 1. slang for the last man or squad in a patrol or a platoon column. 2. slang for a backup squad used to give some security to the rear. 3. a flight dynamics term for the force opposed by thrust.

***Dragon Lady*** 1. slang for a female VIET CONG terrorist who killed several people in SAIGON and CHOLON in 1967. 2. slang for ACAV (Armored Cavalry Assault Vehicles). 3. code for a clandestine U–2 recon operation in Bien Hoa in December 1963. 4. slang for Madame Ngo Dinh Nhu, the sister-in-law of South Vietnamese President Ngo Dinh Diem.

***dragon ship*** 1. slang for a transport plane converted into a GUNSHIP, an aircraft fitted out with GATLING-type machine guns and ILLUM-FLARES. 2. another name for Puff, Puff the Magic Dragon, or Spooky. 3. a DC–3 equipped with three GATLING guns.

***Dragon's Jaw*** see BRIDGE AT THANH HOA.

***Dragonfly*** see A–37.

***draw ambush*** a type of ambush which is carried out by using some type of bait, such as a few C-RATION cans or a pack of matches. Also called a mouse trap.

***dream sheet*** slang for the paper on which the soldier listed where he'd most like to serve. This rarely resulted in being stationed there.

**Dreary Road, The** translation of French slang for Route 1 in South Vietnam.

**Drill Instructor** the trainer of BOOTS and new recruits; he taught them to be effective soldiers or marines. His rank was usually that of sergeant.

**D-ring** a D-shaped metal snap link used to hold gear together.

**driver** slang for an aircraft pilot.

**DRO** abbr. for Dining Room Orderly.

**drogue chute** a chute used to drop cargo from the rear door of an aircraft while it was near the ground.

**drone** aerial term for a pilotless aircraft.

**drop zone** the preplanned landing area for parachuted men or equipment.

**drops** shortening the length of servicemen's tours in Vietnam when the United States began reducing and withdrawing its forces. The term *drop* was used for any reason except medical evacuation.

**drugs** a major problem in Vietnam, particularly after 1970. Before 1970 those found using drugs were prosecuted by the army as criminals and given dishonorable discharges. Later viewed as a medical problem, by the mid-1970s drug users who turned themselves in were promised drug treatment and an honorable discharge. The marines used administrative discharges. Commanders could get rid of drug-using marines by putting into their records "substandard performance of duty," "numerous minor discipline infractions," or "character behavior disorders." With the with-drawal and discharge of troops, the drug and alcohol problem was transported to the United States. Marijuana was the most widely used drug in Vietnam, followed by heroin and opium.

**drum** metal container for fuel.

**DRV** abbr. for Democratic Republic of Vietnam, the official name for North Vietnam; also spelled DRVN. After the formal unification of North and South in 1976, the name of the country became the Socialist Republic of Vietnam.

**dry fire** rifle practice without live ammunition.

**dry run** firing exercise in which live ammunition is not used.

**DSC** abbr. for DISTINGUISHED SERVICE CROSS.

**DSCOPS** abbr. for Deputy Chief of Staff, Operations. The DSCOPS was the staff officer working with tactical plans and operations.

**D-7 Tractor** the ROME PLOW.

**DSU** 1. abbr. for Direct Support Unit. 2. abbr. for Direct Supply Unit.

**Dtd** abbr. for dated.

**DTOC** abbr. for Division Tactical Operational Center; also called TOC.

**DTs** abbr. for DEFENSIVE TARGETS. These were also known as Delta Tangoes.

**Duan** a MONTAGNARD tribe living mainly in KONTUM Province.

**Duck Hook** an early code name for an operation to mine ports and harbors of North Vietnam, mainly HAIPHONG. This operation was carried out in May 1972 under the code name Pocket Money.

**Duck Pond** nickname for KHE SANH, a town just below the Demilitarized Zone in South Vietnam where the marines had a large combat base.

**duckbill** a 12–gauge shotgun tested in Vietnam, called that because of its shape.

**ducks** slang for American POWs who cooperated with the North Vietnamese.

**Ducky** nickname for LE DUC THO.

**dud** any explosive that does not discharge when activated.

**duffel bag** 1. long and cylindrically shaped canvas luggage issued to soldiers to hold their belongings. 2. slang for the use of seismic or acoustical devices to locate movement.

**duffel drag** a short-timer expression for the end of service in Vietnam. For example, "four and a duffel drag" would indicate a soldier had four more days to serve and then was going home.

**dumb bomb** slang for a bomb that is dropped over its target rather than being guided to it. See SMART BOMB.

**dummy cord** slang for the olive drab suspension line used to hold equipment and attached to the LBE (Load Bearing Equipment). The LBE had suspender straps and web belts to hold objects that soldiers carried in the FIELD.

**dump, the** slang for the mortuary.

**dumpster diving** slang for salvaging food discarded from the mess halls. Vietnamese adults and children engaged in this activity.

**dúng lai** Vietnamese for halt or don't move.

**dùng lo** Vietnamese for "Don't worry about it."

**Dung, Van Tien** see VAN TIEN DUNG.

**Duong Cua Dan (People's Road)** an operation by the Ninth Infantry Division to protect and upgrade Highway 4 northwest of My Tho in DINH TUONG Province. Its other purpose was to conduct RECONNAISSANCE IN FORCE operations on both sides of Highway 4 during March through July 1968.

**Duong Van Minh** South Vietnamese president appointed after the resignation of Nguyen Van Thieu.

**Durbrow, Elbridge** U.S. ambassador to South Vietnam, 1957–1961.

**durian** a large oval fruit in Vietnam that had a terrible odor but a delicious taste, similar to a peach.

**dust of life** children born to Vietnamese mothers and American soldier fathers. These children are considered by Vietnamese to be as insignificant as dust.

**dust, to** slang meaning to kill.

**Duster** 1. Army light tank of World War II vintage. 2. the nickname of an M–42 tracked vehicle with two 40mm antiaircraft guns, used mainly as ground support in Vietnam.

**dust-off** medical evacuation by helicopter, also called medevac. The term came from the great amount of dust thrown up by the rotors as the medevacs came in to land. Dust Off was also the radio sign for the Medevac Helicopter, named after the call sign of Major Charles Kelly, an early medevac pilot killed while rescuing the wounded in Vietnam. See MEDEVAC.

**dust-off chopper**    the helicopter used for DUST-OFF.

**dust-off line number**    a number each man was given on reporting in Vietnam. Lists of the numbers were kept on rosters at headquarters. When a man was killed or wounded, the report on the radio listed him by line number rather than by name.

**Dutch Mill**    nickname for the IN-FILTRATION SURVEILLANCE CENTER at Nakhon Phonom, a U.S. Air Force base in Thailand, operated by TASK FORCE ALPHA. The center was called that because of the shape of its antenna.

**DX**    1. abbr. for Direct Exchange, usually meaning the exchange of old equipment for new. 2. slang meaning to kill someone.

**Dye Marker**    code name for the MCNAMARA LINE.

**DZ**    abbr. for Drop Zone, the prearranged landing area for parachuted men or equipment.

# E

**E & E** 1. abbr. for ESCAPE AND EVA-SION, the tactic of the U.S. combat soldier if captured or cut-off from his unit. 2. slang for ducking hazardous assignments.

**Eagle** see KEYSTONE.

**eagle eye** spot checks for the VIET CONG or North Vietnamese Army among peasants, villages, or oxcarts.

**eagle flight** 1. swiftly carried out operation by Hueys, with troops aboard who flushed out Viet Cong from villages. 2. any air-delivered combat force of infantry, or a tactical operation that used a helicopter assault force to reconnoiter enemy positions. 3. a tactical operation that used a HELI-BORNE assault force or squad of larger size to reconnoiter enemy positions, often used as emergency reaction forces. First used in the DELTA in 1963, they became widely used throughout Vietnam. Because eagle flights could react very quickly, they were effective during the war. Eagle flights were also called eagle strikes.

**Eagle Pull** code for the operation involving the evacuation of the U.S. embassy and military personnel from Pnomh Penh, Cambodia, in April 1975, the final U.S. evacuation from Cambodia.

**eagle strike** see EAGLE FLIGHT.

**Eagle Thrust** code name of the operation in which 10,000 men of the 101st Airborne Division were taken for duty from Fort Campbell, Ken-tucky, to Bien Hoa, Vietnam, in a 27 hour period.

**Eagle's Claw** nickname for the Kim Son Valley about twenty miles north west of Phu My. Its seven small valleys resembled a bird's talons when seen on maps. This area was also called CROW'S FOOT.

**early out** an unscheduled early end of a military tour of duty. The usual result was an honorable dis-charge "for the good of the service"; this was common during reductions in force.

**earthquake bomb** nickname for the CBU–55 (Canistered or Clustered Bomblet Unit), one of several air-delivered weapons containing and dis-persing many smaller bomblets.

**Eastertide Offensive** an attempt beginning on March 30, 1972 to overrun South Vietnam by a cross-border attack; this was one of the major North Vietnamese miscalculations of the war. Twelve North Vietnamese divi-sions attacked Quang Tri, Kontum, and An Loc in South Vietnam. On May 1, the Communists raised their flag over Quang Tri. Stopped by the de-fending South Vietnamese divisions and American firepower, they were forced out four months later by a large U.S. air campaign. North Vietnam had expected a major victory but the offen-sive failed. Their casualties were more than 100,000 plus a significant loss of equipment. This campaign was also called the Easter Offensive.

**Eat the Apple and Fuck the Corps** marine phrase for dissatisfaction or unhappiness with the U.S. Marine Corps.

**EB–66** a light reconnaissance bomber with several configurations. It was used for gathering electronic intelligence data and for radio jamming to provide protection for strike forces.

**EC** abbr. for Engineering Corps.

**ECCM** abbr. for Electronic Counter-Countermeasures. These were devices to cancel or mislead the enemy's ECM.

**echelon** an aerial formation in which flight members are positioned sequentially on one side of the lead aircraft.

**echo** 1. military phonetic for the letter E. 2. to listen in undetected on someone's radio transmission.

**ECM** abbr. for Electronic Countermeasures. These were techniques used to jam or disrupt enemy radar or radio. Specialized aircraft were often used for this purpose.

**ECM pod** pylon or fuselage-mounted containers which held multiple transmitters and other electronic devices with the capacity to penetrate electronically controlled ground-to-air defense systems.

**EC–121** the Constellation, Lockheed's military piston-driven airliner, used for AIRBORNE COMMAND AND CONTROL of fighter aircraft over North Vietnam and in Laos.

**Ede** short for RHADE, a tribe of MONTAGNARDS.

**Edsel** see F–111.

**EE–8** a field phone.

**EEI** abbr. for Essential Elements of Intelligence. These are details on the ground for which a pilot was supposed to search.

**E–8** 1. grade for first sergeant or master sergeant in the U.S. Army, (first sergeant or master sergeant in the U.S. Marine Corps, senior master sergeant in the U.S. Air Force, and senior petty officer in the U.S. Navy). 2. an expendable, easy-to-carry launcher. It had the capacity to fire riot-control canisters which produced large amounts of a chemical cloud.

**EENT** abbr. for END OF EVENING NAUTICAL TWILIGHT.

**effective range** the maximum distance at which a weapon could be expected to hit its target and inflict damage. Effective range was always less than the maximum range, which was the absolute distance the weapon's fire traveled.

**efficiency expert** nickname for SPECIAL FORCES troops.

**efficiency report** the periodic rating that was made of officers by their superiors. Efficiency reports were also done for enlisted personnel at the end of their tours of duty.

**E–5** grade for the lowest-ranking noncommissioned officer, a sergeant or specialist-5 in the U.S. Army (sergeant in the U.S. Marine Corps, staff sergeant in the U.S. Air Force, and petty officer-2d class in the U.S. Navy).

**E–4** grade for corporal or specialist-4 in the U.S. Army (corporal in the U.S. Marine Corps, sergeant or senior Airman in the U.S. Air Force, and petty officer-3d class in the U.S. Navy).

***egg sucker***    slang for a soldier who was a kiss-ass or brown-nose.

***EGT***    abbr. for Exhaust Gas Temperature. The EGT is one of the main parameters for thrust in a turbojet engine.

***eidal laundry***    a laundry unit on a trailer covered with canvas.

***Eiffel bridge***    a French-designed metal military bridge. A few remained in Vietnam, built by the French.

***81***    short for the M–29 81mm MORTAR.

***Eighty Deuce***    nickname for the 82d Airborne Division.

***Eighty Niggers and Two White Men***    slang for the 82d Airborne Division, called that from the numerals 82 and also because there was believed to be racial imbalance in the division.

***Eighty-one Mike Mike***    nickname for the 81mm MORTAR.

***el cid***    1. slang for spies in general. 2. slang for the CIA.

***El Tee***    lieutenant, from the letters LT.

***Electric Strawberry***    nickname for the 25th Infantry Division, called that because the design of their shoulder patch represented tropic lightning. The patch itself was strawberry-shaped.

***electronics intelligence***    technical and intelligence information received from special electromagnetic radiations coming from other than radioactive sources. It was usually called Elint and was used for air missions in Vietnam and Laos.

***electronic fence***    a proposed U.S. program to build an electronic obstacle across the demilitarized zone between North and South Vietnam. It was to contain several antitrespass mechanisms and alerting systems. Never built, this fence was the idea of Robert MCNAMARA and was often called the MCNAMARA FENCE.

***element***    USAF term for the basic fighting unit of two aircraft.

***elephant grass***    tall, razor-edged tropical plant indigenous to certain parts of Vietnam, especially the highlands.

***elephant gun***    slang for the M–79 grenade launcher.

***elephant pill***    slang for the antimalarial CHLOROQUINE-PRIMEQUINE tablet taken once a week by the servicemen in Vietnam.

***elephant's intestines***    slang for the long canvas tube used by Viet Cong guerrillas to carry rice.

***elephants***    an important load-bearing animal used by the Vietnamese.

***eleven bang-bang***    slang for an INFANTRYMAN, taken from his MOS code, 11–B.

***eleven bravo***    slang for an INFANTRYMAN, taken from his MOS, 11–B.

***eleven bush***    slang for an INFANTRYMAN, taken from his MOS, 11–B.

***ELINT***    see ELECTRONICS INTELLIGENCE.

***Ellsberg, Daniel***    senior liaison officer, American Embassy, South Vietnam, 1965–1966 and a marine officer. Assistant to the deputy U.S. ambassador to South Vietnam, 1967. After participating in a study of U.S. involvement in Southeast Asia, he was convinced that the war was unjust. He obtained a copy of the study from the Pentagon and was reported to have leaked it to the press in 1971. Ellsberg was indicted and tried, but all charges were dropped in May 1973. He was active in the antiwar movement. See PENTAGON PAPERS.

**elm(s)**  abbr. for element(s).

**ELS**  abbr. for Entry Level Separation, which means the discharge of a recruit.

**EM**  abbr. for enlisted man.

**em**  1. Vietnamese for brother or good friend. 2. Vietnamese word used as a familiar reference to a servant, wife, or girlfriend.

**EM club**  abbr. for enlisted men's club.

**embassy ceiling price**  i r o n i c slang for cost limitations for real estate and other deals in Vietnam. The United States tried to set limits to moderate black market prices and to solve other economic problems.

**Embtel**  abbr. for Embassy Telegram.

**emergency medevac**  (or dust-off) those wounded who were near death. Also called urgent medevac. Compare to PRIORITY MEDEVAC and ROUTINE MEDEVAC.

**emergency resupply**  s u p p l i e s consisting of ammunition and water. When units ran short of supplies in the field and helicopter use was limited by fire, only requests for ammunition and drinking water were honored. Food was not considered an emergency request.

**EMID**  a type of electromagnetic sensor.

**En**  abbr. for Engineer.

**enclave strategy**  a program in which U.S. troops would CLEAR AND HOLD specific areas, especially along the South Vietnam coast.

**encounter**  aerial term for a series of time-continuous actions between specific U.S. and enemy aircraft.

**End of Evening Nautical Twilight**  naval term for period of the day when darkness has fallen completely.

**Endsweep**  code for mine-sweeping operations in North Vietnam during 1973 by the United States as set out by the PARIS PEACE ACCORDS. One of the final actions taken by the U.S. Navy in Vietnam was clearing the port of Haiphong of bombs planted by Americans.

**endurance**  an aircraft's capacity to continue in flight without refueling.

**ENENG**  abbr. for Enemy Engagement.

**engagement**  an encounter which involved hostile or aggressive action by one or more participants.

**Engr**  abbr. for engineer.

**ENGR CMD**  abbr. for Engineer Command.

**Enhance Plus**  code for the massive six-week program involving delivery of military equipment and aircraft to the Republic of Vietnam Armed Forces before the signing of the PARIS PEACE ACCORDS. This was to show support for President Nguyen Van Thieu and to raise the level of assistance that would be permitted under the Paris Agreement.

**ENI**  abbr. for Enemy-Initiated Incident.

**ENIFF** abbr. for Enemy-Initiated Firefight.

**E-9** grade for sergeant major or command sergeant major in the U.S. Army (master gunnery sergeant major in the U.S. Marine Corps, chief master sergeant in the U.S. Air Force, and master chief petty officer in the U.S. Navy).

**ENSURE** abbr. for Expedited Non-standard Urgent Requirement for Equipment. When a unit in the field had an urgent request and could suggest how the need could be met, items could be bought commercially, even from the states such as through Sears, Roebuck & Company, and shipped by air back to the unit which requested it.

**entrenching tool** a small folding shovel, pick, and mattock combined into one instrument; used by infantrymen. It was often called by the slang terms of Army banjo, Irish Banjo, ET, and E-tool. The formal military term for this tool was combat emplacement evacuator.

**envelope** aerial term for a volume of airspace within which a particular weapon must operate to get maximum effectiveness.

**EOD** 1. abbr. for Explosive Ordnance Disposal, disarming explosive devices. 2. abbr. for Explosive Ordnance Demolition.

**EOD team** those who disposed of explosive ordnance and deactivated mines and booby traps.

**EOGB** abbr. for Electro-Optically Guided Bomb, the SMART BOMB, first used in Vietnam in 1972 to home in on targets sighted by those aboard an aircraft.

**E-1** grade for private one, the lowest grade in the U.S. Army (private in the U.S. Marine Corps, airman basic in the U.S. Air Force, and seaman recruit in the U.S. Navy).

**ER** see EFFICIENCY REPORTS.

**Erawan** the mythical three-headed white elephant which symbolized Laos.

**Errand Boy** slang for the daily scheduled courier flights. They were also called the Pony Express.

**escape and evasion** 1. the tactic of U.S. combat soldiers if captured or cut-off from their units. 2. slang for ducking hazardous assignments. Also called E & E.

**escort** 1. an armed helicopter escort, usually a Cobra. 2. a plane flying to protect other aircraft.

**E-7** grade for sergeant first class or specialist-7 in the U.S. Army (gunnery sergeant in the U.S. Marine Corps, master sergeant in the U.S. Air Force, and chief petty officer in the U.S. Navy).

**E-6** grade for staff sergeant or specialist-6 in the U.S. Army (staff sergeant in the U.S. Marine Corps, technical sergeant in the U.S. Air Force, and petty officer first class in the U.S. Navy).

**EST** abbr. for Essential Subjects Test, the annual academic examination for all ranks below sergeant.

**ET** 1. abbr. for an Entrenching Tool. 2. abbr. for Electronics Technician.

**ETA** abbr. for Estimated Time of Arrival.

**ETD** abbr. for Estimated Time of Departure.

**E–3** grade for private first class in the U.S. Army (lance corporal in the U.S. Marine Corps, airman first class in the U.S. Air Force, and seaman in the U.S. Navy).

**E-Tool** short for an ENTRENCHING TOOL.

**ETOUSA** abbr. for European Theater of Operations, U.S. Army.

**ETS** 1. abbr. for Estimated Time of Separation (from service). 2. abbr. for Estimated Termination of Service; the scheduled date for getting out of the service. 3. abbr. for End of Tour of Service.

**E–2** 1. grade for private two in the U.S. Army (private first class in the U.S. Marine Corps, airman in the U.S. Air Force, and seaman apprentice in the U.S. Navy). 2. the Grumman HAWKEYE carrier-based airborne early-warning aircraft. It had a five-man crew and a radar dish mounted on its fuselage.

**EUSAK** abbr. for Eighth U.S. Army, Korea.

**EV** abbr. for Escort Vehicle.

**evac** short for evacuation hospital or a medical evacuation helicopter.

**evac'd** short for evacuated.

**EW** abbr. for Electronic Warfare.

**EWO** 1. abbr. for Electronic Warfare Officer. 2. abbr. for Electronic Weapons Officer.

**exec** abbr. for Executive Officer.

**expectants** casualties who are expected to die.

**Expeditionary Medal** a medal awarded to recognize service members serving before July 3, 1965, and after May 28, 1973, in either Vietnam, Laos, Thailand, or Cambodia. Those who served between those dates were eligible for the VIETNAM CAMPAIGN SERVICE MEDAL.

**extend** voluntarily staying longer than the required overseas tour of enlistment.

**extract** to pull out by helicopter.

**extraction** withdrawal of troops from the field, usually by helicopter.

**eyes in the sky** nickname for the airborne heat-sensitive detectors used to detect enemy activity over the HO CHI MINH TRAIL.

# F

**FA** abbr. for Field Artillery.

**FAA** abbr. for Federal Aviation Administration.

**FAC** abbr. for FORWARD AIR CONTROLLER.

**FAC(A)** abbr. for FORWARD AIR CONTROLLER (Airborne).

**Faceplate** the North Atlantic Treaty Organization designation for early models of the MiG–21.

**FAC-U** slang for Phan Rhang, where FORWARD AIR CONTROLLERS were trained.

**FAE** abbr. for Fuel-Air-Explosive, a highly destructive bomb. FAE was used mainly for clearing sites for helicopter LANDING ZONES; it sprayed fuel when dropped in clusters from planes. When it exploded, FAE burned up all available oxygen and its victims choked. Shock waves from this bomb destroyed everything it its path. Also spelled FAY.

**FAG** abbr. for Forward Air Guide. The FAG was often an indigenous soldier who directed air strikes from the ground.

**FAL** abbr. for Forces d'Armée of Laos, the pro-U.S. Royal Armed Forces of Laos. Also abbreviated FAR.

**falciparum** one of the two main types of malaria soldiers contracted in South Vietnam; the other was vivax. See MALARIA.

**Falcon** nickname of the infra-red AIM–4 air-to-air missile.

**fall in** call to assume military formation.

**FAME** abbr. for Floating Aircraft Maintenance Facility, which serviced combat aircraft in South Vietnam. Also called Flattop.

**Famous Fourth** a nickname of the Fourth Army Division. It was also called the Funky Fourth, and the Poison Ivy Division, because of the four ivy leaves on its shoulder patch.

**Fan Song** NATO code for the Soviet-built fire-control radar for the SA–2 missile system, used to target missile systems.

**FANK** abbr. for Forces Armées Nationale Khmer, the army of the LON NOL government in Cambodia. This training command was made up of U.S. Army Special Forces personnel, who trained Cambodian light infantry and marine battalions for the Khmer Republic. It closed down in January 1973.

**farangs** slang for foreigners.

**FARK** abbr. for Royal Cambodian Armed Forces.

**Farmer** the North Atlantic Treaty Organization designation for the MiG–19, a single-seat fighter capable of supersonic speeds, and rarely seen over Vietnam.

**Farmgate** code for the U.S. Air Force advisory support of the South Vietnamese Air Force early in the war.

**Farnsworth** a POW camp southwest of Hanoi.

**fast bird**  nickname for jet attack aircraft.

**fast CAP**  the Combat Air Patrol's strike aircraft, especially fighters. Compare with SLOW CAP.

**fast mover**  nickname for a jet aircraft, especially the U.S. Air Force F–4 PHANTOM jet.

**fast-FAC**  a FORWARD AIR CONTROLLER in an F–4 or other fighter aircraft.

**Fat City**  nickname for Military Assistance Command, Vietnam (MACV) Headquarters.

**fatigues**  standard green combat uniform.

**fatikees**  slang for jungle fatigues.

**FAVN**  abbr. for Armed Forces of [South] Vietnam.

**favorable kill ratio**  more enemy than American troops were killed.

**FAY**  abbr. for Fuel-Air-Explosive. See FAE.

**FB**  abbr. for Fire Base.

**FBIS**  abbr. for Foreign Broadcast Information Service.

**FC**  1. abbr. for Forward Controller, the air or land officer who had command of all planes and ARTILLERY when there was an attack against an enemy. 2. abbr. for Fire Control.

**FCC**  abbr. for Federal Communications Commission.

**FCT**  abbr. for Fire Control Tower. The FCT was an an elevated structure protected by sandbags, and used in camps to direct ARTILLERY, machine guns, and MORTARS when the camp was under attack.

**FDC**  abbr. for Fire-Direction Control Center. Here requests for fire support were interpreted into specific information for ground ARTILLERY. FDC also coordinated artillery and mortar fire.

**FEBA**  abbr. for Forward Edge of Battle Area.

**FDO**  abbr. for Fire Direction Officer, in command of FDC.

**FEC**  abbr. for Far East Command.

**feet dry**  a radio call to indicate that an aircraft had crossed the shore and was over land.

**feet wet**  a radio call to indicate that an aircraft was over water and no longer over land.

**F–8**  Chance-Vought's carrier-based fighter the Crusader was used briefly by the U.S. Marine Corps and Navy during the early days of the war. As the first MACH–2 shipboard fighter, it was best known for its unusual appearance with its wings mounted above the fuselage. Armed with 20mm cannons and with SIDEWINDERS, it had a single seat and one engine.

**Felt, Harry D**  commander in chief, Pacific Command (CINCPAC) until 1964.

**fenugie**  slang for Fuckin' New Guy (see FNG).

**FF**  abbr. for Fire Fighter Vehicle.

**FFAR**  abbr. for Folding Fin Aircraft Rocket.

**FFE**  abbr. for FIRE FOR EFFECT.

**F–5**  Northrop Aircraft's lightweight fighter/bomber known as the Freedom Fighter and nicknamed Scoshie Tiger. It was developed for the U.S. Air Force but given to the South Vietnamese Air Force. The VNAF's F–5s fell into North Vietnamese hands at the end of the hostilities.

**FFM** abbr. for Flight Facilities, Mobile.

**F–4** the McDonnell/Douglas MACH–2 fighter-bomber, nicknamed the Phantom. This versatile aircraft was developed for the navy and adopted by the air force. McDonnell Aircraft's first jet could carry as much as 16,000 pounds of ORDNANCE. One of the main bombers of the war, it was also called Fours.

**F–4B** the McDonnell Phantom II was a twin-engine, two-seat, long-range all-weather jet interceptor and attack bomber used by the marines and used as an all-weather fighter by the Navy. Also called Fox Four.

**F–4C** U.S. Air Force version of the F–4B.

**FFV** abbr. for Field Force, Vietnam; the U.S. Headquarters at the CORPS level.

**FFZ** abbreviation for FREE FIRE ZONE.

**fib** a tactic used to make a small team seem larger. A distraction was staged so that action could be taken at another location.

**FID** abbr. for Foreign Internal Defense, a basic mission of the SPECIAL FORCES and a type of unconventional warfare. It included the training of friendly foreign forces in various military skills.

**FIDO** abbr. for "Fuck It, Drive On," a phrase used when in a vehicle and trouble loomed ahead.

**field** 1. any place outside a base, where CONTACT with the enemy is a possibility. 2. any training or battle area.

**field cross** the arrangement of the rifle, boots, and helmet of a fallen comrade as part of a memorial service for him.

**field day** marine term for cleaning the barracks.

**field fire** marksmanship practice in a simulated battle environment.

**Field Force** the designation used during much of the Vietnam War to classify U.S. Military corps-level tactical control headquarters. Field Force I commanded I CORPS and II CORPS and Field Force II commanded III CORPS and IV CORPS.

**Field Goal** code for the RT–33 reconnaissance SORTIES over Laos in the spring of 1961.

**field grade** officers above the rank of captain, but below the rank of brigadier general.

**field jacket** a weatherproof jacket with a zippered liner worn in cold, damp weather.

**field of fire** area that a weapon or weapons can cover successfully with fire from a specified point.

**field phone** the hand-generated portable phones used in BUNKERS.

**field scarf** marine term for a necktie.

**field strip** tearing up and dispersing a used cigarette into scraps of paper and shreds, to avoid alerting the enemy that someone had been in the area.

*field transport pack*  m a r i n e term for a way of packing field gear when in transit, using a knapsack, CAR-TRIDGE BELT, HAVERSACK, suspender straps, and other equipment.

*fifteen and two*  15 days of restriction plus two hours a day of extra duty, a common penalty under ARTI-CLE 15.

*.50 caliber*  the .50 caliber Browning machine gun that was often referred to simply as "50."

**55**  number scratched into the ground by American POWs to indicate the sites of their prison camps so they would not be bombed by U.S. aircraft.

*.51 caliber*  a heavy machine gun used by the enemy.

*fighter*  aircraft designed for maneuverability and speed; used primarily for air-to-air combat.

*fighter-bomber*  fighter aircraft which could double as an attack bomber.

*fighting hole*  Viet Cong term for their foxholes.

*fighting wing*  an aerial formation in which the WINGMAN could give ideal coverage and sustain maneuverability during maximum performance maneuvers.

**FIIGMO**  (pronounced "Fig-Mo") abbr. for "Fuck it, I've Got My Orders." Often used by someone leaving a unit and indifferent to what he was leaving behind.

*fin*  a derogatory term for one who is not SCUBA qualified. Also called guppy or straight fin.

*finger charge*  an explosive booby-trap, called that because of its size and shape.

*fingertip*  a four-aircraft formation in which the aircraft occupy positions resembling the four fingertips of a hand.

*fini*  Vietnamese for stop or the end; derived from the French.

*fire*  1. command to discharge a weapon. 2. to use a firing system to detonate an explosive charge.

*fire arrow*  a large, wooden arrow with burning gasoline cans fastened to it. These were used in SPECIAL FORCES camps to indicate the direction of enemy troops for close air support at night.

*fire ball*  blasting an area with large amounts of ARTILLERY fire.

*fire base*  1. a temporary ARTIL-LERY encampment used for fire support of forward ground operations. 2. a self-contained and self-defended artillery base. 3. an ARTILLERY firing position, usually fortified with IN-FANTRY.

*fire brigade*  a highly mobile unit which rushed to the scene of an enemy attack.

*Firecan*  NATO code for Soviet fire-control radar for directing antiaircraft weapons.

*fire for effect*  a fire message suggesting that the adjustment is effective and asking for fire for effect. When calling in ARTILLERY or MORTAR fire, a SPOTTER ROUND was called first. After finding the enemy position with the spotter rounds, firing for effect was carried out. In doing this, the target was leveled.

***fire for record*** the process of testing an individual or a unit for proficiency in using weapons. A soldier fired small arms in the U.S. Army to became qualified as a marksman, a sharpshooter, or an expert.

***fire in the hole*** warning shouted by soldiers when there is to be a planned demolition.

***fire mission*** the authorization for ARTILLERY to fire on a specified target.

***fire support base*** a defended perimeter with supporting artillery and mortar units. An FSB was usually a semipermanent base built to give support to allied unit operations.

***fire team*** a Marine Corps basic unit of four men. The unit contained a fire team leader, an automatic rifleman, an assistant automatic rifleman, and a rifleman/scout.

***fire track*** slang for a FLAMETHROWER tank or an ARMORED PERSONNEL CARRIER.

***fireball*** the rapid use of an artillery battery to bolster a maneuver. The term *fireball* referred to an operation requiring less than eight hours.

***fireballing*** 1. extensive amounts of artillery fire in an area. 2. slang for vehicles moving rapidly.

***fire base psychosis*** slang for U.S. Army units later in the war that were so dependent on FIRE SUPPORT BASE that the troops would not leave their guarded areas.

***firebee*** aerial term for a pilotless aircraft.

***firecracker*** see COFRAM.

***firefight*** a battle between opposing units or an exchange of fire with the enemy, usually with small-arms fire.

***firefly*** 1. helicopter team with one helicopter furnished with a search light plus two GUNSHIPS. Also called Lightning Bug and used for night missions. 2. a call sign for flareships.

***First Field Force*** one of two approximately equal areas of South Vietnam, split for administrative purposes.

***First John*** slang for FIRST LIEUTENANT.

***First Lieutenant*** The second rank of officer, just above second lieutenant. The symbol for this rank is a silver bar. Also called first louie.

***1st Lt*** abbr. for FIRST LIEUTENANT.

***first log*** slang for the First Logistical Command, which was the main support for U.S. troops. They were responsible for storing supplies, fuel, and ammunition in DA NANG and in SAIGON.

***First Louie*** slang for FIRST LIEUTENANT.

***first pig*** derogatory nickname for FIRST SERGEANT.

***first sergeant*** senior noncommissioned officer in charge of personnel. He was also called First Shirt, First Sleeve, Top, Topper, and Top Kick.

***first shirt*** slang for FIRST SERGEANT, the NCO in charge of personnel.

***first sleeve*** slang for FIRST SERGEANT.

***First Team*** nickname for the U.S. First Cavalry Division.

**first up**   the first or lead helicopter in a mission, or the first aircraft to fly out on a mission.

**Fish Hook**   1. code term for the target area of the Cambodian invasion in 1970. 2. the area of Cambodia that juts into South Vietnam.

**Fishbed**   the North Atlantic Treaty Organization designation for late models of the MiG–21.

**five**   radio call for the executive officer of a unit.

**five by five**   a signal that one is receiving a radio transmission loud and clear.

**five fingers**   procedure for buying hashish in villages. A large block of hashish was scraped with one's fingernails, and the hashish was priced according to the number of fingers used.

**555**   a brand of British cigarettes very much favored by the Vietnamese.

**five o'clock follies**   slang for the daily press briefings which reported North Vietnamese Army body counts and allied victories.

**fix**   1. to deter the enemy from moving from one area to another. 2. term for location.

**flag officer**   an admiral in the navy. Compare to GENERAL OFFICER in the army.

**Flag Plot**   slang for the Naval Command Center, Washington.

**flak**   antiaircraft fire SHRAPNEL fragments.

**flak envelope**   aerial term for a vertical unit of airspace in which a specific type of antiaircraft ARTILLERY is accurate.

**flak girdle**   protective body armor, pulled on like pants, used by helicopter pilots and crew.

**flak jacket**   INFANTRY body armor, filled with heavy fiberglass, and worn as a vest for protection against SHRAPNEL. Regardless of the protection they provided, flak jackets were hot and heavy and despite regulations were often not used. When they were worn at all, they were usually left unfastened down the front. Men in helicopters often sat on them.

**flak trap**   slang for a North Vietnamese ploy in which fire was withheld until rescue aircraft came near a downed pilot.

**flak vest**   see FLAK JACKET.

**flaky**   1. slang for bad soldier, one who made mistakes. 2. to be in a state of mental disarray, or spacy. Flaky often referred to various irrational fears.

**flame bath**   incendiary bombardment by a UH–1 helicopter which carried three 55-gallon drums of diesel fuel or JP4. These were dropped and ignited by TRIP FLARES, causing a widespread fire.

**flame out**   aerial term for the extinguishing of the flame in an engine, particularly a jet engine.

**flamethrower**   a weapon that hurled and ignited incendiary fuel.

**Flaming Dart**   1. code name for U.S. bombing operations in which 50 jets from the carriers Hancock and Coral Sea bombed Dong Hoi in North Vietnam in retaliation for an attack on a military compound in Pleiku in February 1965. Flaming Dart, called the Rolling Thunder Operation, started in

March 1965 and continued until November, 1968. 2. Flaming Dart II was code for an air operation over North Vietnam in retaliation for Communist guerrillas attacking a barracks full of U.S. personnel in Qui Nhon on February 11, 1965.

***flaming horse turd***   see FLAMING ONION.

***flaming onion***   slang for the insignia of the Ordnance Corps (a flaming grenade). Also called flaming horse turd and flaming piss pot.

***flaming piss pot***   1. slang for the insignia of the Ordnance Corps (a flaming grenade). 2. slang for the shoulder patch worn by personnel attached to the U.S. Army JFK Center for Special Warfare at Fort Bragg, North Carolina.

***flare***   signaling devices which were hand-fired or shot from ARTILLERY, MORTARS, or aircraft. Green flares designated an encounter with friendly forces, red designated enemy troops, and white flares were used for illumination. A hand-held flare was nicknamed a jackoff flare.

***flare and strike***   the use of aerial flares dropped from a CHINOOK HELICOPTER to allow night operations by the South Vietnamese Air Force.

***flare kicker***   slang for the crewman who operated the FLARE dispenser on PUFF THE MAGIC DRAGON night missions.

***flare ship***   1. an air force cargo aircraft modified to give battlefield illumination by dropping aerial flares. 2. any aircraft, helicopter or fixed wing, capable of dropping illumination flares.

***flattop***   1. slang for an aircraft carrier. 2. a project of the U.S. Army to service combat aircraft in Southeast Asia, formally called the Floating Aircraft Maintenance Facility. 3. slang for a very short crew cut.

***flechette***   1. small projectiles clustered in an explosive warhead. 2. antipersonnel rounds which burst after traversing a set range, spraying the area with dart-shaped nails meant to wound and kill. Also spelled fleshette.

***fleshette***   see FLECHETTE.

***flexgun***   the improved M–60 machine gun, the 7.62mm M60CA1 machine gun.

***flight***   U.S. Air Force term for a tactical fighter unit. It usually consisted of two elements, with two aircraft to each element.

***flight integrity***   aerial term for aircraft maneuvering in relation to and in support of one another.

***fling wing***   slang for helicopter.

***flip-flop***   inserting a team while extracting another team from the same spot. It was used to mislead the enemy into believing that troops had left the area.

***FLIR***   abbr. for Forward Looking Infrared Device. The FLIR recorded small thermal differences among objects.

***float***   marine term for sea duty on a marine unit.

***Floating Aircraft Maintenance Facility***   an army project that serviced combat aircraft in South Vietnam. Also called Flattop.

***Flower Power***   nickname for the Ninth Infantry Division, called that because of the octofoil design on its shoulder patch. This division was also nicknamed Psychedelic Cookie because of its patch and called the Cookie Division.

*fluff 'n' buff*  slang for work uniforms that went through wash-and-wear laundering, and boots that were lightly buffed rather than spit-shined.

*fly by*  air force planes flying past a ceremony or an observer, similar to the army's custom of marching past in review.

*fly-boy*  slang for an individual serving in the U.S. Air Force.

*flycatcher*  code for the supply of aircraft to the Khmer [Cambodian] Air Force in 1974.

*flying bananas*  slang for the H–21 helicopter, used extensively in the early years of the Vietnam War.

*flying battle cruiser*  slang for the B–52 Stratofortress.

*flying box car*  slang for the C–119.

*flying cow*  nickname for the C–123 or C–130 aircraft furnished with rubberized drums and a large pump.

*Flying Crane*  nickname for the CH–54 helicopter.

*flying gas station*  nickname for the KC–135 Stratotanker, used by the air force for air refueling.

*flying lesson*  slang for "disposing" of prisoners via helicopter, resulting in their deaths.

*Flying Oscar*  a CHINOOK nicknamed that because of its resemblance to an Oscar Meyer wiener.

*Flying Telephone Poles*  nickname for SA–2 missiles.

*FM*  1. abbr. for Field Manual. 2. abbr. for Frequency Modulation, a radio term for operating in a specific, static-free band.

*FMFPAC*  abbr. for Fleet Marine Force, Pacific Command. This was the U.S. Marines Pacific command.

*FNG*  abbr. for Fuckin' new guy, also referred to as newby, newfer, cherry, cherry boy, new meat, fenugie, greenseed and twink. The FNG was usually avoided and shunned by others in the unit for fear of his making a serious mistake or having an accident that could affect others. Because soldiers were often transferred individually into units, being an FNG was particularly lonely and frightening.

*FO*  1. abbr. for FORWARD OBSERVER. 2. abbr. for Field Officer.

*FOB*  1. abbr. for Forward Operating Base, a command post and logistical base in the field of a battalion or of a Special Forces unit. 2. abbr. for Fly-Over-Border mission, usually referring to Cambodia or Laos.

*Fogbound*  code for the ECM/ESM missions over North Vietnam by Marine EF–10Bs.

*Fonda, Jane*  an Academy-Award-winning American actress who was an active antiwar demonstrator in 1969 and 1970. She donated funds for the WINTER SOLDIER INVESTIGATION in 1971. In 1972 she traveled to Hanoi, in North Vietnam, to broadcast over the radio to American servicemen about the futility of the war. Nicknamed Hanoi Jane, she is not well-loved by many Vietnam veterans.

**FORCAP** abbr. for Force Combat Air Force. These patrols of fighters maintained control over task forces, intercepting and destroying any threatening enemy aircraft.

**force recon** special Marine RECON units. Force recon's mission was to provide intelligence for the entire Fleet Marine command. Force recon marines were usually more highly experienced than other recon groups, and the qualifications were higher: Volunteers had to score high on specialized tests, be excellent swimmers, score high in physical fitness, and have normal color vision. Members were then selected from among those who met the requirements. Force recon marines referred to themselves as an "elite group within an elite group (marines)."

**Forest of Assassins** the translation of RUNG SAT, the swampy area of mud and mangrove between the Saigon and Dong Nai rivers.

**Forest of Darkness** nickname for the U MINH FOREST.

**forest penetrator** an apparatus for withdrawing a person by helicopter from a jungle area by means of a cable which could be raised and lowered. The penetrator folded to prevent its getting caught in trees and opened up into a seat which protected the passenger being rescued.

**Forget-Me-Not Bar** a well-known bar in DA NANG.

**formations** air force formations are listed by type in this volume. Included are CRUISE, DIVISION, PARADE, RECCE, SECTION, SPREAD, and TRAIL.

**F–111** General Dynamic's swing-wing multipurpose attack aircraft, known as the Aardvark and the TFX.

It was also called the Edsel because like the automobile of that name, it was a clunker.

**F–100** the Super Sabre, North American Aviation's bomber, was nicknamed the Lead Sled and the Hun.

**F–105** Republic Aircraft's medium attack aircraft nicknamed the Thunderchief (THUD). This plane flew 75 percent of all airstrikes into North Vietnam during the ROLLING THUNDER OPERATION in 1965 to 1968. It was the largest single-seater and endured the most losses during the war. Also called Lead Sled, Ultra hot and Squash Bomber.

**F–101** McDonnell Aviation's Voodoo was used mainly for air-to-air STRIP ALERTs until replaced by the F–4. The reconnaissance version of the Voodoo was used in North and South Vietnam and Laos.

**F–106** General Dynamic's Delta Dagger, a follow-up to the F–102, was originally designed to be part of the Sage system for air defense. The F–106 was replaced by the Phantom.

**F–102** General Dynamic's Delta Dart was used mainly on STRIP ALERT until it was replaced by the F–4.

**food tube** device in which North Vietnamese soldiers carried a one-week supply of rations and rice.

**foo-gas** see FU-GAS.

**foot-pounder** slang for INFANTRYMAN.

**foot-slogger** slang for INFANTRYMAN.

**Fort Hood Three** nickname for the three U.S. soldiers who in 1966 publicly stated that they refused to go to Vietnam. They were all COURT-MARTIALED and served 10 years in prison.

**Fort Knox East**  nickname for the U.S. Army Central Finance and Accounting Office at TAN SON NHUT airbase in SAIGON. Enormous sums of money were stored here to pay the troops and others in Vietnam.

**Fort Lost in the Woods**  slang for Fort Leonard Wood, Missouri.

**Fort Fucker**  slang for Fort Rucker, Alabama.

**Fort Piss**  slang for Fort Bliss, Texas.

**Fort Pricks**  slang for Fort Dix, New Jersey.

**Fort Puke**  slang for Fort Polk, Louisiana.

**Fort Screw Us**  slang for Fort Lewis, Washington.

**Fort Smell**  slang for Fort Sill, Oklahoma.

**Fort Turd**  slang for Fort Ord, California.

**Fort Useless**  slang for Fort Eustis, Virginia.

**forty-five**  the U.S. .45 caliber M–1911 automatic pistol.

**forward air controller**  the person airborne or on the ground who coordinated air strikes. He directed attacking aircraft in close air support of ground troops. Also called FAC and FC (forward controller); see FC.

**forward observer**  an observer near the front line who coordinated and regulated ground or naval fire and reported back battlefield information. In the absence of a FORWARD AIR CON-TROLLER, the forward observer could also control close air support. Telephones and/or radios were used to communicate with weapons personnel. The forward observer is usually an ARTILLERY officer attached to an INFANTRY or ARMORED unit.

**forward roll**  a type of parachute landing.

**forward support area**  a permanent or semipermanent area used as a forward logistical base.

**IV–A**  according to SELECTIVE SERVICE classification, a registrant who had completed service and was a sole surviving son.

**IV–B**  according to SELECTIVE SERVICE classification, an official deferred by law.

**IV–C**  an alien, according to SELECTIVE SERVICE classification.

**Four Corners**  slang for the town of Di An in South Vietnam. The term came to mean, however, any town near a U.S. military installation.

**IV Corps**  fourth allied military zone including the MEKONG DELTA region.

**IV–D**  according to SELECTIVE SERVICE classification, a deferment for a minister of religion or divinity student.

**Four Deuce**  slang for the U.S. 4.2 heavy mortar.

**IV–F**  according to SELECTIVE SERVICE, a registrant not qualified for any military service due to a physical handicap or mental deficit.

**Fours (4s)**  nickname for F–4 Phantom jet fighter-bombers.

***fourteen and two*** a punishment under ARTICLE 15 consisting of restriction to barracks during off-duty hours for 14 days plus two hours of extra duty each day for the 14 days.

***Fox Four*** slang for the F–4 Phantom II jet fighter.

***Fox Mike*** FM radio.

***Fox One*** radio call indicating launch of a Sparrow.

***Fox Two*** radio call indicating launch of a Sidewinder.

***foxtail*** slang for the short-handled brush used to sweep rubbish into a dust pan.

***foxtrot*** 1. the military phonetic for the letter F. 2. slang for Vietnamese female.

***foxtrot tosser*** slang for a FLAME-THROWER.

***Foxtrot Yankee*** phonetic alphabet for "Fuck You."

***FPJMC*** abbr. for Four Party Joint Military Commission. Based in Saigon, it consisted of delegations from the United States, South Vietnam, North Vietnam, and the Viet Cong. The purposes of the group were to establish a cease-fire, to supervise the withdrawal of the remaining U.S. troops, and to exchange prisoners of war. This commission began in January 1973 and ended in March 1973.

***FPJMT*** abbr. for Four Party Joint Military Team. The successor to the FPJMC, it began in March 1973. It was based in Saigon with the same delegates from the United States, South Vietnam, North Vietnam, and the Viet Cong. Their goal was to accomplish the objectives of the FPJMC. Consid-

ered even less successful than its predecessor, this organization disbanded and withdrew in April, 1975.

***FPO*** abbr. for Fleet Post Office for navy and marine corps or Field Post Office for the army.

***frag*** 1. abbr. for fragmentation hand grenade. 2. short for a fragment of a shell. 3. using a fragmentation grenade to wound or kill one's own officer or NCO or a LIFER, often because of perceived incompetence. This was usually done by rolling a grenade under the tent flaps of a targeted person while he was sleeping. The fragmentation grenade left no trace. Although fragging increased as the war went on, note that most previous U.S. wars also had fragging incidents.

***frag grenade*** the M–26 fragmentation grenade. The M–26 weighed about one pound and held an explosive charge which shattered into small pieces in all directions. The range was about 40 meters. Also called a hand frag and a fragmentation hand grenade when tossed by hand.

***frag order*** short for fragmentation operations order, which was a day-to-day addendum to standard operations orders directing the handling of a particular military objective involving air flights or missions.

***fragged*** 1. a mission or flight directed by fragmentary operational orders from higher headquarters. 2. having been the target of a fragmentation grenade.

***fragging*** see FRAG.

***fragmentation grenade*** see FRAG GRENADE.

*frankenstein*    slang for a spool of barbed wire with a piece of C–4 plastic explosive in the center for detonation.

*freak*    1. short for radio frequency; also spelled freq. 2. slang for a pothead or junkie.

*free drop zones*    areas designated for random bombing, with the view that anyone or anything within the area was an enemy.

*free fire zone*    an area cleared of civilians within which ARTILLERY and aircraft could fire without having to obtain clearance. Any persons found within a free fire zone were presumed to be an enemy. The South Vietnamese authorities usually approved only uninhabited areas or areas under enemy control. In 1965 the official designation of these areas was changed to Specified Strike Zones.

*free strike area*    see FREE FIRE ZONE.

*free strike zone*    see FREE FIRE ZONE.

*freedom arch*    nickname for the doorway to the building at Long Binh where outprocessing took place just prior to one's ending a tour of duty.

*freedom birds*    slang for the planes that brought American soldiers back to the States after their tour of duty in Vietnam.

*Freedom Deal*    code for the May 1970 operation in support of U.S./South Vietnamese military moves involving the invasion of Cambodia. Freedom Deal was a continuation of the B–52 operations in Cambodia, coded operation MENU.

*Freedom Fighter*    the Northrop Aircraft's lightweight fighter-bomber, the F–5.

*Freedom Train*    code for Joint Chiefs of Staff-directed USAF bombing strikes against targets in North Vietnam from early April to early May, 1972. The bombings were in response to North Vietnam's invasion into South Vietnam in March 1972. The code Freedom Train was replaced by the code name Operation LINEBACKER I. The code following was Operation LINEBACKER II, also called the CHRISTMAS BOMBINGS.

*Freeze*    code for a marine operation to combat FRAGGING. When a fragging incident was reported, the suspect unit was isolated. Leaves and rotations were canceled and each marine was questioned. Each was promised rotation out of Vietnam if he provided information. The guilty persons were often found out and court-martialed, and units returned to their usual functioning.

*French Expeditionary Corps*    the colonial French army, predating American involvement in Vietnam.

*French Fort*    the distinctive, triangular structures built by the French in Vietnam.

*FRENG*    abbr. for Friendly-Initiated Engagement.

*freq*    short for radio frequency, also spelled freak.

*Frequent Wind*    code name of the final evacuation of U.S. Embassy and military personnel from Saigon in April 1975, originally called Talon Vise.

**Fresco** the North Atlantic Treaty Organization designation for the MiG–17.

**fresh meat** slang for a replacement soldier.

**Freshwater Navy** the U.S. COAST GUARD, so called because it operated inland in fresh water.

**friendlies** 1. the aircraft belonging to or held by one's own forces or the forces of an ally. 2. our allies who supported the war. Anyone on our side was called a friendly.

**friendly fire** accidental attacks on U.S. or allied soldiers by other U.S. or allied forces.

**friendly wounds** accidental wounding of an American or allied soldier from FRIENDLY FIRE.

**friendship kits** gifts given to the Vietnamese, in the anticipation of winning their HEARTS AND MINDS.

**frisbees** slang for C-RATION crackers.

**Froines, John** one of the CHICAGO SEVEN.

**front** 1. the person in the front seat of the F–4 Phantom bomber. 2. an aircraft commander.

**front time** time spent in a forward area, on combat duty. See BACK TIME.

**"Front Toward Enemy"** instruction inscribed on the front of CLAYMORE mines.

**FRTS** abbr. for Armed Forces Radio and Television Service.

**fruit salad** slang for ribbons and decorations, a phrase left over from previous wars.

**FSA** abbr. for Fire Support Area.

**FSB** abbr. for FIRE SUPPORT BASE.

**FT** abbr. for FLAMETHROWER.

**FTA** 1 abbr. for Fuck The Army, which was inscribed almost everywhere on Army installations. 2. abbr. for "Fun, Travel and Adventure," used in army promotional material.

**F–10** Douglas Aircraft's Sky Knight, also known as F–3D. It was a two-seat fighter used in the early part of the Vietnam War by the U.S. Marine Corps for ELINT and ECM.

**F–3D** Douglas Aircraft's Sky Knight. See F–10.

**FTR** abbr. for Failure To Return.

**Ftr** abbr. for fighter.

**FTU** abbr. for Field Training Unit.

**FTX** abbr. for Field Training Exercise.

**fu-gas** from *fou gasse*, French military slang for a type of land mine. In American usage it referred to a homemade antipersonnel mine consisting of a buried 50-gallon drum filled with jellied gas. It was usually detonated by blasting caps attached to hand generators. Also spelled foo-gas, phugas and phougas.

**FUBAR** abbr. for Fucked Up Beyond All Recognition (or Repair).

**fuck** the most commonly used expletive of U.S. personnel in Vietnam.

**fuck 'em if they can't take a joke** expression used when things went very wrong. For example, when friendly troops were bombed or accidentally shelled or rocketed.

**fuck the duck** slang generally meaning to loaf or to sleep.

**fucked up** 1 slang for being killed. 2. slang for being wounded. 3. slang for being drunk or high on drugs.

**fuckin' new guy** new arrival in Vietnam. See FNG.

**fuckstick** slang used by CYCLO GIRLS for a GI's penis.

**fuck-you lizard** a gecko lizard in Vietnam which made a call which sounded remarkably like "fuck you."

**Fugazi** slang for crazy or screwed up.

**Fulbright, William J.** Senator who assisted in guiding the GULF OF TONKIN RESOLUTION through the Senate and later an outspoken opponent of the war.

**full bird** slang for a colonel.

**full suppression** troops could fire all the way in on a landing, according to the RULES OF ENGAGEMENT.

**FULRO** abbr. for Front Unifie de Lutte de la Race Opprimée [United Front for the Struggle of Oppressed Races], a movement for MONTAGNARD autonomy. A resistance organization in the HIGHLANDS of Montagnards, CHAM, and ethnic KHMER that conducted fierce resistance to Communist operations designed to suppress indigenous tribes.

**Fulton Recovery** an air rescue method for retrieving downed pilots out of remote places.

**FUNCINPEC** abbr. for National United Front for an Independent, Neutral, Peaceful, and Cooperative Cambodia. In 1982, FUNCINPEC became part of the Cambodian coalition government and it shared the seat at the United Nations.

**FUNK** abbr. for National United Front of Kampuchea, the government established by Prince Norodom SIHANOUK after he had been removed from power and exiled from Cambodia.

**Funky Fourth** see FAMOUS FOURTH.

**funny bombs** slang for fragmenting explosives, also called CBUs and soft bombs.

**funny money** slang for MILITARY PAYMENT CERTIFICATES.

**funny papers** slang for topographic maps, also called comics.

**FUO** abbr. for Fever of Unknown Origin, a serious problem for medical personnel and their patients in Vietnam because of the many virulent bacteria and tropical diseases.

**fuse lighter** slang for an ARTILLERYMAN.

**FV** abbr. for Field Force, Vietnam.

**Fwd** abbr. for forward.

**FWMAF** abbr. for Free World Military Assistance Forces, the ALLIES of South Vietnam.

# G

**G** abbr. for acceleration due to gravity.

**Gabby** call sign for psychological warfare aircraft.

**Gabby Hayes hat** slang for the field hat worn in Vietnam. It had a narrow brim and a low crown, similar to the hat worn by Gabby Hayes, an actor in Western films.

**gaggle** a number of aircraft operating close to each other, but not necessarily in formation.

**Gainful** NATO code for a surface-to-air missile.

**Galaxy** the Lockheed C5A, a transport aircraft developed for the U.S. Air Force and first used in 1968.

**GAM** 1. abbr. for Ground-to-Air Missile. 2. abbr. for Guided Aircraft Missile.

**Game Warden** code name for a long-running project of the U.S. Navy to keep South Vietnam's internal waterways open and hinder the Viet Cong's use of the waterways as supply and penetration routes.

**gangplank policy** slang for a policy that allowed a soldier to extend his overseas tour any time up to the moment when he was about to depart for home.

**GAO** abbr. for General Accounting Office. This congressional body studied the effectiveness and efficiency of various government programs.

**Garage, The** slang for a section of the HANOI HILTON.

**GARAND** the M–1 RIFLE issued to the South Vietnamese early in the war. It was replaced by the M–14.

**Garden of Honor** a veterans' cemetery.

**garitrooper** (spelled several ways) slang for service personnel in the rear who acted as though they were involved in heavy action.

**GAS** abbr. for ground speed, an aircraft's velocity over the ground.

**gas station in the sky** nickname for the KC–135 Stratotanker.

**gate** 1. aerial term meaning to fly at maximum possible speed or power. 2. short for Range Gate, the indication on F–4 radar of the distance between the target and the interceptor.

**gate ghetto** bars and other places that tended to cluster around the gates of military installations.

**gatling** a MACHINE GUN designed by Richard Gatling in 1962. It was manually operated with automatic loading and cartridge ejection and considered semiautomatic, capable of firing up to 4,000 rounds per minute.

**gator clip** an instant quick release device. This is the toggle fastener which attached the IBS DOUGHNUT rope to another craft. Gator clip is short for alligator clip.

**Gayler, Noel** commander in chief, Pacific Command (CINCPAC), 1972–1975.

**GBU** abbr. for God Bless You, the message that POWs frequently communicated to each other for camaraderie and support.

**GCA** abbr. for Ground Controlled Approach. This was an all-weather landing assistance system used mainly by the navy. A ground-based controller transmitted azimuth and elevation information to the pilot, and talked him through a landing, by using instruments and instructions.

**GCI** abbr. for Ground Controller Intercept. This was a ground-based radar system for directing and vectoring friendly aircraft to take on hostile forces.

**GCR** abbr. for Ground Controlled Radar.

**gear** equipment.

**gear locker** a room housing brooms and other cleaning equipment.

**gecko** the lizard in Vietnam commonly known as the Fuck You lizard, because its call sounded like "Fuck you."

**GED** abbr. for General Equivalency Diploma. If passed, this test for non-high school graduates was the equivalent of a high school diploma. It was administered by the U.S. Armed Services.

**geedunk** marine slang for junk food. Also called slopshoot.

**geese** The South Vietnamese used geese at night to guard the four main bridges connecting SAIGON to its neighboring regions. The geese were on a schedule that resulted in their being very hungry when they were on duty. When a strangers would come near the bridge they would honk nois-ily in hopes of being fed. The honking thus alerted the human guards.

**General Classification Test** exams taken following BASIC training to determine the type of advanced schooling each recruit should receive.

**general officer** officer holding a rank between brigadier general and five-star general.

**Generals' Mess** place where general officers took their meals.

**Geneva Accords** a g r e e m e n t signed the night of July 20, 1954, after the Viet Minh victory at DIEN BIEN PHU. These accords put an end to the French war in Indochina and established a border at the 17th parallel. That border separating North and South Vietnam with a 15 mile buffer became the DEMILITARIZED ZONE.

**Genghis Khan of the Air Force** nickname for General Curtis LeMay, the SAC Commander and a member of the Joint Chiefs of Staff in the early 1960s. LeMay was notorious for his remark about the air war against North Vietnam, "We should bomb them back to the Stone Age."

**get it on** marine phrase meaning to fight.

**get some** a slang for killing the enemy.

**get wet** slang meaning to kill with a bayonet or a knife.

**getting smoked** slang for getting shot down.

**G-5** the staff or officer in charge of the military government of occupied territories.

**g-force** force of gravity on the body caused by steep turns or acceleration in an aircraft.

**G–4** the staff or officer in charge of supply and logistics.

**GFU** abbr. for General Fuck-Up, usually referring to specific persons.

**GGM** abbr. for Ground-to-Ground Missile.

**ghe** a medium-sized Vietnamese boat having a small cabin amidships.

**ghost** slang meaning to take it easy or evade duty.

**ghost battalion** nickname for the First Battalion, ninth Marines who had survived CON THIEN and assisted in the defense of KHE SANH; they were called that because of their high number of casualties. Also called the Walking Dead.

**ghost time** slang for free time or time off duty, especially in the sense of being absent and avoiding duty.

**ghosting** slang for goldbricking or sandbagging, taking off, taking it easy, doing nothing, being absent, or shirking duty.

**GHQ** abbr. for General Headquarters.

**GI** 1. abbr. for General Issue. 2. abbr. for Government Issue. 3. slang for soldier, taken from Government Issue, used since World War II.

**GI Bill** nickname for the Serviceman's Readjustment Act, signed in 1944 and regularly updated. These acts provide benefits for eligible discharged veterans. It is generally accepted that benefits for veterans of the Vietnam War were not nearly as generous as in previous wars.

**GI Says** one of many underground newspapers in Vietnam during the war.

**gia** a measure of rice, about 40 liters.

**Gia Dinh** one of the 44 provinces of South Vietnam, located in III CORPS.

**Gia Dinh City** capital of GIA DINH Province.

**Gia Lom** the airport in HANOI, from which released American POWs departed.

**Gia Nghia** capital of QUANG DUC Province.

**giải phóng** Vietnamese for liberation.

**Giap, Vo Nguyen** see VO NGUYEN GIAP.

**GIB** the "guy in back," referring to the backseat crew member in fighter aircraft.

**Gimlets** nickname for the U.S. 21st Infantry Regiment, probably called that because of the cocktail glass shape of its insignia.

**gimme go** Vietnamese for wanting transportation or needing to go somewhere other than by walking.

**gimp** slang for incompetent grunt or poor soldier.

**gink** derogatory slang for Vietnamese.

**giờ** Vietnamese for zero hour.

**GL** abbr. for GRENADE LAUNCHER.

**glad bag** slang for the bag used to wrap a body.

**glide ratio** distance an aircraft glided after engine failure.

**g-load** the force exerted on a pilot and his aircraft by gravity.

**glory hole**    aerial slang for a space in a cloudy sky through which fighters could get to their targets.

**GM**    abbr. for Guided Missile. 2. abbr. for Gunner's Mate.

**GMT**    abbr. for Greenwich Mean Time, the world aeronautical standard time.

**Go Cong**    one of the 44 provinces of South Vietnam, located in IV CORPS.

**Go Cong City**    capital of GO CONG Province.

**go/no go**    the capacity to handle tracked or other vehicles in Vietnam, as in "is it go or no/go?," meaning "can we travel on this road, or not."

**go to hell rag**    nickname for the neckerchief worn around a GRUNT's neck to absorb perspiration, clean weapons, or dry the hands or brow. It was extremely important to him.

**goatscrew**    slang for a disorganized, jumbled mess.

**GOCO**    abbr. for Government-Owned, Contractor-Operated.

**God**    respectful nickname for General Lewis WALT, USMC.

**Go-Go Bird**    nickname for CH–47 helicopter modified for close air support, with two 20mm Vulcan guns, .50 caliber MACHINE GUNS and 40mm GRENADE LAUNCHERs. Also called hook, the shithook, Go-Go ship, or simply Go-Go.

**go-go ship**    slang for a heavily armed CH–47 helicopter. See GO-GO BIRD.

**going downtown**    an air force expression for flying a mission against HANOI.

**going south**    marine slang for traveling from Okinawa to Vietnam.

**Gold Star**    the U.S. Navy, Marine, and Coast Guard award that was equivalent to the U.S. Army's OAK LEAF CLUSTER. It was worn on medal ribbons to indicate a subsequent award of the same medal.

**golden BB**    slang for a bullet aimed at a pilot, meant to kill him.

**golden fleece**    a successful marine rice harvest protection operation. Marines assisted villagers in preventing the VIET CONG from taking part of their rice harvest.

**golden flow**    slang for the urinalysis check for drugs which soldiers were given before they returned from Vietnam to the United States. Beginning in 1971, the government insisted on a drug-free urine specimen as part of a physical examination before discharge from the service. If not drug-free, the soldier could expect to be immediately placed in a treatment facility, rather than being discharged.

**Golden Nugget**    see HANOI HILTON.

**Golden Triangle**    the area bordering Vietnam, Laos, Thailand, and Cambodia, where large amounts of illegal drugs were grown.

**goldie**    nickname for the Advanced Navy/Marine Corps parachutist's insignia.

**Goldiggers**    an all-girl singing group who toured with Bob Hope.

**golf**    the military phonetic for the letter G.

**golf balls and bullets**    slang for C-RATION meatballs and beans.

**Golf Course, The** 1. slang for CAMP RADCLIFF. It was called that because of the smooth, low-cut grass on the helicopter landing area. 2. nickname for An Khe, Army base in II CORPS; it was called that because of its huge size.

**golf time** the zone time applicable to the TONKIN GULF and the Indochinese peninsula. During the time of the Vietnam War, South Vietnam and Washington, D.C. were 13 hours apart. For convenience, this was adjusted so that South Vietnam was 12 hours later than Washington, D.C. Golf time was also called GULF TIME.

**gom dan** Vietnamese for a gathering or herding. The term was used by Vietnamese Communists in describing the resettlement of rural villages in cities and South Vietnamese refugee camps.

**gomer** army nickname for a marine.

**gomers** soldier's slang for North Vietnamese.

**G–1** staff or officer responsible for personnel and for administration.

**gone on a walk** slang for a 30-day contact patrol.

**gong** mocking slang for a medal or decoration.

**Good Conduct Medal** a service award given enlisted men to acknowledge commendable conduct.

**Good Luck** code for the operation of bombing the PATHET LAO positions in the PLAIN OF JARS area in Laos in February 1970.

**Good morning, Vietnam** early morning greeting heard over the Armed Forces Vietnam Network (AFVN radio) in South Vietnam.

**good to go** airborne slang for ready to go, or a mission prepared to depart.

**goodie** slang for a surprise ambush or trap for the enemy.

**Gooey-Looeys** slang for second lieutenant.

**gook** 1. one of several derogatory terms for an Vietnamese person, especially the enemy. Also referred to as dink, dip, dipshit, slant, slope, Luke the gook, Link the Chink, little man, Charles, Charlie, Chuck, Chas, gooner, Zip, zipperhead, and Zit. Gook is the Korean word for *person*, and the term was passed down from Korean war veterans and others who had served in Korea. 2. a generic name for an Oriental person.

**gook band** slang for any of the non-Caucasian (often Filipino) bands who played in the Enlisted Men's clubs. The favorite and most frequently played selections were "Proud Mary," "The Green Green Grass of Home," and "We've Gotta Get Out of This Place."

**gook sore** slang for any skin infection.

**gooner** slang for a North Vietnamese soldier. See GOOK.

**Gooney Bird** slang for a C–47 transport with cargo or passengers. When armed, the Gooney Bird was called Puff the Magic Dragon.

**gork** slang for a person who is brain-dead.

**Government of the Night** slang for the de facto government set up in rural areas in South Vietnam by the VIET CONG. Also called the shadow government. See VCI.

**Government of Vietnam (GVN)** the government below the 17th PARAL-LEL, officially named the Republic of Vietnam and known as South Vietnam from 1954 to 1975.

**GP**   abbr. for General Purpose.

**g-pressure**   1. the force exerted on a pilot and his aircraft by gravity. 2. a reaction to acceleration or deceleration during a change of direction.

**GQ**   abbr. for General Quarters, a call to the battle stations for all.

**GR Point**   abbr. for GRAVES REGIS-TRATION POINT.

**grab them by the balls**   first part of a popular phrase used by grunts that went "grab them by the balls and their hearts and minds will follow." Hearts and Minds was the slogan of the Civil Operations and Rural Development Groups, a U.S. agency established in 1967 under the control of Military As-sistance  Command,  Vietnam (MACV). CORDS was part of the U.S. State Department's pacification pro-gram.

**GRAIL**   the NATO term for the shoulder-fired SA–7 surface-to-air missile.

**gravel**   tiny explosive antipersonnel XM–27 mines discharged in large numbers by low flying aircraft. Gravel mines came in three sizes: regular gravel, small gravel, and microgravel. The regular mines had a three-inch package of cloth-covered explosive which detonated when stepped on or run over.

**gravel crusher**   slang for infan-tryman. See GRUNT.

**gravel mine**   see GRAVEL.

**Graves Registration**   see GRAVES REGISTRATION POINT.

**Graves Registration Point**   a field morgue, the place on a military base where identification, embalming, and processing of dead soldiers took place as part of the quartermaster's duties.

**grazing fire**   bullets that flew par-allel to the ground and attacked the enemy at a low and deadly level.

**grease**   slang for C-RATIONS.

**grease gun**   slang for the U.S. .45 caliber M–3 submachine gun.

**greased**   slang for killed.

**greaser**   originally the M-3 subma-chine gun. More recently it referred to the the M3A–1 .45 caliber submachine gun, which resembled a grease gun.

**Great Dark One, The**   nickname for LON NOL.

**green**   slang meaning safe.

**green bait**   slang for a reenlist-ment cash bonus.

**Green Beanies**   nickname for the Green Berets, the SPECIAL FORCES.

**green belt**   marine term for an as-sistant drill instructor.

**Green Berets**   nickname for elite SPECIAL FORCES of the U.S. Army. These sergeants and officers were awarded green berets to wear as dis-tinctive emblems.

**green door**   a secure location for a team.

**green dragon**  slang for the M-113 Armored Personnel Carrier (APC).

**green-faced frogmen of the Delta**  enemy nickname for navy SEALS.

**green line**  a row of trees at the edge of a field or rice paddy, making a natural defensive location. Also called tree line and wood line.

**Green LZ**  slang for safe LANDING ZONE.

**green machine**  slang for the military bureaucracy or the U.S. Army.

**green tape**  adhesive waterproof tape used in Vietnam for various purposes including taping dog tags together so they would not make noise or glare in the jungle.

**green weenie**  slang for the ARMY COMMENDATION MEDAL. Also spelled wienie.

**greenbacking**  slang for employing mercenaries.

**greenbacks**  slang for U.S. currency.

**Greene, Wallace M.**  commandant of the Marine Corps, 1964–1968.

**green-faced men**  Viet Cong nickname for U.S. Navy SEALS. They were also known as "green-faced frog men of the Delta."

**greens**  the U.S. Army class A uniform.

**greenseed**  slang for new arrival in Vietnam. See FNG.

**grenade**  a hand-held bomb with a short delay fuse. See entries under CONCUSSION GRENADE, CS/CN GRENADE, FRAG GRENADE, ILLUMINATION GRENADE, SMOKE GRENADE, THERMITE GRENADE, WHITE PHOSPHORUS and CHICOM GRENADE.

**Grenade Launcher, M–79**  a single-shot, break-open, breech-loaded shoulder weapon which fired 40mm projectiles and weighed about 6½ pounds when loaded. It had a sustained rate of aimed fire of five to seven rounds per minute and an effective range of 375 meters. Often referred to by one of its nicknames, blooper, bluper, blooker, burp gun, chunker, clunker, elephant gun, thump-gun, and thumper.

**grenadier**  operator of an M–79 GRENADE LAUNCHER.

**Greyhound**  the Grumman C–2, a navy cargo transport plane.

**grid coordinates**  designation of an exact location on a map.

**grid square**  a specific area on a map.

**grids**  maps with lines horizontally and vertically placed with numbered 1,000-meter squares.

**Griffin, Charles D.**  commander, Seventh Fleet, 1960–1961.

**grinder**  marine term for parade deck or drill field.

**grins and shakes**  marine slang for a visitors' tour.

**ground controlled intercept**  a ground-based radar system for directing and vectoring friendly aircraft to take on hostile forces.

**ground effect**  an aerial term for the aerodynamic phenomenon occurring close to the ground. The drag was reduced because of a decrease in the downwash angle of airflow from the edge of the wing.

**ground week**   slang for first week of JUMP SCHOOL.

**groundfire**   various weapons used to shoot at striking aircraft. Shells were frequently fired with TRACERS, and the pilots saw either a black puff during the day or a brilliant flash at night.

**groundpounder**   1. slang for IN-FANTRYMAN. 2. slang for an air force officer who does not fly.

**group**   a U.S. Army designation for a command structure controlling several battalion-sized elements, but subordinate to a brigade. Usually groups were used by support and service commands.

**GRP**   abbr. for GRAVES REGISTRATION POINT, a field morgue.

**Gruening, Ernest Henry**   one of only two senators to vote against the GULF OF TONKIN RESOLUTION.

**Grumman Greyhound**   the C–2, a navy cargo transport plane.

**grunt**   during World War I he was called a doughboy and in World War II and Korea he was called a GI. In Vietnam the word *grunt* originally referred to fighting marines, but later, to any soldier fighting there. Also called by many other nicknames. See INFANTRYMAN.

**Grunt Free Press**   one of many underground magazines in Vietnam during the war. Before 1969 it was called Grunt.

**GS**   abbr. for General Support; usually an ARTILLERY or MORTAR unit that fired in support of several other units.

**g-suit**   a pneumatically inflatable suit that prevented blood from pooling in the abdomen and lower legs during aerial acceleration by exerting pressure on the thorax, calves, and thighs.

**GSW**   abbr. for Gunshot Wound.

**GT**   abbr. for General Technical score, the score one earned on the army GENERAL CLASSIFICATIONS TEST.

**G–3**   staff officer responsible for plans and operations, a tactical advisor.

**G–2**   staff or officer responsible for intelligence and counterintelligence.

**guard**   an emergency communications channel in either the UHF (243.0 mhz) or VHF (121.5 mhz) frequency band.

**guard frequency**   a specific radio frequency used under emergency conditions by pilots.

**guard the radio**   standing by in the communications bunker and listening for incoming messages.

**guava**   a bomb which dropped 500,000 exploding pellets in one SORTIE.

**guerrilla**   an armed element of a paramilitary movement; usually members of small bands of Viet Cong soldiers who performed surprise and unconventional attacks. The word guerrilla comes from the Spanish word *guerra*, which means "little war."

**Guerrilla Theater**   Vietnam Veterans of America's street performances demonstrating the destructiveness of war.

**guerrilla warfare**   military operations undertaken in hostile enemy territory by nonorganized indigenous groups.

**guide** an air-to-air missile which followed the course intended.

**guided missile** unmanned self-propelled mechanisms which could be remotely controlled. The types were air-to-air, surface-to-surface, surface-to-air, air-to-surface, air-to-underwater, surface-to-underwater, underwater-to-air, underwater-to- surface, and underwater-to-underwater.

**Guideline** NATO term for a SA–2 surface-to-air missile.

**Gulf of Tonkin** 1. the waters off South and North Vietnam. 2. The location of the GULF OF TONKIN INCIDENT.

**Gulf of Tonkin Incident** North Vietnamese torpedo boats allegedly attacked U.S. destroyers on August 2–4, 1964. These alleged attacks on the USS *Maddox* and the USS *C. Turner Joy* marked the beginning of the Vietnam War.

**Gulf of Tonkin Resolution** re -solution passed by Congress on August 7, 1964 (88–2 in the Senate and 412–0 in the House of Representatives) which became the president's mechanism for setting policy in Vietnam. The resolution allowed President Lyndon Johnson to "take all necessary measures to repel an armed attack against the forces of the United States and to prevent further aggression." The resolution was repealed by Congress in 1970.

**gulf time** the time actually observed by U.S. Navy ships operating in the area of the Tonkin Gulf, usually the same as South Vietnamese civil time. See GOLF TIME.

**gun** during recent wars, a word sometimes used by new recruits instead of the word *rifle*. When a new recruit referred to his rifle as a gun, he was usually ordered to march with his rifle in one hand and his penis in the other and declare aloud, "This is my rifle, this is my gun. This is for fighting, and this is for fun."

**gun ape** slang for ARTILLERYMAN.

**gun bunny** slang for ARTILLERYMAN.

**gun jeep** slang for an armored vehicle with mounted MACHINE GUNS.

**gunbird** nickname for the COBRA armed helicopter, also called gunship.

**gunboat** a small surface vessel that carried guns as its primary armament.

**gung ho** enthusiastic.

**gunge** a generic term for a tropical disease covering many different infections of the genital area; also called crotch rot.

**gungey** an enthusiastic, gung ho soldier.

**gunney** nickname for a USMC gunnery sergeant, usually an E–7. Also spelled gunny.

**gunny** see GUNNEY.

**gunrun** the path an aircraft takes when expending ORDNANCE.

**guns up** an order for the MACHINE-GUN team to come to the front of the patrol or to another selected place.

**gunship** 1. a helicopter armed with air-to-ground armament. This combat helicopter, commonly a HU–1 HUEY armed with multiple MACHINE GUNs, ROCKETS, and automatic GRENADE LAUNCHERS, was used primarily in support of infantry operations. Gunship also referred to any fixed-wing aircraft or helicopter equipped with rapid-firing guns or cannons to provide close air support for troops in battle. A gunship was also called gunbird. 2. a U.S. Air Force program to change transport aircraft into day or night RE-CONNAISSANCE aircraft equipped with guns, sensors, and lights. Gunship 1, the Douglas AC–47 and Gunship 2, the Lockheed AC–130 were used in Southeast Asia for this program.

**guntruck**  a 5-ton cargo truck armed with .50 caliber or M–60 MA-CHINE GUNS, plus other weapons. The guntruck was used for the security of CONVOYS.

**guppy**  a sarcastic term for one who is not SCUBA qualified. Also referred to as fin or straight fin.

**gurney**  a wheeled stretcher for moving wounded personnel.

**guy in back**  term for the backseat crew member in a fighter aircraft. Usually called GIB.

**GVN**  U.S. abbr. for the Government of South Vietnam.

**gypsy operation**  small unit bases which were often moved around from place to place as needed.

**GySgt**  abbr. for Gunnery Sergeant.

# H

**H & I Fire** abbr. for HARASSMENT AND INTERDICTION (or Interdictory) FIRE.

**H & M S** abbr. for Marine Headquarters and Maintenance Squadron.

**H & S** abbr. for Headquarters and Service unit.

**HA(L)** abbr. for Helicopter Attach (Light) Squadron.

**Hải Quân** Vietnamese for navy.

**Hai Van Pass** a pass on the mountain chain between Danang and Phu Bai. This area was an enemy ambush location and a major B–52 bombing target.

**Haig, Alexander** battalion and brigade commander, First Infantry Division, 1966–1967; regimental commander, deputy commandant, U.S. Military Academy, 1967–1969; military assistant to the president for national security affairs, 1969–1970; deputy assistant to the president for national security affairs, 1970–1973.

**Haiphong** large port in North Vietnam which was mined, immobilizing shipping. See also DUCK HOOK.

**Halang** a MONTAGNARD tribe living mainly in KONTUM Province.

**halazone tablets** used to purify drinking water.

**HALO** abbr. for High-Altitude Low Opening, the placement of troops by helicopters behind enemy lines. The jump was begun from 15,000 feet, fol-lowed by a considerable amount of free-fall time.

**ham** slang for someone in full dress uniform.

**ham and sons of bitches** slang for C-RATION ham and eggs.

**Hàm Rồng** Vietnamese for Dragon's Jaw, their name for the BRIDGE AT THANH HOA.

**Ham Tan** capital of BINH TUY Province.

**Hamburger Hill** site of the May 1969 battle at Ap Bia Mountain, one mile from Laos in the A Shau Valley, staged between the U.S. Army, Marines, and South Vietnamese Army, and the North Vietnamese Army. There were many casualties on both sides. Shortly after this battle, President Richard Nixon proclaimed the first withdrawal of American troops from Vietnam.

**hamlet** a small group of buildings; villages usually contained several hamlets.

**hamlet evaluation system** an evaluation system planned and run by Americans in Saigon, beginning in January 1967. The system necessitated monthly computerized reports from all district senior advisors in South Vietnam. The purpose of rating the hamlets and villages was to show the progress of the pacification program.

**hamlet festival** see COUNTY FAIR.

**hammer and anvil** an infantry tactic to encircle an enemy base area and then add other units to force the enemy out of hiding.

**hand frag** a hand-thrown bomb. See FRAG GRENADE.

**Hanoi** the capital of North Vietnam.

**Hanoi Hilton** 1. slang for large, well-furnished enemy bunkers or tunnel complexes in South Vietnam. 2. the nickname for Hoa Lo Prison, a highly feared prisoner-of-war camp in North Vietnam. It held American prisoners in a number of different sections; such as the Quiz Room, Golden Nugget, Riviera, Power Plant, Heartbreak Village, New Guy Village and Heartbreak Hotel. Also called the Honoi Hilton.

**Hanoi Jane** derogatory nickname for Jane FONDA.

**Happiness is a Cold LZ** popular saying in Vietnam. Landing in a Cold Landing Zone meant that no one was firing at them.

**Happy Valley** 1. nickname for an area near DA NANG. 2. slang for any especially bloody battlefield after a tough firefight.

**harassing fire** fire intended to interfere with the sleep of enemy troops. This cut back on troop movements and lowered their morale.

**Harassment and Interdiction (or Interdictory)** 1. ARTILLERY fired so that the enemy could not move freely. 2. artillery bombardment used to deny the enemy terrain which they could find useful. Targets for H & I were general areas, rather than specific and confirmed military centers; artillery fire was often randomly fired toward the enemy.

**harbor sites** marine term for the way a team established an overnight position.

**hard bomb** a conventional non-fragmenting explosive.

**hard core** grunt slang for North Vietnamese or Viet Cong regulars.

**hard hats** slang for the elite units of Viet Cong who wore metal or fiberglass helmets. They were usually full-time soldiers and not guerrillas.

**hard spot** 1. slang for a tank AMBUSH. 2. slang for a temporary infantry position, usually overnight.

**hardly working** slang for doing a hard assignment with a good attitude.

**hardstand** a pierced steel plate platform placed over sand to hold vehicles or aircraft.

**hard-stripe sergeant** a sergeant with rank indicated by chevron insignia, which implied some authority.

**Harkins, Paul D.** first commander of MACV, February 1962 through June 1964.

**Harriman, Averell** one of the WISE OLD MEN, a group of Americans who advised President Lyndon Johnson about the Vietnam War. He was the U.S. ambassador to the PARIS PEACE ACCORDS in 1968–1969.

**hash mark** stripe indicating three years of active service, also called Zebras. See SERVICE STRIPE.

**hasty defense** a defensive maneuver arranged on the spot, while in contact with the enemy.

**hat** marine slang for a DRILL INSTRUCTOR.

**hatch** naval term for a door.

**hatchet team** Special Operations Groups exploitation forces who neutralize targets discovered by RECONNAISSANCE teams.

**Hau Nghia** one of the 44 provinces of South Vietnam, located in III CORPS.

**haversack** marine term for their primary pack, in which clothing, C-rations, toilet articles, and other gear were carried.

**HAW** 1. abbr. for Heavy Antitank Weapon. 2. abbr. for Heavy Assault Weapon.

**HAWK** a surface-to-air guided missile designed to defend against low-flying aircraft and short-range missiles, and referred to as a Homing-All-the-Way-Killer.

**Hawkeye** the Grumman carrier-based airborne early-warning aircraft. It had a five-man crew and a radar dish mounted on its fuselage.

**hawks** slang for Americans who supported the war effort or who wanted to raise the level of fighting in Vietnam.

**Hayden, Tom** one of the CHICAGO SEVEN.

**Haylift** code name for the operation that sent South Vietnamese saboteurs to North Vietnam to destroy weapons, vehicles, and other war-related items.

**HE** 1. abbr. for High-Explosive, a type of artillery, mortar, or rocket round designed to be highly destructive. 2. abbr. for HERCULES missile.

**head** 1. marine and navy term for a bathroom. 2. slang for pot smokers.

**head call** marine and navy term for a trip to a bathroom.

**head detail** personnel assigned to clean up the HEAD.

**headache bar** slang for the protective safety bar in the roof over the driver's seat in a ROME PLOW (bulldozer).

**heart** short for PURPLE HEART.

**Heartbreak Hotel** a section of Hoa Lo Prison for new prisoners. See HANOI HILTON.

**Heartbreak Village** see HANOI HILTON.

**hearts and minds** the reason Americans were supposedly in Vietnam; that is, to win the hearts and minds of the Vietnamese people through various pacification programs. However, the gun ruled in South Vietnam, and the U.S. Army turned from pacification to the large unit war. Efforts toward pacification did not work in South Vietnam and were discontinued as U.S. withdrawals began.

**HEAT** abbr. for High Explosive Anti Tank, a type of ARTILLERY ROUND.

**heat tabs** an inflammable stick tablet made of trioxane used for heating C-RATIONS or boiling water.

**heavy arty** B–52 bombing strikes.

**heavy duty** slang meaning intense or serious.

**heavy fire team** three helicopters armed with machine guns, rockets, and 40mm cannons.

**heavy gun team** three armed helicopters flying at the same time in close contact with each other.

**heavy stuff** slang for heavy ARTILLERY.

**hedgehogs** isolated outposts in which the French high command had concentrated their troops.

**hedgerow** a thick row of bushes or trees set out as a hedge.

**Heinemann's Hotrod** nickname for the Skyhawk aircraft, named for Ed Heinemann, who developed the A–4 Skyhawk.

**heliborne** being aloft in a helicopter.

**Helicopter Valley** a nickname for the Song Ngan Valley south of the Demilitarized Zone; called that because of several disastrous occurrences in July of 1966 involving marines. An area just east of Nue Cay Tre was also known by this nickname.

**Heligoland** a Red Cross hospital ship, it cared for sick and wounded American civilians during the war. It operated off the coast of Vietnam.

**helipad** a helicopter landing area.

**Hell Island** nickname for POULO CONDOR (Con Son in Vietnamese), an island south of SAIGON used as a prison and known for its TIGER CAGES.

**Hell's Angels** nickname for the POWs at CAMP UNITY who got together and made trouble for their Viet Cong captors.

**Hell's Half Acre** nickname for an area just north of CU CHI.

**helo** helicopter.

**helo cast** a method of quickly INSERTing men into the water with a low-flying helicopter and an insertion platform.

**hen** recon nickname for the Sea Knight medium helicopter.

**HEP** abbr. for high explosive plastic (C4).

**herbicides** chemicals used to destroy vegetation to deny the enemy natural cover and to destroy crops. See AGENT ORANGE.

**Hercules** 1. Lockheed's C–130, a respected medium transport used by the air force for supply and used by the marine corps for supply and refueling. Its nickname was Herky bird. 2. one of the chemical companies that manufactured the defoliant AGENT ORANGE.

**Herd, the** nickname of the 173d Airborne Brigade, a paratrooper outfit that was the first major army combat unit sent into Vietnam, in May, 1965. Because of the very congenial relations between the black and white soldiers, they were sometimes called the Two Shades of Soul; they were also nicknamed the Sky Soldiers.

**Herky Bird** nickname for the HERCULES C–130 transport plane.

**herringbone formation** a formation used by mechanized and armor units in which armored vehicles turn alternately to the sides of the direction of march, putting their main armament and heaviest armor obliquely toward the flanks. The center is left open to provide freedom of movement within the column and as a refuge for vehicles without armor flanks.

**Hershey, Lewis** director of Selective Service, 1948–1970.

**Hershey Tropical Bar** the C-RATION Hershey chocolate bar which did not melt even when exposed to high temperatures.

**HES** abbr. for HAMLET EVALUATION SYSTEM.

**HESH** abbr. for High Explosive Squash Bomb, a round bomb, with a collapsible head and a shaped charge.

**Hester** the name of the severe typhoon which hit Vietnam in October 1971, destroying the AMERICAL division's headquarters at CHU LAI.

**hex tent** a small hexagonal tent holding five men. A larger size held eight to 10 men.

**H–46** the Vertol Sea Knight, a twin-engine transport and assault helicopter manufactured by Boeing and used mainly by the marines.

**HG** abbr. for HAND GRENADE.

**HH–43** HUSKIE, a turbine-engined rescue helicopter, manufactured by Kaman.

**H-Hour** the specific hour a planned operation begins.

**HH–3E** see JOLLY GREEN GIANT.

**Hickory** code name for a U.S. Marine ground operation in May 1967. This was the first major U.S. incursion into the Demilitarized Zone.

**high and tight** slang for a haircut shaved on the top and sides, with a quarter inch of hair on the top.

**high angle hell** slang for MORTAR fire.

**High Drink** code for refueling of hovering rescue helicopters by U.S. Navy vessels in the GULF OF TONKIN.

**high points** CIA and MACV term for short intervals of intense enemy activity, usually attacks against towns or military posts.

**high speed-low drag** slang for someone or something very competent and reliable, or something new and advanced.

**higher-higher** slang for the command or commanders.

**high-G** aerial term for the g-load increase during aircraft maneuvering.

**Highway 548** highway running through the A SHAU VALLEY.

**Highway 1** the main north-south highway in Vietnam and a main supply route. Years before, in attempting to clear this road the French named it the Street Without Joy.

**Highway 13** the highway in South Vietnam from Saigon to towns near the Cambodian border. It gave access to An Loc, Loc Ninh, and Quan Loi. It was important for the United States to hold the road and secure the border against North Vietnamese infiltration into these towns. Enemy base camps and tunnels were in this area. A THUNDER RUN maneuver was exercised often, involving columns of tanks firing H & I fire into suspected enemy areas along the highway. The highway then became known as Thunder Road.

**Hill (followed by a numeral)** during the Vietnam War, hills were given numbers corresponding to their height in meters.

**Hill 875** see DAK TO.

**Hill of Angels** English name for CON THIEN.

**Hilo Hattie** code for the C–54 fitted with infrared reconnaissance equipment; it operated in South Vietnam early in the war.

**HISASS** slang for HSAS (Headquarters Support Activity, Saigon), the navy command that furnished support to the Military Assistance Command, Vietnam. The army took this over in April 1966.

**HistOff** abbr. for Historical Office.

**hit team** slang for KATY, which was taken from KT or Kill Team. Hit teams were usually composed of two recon-trained scouts designated for missions. Also called ding teams.

**hitting someone** slang for trying to persuade someone.

**HJ** abbr. for the Honest John missile.

**HM** abbr. for navy hospital corpsman, a MEDIC.

**HMG** abbr. for Heavy Machine Gun.

**Hmong** a dominant Laotian hill tribe, also called the MEO.

**Ho Bo Woods** jungle area between CU CHI and the Cambodian border in WAR ZONE C.

**Ho Chi Minh** an alias for Nguyen Ai Quoc, founder and leader of the modern Vietnamese revolution. He worked and fought for the independence and the unity of Vietnam. Ho died in HANOI on September 3, 1969. Ho Chi Minh in Vietnamese means "he who enlightens."

**Ho Chi Minh City** the North Vietnamese name for SAIGON after 1975.

**Ho Chi Minh's Curse** slang for diarrhea.

**Ho Chi Minh Sandals** slang for sandals made out of old rubber tires. The soles were made from the tread and the straps were made from the inner tubes. They were also called Ho Chi Minh Slippers, or simply Ho Chi Minhs.

**Ho Chi Minh Trail** the infiltration route used extensively by the North Vietnamese Army to move troops and supplies from North Vietnam through Laos and Cambodia to all parts of South Vietnam. Before 1973 this was the major NVA infiltration route bringing men and materiel into South Vietnam. This principle north-south supply line became a strategic part of the war. The trail expanded as the war continued on. The U.S. recognized the strategic importance of the trail and attempted in many ways to interrupt it, but was not successful in lessening its value.

**hòa bình** Vietnamese for peace.

**Hoa** ethnic Chinese of Vietnam.

**hỏa châu** Vietnamese for flare.

**Hoa Hoa** a sect of the Buddhist religion originating in the MEKONG DELTA in the early 1900s. Often at odds with the central government in Saigon, the sect was also strongly anti-Communist.

**Hoa Lo Prison** a prison camp in North Vietnam where American POWs were held. See HANOI HILTON.

**hỏa-tiển** Vietnamese for rocket.

**HOBOS** abbr. for Homing Bombing Systems. These were TV-guided SMART BOMBS used toward the end of the Vietnam War.

**hộp tác** Vietnamese for reeducation.

**học tập trại or trại cải tạo**  Vietnamese for reeducation camps.

**Hoffman, Abbie**  one of the CHICAGO SEVEN and leader of the Yippies movement.

**Hoffman, Judge Julius**  judge at the trial of the CHICAGO SEVEN.

**hog**  1. nickname for a model UH–1B HUEY with 48 2.75 inch rockets and four M–60s. 2. slang for the M–60 MACHINE GUN.

**hog board**  marine nickname for a bulletin board where family photos were displayed.

**hog flight**  helicopter with a cannon and other weapons used for direct fire support.

**hog jaws**  nickname for the ROME PLOW.

**HOG–60**  slang for the M–60 MACHINE GUN; also called the pig.

**Hoi An**  capital of QUANG NAM province.

**Hoi Chanh**  a VIET CONG defector under the CHIEU HOI amnesty program.

**Holloway, James L.**  chief of naval operations, 1974–1975.

**home**  a missile guiding itself toward the target on heat waves, radar, echoes, or radio waves.

**home plate**  1. slang for one's base of origin. 2. the airfield or carrier where an aircraft is based.

**Homecoming**  code for the operation bringing POWs home after the signing of the PARIS PEACE ACCORDS in 1972, resulting in the release of about 600 POWs in early 1973.

**homerunner**  slang for an ARTILLERY shell landing on target.

**homesteader**  an American who served in Vietnam for five years or longer. Some homesteaders stayed in Vietnam for up to 10 years and raised families there. They usually had married Vietnamese women.

**Homing All the Way Killer**  nickname for the Hawk, a surface-to-air guided missile designed to defend against flying aircraft and short-range missiles.

**Hon Gai**  a major port in North Vietnam mined by the United States to immobilize shipping.

**Hon Gio**  see TIGER ISLAND.

**Hon Me**  an island in the TONKIN GULF.

**Hon Ngu**  an island in the TONKIN GULF.

**honcho**  Vietnamese slang for unit leader or the officer or sergeant in charge. When a Vietnamese wanted something he would always ask the honcho.

**Honda**  Japanese make of motorcycle which became a generic word for motorcycle in Vietnam.

**Honest Abe**  nickname for General Creighton ABRAMS, MACV.

**Honest John**  a surface-to-surface missile with both nuclear and nonnuclear warhead capability. It could hit targets up to 40,000 meters away.

**Hong Kong**  1. Vietnamese slang for anything cheap or false. 2. a padded brassiere.

**Hong Ngu**  the northernmost MEKONG RIVER town in KIEN PHONG Province. The town was only a few miles from the Cambodian border and carried out an active contraband trade.

**Honoi Hilton** see HANOI HILTON.

**Honolulu Conference** a discussion between President Lyndon Johnson and South Vietnamese Premier Nguyen Cao Ky in February 1966 which resulted in the premier's pledge to reform the South Vietnamese government and the president's promise to maintain American aid to South Vietnam. After the talks, President Johnson requested $700 million from Congress to pay for the war; the House approved that figure 408–7, as did the Senate, 88–3.

**Hook** 1. nickname for the CH–47 CHINOOK helicopter. 2. a radio or radio handset. 3. taking a prisoner.

**Hooker** one of the chemical companies that manufactured the defoliant AGENT ORANGE.

**hootch (hooch)** 1. a hut or simple dwelling, either military or civilian; it protected one from the elements although it was often very primitive. 2. a combination tent and shack used to house military personnel in base camps. 3. the thatched and bamboo homes of rural Vietnamese people.

**hootchgirl** young Vietnamese women employed by the American military as maids and laundresses.

**hợp tác** 1. Vietnamese for cooperation. 2. the name of the unsuccessful pacification program begun in 1964 and concentrated in one seven-province area near Saigon. 3. code for the program to increase security in the Saigon area in the fall of 1964.

**horn** 1. a radio handset or microphone or telephone. 2. a specific radio operation that used satellites to rebroadcast messages.

**horse pill** slang for the orange CHLOROQUINE PRIMAQUINE (CP pill).

**horsecollar** a helicopter personnel retractor device for water pickup. A downed crewman could put his torso and arms through a ring and his own weight would hold him in place during retraction and rescue.

**Horseshit Man** derogatory term for HO CHI MINH.

**hose** slang for directing a powerful stream of gunfire toward a target.

**hosing** infantry slang for opening fire on an area, often with automatic fire.

**hot** 1. slang for dangerous area or area under fire. Compare to COLD. 2. slang for a show-off.

**hot hole** slang for a tunnel with Viet Cong in it.

**hot landing zone** a LANDING ZONE which was taking fire, also a hot LZ or a red LZ.

**hot pursuit** slang for letting the U.S. military chase Viet Cong and North Vietnamese soldiers into Cambodia.

**hot sheets** sheets of steel laid out as sidewalks, roads, or runways and heated by the sun.

**HOT/SOP** abbr. for Hot Standard Operating Procedure, in effect from April 15 to October 15. Between those dates certain precautions were in force to avoid heat-related health problems. Compare with COLD/SOP.

***Hot Tip*** code for the operation that involved setting fire to large areas of land to clear it.

***hotdog*** slang for a show-off.

***Hotel*** the military phonetic for the letter H.

***Hotel Alpha*** phonetic alphabetization of HA, meaning to haul ass, or move right now.

***Hotel Caravelle*** a hotel in SAIGON.

***Hotel Echo*** phonetic alphabetization of HE, for high-explosive artillery or mortar rounds.

***Hotel Three*** code for helicopter landing area at TAN SON NHUT airport.

***hound dogs*** slang for air-to-ground missiles.

***house cat*** derogatory slang for a REMF.

***house mouse*** slang for maid or concubine.

***house of dark shadows*** slang expression for Vietnamese dwelling inhabited by CHARLIE.

***housewife*** marine slang for a sewing kit.

***hovercraft*** synonym for the PACV, or patrol air cushion vehicle, a device that moved above the surface of water on a bubble of air which it generated. Its top speed was 75 knots. The navy used this device to assist South Vietnamese operations in the DELTA, especially during monsoon season.

***HOW*** short for HOWITZER.

***Howard Johnson*** slang for the pushcarts that food vendors hauled on city streets in Vietnam.

***howitzer*** a short cannon used to fire shells at medium velocity and with relatively high trajectories.

***howitzer, M–110*** an 8-inch U.S. artillery piece with a 17,000 meter range. This weapon had the capability for nuclear weaponry, which was never utilized during the Vietnam War.

***howitzer, 106mm*** the standard marine ARTILLERY piece, which could fire four rounds per minute.

***HQ*** abbr. for Headquarters.

***HQC*** abbr. for Headquarters Command.

***Hre*** a MONTAGNARD tribe living mainly in QUANG NGIA Province.

***Hroy*** a MONTAGNARD tribe living mainly in PHU BON and PHY YEN provinces.

***HSAS*** abbr. for Headquarters Support Activity, SAIGON. See HISASS.

***HST*** abbr. for Helicopter Support Team.

***H–34*** the Army version of the CH–34 Sikorsky helicopter, the Sea Horse, a medium-sized transport.

***H–21*** the Shawnee tandem-rotor helicopter manufactured by Piasecki and used mainly by the army.

***HUAC*** See HOUSE UN-AMERICAN ACTIVITIES COMMITTEE.

***Hub, The*** slang for a mountainous area northwest of Tuy Hoa.

***Hue*** 1. one of the 11 AUTONOMOUS CITIES of South Vietnam. 2. the former imperial capital of a united Vietnam where Communists executed more than 2,000 noncombatants during the TET OFFENSIVE in February 1968; much of the city was destroyed. Communist troops captured Hue during the offensive and held it for more than three weeks. Marines fought in house-to-house and hand-to-hand combat here. On March 2, 1968, the battle for Hue was declared officially over, when the remaining troops of the North Vietnamese Army fled to Laos.

**Huey** nickname for the Bell UH (utility helicopter) series of helicopters. Huey evolved from its previous name, HU for helicopter, utility. Hueys were the most widely used helicopter of the Vietnam war. Also called HUEY GUNSHIP, Huey Slick, and Iroquois.

**Huey Gunship** nickname for the UH–1 series assault support, multipurpose helicopter.

**Huey Slick** nickname for the UH–1 assault support multipurpose helicopter. Slick meant that it was not carrying weapons.

**HU–5** a U.S. Marine helicopter.

**hug** to close in tight on the enemy or to be pinned down by the enemy.

**hull** the lower part of a tank, where the driver, ammunition, fuel, and engine were.

**Humanitarian Service Medal** medal authorized in 1975 to recognize meritorious direct participation in a significant military act or operation of a humanitarian nature, especially that of evacuating refugees.

**Hummer** The C–117 aircraft, stretched version of the C–47, used by marines for transport and flare missions.

**hump** 1. slang meaning to walk. 2. slang meaning a rotation of 25 percent

or more of a unit within a 30-day period, called a rotational hump. 3. slang meaning to do any laborious job. 4. slang for a rotation period, usually about 25 days in the field. 5. slang for carrying on one's back.

**humping** slang for marching with a heavy load.

**Hunter-Killer** 1. an IRON HAND mission against targets of opportunity flown by a flight of two specially equipped F–105s and two F–4s. Hunter-Killer was called Sam strike team earlier in the war. 2. helicopters, specifically the OH–6 Cayuse, escorted by a Cobra gunship that provided low-level reconnaissance at landing zones. Also called Pink Teams.

**Huong, Van Tran** see TRAN VAN HUONG.

**hush puppy** nickname for the Smith & Wesson 9mm pistol that U.S. Navy SEALs carried. It was called that because of its ostensible purpose of killing enemy guard dogs.

**HU–16** a Grumman amphibian plane, the Albatross.

**Huskie** a search and rescue helicopter, the HH–43 manufactured by Kaman, and used by U.S. Air Force Air Rescue Teams.

**HUT** abbr. for Hamlet Upgrading Team., a U.S. Army program for teaching and improving REGIONAL FORCES and POPULAR FORCES troops. This training program was part of VIETNAM-IZATION.

**HVAR** abbr. for High Velocity Aircraft Rockets.

# I

**I & I**  1. abbr. for Intercourse and Intoxication. See R & R. 2. abbr. for INTELLIGENCE AND INTERDICTION, a stratagem using night artillery to disturb the enemy's sleep.

**I & R**  abbr. for Intelligence and Reconnaissance Platoon.

**I Corps**  (pronounced "eye core") the northernmost military tactical zone.

**Ia Drang**  location of the first major battle between U.S. and North Vietnamese troops, in October 1965. See BATTLE OF THE IA DRANG VALLEY.

**IAS**  abbr. for Indicated Airspeed, the aircraft velocity displayed to the pilot.

**IBS**  abbr. for Inflatable Boat, Small.

**IBS doughnut**  nickname for the IBS. This was a seven-person, air-inflated rubber boat used for various insertions and patrols. Usually paddled, it was nicknamed doughnut because of its shape.

**IC**  1. abbr. for Innocent Civilian. 2. abbr. for Installation Commander.

**ICC**  abbr. for International Control Commission. Consisting of Canada, India, and Poland, this commission was set up by the Geneva agreement in 1954 to monitor the armistice between the French and the VIET MINH for Laos and Vietnam. In 1973 the PARIS PEACE ACCORDS established a similar four-nation group.

**ICCS**  abbr. for International Commission of Control and Supervision, which was set up to monitor the PARIS PEACE ACCORDS. Its members were Canada, Indonesia, Poland, and Hungary; the group was located at Tan Son Nhut Air Base. After two months, the Canadian delegation withdrew and its place was taken by Iran.

**ice cream cone with wings**  slang for the parachutist's badge, which resembled one.

**ice it**  slang phrase used by RECONNAISSANCE for getting extracted after finishing an objective or mission.

**ICM**  abbr. for Improved Conventional Munitions; also called FIRECRACKER.

**ICRC**  abbr. for International Committee of the Red Cross.

**ICS**  1. abbr. for Inter-Communications System which allowed communication between crew members in a cockpit. 2. abbr. for Integrated Communication System. This system consisted of 53 Vietnamese locations furnishing the army with strategic and tactical communication, and enabling it to be linked to worldwide communication systems.

**ICSC**  abbr. for International Commission for Supervision and Control in Vietnam. See ICCS.

**ICT**  abbr. for Individual Combat Training.

**ID**  1. abbr. for Infantry Division. 2. abbr. for Identification.

**IDA**  abbr. for Institute for Defense Analysis, an independent group that engaged in research for the Department of Defense. One of its ideas was for an electronic barrier along the Demilitarized Zone. The IDA was associated with several U.S. universities. See ELECTRONIC FENCE and the MCNAMARA LINE.

**IDAD**  abbr. for Internal Defense and Development. This U.S. group attempted to pacify the indigenous people of Vietnam. They worked through pacification, revolutionary development, internal security, and rural construction.

**identification tags**  used to identify wounded and dead soldiers. Identification tags had the name, service number, blood type, and religious preference of the wearer inscribed on them. Also called dog tags.

**IDT boxes**  abbr. for Indirect Transmission Devices. These were book-size secure transmitting and receiving devices, with built-in display screens.

**IFF**  abbr. for Identification Friend or Foe. This system used a radar pulse to respond to a received interrogation signal from a FRIENDLY radar.

**Igloo White**  1. code name of a program for developing an electronic battlefield. 2. code for the surveillance system of hand-implanted and air-delivered sensors, relay aircraft, and an infiltration system. 3. the code for the remote surveillance of the HO CHI MINH TRAIL monitored by an Infiltration Surveillance Center in Thailand. Igloo White was previously coded Muscle Shoals and Mud River.

**IHTFP**  abbr. for I Hate This Fucking Place, scrawled throughout Vietnam.

**II Corps**  second allied military tactical zone including the CENTRAL HIGHLANDS and adjoining coastal lowlands.

**IIFFORCEV**  abbr. for II Field Force, Vietnam.

**III Corp Tactical**  South Vietnamese military region, the land between the MEKONG DELTA and the CENTRAL HIGHLANDS of South Vietnam.

**III Corps**  the third allied military tactical zone encompassing the area from the northern MEKONG DELTA to the southern CENTRAL HIGHLANDS.

**IIR**  abbr. for Imaging Infrared Sensors. These devices gave gunships the capacity to find targets at night.

**Illinois City**  see PROJECT PRACTICE NINE.

**illum**  1. short for an illumination flare, usually fired by a mortar or artillery weapon. 2. to illuminate with flares or searchlights.

**illumination flare**  a white flare that provided light. These flares were hand-fired or shot from artillery, mortars, or aircraft.

**illumination grenade**  a small hand grenade used if noise or motion were heard ahead of one's position.

**Immelmann**  an aerial maneuver in which the aircraft completes the first half of a loop and then rolls over to an upright position.

**immersion foot**  skin condition suffered by many GRUNTS, the consequence of feet being in water for long periods of time, causing splitting of the skin and bleeding.

**IMN**  abbr. for Indicated MACH Number. This was the relationship of an aircraft's speed to the speed of sound without adjustment for sensor or instrument error.

*impact award*    an award for valorous action presented by a high-ranking officer very soon after that action.

*in the field*    any combat area or any area outside of an established BASE CAMP or town.

*inactivate*    to transfer a discontinued unit from the active to the inactive list. Also called disband, demobilize, and deactivate.

*incendiary bomb*    bombs which set on fire anything that they hit.

*incident counts*    a MACV term for keeping score during the war.

*INCOC*    abbr. for Infantry Noncommissioned Officer Course, an accelerated program to produce NCOs. Instant INCOC was slang for a graduate of INCOC.

*incoming*    1. receiving enemy fire such as MORTARS, ROCKETS, or ARTILLERY. 2. a warning call for enemy fire.

*incontinent ordnance*    bombs that hit where they were not meant to, as in one's own troops. This was sometimes termed by the military as "the accidental delivery of ORDNANCE equipment."

*in-country*    in Vietnam.

*increments*    the removable charges attached to MORTAR fins. If they became wet, the mortar round misfired and fell short.

*incursion*    1. an invasion, as in the incursion into Laos in 1971 by South Vietnamese soldiers, assisted by U.S. planes and artillery. 2. the term that President Richard Nixon used to describe a large combined U.S. and South Vietnamese ground action after the United States had begun withdrawal from Vietnam. The object of the incursion was to destroy North Vietnamese staging grounds inside Cambodia.

*india*    the military phonetic for the letter I.

*Indian Country*    1. slang for areas controlled by the Viet Cong, or North Vietnamese Army, or anywhere the enemy was. Also called Injun Country. 2. often referred to the CENTRAL HIGHLANDS.

*Indian Heads*    nickname for the Second Infantry Division, called that because of their insignia.

*indigenous*    local people.

*indirect fire*    a MORTAR or ARTILLERY attack where shells went on a flight path to an unseen target.

*Indochinese gibbon*    an ape found in Vietnam.

*Inf*    abbr. for INFANTRY.

*INFANT*    abbr. for Iroquois Night Fighter and Night Tracker, a HUEY which went out at night with GATLING guns and rocket launchers.

*Infantry*    in this branch of the army, soldiers were trained to fight on foot. The Infantry was the basic fighting unit of the land war. Also called the "queen of battle," the origin perhaps stemming from the game of chess.

*Infantryman*    a GRUNT, living and fighting out in the FIELD. They were nicknamed Line Doggie, Ground-Pounder, Crunchies, Dogface, Boonie Rat, Foot-Pounder, Foot-Slogger, Gravel-Crusher, and Stump-Jumper.

**infiltration course**  going through an obstacle course under simulated conditions.

**Infiltration Surveillance Center**  a system in Thailand which monitored information from the IGLOO WHITE operations.

**inflatoplane**  a rubber airplane parachuted down in a 55-gallon drum.

**infrastructure**  the government term for the apparatus at the VILLAGE and DISTRICT levels of South Vietnam.

**infusion**  a military program for transferring personnel to shorten the time spent in the field.

**ingress**  U.S. Air Force term for flight into a combat area.

**insert**  to be dropped into a tactical or combat area by helicopter or parachute, usually in secret.

**insertion**  helicopter placement of combat troops in an operational area, usually secret.

**instant detonation**  an instant explosion of a HAND GRENADE. When the four-second time delay section was removed, an instant explosion occurred when the pin was removed and the spoon released.

**instant INCOC**  slang for a new graduate of INCOC (Infantry Noncommissioned Officers Course).

**instant NCO**  a noncommissioned Officer who gets his STRIPES immediately after the course in a particular MOS. Also called Shake 'n' Bake, Ready Whip, and Nestle's quick.

**insurgency**  a situation following a revolt or insurrection against an established government. An insurgency is less disruptive than a civil war.

**Intel**  slang for intelligence.

**intelligence**  any information about the enemy that is useful in planning a mission. Information regarding enemy troop movements, strength, weapons, weather, and terrain could be useful in planning strategy.

**intelligence and interdiction**  also called I & I, it usually meant planned night artillery fire toward enemy locations. The purpose was to disrupt the enemy's sleep and make movement and effectiveness more difficult.

**interceptor**  an aircraft designed to combat other aircraft.

**intercourse and intoxication**  often called I & I, this referred to the activities while on R & R.

**interdiction**  interference with enemy movement and communication by using gunfire, bombs, or shells, with the purpose of making the enemy less mobile.

**interdiction fire**  fire put on an area to block the enemy from using that area.

**interlock switch**  aerial term for a two-position in and out switch on a F–4 front cockpit missile control panel, with the in position preventing AIM–7s from firing.

**internal defense**  means taken by a government to stay in power.

**intervalometer**  cockpit equipment which selected ORDNANCE and the rate of fire.

**Intruder**  the A–6, Grumman's all-weather, medium-sized attack plane.

*iodine spiller* slang for an enlisted man of the Medical Corps, a MEDIC.

**IP** 1. abbr. for Initial Point, a well-defined point used as a starting point for a bomb run to a target or for other tactical purposes. 2. abbr. for Instructor Pilot. 3. that point in a mission where descent toward the target started.

**IPW** abbr. for Prisoner of War Interrogation.

**IR** 1. abbr. for infrared. 2. abbr. for Intelligence Reports.

**IR missile** an infrared, heat-seeking missile.

**IRB** abbr. for Infrared Binoculars.

**IR8** MIRACLE RICE, a United States-developed strain of high-yield rice. Other high-yield strains of rice were also developed by the United States for the South Vietnamese during the war.

*Irene's Bar* a well-known bar in VUNG TAU.

*Irish Banjo* slang for ENTRENCHING TOOL.

*Irish pennant* marine slang for a dangling fiber or thread, especially on a recruit's uniform.

*iron bombs* conventional bombs.

*Iron Brigade* nickname for the Third Brigade, First Infantry. This nickname goes back as far as the Civil War and probably was first used by a war reporter.

*Iron Hand* code for a U.S. flight with specific ORDNANCE and avionics equipment, used to seek and destroy enemy surface-to-air missiles and radar-directed antiaircraft artillery sites.

*Iron Triangle* a jungle area dominated by the Viet Cong between the Thi Tinh and Saigon rivers, next to CU CHI district and about 20 miles northwest of SAIGON. Home to the VC, it occupied about 60 square miles in Military Region IV. The scene of heavy fighting between U.S. and Communist forces the Iron Triangle was the location of operation CEDAR FALLS. This area was also known as War Zone 1.

*ironing a village* Vietnamese slang used to describe the bombing and bulldozing of a village.

*Iroquois* see UH–1.

*irregulars* persons and groups in Vietnam who were armed but not in the armed forces or police force.

*Island of the Phoenix* an island in the MEKONG RIVER.

*I/T* abbr. for Interpreter/Translator (Vietnamese).

*it don't mean nothin'* a phrase said and heard frequently by servicemen, usually meaning the opposite. It was used, for example, on hearing that a buddy had gotten hurt, or on receiving a DEAR JOHN letter, or when the mail helicopter did not get to a unit.

*Ivory Coast* code for the raid on SON TAY PRISON in 1970.

*Ivory Tower* slang for the Pentagon.

*Ivy* nickname for the Fourth Army Division, because of both the design of its shoulder patch and the roman numeral IV. See the FAMOUS FOURTH.

# J

**j's or jay** 1. slang for marijuana cigarettes. 2. a nickname for the PLAIN OF JARS.

**jack** 1. a shark alert when divers were in the water on operations, also called smiling jack.

**jackfruit** a fruit found in the FISH HOOK region of Southeast Asia.

**jacking** evasive maneuvers in an aircraft, also called janking and jinking.

**jackoff flare** slang for a hand-held flare.

**Jacob's ladder** a strong rope ladder used aboard ship, and also dropped by helicopter for an individual to climb down through thick foliage onto the ground. It was used where the ground was too rough for helicopters to land.

**JAG** abbr. for Judge Advocate General, the legal department of the military.

**jail chokers** slang for shoelaces.

**jam** making radio or radar useless by various means of blocking it.

**jank** evasive maneuver in an aircraft, used to avoid getting hit. Also called jack and jink.

**January 27, 1973** 1. date the draft ended. 2. date of the signing of the PARIS PEACE ACCORDS.

**Jarai** a MONTAGNARD tribe living mainly in PLEIKU and PHU BON provinces.

**jarhead** slang for a marine.

**Jasons** code name of a top secret U.S. intelligence group. A team of scientists and professors from this study group conceived of the MCNAMARA LINE.

**JATO** abbr. for Jet Assisted Take Off, used to cut the takeoff roll or to provide obstacle clearance after take-off.

**JCRC** abbr. for JOINT CASUALTY RESOLUTION CENTER.

**JCS** abbr. for U.S. JOINT CHIEFS OF STAFF.

**JCS target** a target appearing on the JCS target lists.

**Jeep** the Ford M–151 quarter-ton. Black Jeeps were used almost exclusively by U.S. intelligence personnel.

**Jefferson Glenn** code for the last large U.S. ground combat operation in South Vietnam, which took place south of Hue, in THUA THIEN Province from September 1970 to October 1971, involving the 101st Airborne Division.

**Jeh** a MONTAGNARD tribe living mainly in QUANG TIN, QUANG NAM and KONTUM provinces.

**jelly donut** slang for an over-weight Red Cross Woman.

**Jesus nut** nickname for the bolt that held the rotor blade to the helicopter. Called that because one prayed to Jesus that the bolt would hold.

**jet jockey** 1. negative term for a combat veteran who extended his tour several times and so had made several trips back to the WORLD. 2. USAF fighter pilots in general.

***Jet Ranger*** nickname for the Bell OH–58 helicopter.

***JG*** abbr. for Junior Grade.

***JGS*** abbr. for Joint General Staff, the South Vietnamese counterpart to Military Assistance Command, Vietnam and the equivalent of the U.S. Joint Chiefs of Staff.

***jinking*** evasive maneuvers in an aircraft; also called jacking and janking.

***JM*** abbr. for Jump Master, the person on an aircraft responsible for troop safety, correct procedures, and spotting and supervising the jumps of the parachutists. Pronounced "Jim," it is sometimes spelled that way.

***JMC*** abbr. for Joint Military Commission. This group consisted of representatives of North Vietnam, the Provincial Revolutionary Government, the United States, and the Republic of Vietnam. Its mission was to ensure that the concerned parties implemented and abided by the agreement detailing how to account for prisoners and MIAs.

***Jody*** generic name for the guy back home who took the wife or girlfriend of a soldier at war.

***Jody calls*** the rhythmic cadence called out to keep marchers in step.

***John Wayne*** marine slang for a P–38 can opener, or bulldozer tank.

***John Wayne bar*** nickname for a candy wafer found in freeze-dried rations, available in vanilla, chocolate, maple, and coconut flavors.

***John Wayne High School*** nickname for the Special Warfare Training School at Fort Bragg, North Carolina.

***John Wayneing it*** slang for acting macho or like a hero.

***Johnny Thunder*** slang for the combination of an M–16 and an M–79 GRENADE LAUNCHER. Also called an over and under.

***Johnson, Harold K.*** chief of staff, U.S. Army, 1964–1968.

***Johnson, Roy L.*** commander in chief, Pacific Fleet, 1965–1967 and Commander of the Seventh Fleet, 1964–1965.

***joint*** slang for a marijuana cigarette.

***Joint Casualty Resolution Center*** organization established as a successor to MACV's Personnel Recovery Center. The JCRC attempted to recover Americans still missing in action after the war.

***Joint Chiefs of Staff*** the senior officers of the U.S. Armed Services, consisting of the chairman, the U.S. Army chief of staff, the chief of Naval Operations, the U.S. Air Force chief of staff, and the U.S. Marine commandant. During the Vietnam War, the chairmen of the Joint Chiefs of Staff were General Nathan Twining, 1957–1960; General Lyman Lemnitzer, 1960–1961; General Maxwell Taylor, 1961–1964; General Earle Wheeler, 1964–1970; Admiral Thomas Moorer, 1970–1974; and General George S. Brown, 1974–1978.

***Joint Service Commendation Medal*** an award to any member of the U.S. Armed Forces serving with the Joint Chiefs of Staff or other agencies for meritorious achievement or service. The degree of merit must be distinctive as this medal ranks just below the AIR MEDAL.

**Joint Task Force** a task force is a temporary grouping of units, under one commander to carry out a specific mission. Joint Task Force refers to a temporary grouping of assigned elements of the army, the navy and the air force or any two of these services, for a specific mission or operation.

**joker** slang for fuel planning information.

**Jolly** slang for JOLLY GREEN GIANT, and also for the HH–53 rescue helicopter used widely in Vietnam.

**Jolly Green Giant** 1. nickname for the largest helicopters used for transporting troops and materiel supplied to the American forces. They were usually heavily armed. 2. an air force HH–53 heavy rescue helicopter. 3. the navy Sikorsky HH–3E helicopter. 4. the CH–54, the Flying Crane and Sikorsky's CH–3.

**Jolly Green SAR** a search and rescue unit responsible for the recovery of hundreds of aviators in North and South Vietnam. These were very highly respected airmen.

**Jones, David C.** air force chief of staff, 1974–1975.

**Jones, William K.** commander of the Fleet Marine force, 1970–1973.

**joypop** flying in a helicopter fast and close to the ground.

**JP–5** a kerosene-based fuel used for jet engines; one of several grades of jet fuel.

**JP–4** a kerosene-based fuel used for turbine engines; one of several grades of jet fuel.

**JPRC** abbr. for Joint Personnel Recovery Group which, within MACV, kept records on and attempted rescues for all POWs in the Vietnam War.

**JTF** abbr. for JOINT TASK FORCE.

**judy** aerial term used to indicate that the interceptor had contact with the target and was assuming control of the engagement.

**juicer** slang for heavy drinkers of alcohol.

**jujube** a thorny Vietnamese fruit tree whose fruit is used as a flavoring for candy.

**juliet** the military phonetic for the letter J.

**jump CP** slang for a temporary command post used for a short operation and usually including only critical personnel and equipment needed for that particular operation.

**jump pay** those who maintained their jump status by jumping from aircraft in flight at least once every three months were given extra pay of $55 per month.

**Jump Week** the final week of jump school training.

**jumping junkie** 1. slang for paratroopers or parachute-qualified troops. 2. a drug-using paratrooper.

**Junction City** code name for a large ground operation in March 1967 in TAY NINH Province where American and South Vietnamese troops tried to destroy COSVN, the Central Office for South Vietnam, the Communist headquarters. This was the only operation during the Vietnam War where battalion-sized combat parachute jumps took place. Junction City, a large SEARCH AND DESTROY operation in War Zone C, was thought to be militarily successful.

***June 8, 1969*** the date that President Richard Nixon announced the start of the U.S. withdrawal from Vietnam. This was part of a 10-part plan proposed by the NATIONAL LIBERATION FRONT in May 1969. Nixon proposed a mutual withdrawal of U.S. allied, and North Vietnamese forces from South Vietnam over a one-year period.

***jungle boots*** footwear that looked like a combination combat boot and canvas sneaker. Although the tops were nylon, the boots had thin plates of steel in the soles. Jungle boots were used by the U.S. military in tropical climates, where leather rotted quickly because of the humidity. The canvas material dried faster after soldiers waded through water.

***jungle eater*** nickname for the ROME PLOW.

***jungle fatigues*** the lightweight fatigue uniforms used by all personnel in Vietnam; also called tropical combat uniforms and hot weather uniforms.

***jungle penetrator*** a device lowered and raised by cable from a helicopter to extract a grunt, often a wounded soldier, from heavy jungle brush.

***jungle rot*** slang for a skin rash caused by the damp environment, affecting mainly the feet and crotch area. Also called crotch rot.

***jungle utilities*** lightweight tropical fatigues.

***jungle-busting*** using a tank or armored vehicle to cut trails through the jungle.

***junk-on-the-bunk*** slang for all gear laid out on beds for inspection. Also called things–on–the–springs.

# K

**k** abbr. for a KILOMETER.

**Kalashnikov** see AK–47.

**Kaman HH–43 Huskie** a rescue helicopter.

**Kampuchea** the new spelling for Cambodia used by the KHMER ROUGE after 1975.

**karst** the limestone mountain ridges of Laos.

**Katu** a MONTAGNARD tribe living mainly in QUANG TIN and QUANG NAM provinces.

**KATY** derived from KT, for kill team. These were usually two recon-trained scouts designated for missions. Also called ding team and hit team.

**KBA** 1. abbr. for Killed By Air, the body count after an air attack. 2 abbr. for Killed By Artillery.

**K-bar or Kabar** a military knife, derived from the Bowie knife; the basic survival knife used by marines in the FIELD.

**KBH** abbr. for Killed By Helicopter.

**KC–103** the in-flight refueling tanker configuration of the C–130 Lockheed HERCULES.

**KC–135** Boeing's Stratotanker, used by the air force for air refueling. It was nicknamed the "gas station in the sky" and the "flying gas station."

**KCS** abbr. for KIT CARSON SCOUT. A KCS was a former Viet Cong soldier working with an American unit as an interpreter and scout.

**KD** abbr. for Known Distance, referring to a rifle course.

**Keep Connie Home** antiwar movement slogan referring to the USS *Constellation*, a carrier that sailed from San Diego in October 1971 for her sixth deployment off the coast of Vietnam.

**Kennan, George** one of the WISE OLD MEN, a group of Americans who advised President Lyndon Johnson about the Vietnam War.

**Kentucky windage** to adjust a rifle's aim by intuition.

**Kep Ha** site of a MiG base in North Vietnam.

**Kerner Commission** the National Advisory Commission on Civil Disorders headed by Governor Otto Kerner of Illinois. In 1968 it described and evaluated racial riots and their causes.

**key terrain** an area whose domination gave the possessor a clear advantage.

**Keystone** the operational code word for the U.S. Army's withdrawal from Vietnam. Divided into Keystone Eagle, Cardinal, Blue Jay, Robin, Oriole, Mallard, and Owl, the stages ran from July 1969 through November 1972.

**Keystoned** applied to a unit as it turned in its equipment and moved on during Operation KEYSTONE.

**K–50** Chinese Communist 7.62mm submachine gun, used by the Viet Cong.

**K–44**  a Russian-made rifle.

**Kha**  Laotian tribesmen recruited by the Communists.

**KHA**  abbr. for Killed in Hostile Action. The United States could not use the official term KIA (Killed in Action) because war was never declared; therefore, KHA was used for the American dead and KIA for enemy dead.

**khakis**  the tropical class A uniform.

**Khanh Hoa**  one of the 44 provinces of South Vietnam, located in II CORPS.

**Khanh Hung**  capital of BA XUYEN Province.

**Khe Sanh**  this marine base near the Demilitarized Zone was attacked on January 21, 1968. In the siege of Khe Sanh, which lasted 77 days, 205 American marines lost their lives. Khe Sanh was evacuated by the Americans later in 1968 and rebuilt into a base in 1971.

**Khiem Cuong**  capital of HAU NGHIA Province.

**Khmer**  Cambodians living mainly in the MEKONG DELTA. Khmers were taller and darker than the Vietnamese and wore a different type of dress. During the Vietnam War, thousands of Khmers fled across the border to Cambodia to escape the fighting.

**Khmer Rouge**  the Communist party in Cambodia, literally "Red Cambodians."

**Khmer Serai**  independent, anti-Communist Cambodians often living in Vietnam and organized by the CIA.

**Khmers Rouges**  members of the Cambodian leftist party, named Khmers Rouges by Prince Norodom Sihanouk to distinguish them from right wing individuals. They took power in 1975 and killed 2 million Cambodians. In December 1978, the North Vietnamese invaded Cambodia and took control. The Khmer Rouge then returned to the jungle and continued guerrilla activities against the Vietnamese.

**không**  Vietnamese for no.

**không biết**  Vietnamese for "I don't know."

**không dủớc khỏe**  Vietnamese for good or well.

**không giờ**  Vietnamese for zero hour.

**Không Quân**  Vietnamese for air force.

**Không xấu**  Vietnamese for "Don't worry about it," or literally, "not bad."

**KIA**  abbr. for Killed In Action. KIA was not authorized by the Department of Defense because war had never been declared, so KIA usually referred to enemy dead. Americans were said to be KHA, meaning Killed in Hostile Action.

**KIA (BNR)**  abbr. for Killed In Action (Body Not Recovered).

**kickers**  slang for personnel of civilian flight companies who dropped equipment into inaccessible locations. The packages were literally kicked out of aircraft doors.

**kicking pots**  slang for kitchen police, mess hall duty.

**kicks**  slang for shoes or boots.

**Kien Giang** one of the 44 provinces of South Vietnam, located in IV CORPS.

**Kien Hoa** one of the 44 provinces of South Vietnam, located in IV CORPS.

**Kien Phong** one of the 44 provinces of South Vietnam, located in IV CORPS.

**Kien Tuong** one of the 44 provinces of South Vietnam, located in IV CORPS.

**kill** aerial term for an enemy plane shot down or otherwise destroyed by military action while in flight.

**kill fire** a barrage of gunfire so accurate that it leaves no one able to return fire.

**kill ratio** a MACV term for keeping score during the war.

**kill team** two recon-trained scouts designated for missions. Also called Katy, and ding team, hit team, and KT.

**kill zone** the radius of a circle around an explosive device. In this circle, an estimated 95 percent of the troops were killed when the device exploded.

**Killer Junior** 1. direct defensive fires by 105mm and 155mm guns. "Killer" methodology was used in taking out snipers from nearby base areas. The name "Killer" came from the radio call sign of the battalion that developed the techniques. See KILLER SENIOR. 2. slang for a high explosive with a time fuse, fired with a short fuse setting, and used for close-in defensive fire.

**Killer Kane** nickname for assassination specialists who operated behind enemy lines at night.

**killer MOS** slang for any combat MOS such as a gunner, rifleman, or tank crew.

**Killer Senior** direct defensive fires using 8-inch HOWITZERS. "Killer" methodology was used in taking out snipers from nearby base areas. The name "Killer" came from the radio call sign of the battalion that developed the techniques. See KILLER JUNIOR.

**killer team** 1. slang for a marine mobile ambush team. 2. slang for any roving patrol.

**killing zone** the area within an ambush where everyone is killed or wounded.

**kilo** military phonetic for the letter K.

**kilometer** 1,000 meters, or 0.62 miles; abbreviated as click, k, klik, and klick.

**king of battle** term referring to artillery. Infantry was called the queen of battle. The origin may stem from the game of chess.

**Kiowa** an observation helicopter manufactured by Bell and used by the army.

**Kissinger, Henry** special assistant to the president for national security affairs (1969–1973) and secretary of state (1973–1977). Kissinger was pivotal in negotiating the settlement of the war. He held many secret talks outside of the formal peace talks in Paris. In January 1973, he and Le Duc Tho of North Vietnam worked out a formal agreement. Soon after, they were jointly awarded a Nobel peace prize, although Le Duc Tho refused to accept his share.

**Kit Carson scouts** former Viet Cong soldiers acting as guides or interpreters for U.S. units. After defecting, they actively aided the American troops.

**kitchen police** cleaning and maintaining mess halls, or one who is assigned that duty.

**kiwi** marine slang for a goof-off.

**KKK** Khmer Kampuchea Krom, a pro-U.S. Cambodian exile group.

**klick** short for kilometer, or 1,000 meters.

**knapsack** an auxiliary pack carried by marines in the field. Knapsacks held extra clothing, and could be attached to the bottom of the larger HAVERSACKs they carried.

**kneeboard cards** cards that pilots held on their knees containing classified information, such as their fuel loads, dive angles, bomb settings, and ordnance carried.

**Koho** a MONTAGNARD tribe living mainly in LAM DONG and TUYEN DUC provinces.

**Komer, Robert** General William WESTMORELAND's assistant in charge of CORDS. In 1967, he took charge of the pacification program and initiated the CHIEU HOI program.

**Kontum** one of the 44 provinces of South Vietnam, located in II CORPS.

**Kontum City** capital of KONTUM Province.

**kool aid** 1. slang for killed in action. 2. a beverage often made by the troops in Vietnam to mask the taste of the drinking water. Presweetened Kool-Aid packets were mailed by friends and relatives in the United States.

**Kools** favorite cigarette of Vietnamese people, especially the mentholated variety.

**KP** abbr. for kitchen police, also known as mess-hall duty.

**kpung** a poisonous nettle that caused excruciating and long-lasting pain. These nettles were used as barriers around villages to prevent Viet Cong attacks.

**krait** a small, deadly snake found in Vietnam.

**KSCB** abbr. for KHE SANH Combat Base.

**Kt** abbr. for knot, one nautical mile per hour, or 6,080.20 feet.

**KT** abbr. for KILL TEAM.

**Ky, Nguyen Cao** see NGUYEN CAO KY.

# L

**L, V, and X** various ambush set-ups named after their shapes.

**LA** 1. the western direction, referring to Los Angeles as west. 2. abbr. for Light Armored.

**laager** 1. all-around night defensive position set by mechanized vehicles. *Laager* is a Dutch term from the Boer War, also spelled lager, when the settlers placed their wagons in a circle, facing outward for mutual defense. 2. placing of helicopters in a secure forward area in order for weapons to be used in defense.

**LAAW** abbr. for Light Antiarmor Assault Weapon or Light Antitank Assault Weapon. See LAW.

**ladder** naval and marine term for stairway.

**lager** see LAAGER.

**lai dâi** Vietnamese for come here.

**Laird, Melvin** secretary of defense from January 1969 to January 1972, and domestic advisor to the president, 1973–1974.

**Lam Dong** one of the 44 provinces of South Vietnam, located in II CORPS.

**Lam Son 719** code name for the invasion of Laos by the Army of the Republic of Vietnam in February 1971 during which they attempted to cut the HO CHI MINH TRAIL in southern Laos. The South Vietnamese troops attempted a large cross-border engagement with the assistance of U.S. troops.

**lancer** a wartime scout dog.

**land of the big PX** slang for the United States, with its big department stores and supermarkets.

**land of the tall American** slang for the United States because Americans were generally taller than the average Vietnamese. Even today, some Vietnamese and Cambodian refugees tell immigration officials they want to go to the land of the tall American.

**land of the 24-hour generator** slang for the United States because in Vietnam power failures were regular occurrences.

**land tail** those in an air-transport unit who joined the unit via land.

**Land to the Tiller Program** President NGUYEN VAN THIEU's plan in 1970 to give peasants their own land at no cost. This program resulted in 400,000 peasants receiving land titles to more than 2 million acres. By 1973 most farmers in South Vietnam owned the land they farmed.

**Landgrab '73** phrase for the pre-cease-fire attempts on the part of both Communist and Saigon forces to gain control of strategic points in 1973.

**Landing Zone** a small clearing secured temporarily for the landing of helicopters to unload men and cargo. The term was usually shortened to LZ and designated hot or cold depending on whether or not it was under fire. Some become more permanent and eventually became base camps.

**landlines** the network of buried or above-ground telephone lines. Often referred to as lima lima or lema lema.

**lang** term used in the central part of South Vietnam for villages.

**Lang Vei** site of a Special Forces camp where North Vietnamese employed tanks for the first time in February 1968.

**Lansdale, Major General Edward** special assistant to the U.S. ambassador to South Vietnam, 1965–1968.

**Lao Dong Party** the Vietnamese Workers' (Communist) party. The Communist party assumed this name in 1951, six years after it was supposedly abandoned by Ho Chi Minh so that he could guide the VIET MINH. Ho believed that the Viet Minh would end French power in Vietnam. In 1976, the name was changed officially to the Communist party.

**lao green** slang for local marijuana.

**Laotian red** a type of marijuana.

**LAPES** abbr. for Low-Altitude Parachute Extraction System, which referred to a free-fall at low altitude. It was a fast method of INSERTING trucks, ammo, or light tanks without the aircraft having to land.

**Las Vegas** a section of Hoa Lo Prison. See HANOI HILTON.

**laser** when an aircraft expends all its ordnance at once. Also called a salvo.

**laser-guided bomb** a bomb that could attack targets illuminated by laser beams and home in on any target sighted by those on board the aircraft.

They were used for the first time in March 1972 against North Vietnamese targets. Also called LGB and smart bombs.

**laterite** the red, rocky, claylike soil in Vietnam.

**LAW** abbr. for Light Antitank Weapon or Light Antitank Assault Weapon. A shoulder-launched, high-explosive, 66mm antitank rocket in a disposable fiberglass rocket-launcher tube. Also spelled LAAW (Light Anti-Armor Weapon).

**lay chilly** slang meaning to freeze, or stop all motion.

**lay dead** slang for goofing off.

**lay dog** slang of recon patrols meaning to lie low in the jungle.

**lazy dog** 1. nickname for a bomb that exploded hundreds of little darts about 30 yards above the ground. 2. an air-to-ground antipersonnel rocket used by the U.S. Air Force in Southeast Asia.

**LB** 1. abbr. for Landing Barge. 2. abbr. for Light Bomber.

**LBE** abbr. for Load-Bearing Equipment, a system of suspender straps and web belts on which most of a soldier's gear was carried.

**LBFM** abbr. for Little Brown Fucking Machine, a derogatory term for the enemy.

**LBJ** 1. slang for Long Binh Jail, a U.S. military stockade on the Long Binh post in South Vietnam. 2. slang for Long Binh Junction, the headquarters for the U.S. Army in Vietnam.

**LBJ Ranch** slang for Long Binh jail.

**LC**   abbr. for Landing Craft.

**LC-1 combat outfit**   a combat harness assembly.

**LCpl**   abbr. for Lance Corporal in the U.S. Marines.

**LDNN**   abbr. for Lin Dei Nugel Nghia, the Vietnamese version of U.S. Navy SEALS.

**Le Duc Tho**   a member of the Political Bureau of the Lao Dong party and the commander during the war against the French. He was also senior advisor to the North Vietnamese delegation at the PARIS PEACE ACCORDS and instrumental in the negotiations with HENRY KISSINGER. His nickname was Ducky. Le Duc Tho was awarded the Nobel Peace Prize in 1973, although he refused to accept it.

**Le, Nguyen Thanh**   see NGUYEN THANH LE.

**lead**   1. the first aircraft in a flight or element. 2. a specific lead aircraft or its pilot.

**lead angle**   the angle between the line of sight to a moving target and the line of sight to the predicted position of the target at the time the projectile intercepts the target.

**Lead Sled**   1. nickname for the F-100 Super Sabre aircraft. Also called the Hun. The F-105 Thunderchief was also called the Lead Sled. 2. synonym for permit, the basic parachutist's insignia.

**leapfrog**   a movement in which supporting groups advanced through or past one another so that each team could cover the other as it moved.

**Leaping Lena**   see PROJECT DELTA.

**Leatherneck**   nickname for a marine.

**Leatherneck Square**   nickname for four marine combat bases in I CORPS in South Vietnam, where they formed a quadrilateral: CON THIEN, Gio Linh, Dong Ha, and Cam Lo.

**leave**   an authorized and extended absence from duty.

**leeches**   bloodsuckers that attached to the human body and were common to parts of Vietnam. To protect their legs, grunts would cross their boot laces from the top to just below the knee and tie them tightly; sometimes they wore condoms to protect their organs.

**Legion of Merit**   award to heads of foreign states or to supreme commanders of foreign military who distinguished themselves by exceptionally meritorious conduct in performing service to the United States. It ranks just below the DEFENSE SUPERIOR SERVICE MEDAL.

**lego**   slang for a soldier who is not AIRBORNE.

**legs**   infantry, as contrasted to parachutists.

**lema lema line**   phone line above or below the ground. Also spelled Lima Lima.

**LeMay, Curtis**   USAF chief of staff, 1961–1965, nicknamed Genghis Khan. He is the originator of the statement about North Vietnam, "We should bomb them back to the Stone Age."

**Lemnitzer, Lyman L.**   chairman, Joint Chiefs of Staff, 1960–1961; and chief of staff, U.S. Army, 1959–1960.

**leroy** nickname that white GIs used for black GIs from rural areas, or for GIs who saw a lot of duty out in the field.

**let's do it/let's get it done** all-purpose phrase used by NCOs and officers, meaning generally "go ahead," sometimes referring to such activities as "let's burn the village."

**lethal envelope** aerial term for the space within which the successful use of a specific weapons systems can be ensured.

**lethal radius** the area within which one-half of visible enemy soldiers became casualties.

**LeTourneau Tree Crusher** a huge machine used to clear heavy jungle. Too large and cumbersome to be effective, it was replaced by the ROME PLOW.

**LF** abbr. for Low Frequency, referring to signals which could be received on the ground.

**LGB** abbr. for LASER-GUIDED BOMB.

**LGH** abbr. for the slang term Large Green Helicopter.

**L-hour** the specific time helicopters land in a landing zone during a planned helicopter operation.

**LI** abbr. for Light Infantry.

**liberation radio** slang for the underground and secret radio station on which the Viet Cong broadcast.

**liberty** naval term for an authorized absence from duty of less than 72 hours.

**licensed** short for "licensed to kill," as were combat soldiers.

**lick** slang for an error or anything bad or wrong, including a military disaster.

**liên dội** Vietnamese for company group, a Vietnamese military unit consisting of three militia infantry companies.

**lifeline** the straps holding the GUNNY on the helicopter while he fires his M–60. Also called a monkey strap.

**lifer** slang for a career soldier, often used in a derogatory manner.

**LIFT** abbr. for Local Improvement of Forces Team. This was a training program for REGIONAL FORCES and POPULAR FORCES as part of VIETNAMIZATION.

**lift** 1. one helicopter trip carrying cargo or troops from a loading area to a LANDING ZONE. 2. any number of helicopters in flight.

**liftbird** nickname for a troop transport, fixed-wing or rotary-wing.

**light at the end of the tunnel** expression often used to describe the defeat of the Viet Cong and the North Vietnamese Army.

**light fire team** two Cobra or UH–1 gunships armed with rockets, machine guns, and a 40mm cannon.

**light infantry** units that carried lighter weight weapons than the infantry traditionally carried.

**light observation helicopter** see OH–6.

**light off** slang for light, light up, or turn on. Often heard in the past tense as lit off.

**light scout team** a group consisting of one LOH armed with two

M–60 machine guns and one heavy COBRA. The LOH hovered at a low level and searched out enemy emplacements. Once the position was marked, the Cobra expended ORDNANCE on the target.

**light-green** marine slang for a Caucasian, as "He's a light-green marine."

**lightning bolts from heaven** marine slang for artillery.

**Lightning Bug** slang for helicopters equipped with searchlights, used for spotting targets at night. Also called firefly.

**lima** military phonetic for the letter L.

**Lima Charley Hotel Mike** radio operator's term for Loud and Clear How Me meaning "I can hear you; can you hear me?"

**lima lima** landlines, telephone communications between two points on the ground. Also spelled lema lema.

**Lima Site** code for the primitive airstrips in Laos used for U.S. covert operations.

**Lima Zulu** international phonetic alphabet for LZ, or landing zone.

**limited conventional war** U.S. Department of Defense designation for conflict involving American units larger than 4,000 men. This term was used by the Pentagon to reclassify the Vietnam War from a guerrilla war.

**Lin Dei Nugel Nghia** the Vietnamese version of U.S. Navy SEALS.

**lindane powder** an insecticide used in Vietnam.

**line doggy/doggie** slang for INFANTRYMAN.

**line haul** long-distance military truck convoys. Also called long haul.

**line number** see DUST-OFF LINE NUMBER.

**line of arrival** a grid line on a map that denoted the end point of an operation.

**line of departure** a grid line on a map that indicated the no-turning-back point in an operation.

**line, the** being on duty with an infantry unit in the field.

**Linebacker** code name for a series of USAF strikes against targets in North Vietnam; Linebacker I began May 9, 1972, in response to the North Vietnamese EASTERTIDE OFFENSIVE. Operation Linebacker II was massive USAF fighter-bomber strikes over Hanoi during Christmas 1972. Soon after Linebacker II, the North Vietnamese returned to negotiating and the PARIS PEACE ACCORDS were signed shortly afterwards, in January 1973.

**Linebacker II** See LINE-BACKER.

**lines** naval term for ropes.

**Link the Chink** derogatory slang for a Vietnamese.

**links** the metal strip holding an ammo belt together.

**listen up** request to pay attention.

**listening post** a position enabling one to detect any sound or movement that might disclose enemy activity in the area.

**litter** stretcher to carry wounded and dead.

**litter case** a combatant wounded in action who could not walk and was placed on a litter and then MEDEVACED.

**Litterbug** code for Remotely Piloted Vehicle (RPV) operations in which propaganda leaflets were dropped over North Vietnam.

**Little Appalachia** nickname for the headquarters of the First Infantry Division, in the towns of Di An and Lai Khe. It was called that because of its similarity to the environment in parts of the Appalachian Mountains in the United States.

**Little Brother** code for the use of Cessna O–2s fitted with side-firing MINIGUNS.

**Little Detroit** nickname for the North Vietnam city of Van Dien, called that because of its factories.

**Little IRT** nickname for the CU CHI tunnel system, named after a New York City subway system.

**Little Men** slang for Viet Cong or North Vietnamese soldiers.

**Little People** slang for the enemy, the North Vietnamese people.

**Little R** slang for Rest and Recouperation (R & R). Compare with Big R, a ROTATION home.

**Little Vegas** a section of the Hoa Lo Prison, nicknamed the HANOI HILTON.

**LLDB** abbr. for LUC LUONG DAC BIET, the South Vietnamese Special Forces. Many were minority group tribesmen including Nung Chinese, Montagnards and others.

**LMG** abbr. for Light Machine Gun.

**LN** abbr. for Liaison.

**LOACH** abbr. for Hughes OH–6 LIGHT OBSERVATION HELICOPTER. See LOCH.

**Load Bearing Equipment** see LBE.

**LOC** abbr. for Line Of Communication. These were land, water, and air routes along which supplies and reinforcements moved from rear bases to troops in the field.

**Loc Ninh** a village in BINH LONG Province in III CORPS, north of SAIGON near the Cambodian border. Loc Ninh was overrun in April 1972 by the North Vietnamese Army.

**local force** a Viet Cong combat unit secondary to a DISTRICT or PROVINCE headquarters.

**Loch** the Hughes OH–6 LIGHT OBSERVATION HELICOPTER. Also called Loach, LOH, Tadpole and White Bird.

**lock and load** phrase meaning to prepare for firing. One loaded a round into the rifle's chamber and made sure that the safety was on.

**lock-on** aerial term meaning to follow a target automatically in one or more dimensions.

**LOCSTAT** abbr. for Location Statement, an indication of the present location.

**Lodge, Henry Cabot** ambassador to South Vietnam, 1963–1964, and again 1965–1967.

**log run** an aerial logistical resupply mission.

**logbird** slang for a logistical supply helicopter that flies resupply missions to a unit's forward elements.

**logging** sending logistics helicopters loaded with supplies to the troops.

**LOH** (pronounced loach) abbr. for Light Observation Helicopter, especially the Hughes OH–6.

**Lomotil** medication used by GIs to relieve diarrhea and dysentery.

**Lon Nol** Minister of defense and commander-in-chief of Cambodia's armed forces until 1967 when he became prime minister. In 1970 he overthrew Prince Norodom Sihanouk with the aid of the United States, and became the leader of Cambodia. Although the KHMER ROUGE was beginning to control the country, Lon Nol rigged an election in 1972 and became president with full power. His government collapsed, however, and he abdicated and fled to Indonesia in April, 1975. He then fled to exile in Hawaii.

**L–19** the military version of the Cessna C–37, an unarmed spotter aircraft, also known as the O–1 Birddog.

**L–119** small American-made plane used for scouting by the Saigon air force.

**Long An** one of the 44 provinces of South Vietnam, located in III CORPS.

**Long Binh** 1. headquarters for the U.S. Army in Vietnam. This large complex just outside of Bien Hoa in III Corps was established in 1966–67. On November 11, 1972, it was closed down, ending direct U.S. participation in the Vietnam War. 2. Long Binh was also the site of a large military stockade, nicknamed LBJ for Long Binh Jail.

**Long Binh Jail** slang for the Long Binh Stockade.

**long green line** slang for a line of infantry humping through the jungle.

**long haul** long-distance military truck convoys. Also called line haul.

**Long John** nickname for 175mm gun. Also called Long Tom.

**Long Khanh** one of the 44 provinces of South Vietnam, located in III CORPS.

**long line** slang for an all-night sexual encounter.

**long nose** Vietnamese slang for an American.

**Long Tau** a main shipping lane between SAIGON and the sea.

**Long Tom** slang for the M–107 175mm long-range artillery gun. Also called Long John.

**Long Xuyen** capital of AN GIANG Province in South Vietnam.

**longan** a Vietnamese fruit related to the lichee.

**longtime** slang for all-night intercourse.

**loose deuce** aerial term for fighter tactics in which two to four aircraft maneuvers provided mutual support and increased firepower.

**LORAN** abbr. for Long-Range Airborne Navigation, a radio navigation aid.

**LORAPL** abbr. for Long Range Planning Task Group. This group was created in July 1968 by General Creighton ABRAMS to examine U.S. tactics in Vietnam during the previous four years; it attempted to effect changes where necessary.

**lottery, draft** see DRAFT LOT-
TERY which began in December 1969.

**Lovett, Robert** one of the WISE
OLD MEN, a group of distinguished
Americans who advised President
Lyndon Johnson about the Vietnam
War.

**LOX** abbr. for Liquid Oxygen,
which is converted to gaseous oxygen
to enable breathing.

**LP** 1. abbr. for listening post, a two-
or three-man position set up at night
outside the perimeter away from the
main body of troops; it acted as an
early warning system against attack. 2.
an amphibious landing platform used
by the infantry.

**LRP** (pronounced "lurp") abbr. for
Long-Range Patrol. It was formerly
called LRRP (Long-Range Reconnaissance Patrol); LRPs became known as
rangers after 1969.

**LRPR** abbr. for Long-Range Patrol
Rations, also called lurps. These
freeze-dried, precooked meals came in
small packets. Water was added to reconstitute them, and the troops much
preferred them to C-RATIONS.

**LRRP** 1. long-Range Reconnaissance Patrol, an elite team usually
composed of five to seven men who
would go deep into the jungle to observe enemy activity without initiating
contact. A unit was considered long-
range if it was out of normal artillery-
support range, approximately 10
kilometers. Also spelled LRP and
LURP, and pronounced lurp. These
units were called rangers after 1969. 2.
reconnaissance units of various types.

**LS** 1. abbr. for LIMA SITE, a temporary aircraft landing site. 2. abbr. for
Landing Site.

**LSA** abbr. for Lubricant, Small
Arms, a gun oil for small arms.

**LtCdr** abbr. for Lieutenant Commander.

**LtCol** abbr. for Lieutenant Colonel,
also abbreviated LTC.

**LtGen** abbr. for Lieutenant General.

**LTL** designation of the Vietnamese
Interprovincial Route, or Highway.

**Ltr** abbr. for Letter.

**Lửa** Vietnamese for fire or flame.

**luât chiến-tranh** Vietnamese
for laws of war.

**Luc Luong Dac Biet** Vietnamese
for South Vietnamese Special Forces.
Often referred to by their initials
LLDB, which were frequently used in
a derogatory manner as Look Long,
Duck Back and Lousy Little Dink Bastards, as their effectiveness was considered minimal.

**L;aluc Quân** Vietnamese for
army.

**Lufberry Circle** a circular tail
chase.

**Luke the Gook** derogatory slang
for Vietnamese.

**Lunch** see MENU.

**Lurp** 1. slang for freeze-dried rations carried on LRRP missions. 2. nickname for a someone who participates
in a LRRP.

**lựu dạn** Vietnamese for grenade.

**lựu dạn cay** Vietnamese for
teargas grenade.

**lựu dạn hỏi ngạt** Vietnamese
for gas grenade.

**lừu dạn khói**   Vietnamese for smoke grenade.

**LWL**   abbr. for Limited War Laboratory.

**LZ**   abbr. for LANDING ZONE.

**LZ Prep**   airstrikes and artillery fires on a proposed LZ, in preparation for its use.

**LZ Stud**   nickname for the First Cavalry's landing zone near Khe Sanh in northern South Vietnam, near the Demilitarized Zone.

# M

**M** abbr. for model. 2. abbr. for mechanized. 3. abbr. for MACH.

**M'Nong** a MONTAGNARD tribe living mainly in QUANG DUC Province.

**M/Sgt** abbr. for Master Sergeant.

**MA** abbr. for MECHANICAL AMBUSH, a booby-trap set by U.S. forces or our allies.

**Ma Deuce** nickname for the M–50 heavy machine gun.

**MAAG** abbr. for Military Assistance Advisory Group. MAAG merged into MACV in May 1964.

**MABS** abbr. for Marine Air Base Squadron. MABS was a repository of an air group's nontactical support elements, plus a catchall for unskilled personnel.

**MAC** 1. abbr. for Military Airlift (or Air) Command, which airlifted on a continuing basis men and materiel from the United States to Southeast Asia. 2. abbr. for Marine Amphibious Corps.

**mace** Viet Cong booby trap consisting of a spiked rock on a camouflaged rope held overhead. A tripwire released the mace, causing it to swing down the trail striking everyone in its path.

**Mach** the unit of velocity relating to the speed of sound and named for physicist Ernst Mach.

**machete** a sharp hacking tool used for cutting through the jungle.

**machine gun, .50 caliber, M–2** a belt-fed, recoil-operated, air-cooled automatic weapon, weighing about 80 pounds. It could fire 450–550 rounds per minute to a range of 1,450 meters.

**machine gun, 7.62mm, M–60** a belt-fed, gas-operated, air-cooled automatic weapon, weighing about 22 pounds. It could fire 100 rounds per minute to a range of 1,450 meters. It was nicknamed the pig, the hog, and the hog–60.

**MACOV** abbr. for Mechanized and Armor Combat Operations in Vietnam.

**MACV** (pronounced macvee) abbr. for Military Assistance Command, Vietnam. This was the American military headquarters of the senior general staff of the American expeditionary corps in Vietnam, located at the TAN SON NHUT air base. Established in 1962, it was closed on March 29, 1973, which ended U.S. combat presence in Vietnam. Civilian newsmen nicknamed it the Pentagon East, or Pentagon of the East, while soldiers called it the puzzle palace and the madhouse.

**MACV 525–13** see RULES OF ENGAGEMENT.

**MACV–SOG** abbr. for Military Assistance Command Vietnam-Studies and Observation Group (Special Operations).

**mad bomber** slang for Mortar Air Delivery System, also called MADS.

**mad mike** see MAD MINUTE.

**mad minute** 1. a 60-second expending of ORDNANCE, a weapons free-fire practice and test session. It was sometimes called mike-mike or mad moment or mad mike. 2. to place heavy fire around a defensive position at night to discourage enemy troops in the area.

**mad moment** when all ORDNANCE or ammunition was fired. See MAD MINUTE.

**mad monkeys** slang for MACV staffers.

**Mademe Nhuyen Thi Minh** see NHUYEN THI MINH, MADAME.

**Maddox** See GULF OF TONKIN INCIDENT.

**madhouse** slang for MACV headquarters in Tan Son Nhut.

**MADS** Mortar Air Delivery System. MADS was also called mad bomber.

**MAF** see Marine Amphibious Force.

**MAG** 1. abbr. for Military Advisory Group. 2. abbr. for Marine Aircraft Group. 3. abbr. for Marine Air Group.

**mag pouch** the magazine holder worn on the web belt.

**magazine** the spring-loaded metal ammo clip which held bullets and fed them into a weapon. Each magazine held 20 or 30 rounds per unit; grunts typically carried seven or eight of them.

**Maggie's drawers** marine slang for the red disc waved from the sidelines or red flag drawn across a rifle target during target practice indicating a clear miss.

**Magpie** a B–57 aircraft with 750-pound bombs.

**mags** short for MAGAZINE.

**Main Force** organized Viet Cong battalions and regiments, as opposed to local VC guerrilla groups.

**Main Force Battalion** the basic Viet Cong fighting force of each province of South Vietnam, usually large and well-equipped.

**Main Force Elements** Viet Cong and North Vietnamese military units subordinate to the Central Office of South Vietnam, the North Vietnamese control headquarters.

**Main Force Unit** regular forces of the North Vietnam Army and Viet Cong military in South Vietnam.

**main line of resistance** the front line against the enemy.

**maint** abbr. for maintenance.

**Maj** abbr. for major.

**Majestic Hotel** 1. a modern hotel on TU DO STREET in SAIGON, with 125 air-conditioned rooms. 2. the hotel in Paris where the PARIS PEACE ACCORDS were signed.

**MajGen** abbr. for Major General.

**make the scene with 18** a phrase heard often on Armed Services Radio and Television to remind soldiers that only 18 rounds of ammo should be put into the standard clip of the M–16 rifle. Although twenty 20-rounds units were taken into the field and rifles could hold 20 rounds, that many would often cause jamming.

**malaria** a disease common in the tropics, which many soldiers developed while in Vietnam. Although it was required that soldiers take both daily and weekly pills to prevent the two most common forms, falciparum and vivax, some soldiers neglected or refused to take them, thus becoming ill. In other cases, the pills were ineffective in preventing the disease. Approximately 120 U.S. servicemen died from malaria while in Vietnam.

**Malay whip**  a booby trap consisting of a large log attached to two trees with rope, and set off by a TRIP WIRE. When the wire was tripped, the log whipped around wildly, striking down anyone in its path. Also called a swinging man trap.

**Malaysian sling**  a doorlike booby-trapped board with PUNJI STAKES protruding from it, ready to spring at anyone who walked by it in the bush.

**Mallard**  see KEYSTONE.

**mama**  slang for the submarine from which teams were inserted.

**mama-san**  G.I. slang for an Oriental female or elderly lady. Mama-sans were respected by the younger generation of Vietnamese.

**man Friday**  slang that white GIs used referring to black GIs whom they believed brown-nosed white superiors to get out of combat or other unwanted assignments.

**man, the**  slang that black soldiers used referring to white authority.

**mangosteen**  a dark red, juicy fruit with a thick rind, found in Vietnam. It was eaten raw or cooked with rice.

**manoi**  Vietnamese for the Vietnamese girlfriend of an American serviceman.

**Manpack Personnel Detector—Chemical**  the formal name of the PEOPLE SNIFFER.

**Marble Mountain**  a small mountain near DA NANG, inland from China Beach. A U.S. base was at its foot, and a Viet Cong hospital and monastery were hidden inside the mountain.

**march order**  an artillery command, meaning to pull up stakes and move to a new location.

**marching fire**  fire dispensed by the infantry during an assault, particularly with the rifle fired rapidly from the shoulder or hip.

**MarDiv**  abbr. for Marine Division.

**Marine Amphibious Force**  the MAF commanded U.S. Marine units in I Corps Tactical Zone, and acted as a corps-level headquarters for U.S. Marine and Army units there. MAF was formerly called the Marine Expeditionary Force, but General William Westmoreland feared that the word *expeditionary* might remind the Vietnamese of the hated French Expeditionary Corps.

**Marine Expeditionary Force**  see MARINE AMPHIBIOUS FORCE.

**Marineland**  slang for I CORPS area.

**mark**  a ground wind-speed indicator.

**marker round**  the first round fired by mortars or artillery used to adjust the following rounds onto the target.

**Market Time**  code for an operation of the U.S. and the South Vietnamese Navy to prevent the infiltration of the North Vietnamese into South Vietnam by sea. The Coast Guard was also involved in this campaign of interdiction along the South Vietnam coast. Market Time began in

March 1965; in late 1969 and throughout 1970 the operation was turned over to the South Vietnamese Navy. The turnover was completed in 1971.

**MARLOG** abbr. for Marine Logistics Flights, a shuttle for men and supplies.

**MAROP** abbr. for Maritime Operation.

**MARS** abbr. for Military Affiliate Radio Station (or System). This was used by soldiers to call home via the Signal Corps plus ham radio equipment.

**Mars Generator** see TUNNEL FLUSHER.

**Marshal Lon Nol** see LON NOL.

**Martin, Graham** the last U.S. ambassador to South Vietnam, serving from 1973 until 1975.

**Marvin Arvin** sarcastic nickname that GIS gave the soldiers of the South Vietnamese Army, from ARVN.

**MASH** abbr. for Mobile Army Surgical Hospital.

**Masher** code for an operation begun in early 1966 by U.S. troops in Binh Dinh Province. It was later renamed White Wing because of President Lyndon Johnson's dissatisfaction with the connotation of the word *Masher*. This was the first large unit operation of the war which crossed corps boundaries, and resulted in a high number of enemy casualties.

**massaged** slang for killed.

**mass-cal** abbr. for mass casualty, a term indicating that seven or more critically wounded G.I.s were brought in.

**MAST** abbr. for Mobile Army Surgical Team.

**mast** nautical term for a hearing. A request mast is held at the request of a serviceman. A CAPTAIN'S MAST is a hearing before the captain.

**Master Sergeant** a senior noncommissioned officer in pay grade E–8.

**Master-At-Arms** the navy and coast guard term for military police.

**MAT** abbr. for Mobile Advisory Team. A six-member team consisting of two U.S. Army Officers, three enlisted men, and an interpreter, responsible for training REGIONAL FORCES and POPULAR FORCES.

**MAT Team** abbr. for Military Assistance and Training Team. Three- or four-man teams of American combat arms advisors lived with Vietnamese units and were associated with them during operations.

**Mặt Trận** Vietnamese for the National Liberation Front.

**Matty Mattel** nickname for the M–16 and also the M–60. The toy-making company, Mattel, was thought to have made some of the parts for these weapons.

**maverick** a government vehicle which was misused or stolen.

**maximum power** aerial term for afterburner power.

**maximum range** the absolute distance a weapon could travel.

**maximum turn-rate** aerial term for the rate or maximum number of degrees per second achieved during a turn.

**máy bay** Vietnamese for airplane.

**mayday** the international distress call.

**MC** 1. abbr. for Marine Corps. 2. abbr. for Medical Corps.

**MCAF** abbr. for Marine Corps Air Facility.

**MCAS** abbr. for Marine Corps Air Station.

**McCain, John.** commander in chief, Pacific Command (CINCPAC), 1968–1972.

**MCCC** abbr. for Marine Corps Command Center.

**McConnell, John P.** air force chief of staff, 1965–1968.

**McDonald, David L.** chief of naval operations, 1963–1965.

**McGuire rig** a device used by SPE-CIAL FORCES for lowering in or lifting out personnel by helicopter. It was frequently used to rescue the wounded.

**MCI** abbr. for Meal, Combat, Individual, which had more variety and more nutrition than C-RATIONS. These were used for selected units later in the war.

**McNamara Line, the** nickname for a proposed electronic fence across the DMZ separating North and South Vietnam; it was to contain barbed wire, seismic and acoustic sensors, and minefields. At first meant to stop activity on the HO CHI MINH TRAIL, the plan was abandoned in 1967. It was also termed McNamara's Wall and electronic fence and was originally coded Illinois city and Operation Dye Marker.

**McNamara, Robert** secretary of defense, 1961–1968. An influential policymaker of the Vietnam war, he believed as early as 1966 that the war could not be won.

**McNamara's Defection** derogatory term following Defense Secretary Robert McNamara's conclusion that the United States could not win the war in Vietnam. In 1967 he tried to persuade President Lyndon Johnson to negotiate a settlement; in November 1967 Johnson asked him to resign as secretary of defense.

**McNamara's Fence** see the MC-NAMARA LINE.

**McNamara's 100,000** see PROJ-ECT 100,000.

**McNamara's Wall** see the MC-NAMARA LINE.

**McPherson, Henry** special counsel to President Lyndon Johnson, 1966–1969.

**meatball** slang for the orange searchlight used for night landings on carriers. Pilots followed these optical landing aids to keep their planes on the right landing approach. Also known simply as ball.

**meat wagon** slang for evacuation transportation.

**Mech** abbr. for mechanized infantry.

**mechanical ambush** booby trap used by U.S. forces; one that is automatically set off by the enemy as he approaches. See BOOBY TRAP.

**mechanical mule** see MULE.

**mechanized platoon** a platoon using tanks and armored personnel carriers.

**MED** abbr. for Message Entry Device, referring to several types of electronic transmission devices.

**Med**   abbr. for medical.

**Medal of Honor (Congressional)**
the highest award given for gallantry
and risk of life above and beyond the
call of duty in actions involving armed
conflict with an enemy. During the
Vietnam War, 238 Medals of Honor
were awarded: 155 recipients were in
the army, 57 in the marines, 14 in the
navy, and 12 in the air force.

**MEDCAP**   abbr. for Medical Civil
Action Program in which U.S. medical
personnel went into the villages to
minister to the local population. Physi-
cians and medical technicians treated
Montagnards and other villagers and
taught personal hygiene and sanita-
tion. Over 150 U.S. medical physi-
cians volunteered to serve in Vietnam.

**MEDEVAC**   1. abbr. for the medical
evacuation of a soldier from the field
by medical helicopter. Helicopter am-
bulances were often brought in to
evacuate the wounded. When patients
were treated on the way to a medical
facility and reached the medical facility alive, the mortality rate was less
than 2 percent. This was the lowest
mortality rate of any war. Medevacs
were classified as emergency
medevacs for those near death, priority
medevacs for those seriously wounded
and unable to walk, and routine
medevacs for those personnel either
ambulatory or dead. 2. the helicopter
carrying emergency medical treatment
supplies and medics. Early in the war
when helicopters went unarmed with
only Red Cross symbols painted on
them for protection, they were often
prime targets for the enemy. Later in
the war, these helicopters were armed
with DOOR GUNNERS and had GUNSHIP
escorts when possible.

**medic**   enlisted men in the Medical
Corps, were called medics or corpsmen. Also called 91 Band-Aid, 91 bedpan, penis machinist, prick smith,
chancre mechanic, bedpan commander, Band-Aid, pecker-checker,
clap-checker, and iodine-spiller.

**MEDMAF**   abbr. for Mekong Delta
Mobile Afloat Force, usually called
Mobile Riverine Force.

**MEDTC**   abbr. for Military Equipment Delivery Team, Cambodia. Set
up by the United States in January
1971 this group gave military aid to
Cambodia.

**meeting engagement**   a collision between two forces, sometimes
occurring when neither is ready for a
conflict.

**MEF**   abbr. for Marine Expeditionary Force. See Marine Amphibious
Force.

**Mekong Delta**   an area in the
southern part of South Vietnam (IV
CORPS) with rivers, streams, and canals. The Delta was heavily cultivated
to produce rice, fruit, and vegetables.
The area was generally inhabited by
ethnic Vietnamese.

**Menu**   collective code name for B–
52 bombing operations against Communist base areas in Cambodia. The
series included Breakfast (near the
Fish Hook area of Cambodia), Lunch
(on the borders of Cambodia, Laos,
and Vietnam), Dinner (in the Fish
Hook area), Snack, Supper (a base area
in Cambodia), and Dessert (an area
north of the Fish Hook area). These
concealed bombings continued from
March 1969 to May 1970, causing civilian casualties in Cambodia. President Richard Nixon took strong

measures to keep Operation Menu from becoming known to Americans at home.

**Meo (also spelled Moi)** 1. a derogatory Vietnamese word, meaning savage used for the MONTAGNARDS and various tribes of indigenous mountain people. 2. the Meo people were also one of the tribes of Laos.

**meritorious promotion** a promotion given without the usual tests and before the expected interval of time required for such a promotion.

**Meritorious Service Medal** award given for outstanding meritorious achievement or service to the United States by any member of the U.S. Armed Forces. It ranked just below the Defense Meritorious Service Medal (for army and air force) and just below the Bronze Star (for navy and marine corps).

**Meritorious Unit Commendation** award to units for exceptionally meritorious conduct, outstanding devotion, and superior performance of outstanding service for at least six continuous months during military operations against an armed enemy.

**mermite** a large insulated food container.

**mess cook** mess hall cook's helper or waiter.

**mess hall** military dining quarters, where GIs took their meals when they were not out in the field.

**meter** 39.37 inches, or 1.09 yards. Distances and other measures, such as weaponry size, used the metric system in Vietnam.

**Metrecal Division** derogatory slang for the AMERICAL division, a reference to a low-calorie beverage popular in the United States taken instead of regular meals.

**MF** abbr. for MIKE FORCE.

**MFC** abbr. for Mortar Fire Controller.

**M–5 bag or M–5 kit** large green bag carried by medics containing bandages, morphine, and other medical supplies.

**M–48** a medium-sized tank, the Patton, used by U.S. forces in Vietnam.

**M–41** an American-made light tank supplied to the South Vietnamese Army and used by U.S. forces prior to the Vietnam War.

**M–46** a Soviet-made 130mm field gun, used by the North Vietnamese Army.

**M–42** a modified M–41 tank with two 40 mm antiaircraft guns used as ground support in Vietnam. It was nicknamed Duster.

**M–14** a standard U.S. rifle in the early 1960s, eventually replaced by the M–16; it fired the standard NATO 7.62mm round.

**MFWs** abbr. for multiple FRAG wounds.

**MG** 1. abbr. for Machine Gun. 2. abbr. for Major General. 3. abbr. for Military Government.

**MGen** abbr. for Major General.

**MGF** abbr. for MOBILE GUERRILLA FORCE.

**MGH** abbr. for Medium Green Helicopter.

**MGySgt** abbr. for Master Gunnery Sergeant.

**MH** abbr. for Medium Helicopter.

**MI**  abbr. for Military Intelligence.

**Mi**  abbr. for mile.

**MI team**  abbr. for Military Intelligence team.

**MIA**  abbr. for Missing In Action. North Vietnam returned almost 600 American prisoners or persons Missing In Action in 1973. By the mid-1980s North Vietnam had returned the remains of about 100 more MIAs. There are still, however, over 2,400 Americans not accounted for and considered either still missing or held prisoner.

**MIA/BNR**  abbr. for Missing In Action/Body Not Recovered.

**Michelin Rubber Plantation**  a French rubber plantation northwest of Saigon. During the war Michelin operated a large rubber plantation which was the base for large Communist units.

**microgravel**  see GRAVEL.

**MICROSID**  a seismic device smaller than the MINISID.

**MICV**  abbr. for Mechanized Infantry Combat Vehicle.

**midnight requisition**  slang for unauthorized supplied acquired by small units. Single serviceman or very small groups would obtain items on their own, without going through proper channels.

**MiG**  all Soviet-built fighter-bombers supplied to the Hanoi Air Force. Actually MiG stands for the Soviet design team of *Mi*koyan-*G*urevich (Arten I. Mikoyan and Mikhail I. Gurevich) which produced many of the leading Russian fighters. Often misspelled as MIG.

**MiG CAP**  Combat Air Patrol directed specifically against MiG aircraft. This section of fighters was free to intercept any airborne threat with the primary mission of downing the aircraft.

**mighty mite**  1. commercial air-blower used for injecting smoke and tear gas into tunnels to clear them. Also spelled Mitey Mite. 2. Marine slang for a jeep.

**MiGSCREEN**  mission where protection of a strike force is provided by placing fighters between the threat and the strike force in a specific area.

**mike**  military phonetic for the letter M.

**Mike Force or MSF**  see MOBILE STRIKE FORCE.

**Mike Papa**  phonetic alphabetization for MILITARY POLICE.

**mike-mike**  1. a military slang for millimeter (mm). 2. the phonetic alphabetization for MAD MINUTE.

**Mil**  an angular measurement of 1/6400 of a circumference, or about 1/18 of a degree. Gunsight settings are in mils.

**Military Assistance Command Vietnam**  See MACV.

**military payment certificate**  GIs were paid in scrip, or MPCs, to minimize inflation and reduce black market trading in South Vietnam. This system of payment began in September 1966, and one year later, over one billion military pay certificates had been handled.

**military police**  the enforcers of military law and order. The military police (MPs) controlled traffic, escorted convoys, and protected property. They operated CHECKPOINTS and security systems and also monitored drug use and prostitution.

**military power**  aerial term for the maximum thrust of an aircraft engine, without use of the afterburner.

**military region**  the term that replaced CORPS TACTICAL ZONE. South Vietnam was divided into four geographic zones, numbered from I to IV for military and civil administration purposes. These military regions were formerly called I Corps, II Corps, III Corps, and IV Corps.

**million-dollar wound**  slang for a noncrippling wound, but one serious enough for the patient to be returned to the United States for treatment.

**MILPHAP**  abbr. for Military Provisional Health Assistance Progress. This was a health program for Vietnamese civilians set up by the medical command in Vietnam. Its main purpose was to assist Vietnamese medical staffs and to help improve clinical and surgical services through the introduction of American methods and technology.

**min**  Vietnamese for mine or landmine.

**minesweeper**  a large amphibious-tractor vehicle with large steel prongs projecting from the front. It was used to uncover and explode mines.

**Minh, Duong Van**  see DUONG VAN MINH.

**mini-arc light**  the combined air and artillery strike delivered over target areas.

**minigun**  an electric GATLING gun, a six barreled, 7.62mm machine gun

which used a system of rapidly rotating barrels to produce a high rate of fire. Electronically controlled, miniguns were capable of firing 6,000 rounds per minute. They were usually mounted on aircraft to be used on ground targets.

**mini-hand SID**  small, hand-implanted SEISMIC INTRUSION DETECTORS.

**MINISID**  a seismic device attached to a Magnetic Intrusion Detector and slightly larger than the MICROSID, which in turn was slightly larger than the PSID (Patrol Seismic Intrusion Device). The latter was small enough to be carried on patrol.

**Mini Tet**  a second wave offensive in May of 1968, following the full-scale TET OFFENSIVE. Rockets and mortars hit downtown Saigon, and 120 additional attacks took place in other parts of South Vietnam.

**Mint, The**  nickname for an area of cells in the Las Vegas section of the Hoa Lo Prison, HANOI HILTON.

**Miracle Division**  derogatory slang for the AMERICAL Division, to imply that it would be a miracle if it performed well.

**Miracle Rice**  a quickly maturing rice strain brought into Vietnam through USAID programs in 1968, Miracle Rice was two and a half times more productive than the domestic South Vietnamese rice. Other high-yield strains of rice were developed during the war.

**misadventure**  MACV euphemism for a nonhostile casualty by FRIENDLY FIRE.

**missile free** the authority to fire missiles if a target is not identified as friendly.

**missile tone** audio signal indicating an AIM–9 is locked on to an infrared source.

**missile-free environment** a sighting or radar contact that could only be the enemy.

**Mission Council** organized by U.S. Ambassador Maxwell Taylor, this group met weekly to coordinate activities among the U.S. agencies in Vietnam. ELLSWORTH BUNKER, WILLIAM WESTMORELAND, and other heads of U.S. agencies met regularly as an executive and advisory committee.

**mission ready** equipment, including helicopters, that was ready to perform designated missions.

**mister zippo** slang for a FLAMETHROWER operator.

**Misty Bronco** OV–10 aircraft flown by a FORWARD AIR CONTROLLER usually armed with fourteen 2.75 HE rockets and 4 M–60s, with 550 rounds per gun and fourteen 2.75 WP rockets.

**Mitey Mite** see MIGHTY MITE.

**Mixmaster** nickname for the Cessna twin-engined FAC Super Skymaster, or O–2.

**MLR** abbr. for Main Line of Resistance.

**mm** abbr. for millimeter.

**MN–19** steel runway panels which were fitted together quickly to make a solid surface for airstrips or ramps.

**MO** abbr. for Medical Officer.

**Mobe, The** short for The National Mobilization Committee to End the War in Vietnam. This group was formed in the United States during the fall of 1966 to coordinate antiwar activities. It organized an antiwar march on the Pentagon in October 1967, with 150,000 people marching. After 1968 it was called THE NEW MOBE.

**Mobile Advisory Team** the army teams put together in 1967 under the guidance of local PROVINCE and DISTRICT advisory teams. Each Mobile Advisory Team had two army officers, three enlisted men, and an interpreter. They gave advice on operations, tactics, ambushes, weapons care, and medical treatment.

**Mobile Guerrilla Force** sometimes abbr. MGF. See MOBILE STRIKE FORCE.

**Mobile Riverine Force** a U.S. Army/Navy Task Force. The army-navy command directing amphibious operations in the MEKONG DELTA was established in 1967. Officially called Mekong Delta Mobile Afloat Force, it was abbreviated MEDMAF.

**Mobile Strike Force** units made up of indigenous personnel and used for reinforcement. They were trained by U.S. SPECIAL FORCES for rescue operations, reaction or standby units and guerrilla operations in Viet Cong-controlled locations. They were called Mobile Guerrilla Forces until 1967, and were also called China boy companies.

**Model K Buffalo Turbine** see TUNNEL FLUSHER.

**mogas** short for motor gas.

**MOH** abbr. for MEDAL OF HONOR.

**Mohave** a transport helicopter manufactured by Sikorsky and used by the army.

**Mohawk**   see OV–1B.

**Moi**   derogatory Vietnamese reference to MONTAGNARDS, meaning savages.

**Molotova truck**   a Soviet model of troop transport truck. It was made in China and supplied to the Viet Cong.

**moment of truth**   marine phrase for the last chance to admit deceitful statements before basic training (boot camp) begins.

**momgram**   marine phrase for the postcard sent home to announce safe arrival at Parris Island, South Carolina, where recruits were trained.

**Monam**   a MONTAGNARD tribe living mainly in KONTUM Province.

**Monday pills**   slang for the large, orange antimalaria pills taken once a week, usually on Mondays.

**M19IIA**   the Colt .45 caliber automatic pistol, a standard issue weapon in Vietnam.

**M–109**   a self-propelled cannon used in Vietnam.

**M–107**   a 175mm self-propelled gun used in Vietnam.

**M–102**   the 105mm howitzer used by First Cavalry artillery units. The M–102 replaced the M–101A1.

**M–113**   American-made ARMORED PERSONNEL CARRIER supplied to the South Vietnamese Army and used by U.S. forces in Vietnam.

**M–16**   the standard U.S. 5.56mm military rifle used in Vietnam, the successor to the M–14. This lightweight semiautomatic Colt weapon could fire automatic bursts or single shots.

**Monitor**   an Assault Support Patrol Boat, a gunboat armed with 40mm and 80mm guns and 81mm direct fire mortars.

**monkey house**   jail, used as slang by Vietnamese who picked up this phrase and others from U.S. Servicemen.

**Monkey Mountain**   the mountain between the DA NANG airfield and the sea.

**Monkey Mountain Airfield**   a large base for marine helicopters.

**monkey strap**   the straps that held the GUNNY on the helicopter as he fired the M–60; also called the lifeline.

**monopoly money**   slang for the military payment certificates soldiers received instead of regular U.S. money.

**Monsanto**   one of the chemical companies that manufactured the defoliant AGENT ORANGE.

**monsoon**   a season of heavy rains that made living in Vietnam even more difficult for servicemen and women. Clothes and socks did not have a chance to dry out, weapons did not fire properly, and visibility was poor. The soil became thick mud and almost everyone became moody and irritable.

**monster, the**   1. slang for the PRC–77, a radio similar to the PRC–25 but with a scrambling device attached. Transmission frequencies on the PRC–77 were called the secure net. 2. 12 to 20 CLAYMORE antipersonnel mines set to go off together. This arrangement was also called the animal.

**Montagnard**   a Vietnamese term for several tribes of mountain people made up of roughly 60 ethnic groups and totaling about 5 million people altogether. They inhabited the highlands of Vietnam near the Cambodian border. They were courted by both sides during the war because of their extensive knowledge of the rugged highland terrain and because of their fighting ability. The word *Montagnard* means "dweller in the mountains." These mountain people were viewed differently from Vietnamese by the U.S. troops. The Montagnards disliked the Vietnamese and many were willing to be organized into CIDG camps. Montagnard-Vietnamese relations were improved by 1971. By the end of the war, almost all of the Montagnards had lost their tribal land.

**Montagnard bracelet**  bracelet given by Montagnards and worn by SPECIAL FORCES working with these mountain people. Other soldiers were honored to receive Montagnard bracelets when working with these warriors in Vietnam.

**moonbeam**  marine slang for flashlight.

**moonglow**  slang for a C–47 aircraft carrying 96 flares.

**moonshine**  1. slang for a flare-carrying aircraft. 2. a call for a flare ship, which is a helicopter with a four-hour supply of aerial flares.

**Moorer, Thomas H.**  chief of naval operations, 1967–1970; chairman Joint Chiefs of Staff, 1970–1974; and commander of the Seventh Fleet, 1962–1964.

**Moose**  1. code for the 1967 movement of U.S. troops away from Saigon to other bases. Saigon was becoming extremely overcrowded with not enough housing nor storage facilities

as the troops built up in number. To manage this situation, GENERAL WESTMORELAND arranged to have Long Binh Post built, about 12 miles from Saigon. Long Binh was completed in 1967, and was a modern post with modern plumbing. 2. slang for Move Out Of Saigon Expeditiously, referring to the Moose operation. 3. nickname for a mistress.

**MOOT**  slang for Move Out Of Town, referring to a program meant to reduce the consolidation of troops in city areas.

**Moratorium, The**  the October 15, 1969, national, nonviolent demonstrations in Washington, D.C. against U.S. participation in Vietnam.

**Morse, Senator Wayne Lyman**  one of only two senators to vote against the GULF OF TONKIN RESOLUTION.

**MORSID**  abbr. for Mortar Delivered SID (SEISMIC INTRUSION DEVICE).

**Mort**  abbr. for MORTAR.

**mortar**  a muzzle-loading cannon that launched low muzzle velocity shells at high angles. It had a short tube in relation to its caliber. Also nicknamed mortie.

**mortar, 81mm, M–29**  a smoothbore, muzzle-loaded, single-shot, high angle of fire weapon, which weighed about 115 pounds when assembled and fired many types of rounds. With a sustained rate of fire of two rounds a minute, the M–29's effective range was 2,200 to 3,650 meters, depending on the ammunition used.

**mortar, 4.2-inch**  a large mortar with a rifled bore and a very large range. The shell's base held a soft metal which expanded into the rifling when the propellant exploded.

**mortar, 122mm** the largest North Vietnamese weapon and their standard artillery piece. This weapon and other mortars were not well-suited to guerrilla warfare because they and their ammunition had to be carried.

**mortar, 6mm** a muzzle-loaded weapon used by the U.S. and North Vietnamese troops.

**mortar, 60mm, M–19** a smooth-bore, muzzle-loaded, single-shot, high angle of fire weapon, which weighed about 45 pounds when assembled and fired a variety of high explosive and pyrotechnic rounds. It had a maximum rate of fire of 30 rounds per minute and a sustained rate of fire of 18 rounds per minute. The effective range was 2,000 yards.

**mortie** slang for MORTAR.

**MOS** abbr. for Military Occupational Specialty, the numerical code for assigned jobs in the army or marines. For example, 11–B was infantryman, 13–B was artilleryman, and 91–B was medical specialist. See NEC for the navy and coast guard code and AFSC for the air force.

**mosquito boat** slang for a torpedo boat.

**most ricky tick** slang for immediately, or right now.

**mother bomb** slang for the outer canister of a GUAVA bomb.

**Mother's Day Medal** slang for the NATIONAL DEFENSE SERVICE MEDAL.

**Mountain Camp** a North Vietnamese POW camp northeast of HANOI.

**mouse** slang for a POINTMAN on a patrol.

**mouse trap** ambush carried out by using some sort of bait, such as a few C-RATION cans or a pack of matches. Also called a draw ambush.

**Mouth of the Dragon** nickname for the MEKONG DELTA.

**move out** call to a patrol to begin walking.

**MP** abbr. for MILITARY POLICE.

**MPC** abbr. for MILITARY PAYMENT CERTIFICATE.

**MR** abbr. for MILITARY REGION.

**Mr. Charlie** slang for the enemy. See VICTOR CHARLIE.

**Mr. No Shoulders** slang for snakes, which were abundant in Vietnam.

**Mr. Refrigerator** the Vietnamese people's nickname for ambassador Ellsworth BUNKER, because he was perceived as very cold.

**Mr. Thirty** slang for tigers. The name Mr. Thirty was taken from the tigers who hunted toward the end of the lunar month when there was little moonlight.

**MRE** abbr. for Meal, Ready-To-Eat. This combat ration replaced C-RATIONS. The troops said MRE stood for Meal, Rejected by Everyone.

**MRF** abbr. for MOBILE RIVERINE FORCE.

**MRP** abbr. for Medical Rehabilitation Platoon, the marine term for the overweight platoon. The recruits so designated had extra physical fitness assignments and were placed on strict diets.

**MS**   abbr. for Medical Service.

**MSC**   1. abbr. for Medical Service Corps. 2. abbr. for the U.S. Navy's Military Sealift Command. This was quite crucial, as almost all of the ammunition, fuel, supplies, and vehicles, needed in Vietnam arrived by sea.

**M–79**   a 40mm U.S. military hand-held grenade launcher that shot spin-armed balls or small grenades. The shoulder-fired weapon resembled a sawed-off, large bored shotgun; it could lob projectiles more than a 100 meters. Nicknamed thumper, thump-gun, blooker, blooper, bluper, clunker, and burp gun, elephant gun, and chunker.

**M–76**   a 9mm submachine gun made by Smith and Wesson and used by SEAL teams and clandestine navy teams in North Vietnam.

**M–72**   see LAW

**M–60**   the standard lightweight 7.62mm MACHINE GUN used by U.S. forces in Vietnam. It was nicknamed the pig.

**M–61**   Vulcan 20mm cannon used on the F–105 and F–4 aircraft.

**M–67**   a 90mm recoilless rifle, a basic weapon for antitank platoons of combat support companies.

**MSS**   1. abbr. for Military Security Service, the South Vietnamese Army's military intelligence organization. MSS was a counterintelligence unit. 2. abbr. for Mission Support Site, a safe-house or a location where administrative duties could be performed.

**M–3**   a .45 caliber submachine gun called a grease gun because of its resemblance to one. Manufactured by Bell Labs, it was used by the Office of Strategic Services in World War II and by SPECIAL FORCES RECON teams in the Vietnam War in the early 1960s.

**M–3 kit**   a small medical kit.

**MTT**   abbr. for Mobile Training Team. These instructors went to foreign countries such as Australia, Korea, or the Philippines to teach the use of weapons and tactics. These AL-LIES then sent troops to Vietnam to fight on our side.

**M–26**   a FRAG GRENADE.

**Muc Hoa**   capital of KIEN TUONG Province.

**Mud River**   early code name for the IGLOO WHITE surveillance system along the HO CHI MINH TRAIL.

**mule**   a small, motorized platform originally designed to carry a 106mm recoilless rifle, but most often used for transporting weapons, heavy equipment, and personnel. Also called mechanical mule.

**Mule Train**   code for the initial deployments of C–123 tactical transports to South Vietnam in early 1972.

**mummy sack**   slang for BODY BAG.

**Muong soldiers**   hill tribesmen used by the French in their counterattack against the VIET MINH.

**Muscle Shoals**   early code for the IGLOO WHITE surveillance system along the HO CHI MINH TRAIL.

**MUST**   abbr. for Medical Unit, Self-contained, Transportable. MUST was a complete 40-bed mobile hospital, transported by a 2 1/2 ton truck, and nicknamed Bubbles because of its resemblance to one.

**mustang**  slang for an up-from-the-ranks officer.

**muster**  a quick gathering of soldiers with little or no forewarning.

**Mutter's Ridge**  hills near Nui Cay Tre just south of the Demilitarized Zone. Marines were engaged in almost constant combat in this area.

**MUV**  abbr. for Marine Unit, Vietnam. This was formerly referred to as SHUFLY (Marine Aviation Task Unit in RVN).

**muy huy duc**  (pronounced me hoy duck). Vietnamese for "kiss my ass." This slang phrase was used by U.S. servicemen but is an unknown expression to the Vietnamese.

**Mxd**  abbr. for mixed artillery of 105mm and 155mm types.

**mỹ**  Vietnamese for American.

**My Canh**  a river boat restaurant near Saigon. It was bombed by terrorists in 1965, killing more than forty American and Vietnamese diners and wounding 85.

**My Lai**  the village where troops of the U.S. AMERICAL Division were believed to have killed many civilians in March 1968. See MY LAI INCIDENT.

**My Lai incident**  on March 16, 1968, in the hamlet of My Lai in Son My village, Quang Ngai Province in I Corps C company, First Battalion, 20th Infantry, 11th Infantry Brigade, AMERICAL Division conducted a heliborne assault to secure the area. Approximately 150 Vietnamese civilians were gunned down and other abusive violence was believed to have been committed. Court-martialed for this incident, Lt. William Calley was later paroled and given a dishonorable discharge in 1974.

**My Tho**  one of the 11 AUTONOMOUS CITIES of South Vietnam.

# N

**NAB** abbr. for Naval Air Base.

**NAF** abbr. for Naval Air Facility.

**Naked Fanny** nickname for NKP (NAKHON PHANOM) airport in Thailand.

**Nakhon Phanom** the airport in Thailand, nicknamed Naked Fanny. A large USAF air base was also located here. Air force computers helped make sure that pilots would not fire missile at civilian aircraft without positive identification.

**Nam, The** slang for Vietnam.

**napalm** an incendiary fluid named for its ingredients, naphthenic and palmitic acids. A jellied gasoline incendiary used in FLAMETHROWERS and bombs napalm was used by both sides in the Vietnam War as a defoliant and as an antipersonnel weapon. Napalm adheres to whatever it touches, including human skin.

**nape** slang for NAPALM.

**naphthenic** one of the ingredients of NAPALM.

**nap-of-the-earth** aerial term for flying as close to the ground as possible and following the earth's contours.

**narrow gate** aerial term for a selection on a radar missile which allows it to home only on targets within a selected range.

**nasties** see NASTY BOAT.

**nasty boat** motor gunboats from Norway, named for the Swedish manufacturer Nasty. They were used as

patrol boats by the U.S. Navy and the South Vietnamese.

**National Cemetery of the Pacific** the cemetery in Honolulu where the missing and dead of World War II, Korea, and Vietnam are recorded.

**National Defense Service Medal** a medal authorized for all members of the U.S. Armed Forces who served on active duty during the Vietnam Era, between January 1, 1961, and August 14, 1974. It was nicknamed the Mother's Day Medal, because everyone who had a mother—that is, everyone who served even one day on active duty—received one.

**National Liberation Front** the South Vietnamese Communist organization that led the fight against the Saigon government and their American allies. Supposedly an independent organization in the South, the National Liberation Front—which became known as the Viet Cong—followed the dictates of the North Vietnamese government.

**native sport** slang for hunting for VIET CONG.

**NATO** 1. abbr. for North Atlantic Treaty Organization. 2. the designation of the standard machine gun round is 7.62 NATO.

**NAVAIDS** abbr. for navigational aids.

**naval flare** a small signal FLARE used to signal aircraft.

**NAVFORV** abbr. for Naval Forces, Vietnam.

**Navy Achievement Medal** award given to officers for outstanding professional achievement or leadership, and awarded to enlisted men for leadership. It ranks just below the NAVY COMMENDATION MEDAL.

**Navy and Marine Corps Medal** awarded for heroism not involving actual armed conflict with an enemy. It ranks just below the DISTINGUISHED FLYING CROSS.

**Navy Commendation Medal** awarded for outstanding performance in combat or non-combat.

**Navy Cross** See DISTINGUISHED SERVICE CROSS (NAVY).

**Navy SEAL** the elite U.S. Navy units qualified in underwater, airborne, and ground combat. The acronym SEAL is taken from Sea, Air, and Land.

**NC** abbr. for Nurse Corps.

**NCO** abbr. for NON-COMMISSIONED OFFICER, usually a squad leader or platoon sergeant. Derided by some to mean "No chance outside," suggesting that an NCO would not be successful in the civilian world.

**NCOIC** abbr. for Non-Commissioned Officer In Charge.

**NCRC** abbr. for National Council of Reconciliation and Concord. This was a group charged by the PARIS PEACE ACCORDS in 1973 to organize general and local elections for a new South Vietnam. This council consisted of the two combatants plus a third force. It was not successful in accomplishing its goals.

**NDB** abbr. for Non-Directional Beacon, a radio beacon used for homing.

**NEC** abbr. for Naval Enlisted Classified, which referred to the numerical code for each assigned job in the navy and coast guard.

**necessary** slang term for latrine.

**neckerchief** standard 36 x 24 inch olive drab cloth used to wipe off sweat and dirt, to clean weapons, to wear on the head, etc. Nicknamed the "Go to hell rag," it was highly valued by GRUNTs.

**negative** radio talk for no.

**negative G** aerial term for the force of gravity exerted on the human body as a result of forward acceleration.

**negative objective** code term used over the radio to declare that a pilot has been found dead.

**negative suppression** term meaning that troops were not to shoot back, according to the RULES OF ENGAGEMENT.

**Nestle's Quick** Slang for an NCO who was fresh out of NCO school. He was also called Shake 'n' Bake, Ready Whip, and Instant NCO.

**net** short for radio network or radio frequency setting, taken from the word network.

**neutralize** 1. to make enemy forces or installations ineffective by military or other action. 2. to assassinate or destroy an unfriendly hamlet.

**New Guy Village** slang for section of the Hoa Lo Prison, also known as the HANOI HILTON.

**New Life Hamlet**   one of a series of hamlet development programs under the Civil Operations and Rural Development (CORDS) program. These programs attempted to move civilians from rural areas to secure hamlets and instill in them respect for the Republic of Vietnam (South Vietnam). Problems arose almost immediately, including the resistance of the people to abandon their land, the meager goods, and the poor security. This program was not well thought out, did not work well, and was abandoned.

**New Life Program**   See STRATEGIC HAMLET PROGRAM.

**new meat**   slang for new guy in Vietnam. See FNG.

**New Mobe, The**   short for the New Mobilization Committee to End the War in Vietnam. Formerly called THE MOBE, the group became the New Mobe after 1968. Changing its name in 1971 to the People's Coalition for Peace and Justice, it continued the work of THE MOBE in coordinating antiwar activities.

**new puppy**   slang for an ensign or second lieutenant.

**newbie**   slang for a new soldier (from new babies). It was also spelled newbee. See FNG.

**newby**   a replacement or new man in a unit. See FNG.

**next**   slang for soldier due for ROTATION in a few days. He was also called short.

**NFO**   short for Naval Flight Officer, a commissioned aircrew member other than a pilot. He could be a school-trained nonaviator, a RIO (Radar Inter-cept Officer), or a B/N (Bombardier/Navigator).

**NFZ**   abbr. for no fire zones. Some heavily populated areas were designated No Fire Zones because almost certain damage and civilian casualties would result.

**NG**   abbr. for National Guard.

**Nghĩa Quân**   Vietnamese for POPULAR FORCES.

**nguời bắc Việt**   Vietnamese for North Vietnamese.

**ngừng**   Vietnamese for stop.

**ngừng bắn**   Vietnamese   for ceasefire.

**nguời thông ngôn**   Vietnamese for interpreter.

**ngụy trang**   Vietnamese for camouflage.

**nguyen**   (pronounced no-win) slang for enemy soldier.

**Nguyen Ai Quoc**   the Communist code name of HO CHI MINH.

**Nguyen Cao Ky**   a French- and U.S.-trained officer who became air vice marshal and commander of South Vietnam's Air Force. He was prime minister in 1965 and became deputy vice president in 1967. Later he fell out of favor with President Nguyen Van THIEU and he withdrew his opposition candidacy in Nguyen Van Thieu's one-man presidential election of October 1971. Nguyen Cao Ky sought exile in the United States in April 1975.

**Nguyen Thanh Le**   spokesman for the Democratic Republic of Vietnam delegation at the PARIS PEACE ACCORDS and deputy editor of the daily paper of the LAO DONG party.

**Nguyen Van Thieu**  president of South Vietnam 1967–1975.

**Nha Trang**  one of the 11 autonomous cities of South Vietnam. A large U.S. air base was located here and it was the headquarters for the SPECIAL FORCES.

**Nhan Dan**  Hanoi's official newspaper.

**niact**  short for night action communications, which brought a response from the listener regardless of the hour of night.

**Niagara**  1. code for a joint U.S. Air Force, Navy, and Marine Corps air campaign in support of the Marine fire base at KHE SANH. It began in January 1968 and played an important part in the successful defense of the base. 2. code for air operations during the siege of Khe Sanh in early 1968. 3. code for a SLAM operation in the spring of 1968 in support of the Khe Sanh Combat Base. The mission was to use intelligence to locate the enemy and apply destructive firepower. In June 1968 Khe Sanh was temporarily forsaken by U.S. forces.

**nickel**  slang for the number five.

**night belongs to Charlie, the**  phrase frequently heard by soldiers in Vietnam, referring to the belief that the U.S. forces controlled the days, but the nights belonged to the enemy.

**night fire program**  random artillery defensive targets shooting at night, often close to landing zones and near trails.

**night kit**  an equipment package for troops that included ammo, c-rations, water, shovel, barbed wire, sandbags, claymore mines, flares, insect repellent, and engineer stakes. These equipment packages were usually flown in.

**night location**  remaining overnight, abbreviated NL. Also called Remain Overnight and RON.

**night observation device**  term for the STARLIGHT scope and other instruments which used Starlight to help troops see when it was very dark. Various types of infrared devices could spot the enemy up to 1,400 yards away.

**night owl**  term for controlled night strike missions, used as training for pilots.

**night vision goggles**  special battery powered goggles for increasing night vision.

**Nighthawk**  1. a UH-1 (Huey) carrying a spotlight and STARLIGHT capabilities. ORDNANCE consisted of one 7.62 MINIGUN and two M-60 MACHINE GUNS carrying between 4,000 and 7,500 rounds. 2. Nighthawk also referred to the UG-1 helicopter which was qualified for night missions.

**Nine Rules**  a card was given to each American soldier entering Vietnam containing nine rules of conduct. The front of the card read "NINE RULES for Personnel of U.S. Military Assistance Command, Vietnam. DISTRIBUTION—1 to each member of the United States Armed Forces in Vietnam. The Vietnamese have paid a heavy price in suffering for their long fight against the communists. We military men are in Vietnam now because their government has asked us to help its soldiers and people in winning their struggle. The Viet Cong will attempt to turn the Vietnamese people against you. You can defeat them at every turn by the strength, understanding, and generosity you display with the people. Here are the nine simple rules:" (Back of card)

"1.   Remember we are guests here. We make no demands and seek no special treatment.

2.   Join with the people! Understand their life, use phrases from their language and honor their customs and laws.

3.   Treat women with politeness and respect.

4.   Make personal friends among the soldiers and common people.

5.   Always give the Vietnamese the right of way.

6.   Be alert to security and ready to react with your military skill.

7.   Don't attract attention by loud, rude, or unusual behavior.

8.   Avoid separating yourself from the people by a display of wealth or privilege.

9.   Above all else, you are members of the U.S. Military Forces on a difficult mission, responsible for all your official and personal actions. Reflect honor upon yourself and the United States of America."

**91 band-aids**   slang for an army medical specialist, MOS 91-B.

**91 bedpans**   slang for an army medical specialist, MOS 91-B.

**91mm**   an artillery piece mounted on a tank chassis.

**niner**   military pronunciation of the number nine.

**nineteen**   the average age of the combat soldier in Vietnam was 19.2 years. In comparison, the average age of the GI in World War II was 26 years.

**ninety**   1. slang for the 90mm long gun used as the main armament on the M–48 series of battle tanks. 2. slang for the M–67 90mm recoilless rifle.

**Ninh Thuan**   one of the 44 provinces of South Vietnam, located in II CORPS.

**Ninth Army Division**   the division whose nickname was Old Reliables.

**NIS**   abbr. for Naval Investigative Service, the navy's detective corps.

**NJP**   abbr. for nonjudicial punishment, usually less than that given out by a court-martial.

**NKP**   abbr. for NAKHON PHANOM, a USAF airbase in Thailand.

**NL**   abbr. for night location, remaining in one place overnight. Also called Remain Overnight and RON.

**NLF**   abbr. for National Liberation Front, the political organization of the guerrilla forces in South Vietnam. It included various other groups besides the Communist Party, including some non-Communists. Its purpose was to overthrow the government of South Vietnam and unite with North Vietnam.

**NLT**   abbr. for no later than.

**NM**   abbr. for nautical mile, which equals 6,076.1 feet.

**no can do, Madame Ni...**   phrase for something that was not possible to accomplish

**no chance outside**   derogatory slang for the NCO (non-commissioned officer).

**no fire zone**   an area in which using any type of firepower by the military must first be cleared by the chain of command. Also called NFZ.

**no joy** 1. term for a radio communication meaning a lack of success. 2. in flying, no joy means no visual contact.

**no man's Nam** slang for Vietnam.

**no sweat** slang for easy, with little effort, or no trouble.

**no visual results** term used in bomb damage assessment. Also abbreviated NVR.

**NOD** See NIGHT OBSERVATION DEVICES.

**no-doze mission** psychological operations' (PSYCHOPS) slang for nighttime airborne broadcasts of audiotapes containing various types of propaganda.

**NOFORN** abbr. for Not For Foreign Eyes (referring to classified messages).

**noise** unwanted sound or disturbances found in a communication system or appearing on a radar scope.

**Nolting, Frederic J.** ambassador to South Vietnam 1961–1963.

**noncom** short for a NON-COMMISSIONED OFFICER.

**noncombatant** military personnel who did not usually have combat duties, such as a cook or mail sorter.

**non-commissioned officer** term for the ranks between E–5 and E–10, the highest ranks of enlisted personnel. Also referred to as NCO. During the Vietnam War, NCOs were given short, intensive training. When they arrived in Vietnam they were nicknamed

Shake 'n' Bake, Ready Whip, and Nestle's Quick.

**non-hacker** slang for an incompetent grunt or poor soldier.

**Nordo** 1. an aircraft with no radio. 2. someone with inadequate communication skills.

**normal rules** troops could return fire for fire received, according to the RULES OF ENGAGEMENT. Also called normal suppression.

**normal suppression** according to the RULES OF ENGAGEMENT, troops could return fire for fire received. Also called normal rules.

**NOROC** the armored panels used for crew protection in helicopters.

**notched** 1. slang for being wounded. 2. slang for wounding someone.

**november** military phonetic for the letter N.

**NS** abbr. for naval station.

**NSAM** abbr. for National Security Action Memorandum. This referred to presidential policy statements determining action on national security issues.

**NSC** abbr. for National Security Council. This group developed defense strategies for the United States. It directed the CIA and was made up of the president; the secretaries of state, defense, army, navy, and air force; and the chairman of the National Security Resources Board.

**nub bush** slang for a black female.

**nugget** 1. slang for a new flight-crew member with little experience. 2. slang for a new second lieutenant.

**Núi Bà Den (also spelled Núi Bà Dinh)** Vietnamese for Black Virgin Mountain, a holy place in the Buddhist religion. The mountaintop arose out of the flat delta south of Saigon. Viet Cong controlled the base of the mountain, although U.S. and South Vietnamese troops held the strategic peaks during the war.

**Number 1** (pronounced "numba one") this was slang for the best or first place.

**Number 60 (Sixty)** slang for the M–60 machine gun.

**Number 10** (pronounced "numba ten") this was slang for the worst, a loser, or the lowest.

**Nungs** tribal people of Chinese origin from the highlands of North Vietnam. The Nung were an ethnic Tai subgroup that inhabited both North and South Vietnam. Their men were known for their ability as warriors; some Nungs who moved south worked with U.S. SPECIAL FORCES as mercenaries.

**nůớc** Vietnamese for water.

**nůớc mam** a strong-smelling sauce made from fish, used by the Vietnamese as a condiment, made by percolating water through large vats of salted fish. The sauce was a basic part of the Vietnamese diet because each bit of food was dipped in the sauce before being eaten. GIs smelled the odor of *nůớc mam* on every

Vietnamese person's breath. It was nicknamed Armpit sauce.

**nử việt công, nửcán bô** Vietnamese for female Viet Cong soldier.

**Nuy Loc Son Basin** a heavily populated rice-growing area along the southern boundary of QUANG NAM Province and the scene of many fierce marine battles.

**NV** abbr. for North Vietnam.

**NVA** abbr. for North Vietnamese Army. The NVA was also called the People's Army of Vietnam (PAVN) and the Vietnam People's Army (VPA). First organized in 1954, the NVA became a well-respected army. It was supported by approximately 30,000 Viet Cong guerrillas in South Vietnam. By 1974, more than half of the North Vietnamese Army was located in South Vietnam and near the borders of Laos and Cambodia.

**NVAF** abbr. for North Vietnamese Air Force.

**NVN** 1. abbr. for Navy of Vietnam. 2. abbr. for North Vietnam (Democratic Republic of Vietnam).

**NVNAF** abbr. for North Vietnamese Air Force.

**NVR** abbr. for No Visual Results, a term used in BOMB DAMAGE ASSESSMENT.

**nylon** slang for parachute.

**NZ** abbr. for New Zealand.

# O

**Oak Leaf Cluster** used by the U.S. Army and Air Force to denote subsequent military decorations worn on the previous medal's ribbon (except for the Air Medal). Subsequent awards for the U.S. Navy, Marine Corps, and Coast Guard were denoted by a metallic gold star.

**oanh-tạc** Vietnamese for bombing.

**OB** abbr. for Order of Battle, a listing of military units.

**observed fire** fire in which the impact can be seen by an observer, and adjustments can be made on the basis of what is observed.

**OC** abbr. for Officer Commanding.

**O-club** club for officers, warrant officers, and their dependents, where food and drink were served and where there was often entertainment.

**OCO** abbr. for Office of Civil Operations. Established in 1966 to coordinate American pacification efforts, its name was changed to CORDS in 1967.

**OCS** 1. abbr. for Officers Candidate School. Each service runs a school to train men and women to become officers. 2. abbr. for On Civilian Streets.

**OCS Manual** slang for comic book.

**OD** 1. abbr. for OLIVE DRAB, the camouflage color, and ARMY SHADE 107. 2. abbr. for Officer of the Day. 3. abbr. for ORDNANCE Department.

**o-dark-thirty** very early in the morning, just after sunrise or about thirty minutes before the sun comes up. It was also called zero-dark-thirty.

**OE-1** the Cessna single-engine observation plane, also known as the O-1B.

**O8** grade for a major general in the U.S. Army, Marine Corps, and Air Force (rear admiral [upper] in the U.S. Navy and U.S. Coast Guard). The symbol for this rank is two stars.

**OER** abbr. for Officer Efficiency Report, an important mechanism for the evaluation of officers for promotion.

**off** slang meaning to kill.

**office hours** marine term for being disciplined by the company commander. On the carpet is the equivalent army term, and captain's mast is the naval term.

**O11** grade for a general of the army or fleet admiral of the navy. The symbol for this rank is five stars.

**O5** grade for a lieutenant colonel in the U.S. Army, Marine Corps, and the Air Force (commander in the U.S. Navy and the U.S. Coast Guard). The symbol for this rank is a silver oak leaf.

**O4** grade for major in the U.S. Army, Marine Corps, and the Air Force (lieutenant commander in the U.S. Navy and the U.S. Coast Guard). The symbol for this rank is a gold oak leaf.

**O9** grade for a lieutenant general in the U.S. Army, Marine Corps, and the Air Force (vice admiral in the U.S.

Navy and the U.S. Coast Guard). The symbol for this rank is three stars.

**O1**    grade for a second lieutenant in the U.S. Army, Marine Corps, and the Air Force (ensign in the U.S. Navy and the U.S. Coast Guard). The symbol for this rank is a gold bar.

**O7**    grade for a brigadier general in the U.S. Army, Marine Corps, and the Air Force (commodore or rear admiral [lower] in the U.S. Navy and the U.S. Coast Guard). The symbol for this rank is one star.

**O6**    grade for colonel in the U.S. Army, Marine Corps, and the Air Force (captain in the U.S. Navy and the U.S. Coast Guard). The symbol for this rank is a spread eagle.

**O3**    grade for a captain in the U.S. Army, Marine Corps, and the Air Force (lieutenant in the U.S. Navy and the U.S. Coast Guard). The symbol for this rank is two silver bars.

**O2**    grade for a first lieutenant in the U.S. Army, Marine Corps, and the Air Force (lieutenant, junior grade in the U.S. Navy and the U.S. Coast Guard). The symbol for this rank is a silver bar.

**OH**    abbr. for Observation Helicopter.

**OH–6**    the Hughes Light Observation Helicopter (LOH), was used to carry a crew of two plus four combat-ready troops in the cargo area. The 101st Airborne used these light and fast helicopters nicknamed sperm, tadpole, and white bird.

**OIC**    abbr. for Officer In Charge.

**oil spot**    slang for a pacified area.

**OJT**    abbr. for On-the-Job Training.

**Old Breed**    nickname for the First Marine Division.

**Old Man, the**    slang for a commanding officer.

**Old Reliables**    nickname for the Ninth Infantry Division.

**ổ liên-thanh**    Vietnamese for machine gun nest.

**olive drab**    the official Army shade 107. This became every GI's least favorite color.

**olive green**    see OLIVE DRAB.

**OMH**    abbr. for Officers' Mess Hall.

**on profile**    being temporarily restricted in physical activities for medical reasons.

**on quota**    marine term for the assignment of a drill instructor to a substitute, alternate training duty, given approximately once in a two-year tour.

**on station**    armed helicopter GUNSHIPS, SLICKS or FAST MOVERS in position to support a ground commander, or in position for a mission or an operation.

**on the carpet**    army slang for being disciplined by the company commander. The equivalent marine term is office hours, and the naval term is captain's mast.

**I CORPS**    (pronounced "eye" corps), the first allied MILITARY REGION in northernmost Vietnam.

**One Five One**    abbr. for the M–151 Jeep.

**I–A**    according to the SELECTIVE SERVICE classification, a man available for military service.

***I–A–O*** according to the SELECTIVE SERVICE classification, a CONSCIENTIOUS OBJECTOR available for non-combatant military service only.

***one-buck*** code for units in the United States ready to be sent to Vietnam on 48-hours' notice.

***I–C*** according to the SELECTIVE SERVICE classification, a member of the U.S. Armed Forces, the Coast and Geodetic Survey, or the Public Health Service.

***I–D*** according to the SELECTIVE SERVICE classification, a member of a reserve component or a student taking military training.

***173d Airborne Brigade*** the first U.S. combat unit sent to Vietnam in May 1965. The 173d was nicknamed Sky Soldiers, the Herd, and Two Shades of Soul, because of the good relations between black and white paratroopers. They were headquartered at BIEN HOA.

***I–O*** according to the SELECTIVE SERVICE classification, a CONSCIENTIOUS OBJECTOR available for civilian work contributing to the maintenance of the national health, safety, or interest.

***One-Oh-Five, One-Oh-Six, etc.*** slang for various artillery pieces.

***One-oh-worst*** nickname for the 101st Airborne Division (Airmobile) based on its numerical designation. Also nicknamed Screaming Eagles, Screaming Chickens, and Puking Buzzards because of the large eagle on the unit's insignia.

***I–S*** according to the SELECTIVE SERVICE classification, a student deferred by statute, usually still in high school.

***one twenty-two*** short for the Russian 122mm ground-launched

rocket, used by North Vietnamese Army.

***I–W*** according to the SELECTIVE SERVICE classification, a CONSCIENTIOUS OBJECTOR performing civilian work contributing to the maintenance of the national health, safety, or interest.

***I–Y*** according to the SELECTIVE SERVICE classification, a registrant available for military service, but qualified for military service only in the event of war or national emergency.

***one zero line*** nickname for the military grid line from Cam Lo to Con Thien, at the northernmost edge of South Vietnam.

***ông*** Vietnamese for Mister.

***ông có nói tiếng anh không*** Vietnamese for "Do you speak English?"

***ONI*** 1. abbr. for Office of Navy Investigation, the U.S. Navy's intelligence section. 2. abbr. for Office of Naval Intelligence.

***ONTOS*** the U.S. Marine Corp tank-killer, a lightly armored tracked vehicle armed with 106mm. recoilless rifles. Originally designed for use against tanks, these were used in Vietnam primarily to support INFANTRY.

***OODA loop*** Short for the sequence of a pilot's mental preparation for action: observation, orientation, decision, action.

***O–1*** Cessna's single-engine, high-winged birddog, a spotter plane.

***O–1B*** Cessna's single-engine observation plane, also known as the OE–1.

***OP*** 1. abbr. for Observation Post. 2. abbr. for Out Post, which was manned during daylight hours to watch for enemy movement.

**open sheaf** a term used in calling artillery in which the artillery rounds are spread out along an axis instead of being concentrated on a single point. A single point would be used for covering a TREE LINE.

**ở phục kích** Vietnamese for ambush.

**Operation Homecoming** code for the Pentagon procedures aimed at easing the transition of the American POWs from Communist prison camps to their homes in the United States.

**OPLAN 34** the program calling for covert action against North Vietnam ordered by President Lyndon Johnson soon after he took office in early 1964. The proposal included propaganda, the interception of Communist ships, and planning for air attacks against North Vietnam.

**OPLAN 37** proposal prepared in the spring of 1964 for U.S. air operations in three phases: attacks against enemy forces retiring into Laos and Cambodia, reprisal strikes, and increasingly heavy bombing of North Vietnam.

**Opns** abbr. for Operations.

**Opposition** the enemy.

**Ops** abbr. for operations.

**OpSum** Operation Summary.

**Option IV** code for the United States military plan for the helicopter evacuation from Saigon on April 29, 1975.

**orange corn flake bar** a delicacy found in LRRP rations, considered a special treat.

**orbit** aerial term for a circular or elliptical pattern flown by aircraft to remain in a specified area.

**Ord** abbr. for ORDNANCE.

**Order of Battle (OB)** the plan and system of the different sections of an army ready for battle.

**orderly room** 1. building where paperwork is done. 2. the site of the recreation area on smaller installations.

**ordnance** ammunition, bombs, rockets, explosives and other military munitions. Also seen as Ord.

**organic** 1. hardware items such as weapons or vehicles which belonged to a given unit. 2. military units, weapons, or equipment which were part of a military organization.

**organize** to bring an active unit into physical existence by assignment of personnel.

**Oriole** see KEYSTONE.

**ORP** abbr. for Objective Rally Point, the location where survivors gather after assaults to verify who came through.

**OSA** abbr. for Office of the Special Assistant to the ambassador in Vietnam.

**Oscar** 1. the military phonetic for the letter O. 2. an observer. 3. radio slang for radio-telephone operator, usually the enlisted man who carried and used the unit's radio.

**Oscar Papa** phonetic alphabetization for outpost.

**OSD** abbr. for Office of Secretary of Defense, including the secretary of defense and his immediate staff.

**OSO/OSD**  abbr. for Office of Special Operations for the OSD.

**OSS**  abbr. for Office of Strategic Services, replaced by the Central Intelligence Agency (CIA) in 1947.

**other theater, the**  the secret air war over Laos.

**OTS**  abbr. for Officer Training School.

**O–2**  Cessna's twin-engined FAC aircraft; the Super Skymaster, also known as the Push Me, Push-You and the Mixmaster. The air force used this aircraft in South Vietnam and Laos.

**out**  slang for being out of Vietnam or out of the military.

**out-country**  that part of Southeast Asia outside of South Vietnam, including Laos, North Vietnam, Thailand, Cambodia, and China.

**outgoing**  friendly fire, especially artillery directed toward the enemy.

**Operation Frequent Wind**  code for the evacuation of the last Americans out of SAIGON.

**Operation Outreach**  the readjustment counseling program for Vietnam veterans. These offices are often storefronts, located apart from VA hospitals and generally staffed by Vietnam vets, as authorized by Congress in 1979. There were 196 Outreach Centers throughout the United States as of 1990, at least one in every state as well as Puerto Rico and the Virgin Islands.

**OUTUS**  abbr. for outside the United States.

**over and under**  1. slang for the combination of an M–16 and an M–79 GRENADE LAUNCHER nicknamed Johnny Thunder. 2. any double barreled shotgun in which one barrel was mounted under the other.

**over the fence**  slang for cross-border movement.

**over the hump**  slang for past the half-way mark through an enlistment. The term sometimes referred to other difficult tasks or periods of time.

**overhead**  navy term for ceiling.

**overhead grenade**  a booby trap in which a GRENADE with its pin pulled was placed inside a can that was attached to a TRIP WIRE and hung from a tree. When a soldier tripped the wire, the grenade exploded.

**override**  the tank commander's personal controls, mounted to the right of the TURRET. The override allows the tank commander to operate all the weapons.

**Oversexed Weekly**  slang for the newspaper *Overseas Weekly*, a privately published paper distributed to service personnel.

**overtake velocity**  aerial term for a sudden gain in speed to come up on another aircraft.

**over-the-border**  crossing into Laos or Cambodia, also called over-the-fence.

**Ovnand, Chester N.**  an American advisor in Vietnam, killed in Vietnam on July 8, 1959 by Viet Cong while watching a movie in a mess hall in Bien Hoa. His is the second name inscribed on the Vietnam Veteran Memorial.

**OV–1B**  Grumman's twin turboprop sensor aircraft, known as Mohawk.

Used by the army it was well-equipped with various SENSOR devices.

**OV–10**   North American's twin tur-boprop counterinsurgency aircraft, the Bronco.

**Owl**   see KEYSTONE.

# P

**P** 1. abbr. for PIASTER, one cent or less in Vietnamese money. 2. abbr. for provisional. 3. abbr. for Pilot.

**P-38** slang for a small, foldable C-RATION can opener that was included in C-ration cases. Usually kept in a pocket or on a keyring, it carried the brand name of Shelby or Speaker.

**PACAF** abbr. for Pacific Air Force.

**pace-man** a soldier in a patrol who counted each step taken. He knew how many of his steps were equivalent to 100 meters and reported each count to his sergeant as he completed it.

**pacification** unofficial term given to several programs of the South Vietnamese and U.S. governments to strengthen security, destroy enemy dominance in the villages, gain support of civilians for the government of South Vietnam, and stabilize the country. These programs included the STRATEGIC HAMLET PROGRAM from 1961 to 1963, the Revolutionary Development Program from 1966 to 1968, the ACCELERATED PACIFICATION PROGRAM from late 1968 to January 1969, and the Community Defense Development Program which was in existence from 1971 until the end of the war. These programs were not successful in attaining their goals.

**pacifier package** a marine quick response helicopter operation using small units instead of full battalion sweeps. They began in 1970.

**pack** radio term for soldier.

**Pacoh** a MONTAGNARD tribe living mainly in THUA THIEN Province.

**PACOM** abbr. for Pacific Command.

**PACV** abbr. for Patrol Air Cushion Vehicle. See HOVERCRAFT.

**padlocked** aerial term meaning that a crew member had sighted BOGIES or BANDITS and had his vision fixed on them.

**PAE-BAG** abbr. for Parachutist's Adjustable Equipment Bag, which held a jumper's equipment in front of him. It was also spelled pay-bag.

**palm** slang for napalm.

**palmitic** one of the ingredients of napalm.

**Panama Control** code for the air traffic control center at DA NANG.

**papa** military phonetic for the letter P.

**papa-san** slang for an Oriental father or much older male who was looked up to and respected by the younger generation. He was considered to be wise simply because of his age.

**papa sierra** phonetic alphabetization for Platoon Sergeant.

**papa-san stick** slang for the walking stick often used by elderly men in Vietnam.

**paper pusher** slang for those with desk jobs. Also called pencil pusher and straphanger.

**parachute flare**  a brilliant pyrotechnic made up of a small rocket and a parachute.

**parade**  an airplane formation used by the air force for close maneuvering at night, in the clouds, or around the field. Sometimes it was used for showing off.

**parade deck**  drill field or parade ground.

**parajumper**  called PJ for short, these enlisted parachute rescue specialists rode in helicopters and were trained in parachuting, helicopter rescue operations, medicine, and survival tactics. They wore maroon berets and combat boots and wore their trousers bloused.

**parakeet mission**  raid mission that included: a light observation helicopter (OH–6) serving as a scout to locate the enemy; a gunship to attack once a target was identified; and a utility helicopter with a team of LRRPS to collect weapons and documents.

**paramilitary**  groups outside of a country's regular armed forces but having in common with them either organization, training, or objective.

**Parasol-Switchback**  code for a 1963 program supplying U.S. funds to civilian irregular defense groups (CIDG) in Vietnam.

**Paris Peace Accords**  agreements signed on January 28, 1973, by representatives of the governments of the Democratic Republic of Vietnam (Hanoi), the Republic of Vietnam (Saigon), the United States, and the Provisional Revolutionary Government (Viet Cong). These accords put an end to American intervention in Vietnam.

**Paris Peace Talks**  the negotiations for peace held in Paris, 1969–1972.

**Paris Control**  code for the air traffic control center at TAN SON NHUT.

**Paris of the Orient**  prewar nickname for SAIGON.

**Parrot's Beak**  a part of Cambodia that extends into Vietnam, located on the PLAIN OF REEDS. Flat and treeless, it is a dry spot on the Cambodian border, covered with undrinkable water during the monsoon season. Parrot's Beak was the location of the first major U.S. INCURSION into Cambodia in April 1970.

**passageway**  naval term for corridor.

**passed over**  slang for not being promoted at the usual time.

**paste**  slang for C-RATION peanut butter.

**PAT**  abbr. for Political Action Team, the forerunner of the Revolutionary Development Teams. These Vietnamese political CADRE were assigned to pacification missions; they represented the government of South Vietnam in the Vietnamese hamlets.

**patch**  slang for a RECONNAISSANCE zone delegated to a team.

**Pathet Lao**  the Laotian Communists, who from their beginning were under the authority of the Vietnamese Communist Party. During operations against the HO CHI MINH TRAIL, the United States dropped over 2 million tons of bombs on Laos between 1965 and 1973. In February 1973, a peace agreement between the Pathet Lao and the Royal Lao government (non-Communist) included a halt to all U.S. bombings. In April 1975, a coalition government was formed but the Pathet Lao continued to flourish and Laos fell to the Communists in August 1975.

**Pathfinder**   airborne infantry teams dropped or air-landed at an objective, often behind enemy lines, to establish a LANDING ZONE or DROP ZONE. They were nicknamed black hats because of their black baseball caps.

**Pathfinder Badge**   a badge awarded by the commandant of the U.S. Army Infantry School at Fort Benning, Georgia, to soldiers who had completed the PATHFINDER course and were trained in land navigation techniques.

**Patio**   code for the operation in April 1970 involving the INCURSION into Cambodia by U.S. and South Vietnamese forces.

**Patricia Lynn**   code for RB–57Es fitted with infrared SENSORs used to detect camouflaged Viet Cong targets.

**patrol air cushion vehicle**   see HOVERCRAFT.

**patrol base**   a semipermanent infantry position, with or without a platoon of light artillery.

**patrol harness**   heavy duty green suspenders issued to Army troops which held a pistol belt, two ammo pouches, two fragmentation grenades, a smoke grenade, a K-BAR, and two canteens for water.

**pattern activity**   plotting enemy activity on maps based on information learned from outside sources over a period of time. Also called pattern activity analysis.

**Patton of Parrot's Beak**   nickname for South Vietnam Lieutenant General Do Cao Tri who fought well in operation LAM SON 719; he was killed in a helicopter crash in 1971.

**Paul Doumer**   name of a bridge in North Vietnam. An important bombing target because of its strategic position as a transportation artery, it was difficult to destroy. A U.S. attack in May 1972 badly damaged the bridge. Repairs began in January 1973 and by early March of that year the Paul Doumer Bridge was reopened.

**PAV**   abbr. for People's Army of Vietnam, also abbreviated PAVN; Later called NVA.

**Pave Eagle**   code for unmanned Beech QU–22 aircraft used as relay platforms for data collected by the IGLOO WHITE surveillance system.

**Pave Knife**   nickname for F–4s equipped with LASER-GUIDED BOMBS.

**Pave Nail**   code for the night observations system using LASER-GUIDED BOMBS. The bombs followed laser beams locked onto the targets. These were used with F–4s for offensive missions.

**Pave Spot**   code for the laser designator fitted to certain USAF OV–10As.

**Paveway**   a LASER-GUIDED BOMB.

**PAVN**   abbr. for People's Army of (North) Vietnam. PAVN was later called the NVA.

**PAVNAF**   abbr. for People's Army of Vietnam Air Force.

**payback**   marine slang for revenge.

**PAY BAG**   see PAE BAG.

**PB**   abbr. for Patrol Boat.

**PBR**   1. abbr. for Patrol Boat, River, the U.S. Navy's designation for the fast, water-jet propelled, 30-foot, heavily armed boats used to protect the major canals, rivers, and tributaries in South Vietnam. PBRs were first used in Vietnam in 1966 and usually carried six infantrymen. 2. abbr. for Pabst Blue Ribbon beer.

**PC**  abbr. for Personnel Carrier.

**PCF**  abbr. for Patrol Craft, Fast; also called SWIFT BOATS.

**PCOD**  abbr. for Pussy Cut Off Date, slang referring to the date when a soldier in Vietnam should stop having sexual relations. After that date there would not be enough time to identify and cure a venereal disease before he departed Vietnam, which would mean that his homecoming would be delayed for mandatory medical treatment.

**PCS**  1. abbr. for Permanent Change of Station usually meaning a transfer out of Vietnam. 2. abbr. for Provincial Security Committee, which judged and sentenced Viet Cong infiltrators caught under the PHOENIX program.

**PDJ**  abbr. for PLAIN OF JARS.

**PDS**  abbr. for Permanent Duty Station.

**Peace Offensive**  a 37-day bombing halt in early January 1966 during which President Lyndon Johnson sought diplomatic ways to come to terms with Hanoi.

**Peacock**  code for the air traffic control center at PLEIKU.

**peanuts**  slang for wounded in action.

**pecker-checker**  slang for MEDIC.

**pee halt**  slang for a comfort stop.

**peepers**  slang for night-vision apparatus.

**pee pipe**  slang for PISS TUBE.

**peepsight**  a rifle's rear sight.

**Peers Inquiry**  the Dept. of Army investigation into the MY LAI INCIDENT, directed by Lt. Gen. William R. Peers.

**Pegasus**  code for the operation giving relief to KHE SANH after its 77-days siege in April 1968.

**Peitun Yunnani**  the air base in southern Red China where the North Vietnamese housed their MiGs.

**pencil pusher**  slang for those with desk jobs. Also called paper pusher and straphanger.

**pencil whip**  marine slang for writing up make-believe events just for the fun of it.

**penis machinist**  slang for a MEDIC.

**penny nickel nickel**  slang for the 155mm howitzer.

**Pentagon East**  the Military Assistance Command, the U.S. headquarters complex in Vietnam at TAN SON NHUT air base, where most of the military aspects of the Vietnam War were directed. See MACV.

**Pentagon Papers**  a once-secret internal Defense Department study of United States-Vietnam relations from 1945 to 1967. They were published in the *New York Times* in 1971. President Richard Nixon opposed publication of these documents, but on June 30, 1971, the U.S. Supreme Court ruled that the *New York Times* had the right to publish these papers. DANIEL ELLSBERG reportedly had stolen the papers and furnished them to the *Times*; he was indicted in June 1971 for illegal possession of government documents and using government property for personal use, plus other charges. In May 1973 all charges were dismissed.

***Pentomic*** an organizational plan laid out for potential nuclear conflict using five divisional elements instead of the usual three regiments.

***People Sniffer*** nickname for Airborne Personnel Detector, APD the long, snoutlike radar that hung from helicopters to register body heat and attempt to sniff out the enemy. It could not, however, distinguish between animal or human urine, or between friend and enemy. Also called smell-o-meter and the manpack personnel detector—chemical.

***People's Army of Vietnam (PAVN)*** original name for the North Vietnamese Army. See NVA.

***People's Liberation Army*** the armed forces of the People's Republic of China, which became the model for HO CHI MINH's People's Army of Vietnam (PAVN). PAVN was the original name for the North Vietnamese Army.

***People's Revolutionary Party*** the southern chapter of the LAO DONG party. Along with the Democratic party and the Radical Socialist party, it formed the beginning of the NATIONAL LIBERATION FRONT.

***Perfume River*** river along the city of HUE.

***perim*** short for the PERIMETER which surrounded fire bases or base camps.

***perimeter*** outer limits and defensive line of any military position, beyond which lay the enemy. The perimeter consisted of any combination of barbed wire, concertina wire,

electronic listening devices, minefields, security lighting, and a variety of weaponry. Also called picket line.

***permit*** the basic parachutist's insignia.

***peta-prime*** the black tarry material that was spread to hold down dust during the dry season. It tended to melt in the sun and stick to everything.

***Peter pilot*** slang for copilot in training.

***Petty Officer*** a noncommissioned officer in the U.S. Navy or Coast Guard, in grades of chief, first, second, and third.

***PF*** abbr. for POPULAR FORCES.

***PFC*** 1. abbr. for Private First Class. 2. abbr. for "Proud Fucking Civilian," derogatory slang.

***PG*** abbr. for Patrol Gunboat.

***phá hủy*** Vietnamese for destroy.

***phải*** Vietnamese for must, used to accentuate verbs.

***Pham Van Dong*** prime minister of the North Vietnamese government from 1959–1975. He was appointed prime minister of the Socialist Republic of Vietnam in 1976.

***Phan Rang*** capital of NINH THUAN province; site of a large U.S. air base. FORWARD AIR CONTROLLERs were trained there.

***Phan Thiet*** the capital of BINH THUAN province on the South China Sea. Phan Thiet was the birthplace of HO CHI MINH.

***Phantom*** nickname for the F–4, the McDonnell/Douglas Mach-2 fighter-bomber. This versatile and rugged aircraft was developed for the navy and adopted by the air force.

**Phantom Blooper**   nickname for what was believed to be an American turncoat who used an M–79 grenade launcher in repeated attacks against U.S. Marines in 1967–68, mainly in I Corps.

**Phantom II**   see F–4B.

**pháo binh**   Vietnamese for artillery.

**pháo dài**   Vietnamese for bunker.

**phi cỏ cánh quạt**   Vietnamese for propeller plane.

**phi cỏ phản lực**   Vietnamese for jet plane.

**phi cỏ trực thắng**   Vietnamese for helicopter.

**phi công**   Vietnamese for pilot.

**pho (also spelled phu)**   a noodle soup sold on the streets in Vietnam.

**Phoenix**   code name for Phuong Hoang a long-running program to identify and destroy the Viet Cong political infrastructure (VCI) through identification and arrest of key party cadres. This South Vietnamese intelligence-gathering program was advised by CORDS. Phoenix was directed by William Colby, who became CIA director in 1973. An estimated 20,000 Viet Cong underground political agents and tax collectors were neutralized (either killed or arrested.)

**phonetic alphabet**   words assigned for each letter of the alphabet; for example, delta for D, and november for N.

**Phong Dinh**   one of the 44 provinces of South Vietnam, located in IV CORPS.

**phosphorus grenades**   GRENADES with white phosphorus, used to mark ground positions.

**Phuong Hoang**   see PHOENIX.

**Phu Cat**   a U.S. air base in Vietnam.

**Phu Vinh**   capital of VINH BINH Province.

**Phu Yen**   one of the 44 provinces of South Vietnam, located in II CORPS.

**Phuc Yen**   an important North Vietnamese base for MiGs.

**Phuoc Long**   one of the 44 provinces of South Vietnam, located in III CORPS.

**Phuoc Long City**   capital of PHUOC LONG province.

**Phuoc Tuy**   one of the 44 provinces of South Vietnam, located in III CORPS.

**Phuoc Tuy City**   capital of PHUOC TUY province.

**Phu Bon**   one of the 44 provinces of South Vietnam, located in II CORPS.

**Phu Cuong**   capital of BINH DUONG Province.

**Phu Dung**   code name adopted in 1971 for what had been previously coded Shining Brass from 1965 until 1968 and Prairie Fire in 1968. The operation involved covert U.S. Army SPECIAL FORCES raids and RECONNAISSANCE missions into Laos to end the North Vietnamese Army's infiltration.

**Phu Tho Racetrack**   a racetrack in Saigon that was the scene of heavy fighting during the 1968 TET OFFENSIVE. Prior to Tet, this racetrack was a Viet Cong stronghold. The Vietnamese ran their horseraces with the horses running clockwise, rather than counterclockwise as it is done in the United States.

**phục xạ thủ** Vietnamese for snipers.

**Phuoc Valley** a heavily populated rice-growing area along the southern boundary of QUANG NAM Province, the scene of many fierce marine battles.

**Phuong Hoang** Vietnamese for PHOENIX, the intelligence program established in 1968 to eliminate the Communist infrastructure.

**piaster** the former currency of South Vietnam. The official exchange before the Liberation (1960) was 755 piasters to the American dollar; 100 piasters was about 85 cents in 1966 and $1.15 in 1970. The piaster was replaced by the DONG in 1978.

**picket line** slang for PERIMETER.

**pickle** radio slang for releasing an aircraft's bomb load by depressing the button atop the control stick.

**pick up zone** 1. helicopter loading area. 2. pick up point for helicopter extractions.

**pictomap** photos which used computer-aided photographic processes to eliminate distortion. These were mosaics of aerial photos and could be used to overlay photos with symbols for trails and waterways to gain a clearer and more accurate view of an area. These processes were used during the Vietnam War.

**piece** 1. nickname for one's rifle. 2. slang for any weapon.

**Pierce Arrow** code for the air strikes over North Vietnam in 1964

after Communists reportedly attacked two U.S. ships in the TONKIN GULF, the USS *Maddox* and the USS *C. Turner Joy.*

**pig, the** slang for the M–60 MACHINE GUN, also called hog and hog–60.

**pigs** nickname for B–52s.

**pigeons** aerial term for the vector to a specific destination or point.

**pile-on** the process of gathering intelligence and then vigorously engaging with and demolishing the enemy. Reaction forces were said to "pile-on" their stuff. Colonel George Smith Patton, son of General George Patton, was credited with developing the pile-on technique which was widely used after 1968.

**pill, the** slang for weekly pill taken by U.S. servicemen to protect against malaria.

**pineapple** 1. slang for a hand grenade. 2. an area of rice fields, fruit orchards, and swamps, west of SAIGON. The Pineapple was a sanctuary for communist forces who came in from Cambodia. It was also called the Pineapple Patch.

**Pink Rose** 1. code for three B–52 missions in 1967 that set fire to jungle areas using INCENDIARY BOMBS. 2. code for a test operation involving spraying a target with DEFOLIANT first and then with a drying agent. Cluster incendiary bombs were then dropped onto the targets, destroying both vegetation and enemy positions.

**Pink Team** an OH–6 Cayuse helicopter escorted by a Cobra gunship, that provided low-level reconnaissance at landing zones. Also called hunter killer.

**Pinkville** nickname for MY LAI, called that because of the number of VIET CONG in the area.

**pip** a spot of light on a radar scope representing the relative position of a reflecting object such as an aircraft. Also called a blip.

**Piranha** code for the marine operation against the VIET CONG in September 1965 at Cape Batangan along the coast, south of Da Nang.

**PIRAZ** see RED CROWN.

**piss-tube** 1. a vertical metal tube two-thirds buried in the ground, for urinating into. This device was also called a pee pipe. 2. piss-tube also referred to a MORTAR.

**pisser** slang for an observer who watched enemy trails.

**pistol, M–1911A1** a .45 caliber pistol carried as a sidearm by some unit leaders and by marines who also carried heavy weapons.

**pitch** aerial term for the displacement of an aircraft about its lateral axis, either nose-up or nose-down.

**pitch liberty** navy term for going ashore.

**pith helmet** a helmet worn by some North Vietnamese Army and VIET CONG units.

**Pittman Apartments, The** the apartment building where helicopters landed during the evacuation of Saigon in 1975.

**PJ** 1. abbr. for PARAJUMPER. 2. abbr. for photojournalist.

**PKIA** abbr. for Presumed Killed In Action.

**PL** abbr. for PATHET LAO, the anti-government Communist forces in Laos.

**PLA** abbr. for People's Liberation Army of South Vietnam. See VIET CONG.

**PLAF** abbr. for People's Liberation Armed Forces. See VIET CONG.

**Plain of Jars** a high plain in northern Laos where hundreds of old vessels believed to be funeral urns were found. Firefights and U.S. airraids took place here. Also called PDJ.

**Plain of Reeds** name of a major VIET CONG base area south of SAIGON in the DELTA.

**Plan 34A Raids** code for secret U.S. air attacks of North Vietnam before the 1964 GULF OF TONKIN episode.

**Plantation, The** nickname for a North Vietnamese prison camp near HANOI.

**plastique** 1. a moldable plastic explosive. 2. a bomb made with plastic explosives.

**platoon** 1. a subdivision of a company-sized military unit, normally consisting of two or more squads or sections, and commanded by a lieutenant. 2. naval designation for a naval gunfire ship.

**play dough** slang for C-RATION bread.

**Pleiku** one of the 44 provinces of South Vietnam located in II CORPS, site of a U.S. air base. VIET CONG guerrillas attacked that base on February 7, 1965, and the United States began bombing

North Vietnam in retaliation. Shortly after this incident, U.S. ground troops began arriving in Vietnam.

**Pleiku City** capital of PLEIKU Province.

**PLF** 1. abbr. for Parachute Landing Fall, the roll that parachutists used when they landed. 2. abbr. for People's Liberation Force. See VIET CONG.

**PLT** abbr. for platoon.

**PO** abbr. for PETTY OFFICER.

**Pocket Money** code name for the mining of major ports and harbors, including Haiphong, off North Vietnam in May 1972. The original code for this operation was Duck Hook.

**pod** aerial term for any one of several aerodyamically configured subsystems carried externally on fighter aircraft.

**pod formation** a formation of two or more aircraft flown in such a way that ECM pods installed on each aircraft offer shared and maximum protection.

**pods** rubberized 500-gallon containers, containing water or fuel.

**pogey bait** marine slang for junk food and snacks and other food not issued by the military.

**pogue** derogatory term for military personnel employed in rear echelon support capacities.

**POI** abbr. for Program Of Instruction.

**point** see POINTMAN.

**point blank canister rounds** close range artillery used at ground level.

**point element** the POINTMAN and those walking SLACK.

**point target** a target which demanded the exact position of bombs or fire.

**pointman** the first man in line as a squad or platoon of men walk along a trail or through the jungle. He kept watch for danger for himself and for those following him. He was also called the Point.

**Pointman Project** an ongoing study exploring the effects of the defoliant AGENT ORANGE on Vietnam veterans.

**Poison Ivy Division** nickname for the Fourth Infantry Division, taken from both the design of its shoulder patch and its official title as the Ivy Division. Also called the Famous Fourth and the Funky Fourth.

**POL** abbr. for Petroleum, Oil, and Lubricants.

**POL point** slang for a GI gas station.

**POL strikes** air strikes against petroleum, oil, and lubricants facilities.

**poles** slang for pants.

**police, to** to clean up, or make tidy.

**polyjohn** a portable toilet, similar to those used at construction sites.

**poncho liner** the light-weight, quilted, military issue rain poncho. Used as blankets or as camouflage, they were were highly treasured by those who had them.

**Pond, The** slang for the Pacific Ocean.

**Ponderosa**  a bar at Military Intelligence Headquarters in SAIGON, the site of a former French villa.

**Pony Express**  daily scheduled courier flight. This courier was also called Errand Boy.

**Pony Soldiers**  slang for a soldier in the First Cavalry Division, probably called that because of the Cavalry's history of using horses.

**pop smoke**  slang for igniting a smoke grenade to identify a location or to signal an aircraft.

**popeye**  a radio transmission from an aircraft indicating that the flight was in the clouds and that there was poor vision to the ground or to any other aircraft.

**popper**  slang for drug user.

**popping caps**  slang for the rapid firing of rifle shots to intimidate or deceive the enemy.

**Popular Forces**  militia units of locally recruited men who organized within each village. The primary duty of these units was to provide village security and undertake offensive operations against guerrilla units in the nearby areas. PF units were supposed to be used only within their local village areas and were the most poorly paid and equipped of the South Vietnamese military units.

**pop-up**  aerial term for a climbing maneuver from a low-altitude position or other position of concealment, used to gain an advantageous position for weapons delivery.

**Portcall**  code for the air traffic control center at Hon Tre.

**pos**  slang for position, usually meaning a friendly location.

**Post-traumatic stress disorder**  the development of a set of symptoms comprising a syndrome after experiencing a psychologically traumatic event or events outside the normal range of human experience. Post-traumatic stress disorder was officially recognized as a syndrome in the 1980 edition of the *Diagnostic and Statistical Manual* that psychiatrists and psychologists use for diagnosis and research. Serving in Vietnam usually meant that one had suffered such trauma. The disorder can be successfully treated, but not totally cured because the original trauma can cause a flare-up of symptoms at any time. It is often abbreviated as PTSD.

**potato masher**  slang for a CHICOM hand GRENADE.

**Poulo Condor**  an island 60 miles due south of Saigon. The Vietnamese name for this island was Con Son, or Hell Island. Used as a penitentiary for many years, it was known for its TIGER CAGES that held prisoners.

**POW**  abbr. for Prisoner Of War.

**powder train**  nickname for a U.S. Navy SEAL explosive expert.

**powdered**  1. destroyed. 2. disintegrated, if an aircraft.

**power band**  slang for a bracelet made of braided bootlaces symbolizing the Black Power spirit of black soldiers. Some white soldiers also wore them.

**Power Plant**  nickname for a section of the North Vietnamese Hoa Lo Prison, called the HANOI HILTON.

***Practice Nine Barrier Brigade*** a brigade intended to guard the MCNA-MARA LINE by using observation posts and electronic sensors to monitor activity. The plan for this brigade was abandoned when plans for the line were dropped.

***Prairie Fire*** code for an operation to stop the North Vietnamese Army's infiltration in Eastern Laos. See SHINING BRASS.

***prang*** a bumpy landing of a helicopter.

***PRC*** abbr. for the People's Republic of China.

***PRC–74*** (pronounced Prick–74) a radio used by MOBILE GUERRILA FORCE units to keep in contact with troops outside the range of the PRC–25.

***PRC–77*** (pronounced Prick–77) a radio similar to the PRC–25, but with a scrambling device attached, also called the monster. Transmission frequencies on the PRC–77 were called the secure net.

***PRC–10*** (pronounced Prick–10) a hand-held portable radio, which could work only over short distances. The battery life was very short which limited its use; it was replaced by the PRC–25 which had a longer-life battery.

***PRC–25*** (pronounced Prick–25) portable radio communications, Model 25, a back-packed FM receiver-transmitter used for short-distance communications. The range of the radio was 5 to 10 KILOMETERS, depending on the weather, and whether it was attached to a special nonportable antenna which could extend the range to 20 or 30 kilometers.

***precleared fire zone*** a term that replaced the term FREE FIRE ZONE because that phrase was connected with the perceived irresponsible and controversial use of American artillery and air strikes which magnified concerns of the American general public about what the United States was accomplishing in Vietnam. Militarily, the use of free fire zones was not very effective.

***prep*** 1. abbr. for preparation, usually meaning bringing fire to a LANDING ZONE before a landing or an attack. 2. the ARTILLERY preparation of a LANDING ZONE.

***prep fire*** see PREPARATION FIRE.

***preparation fire*** fire placed on a target preliminary to an assault.

***Presidential Unit Citation*** an award to units which had shown gallantry, determination, and esprit de corps for a mission under difficult and hazardous conditions. This award required the same degree of heroism as a DISTINGUISHED SERVICE CROSS, NAVY CROSS or AIR FORCE CROSS presented to an individual.

***PRF*** abbr. for Pulse Recurrence Frequency.

***PRG*** abbr. for Provisional Revolutionary Government in South Vietnam. Constituted on June 6, 1969, it was the political organization of the guerrilla NATIONAL LIBERATION FRONT and anti-American resistance.

***PRGVN*** abbr. for Provisional Revolutionary Government of South Vietnam. See PRG.

***Prick–74*** see PRC–74.

***Prick–77*** see PRC–77.

**Prick–10**   see PRC–10.

**Prick–25**   see PRC–25.

**pricksmith**   slang for enlisted men in Medical Corps, medics.

**priority medevac (or dust-off)**   term for those seriously wounded or ill and unable to walk. Later in the war, Army Headquarters changed this category to mean patients requiring medical care not locally available. Compare to EMERGENCY MEDEVAC, ROUTINE MEDEVAC, and URGENT MEDEVAC.

**Private First Class**   see PFC.

**Probe-Eye**   an infrared optical system that could detect humans from nonhumans and armed forces from unarmed forces in the dark.

**profile**   1. a prohibition from certain military duty due to injury or disability. This was also termed on profile. 2. a documented description of medical problems during one's tour of military service.

**prohibited zone**   the areas encircling Hanoi by 10 nautical miles and Haiphong by 4 nautical miles. U.S. aircraft were forbidden to strike these areas unless specifically authorized because of the presence of many civilians. These were more highly restricted than the RESTRICTED ZONES because they were even more densely populated.

**Project Agile**   code for the Department of Defense's program for developing new weapons for use by U.S. servicemen in Vietnam. The agency ACTIV (Army Concept Team In Vietnam) tested these weapons.

**Project Daniel Boone**   code for the SOG RECONNAISSANCE teams that identified North Vietnamese base camps and roads in Cambodia. In 1967 they were permitted to penetrate up to 30 kilometers into the entire Cambodian frontier. Later the Daniel Boone Operation was renamed Salem House, and in the spring of 1971 it took its final name of Thot Not.

**Project Delta**   code for SPECIAL FORCES and RECONNAISSANCE and ROADRUNNER teams who monitored the traffic on the HO CHI MINH TRAIL and performed other secret recon and intelligence-gathering missions. Project Delta's earlier code name was Leaping Lena.

**Project 404**   code name for the secret air force operations in Laos and Thailand.

**Project 100,000**   code for Secretary of Defense Robert McNamara's 100,000 plan. This program was to accept into the service up to 100,000 men who would have been excluded from the armed services because of low mental ability, as measured by the Armed Forces Qualification Test (AFQT). Young men from low-income homes or minority groups and those in foster homes were especially sought. It enabled draft quotas to be met without abolishing existing deferments. The casualty rate of men recruited under Project 100,000 was twice as high as the general population of recruits, and the program was discontinued in 1972.

**Project Phoenix**   code for CIA assassination operations. See PHOENIX.

**Project Practice Nine**   the earliest code name for the MCNAMARA LINE, a proposed barricade that was to extend across the Demilitarized Zone. It was renamed Illinois City in 1967 and later named Dye Marker. The McNamara Line was never built.

**Project Water Pump** code for the secret 1964 United States Air Force training of Laotian pilots to fly fighter-bombers. This was carried out at Udorn Air Force Base in Thailand.

**protective reaction** 1. missions where American bombers escorted reconnaissance aircraft. 2. bombing.

**Proud Deep** code name for the more than 1,000 bombing SORTIES against North Vietnam in the five days beginning December 26, 1971.

**Prov** abbr. for Provisional.

**Provider** see C–123.

**province** South Vietnam was divided into 44 provinces and 11 AUTONOMOUS CITIES. A list of provinces can be found in appendix 1; each province has an entry in the book. The provinces were political subdivisions analogous to states in the United States.

**province chief** the governor of a state-sized administrative territory in South Vietnam, usually a high-ranking military officer.

**province team** the American civilian and military advisors assigned duties at the provincial capitals.

**Provincial Revolutionary Government** see PRG.

**PROVN** abbr. for Program for the Pacification and Long-Term Development of South Vietnam. This resulted in a 1966 secret study by Army Chief of Staff General Harold K. Johnson; he found that there was an overall lack of cohesion among the American advisors. The PROVN Study prescribed that PACIFICATION be given a high priority.

**proword** a code word used to express a prearranged message. Numerals were also used as codes to express prearranged messages.

**PRP** abbr. for PEOPLE'S REVOLUTIONARY PARTY.

**PRU** (pronounced pru.) abbr. for Provincial Reconnaissance Units. These units were intelligence collection and reaction forces established by the CIA; they participated in the PHOENIX program. An irregular unit was organized within each province for the official purpose of reconnoitering guerrilla sanctuaries and collecting intelligence on guerrilla activities.

**PSA** abbr. for PROVINCE Senior Advisor. The senior American advisor in each province in Vietnam was the commander of the province team. While the PSA was usually an American army colonel, the post was sometimes filled by a State Department official.

**PSDF** abbr. for People's Self-Defense Force. These were South Vietnamese irregulars, mainly teenagers and old men, and South Vietnamese village militia. This force was separate from the South Vietnam military.

**pseudomonas** a strain of bacteria that was common in Vietnam and caused many serious infections in service personnel. Its presence gives pus a blue-green color; it is highly resistant to many antibiotics.

**PSG** abbr. for Platoon Sergeant.

**PSP** abbr. for Perforated Steel Plate or Pierced Steel Plank, used for runways and roadways instead of pavement.

**Psychedelic Cookie** nickname for the Ninth Infantry Division, taken from the octofoil design of its shoulder patch. It was also called the Cookie Division.

**psycho-killer** slang for the UG–1 aircraft armed with .50 caliber machine guns, loudspeakers blaring threatening tapes, CS, infrared search lights, and other psychological warfare devices.

**Psychological operations** 1. the planned use of propaganda to influence the enemy's thinking. 2. psychological warfare operations such as dropping leaflets and making loudspeaker broadcasts to lower the enemy's morale. Between October 1965 and December 1971 several U.S. psyops groups utilized these tactics.

**psyops** short for PSYCHOLOGICAL OPERATIONS.

**psywar** abbr. for psychological warfare.

**P-Training** abbr. for Physical Training.

**PT** abbr. for Physical Training.

**PT–76** a Soviet amphibious RECONNAISSANCE vehicle. This North Vietnamese armor entered South Vietnam in February 1968 at the SPECIAL FORCE camp at Lang Vei near Khe Sanh. U.S. intelligence determined that enemy armor did not represent a threat to South Vietnam.

**PTAT** abbr. for Post Telegraph and Telephone System.

**PTSD** abbr. for POST-TRAUMATIC STRESS DISORDER.

**PTT** a Saigon radio station.

**PUC** abbr. for PRESIDENTIAL UNIT CITATION.

**pucker factor** slang for intense fear, meaning a soldier's asshole puckered up tight.

**Puff** 1. nickname for the C–47, a gunned aircraft. See PUFF THE MAGIC DRAGON. 2. slang for POPULAR FORCES (usually MONTAGNARDS).

**Puff the Magic Dragon** nickname for the C–47 with VULCAN MACHINE GUNS set up in the cargo doors. It provided intensive ground fire, with MINIGUNS and FLARES. Also called Puff, Dragon Ship, and Spooky.

**pugil stick** the padded stick used by Marine instructors to indoctrinate recruits with fighting spirit in training for combat.

**Puking Buzzards** nickname for the 101st Airborne Division, taken from the design of the eagle on the unit's shoulder patch and an ironic twist on their common nickname, Screaming Eagles.

**pull device** a wire detonating a booby trap when pulled.

**pull pitch** helicopter pilots' term indicating that they are about to take off.

**pull-up** 1. aerial term for the act of pulling up, a pullout or a recovery from a dive. 2. aerial term referring to bringing up the nose of an aircraft sharply, especially from a level attitude.

**pull the pin, to** slang expression meaning to leave or depart.

**pulling lead** aerial term for the act of aiming the nose of an aircraft ahead of an enemy aircraft.

**Punch Bowl**    nickname for an area near Khe Sanh, probably because of the large bomb craters there.

**punch out**    slang for bailing out from a jet aircraft by using the ejection seat.

**punji pit**    camouflaged hole covering PUNJI STAKES.

**punji stake**    primitive booby traps used by the VIET CONG. Traps consisted of sharpened bamboo stakes hidden under water, at ambush sites, along trails, or in carefully dug hidden pits. Often dipped in feces or poison, these stakes penetrated soldiers' feet. Also spelled pungi stake.

**Purple Heart**    a U.S. military decoration awarded to any member of the armed forces wounded by enemy action. It was often referred to simply as a "Heart." The Three Heart Rule stated that anyone who received three purple hearts could be rotated back to the United States. This rule was not always honored. The Purple Heart ranks just below the Army Achievement Medal, the Air Force Achievement Medal, and the Navy Achievement Medal.

**Purple Heart Trail**    slang for an area west of Da Nang, called that because of heavy U.S. casualties there.

**purple-out zone**    slang for emergency evacuation.

**purple vision**    term for the eye's ability to see in darkness. This ability can be temporarily destroyed by a flash of light.

**Push-me, Pull-you**    nickname for the Cessna twin-engined FAC Super Skymaster (O–2), also known as the Mixmaster.

**push**    slang for radio frequency.

**Pussy Cut Off Date**    see PCOD.

**Puzzle Palace**    1. slang for any headquarters or staff area. 2. slang referring to the Pentagon and to the MACV headquarters.

**Pvt**    abbr. for Private.

**PW**    abbr. for Prisoner Of War, also abbreviated POW.

**PX**    abbr. for Post Exchange, the military store. Merchandise at the PX was tax-free and sold only to American military personnel. In these department and grocery stores soldiers and their families could purchase a wide variety of personal items at a lower cost than in civilian stores.

**PX Hero**    slang for the guy who went to the PX to purchase medals instead of earning them. He then wore them proudly.

**PX issue**    the basic clothing and supply issue.

**pylon**    the projection under an aircraft's wing, designed for suspending ORDNANCE, fuel tanks, or pods.

**Pyramid Control**    code for the air traffic control center at Ban Me Thuot.

**PZ**    abbr. for PICK UP ZONE.

# Q

**Q course** the qualification course for SPECIAL FORCES soldiers. If passed successfully, they were awarded the Special Forces tab.

**QC** 1. abbr. for Quan Cahn, the Vietnamese military police. 2. abbr. for Quartermaster Corps.

**QL** the national highway in Vietnam. See HIGHWAY 1.

**QM** abbr. for Quartermaster, the NCO in charge of supplies.

**QRC–160** abbr. for quick reaction capability noise jamming ECM pod, developed to counter radar threats.

**QT** see QUICK TIME.

**quad** four heavy MACHINE GUNS mounted on a single pedestal and fired at the same time by a single gunner.

**quad–50** four .50-caliber MACHINE GUNS mounted as one unit.

**quad–60** four .60-caliber machine guns mounted as one unit.

**quan bao** Vietnamese for an "NVA intelligence element."

**Quan Cahn** Vietnamese Military Police.

**quân du kích** Vietnamese for guerrilla.

**Quan Long** capital of AN XUYEN Province.

**quan nhảy dù** Vietnamese for airborne troops.

**Quang Duc** one of the 44 provinces of South Vietnam, located in II CORPS.

**Quang Khe** a small North Vietnamese port which was heavily mined, immobilizing shipping. There was a small naval base here, about 50 miles north of the demilitarized zone.

**Quang Nam** one of the 44 provinces of South Vietnam, located in I CORPS.

**Quang Ngai** one of the 44 provinces of South Vietnam, located in I CORPS.

**Quang Ngai City** capital of QUANG NGAI Province.

**Quang Tin** one of the 44 provinces of South Vietnam, located in I CORPS.

**Quang Tri** one of the 44 provinces of South Vietnam, located in I CORPS. This northernmost province took the most casualties during the war. There was especially heavy fighting here during the EASTER OFFENSIVE in 1972.

**Quang Tri City** capital of QUANG TRI Province.

**Quantico** marine training base in Virginia.

**Quartermaster** the NCO in charge of supplies.

**quarters** living space.

**quê lắm** Vietnamese for a backward person or a peasant, used in a derogatory manner.

**quebec**    the military phonetic for the letter Q.

**Queen Bee**    a popular nightclub in Saigon.

**queen of battle**    term referring to the INFANTRY. Artillery was called the king of battle. The origin may stem from the game of chess.

**Que Son Valley**    a heavily populated rice-growing area along the southern boundary of QUANG NAM Province, and the scene of many fierce marine battles.

**Qui Nhon**    one of the 11 AUTONOMOUS CITIES of South Vietnam, a port in BINH DINH Province in II CORPS, and a major supply base. Qui Nhon fell to the North Vietnamese in March 1975.

**quick time**    a marching rate of 120 steps per minute, with steps about 30 inches in length.

**Quiz Room**    nickname for a section of the North Vietnamese Hoa Lo Prison, the HANOI HILTON where prisoners were questioned.

# R

**R & R** abbr. for Rest and Recuperation, a three- to seven-day vacation from the war for soldiers once during their one-year tours. Popular out-of-country R & R locations were Banghok, Hawaii, Australia, Hong Kong, Tokyo, Manila, Kuala Lampur, Singapore, and Taipei. In-country R & R locations were Vung Tau and China Beach. Out-of-country transportation and other expenses were the responsibility of the soldiers. R & R was also called rape and restitution, rape and ruin, rape and run, rest and relaxation, and rest and recreation. Other slang phrases for R & R were I & I, which stood for "intercourse and intoxication," and B & B, which stood for "booze and broads."

**r-max** short for maximum range.

**RA** 1. abbr. for Regular Army, the prefix to the enlistee's or lifer's serial number. See U.S. 2. abbr. for Rear Admiral.

**rabbit** slang used by black soldiers for white soldiers in Vietnam.

**Rach Gia** one of the 11 AUTONOMOUS CITIES of South Vietnam, and the southernmost area for U.S. troops.

**rack** marine slang for bed or cot.

**rack out** phrase meaning to go to bed.

**radar, MQ–74** electronic heat-sensing guide for locating targets, also referred to as snake eye.

**radar position** aerial term for one of three switch positions on the F–4 front cockpit missile control panel, used to select radar-guided missiles (AIM–7s) as ORDNANCE to be fired.

**radar signature** aerial term for characteristics specific to different aircraft which are distinguishable when displayed on a radar scope.

**radar, TPQ 10** an electronic heat SENSOR for locating targets.

**radio** see PRC-74, PRC-77, PRC-10, PRC-25.

**rag** slang for a parachute.

**rag boats** boats holding about 30 men, used mainly in South Vietnamese riverine operations. The acronym for River Assault Group was RAG.

**rag stuffer** nickname for a parachute rigger.

**railroad tracks** slang for a captain's bars.

**rallier** a defector from the VIET CONG, an individual who voluntarily surrendered (rallied) to the government of South Vietnam.

**rally** RECONNAISSANCE marine term for rendezvous.

**RAMF** abbr. for Rear Area Mother Fucker. A variation on REMF.

**ramp** the part of an airport where planes are parked. Also called the apron.

**ramp alert** a fully armed aircraft waiting on the ground and ready for takeoff within 15 minutes.

**ramp tramp** slang for the air force officer who coordinated flight-line activities at an air base.

**ramps** aerial term for movable walls that regulate the position of supersonic shock waves to control inlet airflow to the engines.

**Ranch Hand** 1. code for operations to conduct DEFOLIATION activities from 1962 to 1970. HERBICIDES were assigned code names according to the color of the identification bands on their storage drums. Purple and pink were followed by orange, white, and blue. AGENT ORANGE contained the toxic contaminant dioxin. Ranch Hand's motto was "Only we can prevent forests." 2. the air force unit that flew defoliation missions.

**range card** card used by INFANTRY units to indicate position sectors and direction of fire.

**ranger** soldiers specially trained for RECONNAISSANCE and combat missions. This included elite INFANTRY and commandos and special corps of South Vietnamese Army commandos. Rangers were usually trained in hand-to-hand fighting, and scout and recon missions at Fort Benning, Georgia. After 1969, LRRP units were designated ranger companies.

**ranger roll** a way of wrapping one's clothes to secure them for crossing water, usually by swimming.

**RAP** abbr. for Rear Area Pussy, another derogatory term for support troops not in the action.

**rat fuck** 1. slang for a mission that was jinxed from the start. 2. slang for combat assault.

**rat patrol** nickname for the four-man unit that patrolled the roads in South Vietnam; they traveled in jeeps and were armed with two M–60s.

**ration card** given to soldiers enabling them to buy certain items, such as liquor and cigarettes, in specified amounts.

**ration supply pack** kits issued to servicemen containing cigarettes and pipe tobacco, candy, tissues, stationery, and bootlaces. Also called ration supplement packs and RSP.

**Raven** a utility and observation helicopter manufactured by Hiller and used by the Army.

**Raven FAC** American pilots who flew O–1s and T–28 Nomads. Usually Laotian pilots flew those planes.

**RBF** abbr. for RECON-BY-FIRE.

**RD Cadre** abbr. for Rural Development Cadre, specially trained teams of young American men and women who worked with the villagers in improving their lives. RD cadre wore black pajamas, were armed for self-defense, and collected intelligence on Viet Cong activities. They were trained to use VC political tactics to carry out pacification in South Vietnam.

**rd(s)** abbr. for round(s) of ammunition.

**RDC** Revolutionary Development Cadre. These were friendly South Vietnamese, working at the local level toward HAMLET pacification.

**RE codes** the letter/number combination on DD214 discharge papers referring to eligibility for reenlistment. These codes indicate a veteran's status regarding reenlistment in his or her former branch of service. The codes follow:

### U.S. ARMY

RE I fully qualified for immediate enlistment.

RE II fully qualified for immediate enlistment, separated for convenience of the government under a separation which does not contemplate immediate reenlistment.

RE III not eligible for reenlistment unless a waiver is granted.

RE IV not eligible for reenlistment. Disqualification is unwaivable.

### U.S. NAVY AND MARINE CORPS

RE I recommended for reenlistment.

RE II recommended for reenlistment but ineligible because of status: fleet reservist, retired, commanding officer, warrant officer, midshipman, cadet.

RE III recommended for reenlistment except for disqualifying factor.

RE IV not recommended for reenlistment.

The U.S. Air Force used a similar code. If an RE code is believed to be erroneous, it is possible to have it removed by formally requesting a new DD214 discharge certificate without the code. See SPN code.

**react, the**    slang for a unit assigned to assist another unit which very much needed assistance, usually because of enemy fire.

**reaction force**    standby relief or reenforcement.

**reaction platoon**    an airmobile infantry unit on standby to assist units in contact. Also called blues.

**ready box**    a wooden ammunition box, where extra ammo was kept.

**ready light**    light indicating a particular avionics/munitions system was operating and ready for use.

**Ready Whip**    slang for an INSTANT NCO, one fresh out of NCO school.

**real bush**    slang for a round-eye female.

**real-time** time a computer operates in when it absorbs and processes information as soon as it is received, thus providing an essentially instantaneous output.

**rear area**    the area to the rear of the front line.

**rear area pussy**    derogatory term for support troops. See also REMF.

**Reb**    term used in Vietnam referring to South, probably after the Southern Confederate rebels in the United States Civil War.

**Recce (pronounced "reck ee")** 1. slang for RECONNAISSANCE. 2. an air force formation involving a close combat spread.

**recoilless rifle**    a lightweight ARTILLERY weapon in which the rearward movement (recoil) resulting from firing was essentially eliminated by a compensatory charge forward. It was usually portable.

**recoilless rifle, 106mm**    a single-shot, recoilless, breech-loaded weapon, weighing about 436 pounds when assembled and mounted for firing. It had a sustained rate of fire of six rounds per minute and an effective range of 1,365 meters. It was similar to the recoilless rifle, 57mm.

**recon-by-fire**    a RECONNAISSANCE technique in which suspected enemy positions were fired on so that the enemy would reveal his presence or return fire.

**recon**  see RECONNAISSANCE.

**recon patrol**  a patrol whose function was to get facts about enemy strength, location, and movement.

**recon zone**  a recon patrol's area of responsibility.

**recondo**  (from recon and commando), a school in-country for training U.S. Army troops in performing long-range reconnaissance patrols. The largest school of this type was at NHA TRANG, operated by the Fifth SPECIAL FORCES, 1966–1970.

**reconnaissance**  involved going out into the jungle to observe and identify enemy activity. It was also called recce and recon.

**Reconnaissance in Force (RIF)** 1. various military SWEEPS for finding the enemy. 2. a limited objective operation by a military force to discover and test the enemy's disposition and strength, or to develop other intelligence. 3. general phrase used for SEARCH AND DESTROY, SEARCH AND CLEAR, SWEEPing operations, and reconnaissance force sweeping operations.

**reconstitute**  returning a DEMOBILIZED or DISBANDED unit to the active list, therefore making it available for activation.

**recycled**  slang for repeating part of basic training.

**red**  refers to the enemy, as Red (Communist) North Vietnam.

**red alert**  the most urgent form of warning, signaling an imminent enemy attack.

**red ball**  1. method for expediting requests for repair parts, also the Red Ball Express. 2. an enemy road or trail.

**Red Beach**  spot just north of DA NANG where the first U.S. Marine combat unit arrived in Vietnam in 1965.

**Red Bird**  nickname for a COBRA helicopter.

**red broom handle**  slang for an enemy booby trap in which a communist grenade was taped to a small stick about the size of a broom handle. A piece of fishing line was attached to the grenade handle. The trap would detonate about two feet above the ground, causing painful leg injuries.

**Red Book**  slang for the Uniform Code of Military Justice (UCMJ).

**Red Cross**  the American Red Cross maintained units to serve U.S. servicemen and women in many locations in Vietnam, including Cam Ranh, Da Nang, Saigon, Camp Enari, Camp Eagle, and elsewhere.

**Red Crown**  1. code for radar-warning and aircraft control on U.S. Navy ships, stationed in the GULF OF TONKIN. 2. a navy radar-equipped spotter ship based in the Gulf of Tonkin. 3. call sign for the radar-equipped USS *Long Beach*, the navy's Piraz ship. Piraz stands for positive identification and radar advisory zone. This is a specific area for identifying and following aircraft near an area that is defended by a fleet. Stationed in the northern part of the Gulf of Tonkin, it performed GROUND CONTROL INTERCEPT functions.

**Red Diamond**  slang for the Fifth Infantry Division called that because of its insignia.

**red hats**   slang for TRACER rounds.

**red haze**   RECONNAISSANCE flights detecting heat emissions from the ground.

**red horse**   1. a fast engineering deployment and heavy operational repair squadron. 2. code for air force construction units.

**red legs**   slang for artillery, taken from the time of the Civil War when Union artillerymen's trousers had red stripes.

**red LZ**   a LANDING ZONE under hostile fire. Also called a hot LZ.

**red team**   armed helicopters.

**redball**   slang for an enemy high-speed trail or road.

**Redcatchers**   nickname for the 199th Light Infantry Brigade, called that because of the unit's shoulder patch of a flaming spear embedded in a blue and white shield.

**REDCOM**   abbr. for U.S. Readiness Command. This was a unified command with operational control of the tactical army and air force units in the United States.

**REDCON**   abbr. for the Readiness Condition of troops.

**redesignate**   to change the designation (name or name and number) of a unit.

**reeducation camp**   euphemism for concentration camps. These were political prisons and labor camps of varying size and severity. Such camps throughout South Vietnam were similar to the Soviet gulag system. They were run by the Socialist Republic of Vietnam.

**reefer**   Navy slang for refrigerator.

**Ref**   abbr. for Reference.

**regiment**   a military unit in the marines consisting of three infantry battalions. In the army only the armored cavalry units used regiments.

**Regional Forces**   militia units organized within each DISTRICT in South Vietnam to engage in offensive operations against local VIET CONG forces, controlled by a district chief. RF units were better paid and equipped than PF (Popular Forces) units and could be assigned duties anywhere within the home district. Regional Forces were also called RF strikers and Ruffs.

**Regt**   abbr. for Regiment.

**regular**   a well-geared north Vietnamese Army enemy soldier.

**rehab**   short for rehabilitate or rehabilitation.

**relay Huey**   a communication helicopter.

**Reliable Academy**   nickname for the ninth Infantry Division's Sniper School. The Ninth Division was known as Old Reliable.

**REMF**   abbr. for Rear Echelon Mother Fucker, a putdown used by front-line soldiers to refer to those assigned to duties in the rear. Also called house cat. 2. staff in any higher headquarters who were perceived not to understand the difficulties of any fighting soldier's duties.

**Remington raiders**   slang for Army clerk-typists and office personnel. They were also called Remington Rangers, probably referring to Remington typewriters.

**remote**  a dangerous or primitive assignment; usually this was a post where the military did not allow families to accompany their servicemen.

**Rengao**  a MONTAGNARD tribe living mainly in KONTUM Province.

**repo depo**  1. short for the replacement depot where the lower enlisted men were processed for assignment to a unit. Repo Depo was also called repple depple. 2. the place where the soldier was reprocessed to go home after a tour in South Vietnam.

**Repose, The**  a U.S. Navy hospital ship which began operating at Chu Lai in early 1966 and remained in Vietnam for four years. The other active hospital ship was the *Sanctuary*.

**repple-depple**  slang for Replacement Depot, which handled the transfers of troops. See REPO DEPO.

**Republic of Vietnam Civil Action Medal**  an award to a U.S. unit given by South Vietnam in recognition of meritorious civil action service.

**Republic of Vietnam Gallantry Cross**  an award to a U.S. unit given by South Vietnam in recognition of valorous combat achievement.

**RESCAP**  abbr. for Rescue Combat Air Patrol. See SARCAP.

**resoject**  see TUNNEL FLUSHER.

**rest and recuperation**  see R & R.

**restricted zone**  the areas encircling Hanoi by 30 nautical miles and Haiphong by 10 nautical miles, in which U.S. aircraft were restricted from striking unless specifically authorized because of the presence of civilians. See also PROHIBITED ZONE.

**reticle**  short for the optical sight reticle. This was a system of lines around a DOT in the focus of an optical gunsight that provided a reference for aiming and estimating range and distance to the target.

**retrograde**  movement to the rear.

**retrograde maneuver**  euphemism for a military retreat.

**re-up**  slang for re-enlisting.

**re-up bird**  a native Vietnamese bird which chirped "RE-UP, re-up."

**rev-dev**  see REVOLUTIONARY DEVELOPMENT PROGRAM.

**revetment**  a wall to protect against explosions, made of earth, sandbags, concrete, or stone.

**reveille**  1. a wake-up call. 2. a specific bugle call.

**Revolutionary Development Program**  this program of pacification ran from 1966 to November 1968 and was also called Rural Development. Individuals in this program acted as a liaison between the people and the government. They were first instructed at a training center in VUNG TAU and then formed into groups to work in hamlets for pacification. These individuals lived in the hamlets and organized groups later called POPULAR FORCES. This effort was fairly successful compared to other pacification programs; it dropped in usefulness in 1970, however, and was discontinued in 1971.

**RF–8**  a version of the CRUSADER used by the navy and marines.

**RF–4**  a version of the PHANTOM used by the air force and the marines.

**RF** 1. abbr. for REGIONAL FORCES, for the local military forces working within a DISTRICT. 2. abbr. for Radio Frequency.

**RF/PF** abbr. for REGIONAL and POPULAR FORCES, which were the South Vietnamese National Guard units. Regional Forces were company-size and protected DISTRICT areas, while Popular Forces were platoon-size and guarded their home villages. RF/PF were nicknamed Ruff/Puffs.

**RF Strikers** local military forces recruited and employed inside a DISTRICT, known as REGIONAL FORCES.

**RF-8A** The RECONNAISSANCE version of the F-8 Chance Vought fighter plane.

**RFZ** abbr. for Restrictive Fire Zone. see RESTRICTED ZONE.

**Rhade** a MONTAGNARD tribe living mainly in DARLAC, PHU BON, KHANH HOA and TUYEN DUC provinces.

**RHAW** abbr. for Radar Homing and Warning, on-board aircraft equipment to warn pilots of active enemy defenses.

**Rheault Affair** refers to the imprisonment in mid-1969 of Colonel Robert Rheault, the commander of the U.S. Fifth SPECIAL FORCES Group in Vietnam, and six of his officers charged with the premeditated murder of a Vietnamese Special Forces agent acting as a double agent for the Viet Cong. The CIA withheld classified information and the case was dismissed in September 1969. Colonel Rheault then retired from the U.S. Army.

**Richardson, Eliot** secretary of defense from January to July 1973.

**RIF** 1. abbr. for a RECONNAISSANCE IN FORCE patrol. 2. a reduction in force, a retiring of career soldiers prior to the end of their 20-year terms or dismissal from military or government duties.

**rifle, caliber 7.62mm, M-14** a gas operated, magazine-fed, air-cooled semiautomatic shoulder weapon which weighed about 12 pounds with a full 20-round magazine.

**rifle, caliber 7.62mm, M-14 (modified)** the automatic rifle version of the M-14 which weighed about 14 pounds with a bipod. It had a sustained rate of fire of 40–60 rounds per minute and an effective range of 460 meters.

**rifle grenade, HEAT, M-28** a high-explosive, antitank bomb, fired by a GRENADE LAUNCHER fixed to a rifle. Weighing about 1 1/2 pounds, it had an effective range of 90 meters.

**Rifle Security Companies** INFANTRY companies of the U.S. Army organized to provide security and not to pursue offensive operations.

**rigger** nickname for a U.S. Navy SEAL who assisted the POWDER TRAIN and laid explosive charges.

**rikky-tik** slang for quick or fast.

**ringknocker** slang for a graduate of a military academy, called that because of the academy rings worn by graduates.

**RIO** abbr. for Radio-Intercept-Officer. The naval flight officer occupied the back seat of F-4s and F-14s and was responsible for the use of radar and the conduct of an intercept. The air force term was WSO, Weapons System Officer.

*ripple fire*   rapid sequential firing of two or more missiles.

*Riverine Force*   the river units that operated in the MEKONG DELTA.

*Rivet Top*   code for the experimental EC–121M aircraft which began testing in August 1967; they were equipped with advanced airborne radar.

*Riviera*   nickname for an area of cells in the Las Vegas section of the North Vietnamese Hoa Lo Prison, the HANOI HILTON.

*RL*   abbr. for rocket launcher.

*RLA*   abbr. for Royal Laotian Army.

*RLAF*   abbr. for Royal Laotian Air Force.

*RLG*   abbr. for Royal Laotian Government.

*RMK/BRJ*   the initials of Raymond, Morris, Knudson/Brown, Root, Jones. This large group of construction companies held contracts in Vietnam for such major projects as airports, seaports, airstrips, hospitals, barracks, roads, and bridges.

*RNO*   abbr. for Results Not Observed. This was the same as NVR, No Visual Results. These phrases were used after an air attack or the firing of weapons when it was not possible to view the results.

*roach coach*   slang for a mobile mess. Also called roach wagon.

*road sweep*   checking a road for mines.

*roadrunner*   1. friendly Vietnamese and indigenous force units who dressed in North Vietnamese army uniforms or Viet Cong black pajamas and mingled with the NVA/VC, to report their positions, and lead them into PROJECT DELTA ambushes. 2. RECONNAISSANCE teams who served with SPECIAL FORCES reconnaissance detachments. Selected from the Civilian Irregular Defense Groups, they operated in four-man teams, wore native clothing, and carried captured weapons and equipment. INSERTed by helicopter deep into enemy-held territory, they moved along roads and trails and collected intelligence. 3. slang for surprise road-clearing actions against the enemy.

*roadrunner operation*   1. an operation with a group of vehicles that traveled a road to keep the enemy off balance and to make the presence of friendly forces felt among the local population. 2. a road-clearing operation with the goal of catching local GUERRILLAS by surprise. 3. a special forces trail-watch team.

*roadrunning*   a counterambush technique in which a convoy went past possible enemy positions so quickly that it could not be targeted.

*Robin*   see KEYSTONE.

*ROC*   abbr. for Radio Operator Course.

*rock and roll*   1. army term for setting one's weapon on full automatic fire. 2. putting an M–16 on full automatic fire. Also called busting caps.

*Rock Island East*   slang for a large cache captured by U.S. soldiers in Cambodia. It was named for the Rock Island Arsenal in Illinois because there was a huge amount of antiaircraft and rifle ammunition, rockets, and other material.

**rocker** slang for the first lower stripe of an enlisted man's rank insignia; it is shaped like a curve or rocker.

**rocket** a missile propelled by hot gases and launched by a motor or burning charge. Aerial rocket artillery, later called aerial field artillery, was used in the Vietnam War to support ground operations. Various rocket launchers were used to hold and guide rockets. Rockets were propelled by the M–79 GRENADE LAUNCHER as well as shot from helicopters and from Navy boats.

**rocket belt** the zone around a FRIENDLY area from which the enemy could launch rocket attacks.

**Rocket City** the nickname given to Da Nang, Tay Ninh, to the First Infantry's base camp in Lai Khe, and to many other places in Vietnam where rocket attacks were frequent and intense.

**rocket, 107mm** a light North Vietnamese hand-carried weapon.

**rocket, 122mm** a heavy North Vietnamese weapon.

**rocket pocket** any geographic location from which the enemy could fire rockets.

**Rocket Ridge** nickname for high area near Dak To, about 25 miles north of KONTUM, called that because of the frequency and intensity of rocket attacks.

**Rockpile, The** a 700-foot high peak near the Demilitarized Zone at the intersection of three river valleys and two enemy trails. Near the Rockpile were granite outcroppings with North Vietnamese Army bunkers and mortar emplacements where many FIREFIGHTS were staged.

**ROE** abbr. for RULES OF ENGAGEMENT.

**Roger** radio communication meaning the message was received and understood.

**Rogers, William P.** secretary of state, 1969–1973.

**Roglai** a MONTAGNARD tribe living mainly in BINH THUAN, NINH THUAN, BINH TUY, and KHANH HOA provinces.

**ROK** (pronounced rock), abbr. for Republic of Korea (South Korea). ROK also referred to South Korean troops.

**ROK Marines** marines from the Republic of Korea who were our fighting ALLIES in Vietnam. Known for being especially tough and deadly, they were very much feared by the enemy.

**ROK rats** slang for Korean C-RATIONS.

**ROKAF** abbr. for Republic of Korea Air Force.

**roll** aerial term for the displacement of an aircraft about its longitudinal axis as it banked left or right.

**Rolling Thunder** code for the Joint Chiefs of Staff directed, B–52 USAF strikes against North Vietnam, especially the preplanned strikes. Originally, these bombing strikes were planned to take place for only a short time, but in effect they lasted from 1965 through 1968 with only a few pauses in the bombing. The phases of Rolling Thunder were: Phase I: March 2–May 11, 1965; Phase II: May 18–December 24, 1965; Phase III: January 31–March 1, 1966; Phase IV: January 3–November 1, 1968. By November 1968, 645,000 tons of bombs had been dropped on North Vietnamese targets and 920 aircraft had been lost to North Vietnamese action.

***rollout*** aerial term for the termination of a maneuver or series of maneuvers designed to place an aircraft in a position which would most likely assure completion of its intended activity.

***Rome plow*** a special bulldozer manufactured by the Rome Caterpillar Company of Georgia, and used for cutting brush and small-to-medium trees. Also used for forest or jungle clearing and heavy-duty land clearing, it was nicknamed hog jaws and jungle-eater.

***romeo*** 1. military phonetic for the letter R. 2. slang for RULES OF ENGAGEMENT.

***RON*** abbr. for Remain Overnight position. Also called NL for NIGHT LOCATION.

***rooster*** RECONNAISSANCE nickname for the Sea Stallion marine troop and the CH–53 cargo helicopter.

***Rostow, Walt W.*** special assistant to President Lyndon Johnson for national security affairs, 1966–1969.

***rotate*** to return to the United States after completing a tour of duty. Also referred to as Big R in contrast to Little R, for R & R.

***rotation*** returning to the United States after completing a tour of duty.

***rotational hump*** a ROTATION of 25 percent or more of a unit within a 30-day period.

***ROTC*** abbr. for Reserve Officers Training Corps. This on-campus program led to a commission as a second

lieutenant in the U.S. Army, Navy, Marines, or Air Force.

***rotor*** the overhead helicopter blade.

***rotor wash*** wind blown up by a helicopter.

***rough rider*** slang for the security guard on a vehicle. Also called Shotgun.

***round-eye*** any Occidental, especially a woman.

***round*** bullet or other ammunition.

***Route Package*** any of six areas in North Vietnam specified for flight leader-controlled strikes. This was part of operation ROLLING THUNDER. The six areas—numbered RP–I through RP–VI—were divided up for efficiency and to avoid accidents.

***routine medevac (or dust-off)*** term for those sick or wounded where loss of life or limb was not likely, and the dust-off could safely be delayed from 12 to 24 hours. This term also included those patients who were dead. Compare to EMERGENCY MEDEVAC, PRIORITY MEDEVAC, and URGENT MEDEVAC.

***RP*** 1. abbr. for ROUTE PACKAGE. 2. abbr. for Rendezvous Point.

***RPC*** naval term for River Patrol Craft.

***RPD*** Soviet light MACHINE GUN 7.62mm, bipod mounted, and belt fed. Similar to the American M–60 machine gun the RPD was used by the VIET CONG and NVA.

***RPG*** rocket-propelled grenade. These 77mm and 40mm Russian-made antitank GRENADE LAUNCHERS were used by the VIET CONG and North Vietnamese Army. They were similar to the U.S. LAW. The RPG–3 version would burst in the air, giving it antiaircraft capability against helicopters.

**RPG Screen**   the chain-link fence placed around vehicles to absorb the RPG's blast.

**RPG-2**   a Chinese-made rocket launcher, used by the VIET CONG and the North Vietnamese Army.

**RPV**   abbr. for Remotely Piloted Vehicle, small unmanned aircraft flown by remote control and used for surveillance.

**Rqn**   abbr. for requisition.

**RR**   1. abbr. for recoilless rifle. 2. abbr. for radio relay.

**RSP**   see RATION SUPPLY PACK.

**RSSZ**   abbr. for RUNG SAT SPECIAL ZONE.

**RT**   abbr. for RECONNAISSANCE Team.

**RTAF**   abbr. for Royal Thai Air Force. In the early 60s native workers and American engineers built six jet airfields in Thailand, our ally in Vietnam, including U-Tapao, the largest airfield in Southeast Asia.

**RTB**   abbr. for Return To Base.

**RTO**   abbr. for Radio-Telephone Operator. Most commonly, the man assigned to carry the PRC–25 radio while out on an operation.

**rubber bitch**   slang for the inflatable rubber air mattress issued to troops in the field. Also called a rubber lady.

**rubber lady**   see RUBBER BITCH.

**Rubin, Jerry**   one of the CHICAGO SEVEN.

**Ruby Queens**   a brand of Vietnamese cigarette.

**RUC**   abbr. for Riverine Utility Craft.

**ruck**   also called rucksack, this was the backpack issued to the INFANTRY in Vietnam.

**rudder reversal**   aerial term for a roll reversal using the rudder only. It was usually used in maximum performance, high angle of attack maneuvering.

**Rue Catinet**   former French name of TU DO STREET in SAIGON.

**Ruffs**   slang for REGIONAL FORCES.

**Ruff Puffs**   slang for units or individual soldiers belonging to the REGIONAL FORCES/POPULAR FORCES, also called RF/PF units.

**ruined his whole day**   slang for getting killed.

**Rules of Engagement**   the specific regulations (MACV Directive 525–13) for the conduct of air and surface battles by U.S. and Allied forces during the Vietnam War. These rules were issued from 1965 on to all Vietnam-bound servicemen, and dictated procedures for the control of air power and ARTILLERY to minimize civilian casualties. FULL SUPPRESSION meant they could fire all the way. NORMAL RULES meant they could return fire for fire received. NEGATIVE SUPPRESSION meant they were not to return fire. Also called ROE and romeo.

**Rung Sat Special Zone**   the swampy area of mud and mangrove between the Saigon and the Dong Nai rivers. The 40-mile stretch of rivers and marshes between Saigon and the sea included a main shipping lane, LONG TAU.

VIET CONG hid water mines here, aimed at South Vietnamese ships. Rung Sat means Forest of Assassins and was known as a Viet Cong refuge.

**running a block**  slang for soldier who deliberately drew enemy fire so that his buddies could arrange a counterattack.

**running trails**  setting up and observing enemy trails, but not necessarily using them.

**ruptured duck**  nickname used by American advisors for the badge of the Signal Corps of the Army of the Republic of Vietnam.

**Rural Development Cadre**  s e e RD Cadre.

**Rural Pacification Corps**  this organization of South Vietnamese troops was responsible for searching out suspected VIET CONG, their families, and supporters. The RPC arrested, tortured, and killed those they found.

**rush mat**  the sleeping mats of POWs.

**Rusk, Dean**  secretary of state, 1961–1969.

**Rusty**  nickname of Lt. William CALLEY.

**RVN**  Republic of Vietnam (South Vietnam).

**RVNAF**  1. Republic of Vietnam Armed Forces. 2. abbr. for Republic of Vietnam Air Force.

# S

**S & D** abbr. for SEARCH AND DE-STROY.

**S & S** abbr. for Supply and Service, the designation of a support unit.

**S maneuver** aerial term for a weave in the horizontal plane.

**SA** 1. abbr. for Small Arms. 2. abbr. for Senior Advisor.

**Sa Dec** one of the 44 provinces of South Vietnam, located in IV CORPS.

**Sa Dec City** capital of SA DEC Province.

**SAC** abbr. for U.S. Strategic Air Command, a branch of the USAF developed for extended long-range air operations against enemy targets. The purpose was to eliminate the enemy's ability to engage in war.

**SACADVON** abbr. for Strategic Air Command Advanced Echelon, which was SAC's forward command post at MACV.

**sack** slang for totally destroying an enemy area.

**sack in (or sack out)** to go to bed; also phrased to rack in or rack out.

**SACSA** abbr. for Special Assistant for Counterinsurgency and Special Activities. SACSA directed the top-secret section of the Joint Chiefs of Staff which conducted MACV–SOG operations.

**SAD** abbr. for SEARCH AND DE-STROY.

**saddle** 1. a low area between two hills. 2. the final attack position with the attacker in range.

**saddle up** an order meaning troops were to put on their packs and prepare to march or move on.

**SAF** abbr. for Small Arms Fire.

**SAFE AREA** abbr. for Selected Area For Evasion, meaning the terrain, location, or nearby population made the area a suitable place for ESCAPE AND EVASION.

**safe bar** a place where information from indigenous personnel was shared.

**safe house** a place to make contact with indigenous personnel during covert operations.

**SAGE** a system of air defense.

**Saigon** 1. one of the 11 AUTONO-MOUS CITIES of South Vietnam. 2. the capital of South Vietnam.

**Saigon commando** slang for a soldier who spent his time in the rear, especially in Saigon. He was also called a Saigon warrior.

**Saigon cowboy** slang for a pimp.

**Saigon Daily News** an English language newspaper in South Vietnam.

**Saigon Post** an English language newspaper in South Vietnam.

**Saigon quickstep** slang for diarrhea.

**Saigon tea**  slang for the soda or cold tea drunk by Saigon bar girls.

**Saigon warrior**  slang for a soldier stationed in Saigon. He was also called a Saigon commando.

**Salem House**  see PROJECT DANIEL BOONE.

**salty dog**  slang for an item lost in combat.

**salvo**  firing a battery in unison; also called a laser.

**SAM**  1. abbr. for Surface-to-Air Missile. 2. a strike team, particularly as an early name for HUNTER-KILLER. 3. A training program for REGIONAL FORCES and POPULAR FORCES as a part of the VIETNAMIZATION program. The initials stand for Stamina, Accuracy, and Marksmanship.

**Sam-Song**  U.S. pilot's slang for the radar signals of enemy missile batteries that alert them to their presence.

**Sam Strike Team**  see HUNTER-KILLER.

**Sam Two**  code for the SA–2 GUIDELINE.

**same-same**  the same as, or to do likewise.

**sampan**  a Vietnamese peasant boat.

**San Antonio formula**  a reference to President Lyndon Johnson's statement in a speech in San Antonio, Texas, on September 29, 1967, that he would halt the bombing of North Vietnam if North Vietnam would begin peace negotiations and would not send men or materiel to the south. Johnson did stop the bombing for six months, but North Vietnam would not negotiate at that time.

**Sanctuary**  an offshore hospital ship, where sick and wounded were taken. After going into service in 1967, it served for four years. This was the second hospital ship in Vietnam; the other was the *Repose*.

**sandbags**  fabric containers which soldiers filled with sand and stacked together. They provided some protection from enemy weapons and were placed in bunkers, foxholes, hootches, and anywhere else they were needed.

**Sanctuary Counteroffensive**  campaign from May 1 to June 30, 1970.

**sandwich**  an aerial situation in which an aircraft is positioned between two opposing aircraft.

**Sandy**  nickname for the A–1 Skyraider, used by the U.S. Navy and the Air Force in Vietnam; also called Spad.

**sanitize**  euphemism for assassinate.

**sao**  Vietnamese meaning to lie or to be a liar.

**sapper**  1. a Viet Cong or North Vietnamese Army commando, usually armed with explosives. 2. a specially trained NVA infiltrator who went into a base or camp to destroy lives or property. 3. an NVA or VC demolition assault expert skillful at penetrating ALLIED defenses.

**sapper team**  VIET CONG GUERRILLAS who attempted to infiltrate American and South Vietnamese bases and use explosive devices against aircraft and equipment.

**sappers inside the wire**  a warning called out in the night that soldiers greatly feared. See SAPPER.

**SAR** 1. abbr. for Search And Rescue. 2. abbr. for Sea-Air-Rescue.

**SARC** abbr. for Surveillance and Reconnaissance Center. SARC was a reporting center for combat information at the main operational headquarters.

**SARCAP** abbr. for Search And Rescue Combat Air Patrol, used to cover rescue operations. SARCAP was later changed to RESCAP.

**SARTAF** abbr. for Search And Rescue Task Force.

**SA–7** an antiaircraft missile used by the North Vietnamese Army after 1972. It could be carried by one man and had an infrared homing system that was effective against slow-moving helicopters and aircraft. Grail was the NATO term for this shoulder-fired surface-to-air missile.

**SA–2** a Soviet-built surface-to-air missile (SAM) with an altitude capacity of 60,000 feet and a speed of MACH 2.5. This was the main North Vietnamese antiaircraft missile. It was named Guideline, and nicknamed the Flying Telephone Pole.

**Sat Cong** South Vietnamese slogan meaning "Kill Communists."

**satchel charge** the pack used by the Viet Cong containing explosives. The satchel charge—a canvas bag filled with explosives and thrown or dropped by its handle onto targets—was generally more powerful than the grenades used by SAPPER TEAMS.

**SATS** abbr. for Short Airfield for Tactical Support. This transportable land-based aircraft carrier could be put together quickly. It was capable of launches and recoveries because of its portable catapult.

**Scared horse** nickname for the 11th Armored Cavalry Regiment, called that because of the rearing horse design on its shoulder patch.

**Sch** abbr. for School.

**scheduled fire** fire that has been prearranged to be delivered at a specific time.

**Schlesinger, James** secretary of defense, 1973–1975.

**Schoech, William A.** commander, seventh Fleet, 1961–1962.

**science fiction** nickname for the U.S. Army SPECIAL FORCES.

**scissors** aerial term for the basic air-combat-maneuvering technique in which a series of turn reversals are made in an attempt to attain the offensive after an overshoot by the attacker.

**SCLC** abbr. for SOUTHERN CHRISTIAN LEADERSHIP CONFERENCE.

**Scooter** nickname for the SKY-HAWK plane.

**scope** nickname for the Radio Intercept Officer (RIO).

**scope-tow** a tow for an IBS DOUGHNUT. A line was thrown around the periscope of an underwater submarine for towing.

**scorpions** found in Vietnam and concealed in VIET CONG booby traps. Scorpions had long, narrow sectioned tails, with venomous stingers at the end.

**Scoshie Tiger** 1. nickname for the F–5 Freedom Fighter aircraft. 2. code for the operational evaluation of the Northrop F–5A light fighter.

**Scotland**  code for the operation in defense of KHE SANH.

**scout track**  an armored cavalry assault vehicle (ACAV) operated by a Battalion Recon Platoon.

**scouts out**  a call to action by the cavalry.

**scoutships**  OH–13 or OH–23 helicopters used for surveillance and RECONNAISSANCE.

**scramble**  an alert or call for assistance.

**scrambler**  an instrument that could change radio transmissions so they could not be bugged.

**Screaming Chickens**  sarcastic nickname for members of the 101st Airborne Division, a twist on their affectionate nickname of Screaming Eagles, or their sarcastic nickname of Puking Buzzards.

**Screaming Eagles**  nickname for members of the 101st Airborne Division because of the eagle on their shoulder patches. Also called, sarcastically, Screaming Chickens and Puking Buzzards.

**scrip**  MILITARY PAYMENT CERTIFICATES (MPCs).

**scuba**  abbr. for self-contained underwater breathing apparatus.

**scuttlebutt**  1. slang for rumors. 2. marine slang for a drinking fountain.

**scuz rag**  slang for the rags used for wiping floors.

**SDC**  abbr. for Self-Defense Corps, a local militia of South Vietnam.

**SDS**  abbr. for Students for a Democratic Society. Founded in the 1960s, SDS became the largest radical student organization in the country. It focused its attention and energy on community organization of the poor and opposition to the Vietnam War.

**SEA**  abbr. for Southeast Asia.

**Sea Dragon**  code for a U.S. Navy operation to interrupt North Vietnamese supply lines begun along with the ROLLING THUNDER operation in October 1966. Sea Dragon sunk North Vietnamese boats heading south and continued with the bombardment of the North Vietnam coast. Operation Sea Dragon ended in October 1968 when President Lyndon Johnson announced a bombing halt.

**Sea Horse**  a medium-sized transport helicopter, the army version of the Sikorsky CH–34.

**Sea King**  a search and rescue helicopter manufactured by Sikorsky and used by the navy.

**Sea Knight**  a transportation helicopter manufactured by Boeing and used by marines.

**Sea Sprite**  a utility helicopter manufactured by Kaman and used by the navy.

**Sea Stallion**  a heavy assault helicopter, the CH–53, manufactured by Sikorsky and used by the marines and the navy for transporting troops and material. Nicknamed the rooster.

**seabag**  the canvas bag that held a recruit's gear.

**SEABEE**  abbr. for Naval Construction Battalion Personnel. SEABEE was derived from C.B., which stood for U.S. Navy Construction Battalion. Seabees built airstrips, roads, bridges, housing, wells, and SPECIAL FORCES camps, from 1963 on. They supported combat operations, frequently under enemy fire. They often worked side by side with the South Vietnamese. At their peak strength, in April, 1968, there were 9000 Seabees in South Vietnam.

**seal bins**  500-gallon rubberized containers.

**SEAL Forces**  SEAL stood for Sea-Air-Land units. American and South Vietnam Navy commandos formed an elite navy special warfare force. These units operated in Vietnam with the River Patrol Forces and also with MACV–SOG in secret intelligence operations. They infiltrated enemy territory by land as ranger patrols, using helicopters and parachutes, and by water in small boats as frogmen.

**Seale, Bobby**  one of the CHICAGO SEVEN and a Black Panthers leader.

**SEALORDS**  abbr. for Southeast Asia Lake, Ocean, River, and Delta Strategy, which was an operation of the U.S. and South Vietnamese Navies together with U.S. Army RIVERINE FORCES, and South Vietnam's Army and Marine Corps. Their purpose was to cut enemy supply lines from Cambodia and to interrupt enemy base areas in various waterways. The South Vietnamese Navy took over the U.S. Navy's role in SEALORDS in April 1971.

**search and avoid**  derogatory phrase for South Vietnamese Army activities.

**search and clear**  offensive military operations that swept through regions to find, drive away, and/or destroy the enemy. Also called search and sweep.

**search and delight mission**  slang for R&R activities.

**search and destroy**  an offensive operation in which Americans searched an area to find, fix in place, fight, and destroy enemy forces and their base areas and supplies. The name search and destroy was dropped in 1968 because it was associated with aimless searches and wanton destruction of property. It was then called RECONNAISSANCE IN FORCE or helicopter assault. Search and destroy operations were also called S&D, SAD, and Zippo missions.

**search and evade**  derogatory phrase for South Vietnamese Army activities.

**search and rescue**  missions to locate and rescue troops in trouble.

**Search and Rescue Combat Air Patrol**  see SARCAP.

**SEAsia**  abbr. for Southeast Asia.

**second balloon**  slang for second lieutenant.

**Second Field Force**  one of two approximately equal areas of South Vietnam, split for administrative purposes.

**second hat**  slang for an assistant drill instructor in charge of instruction.

**2d AD**  abbr. for Second Air Division.

**2d Lt**  abbr. for Second Lieutenant.

**SecState**  abbr. for Secretary of State.

**section**  an U.S. Air Force formation involving a two-plane unit made up of a leader and a wingman.

**Section 8** a discharge from the military for mental or emotional problems.

**sector** a military command word corresponding to a South Vietnamese PROVINCE.

**secure** locking up or putting away.

**secure net** scrambled radio transmission on the PRC–77.

**Sedanq** a MONTAGNARD tribe living mainly in KONTUM Province.

**seismic intrusion device** various apparatus for detecting the presence of the enemy. Varieties include PSID, MORSID, MAGID, TURDSID, PIRID, minihand SID, MINISID, and MICROSID.

**seismic sensors** see SENSOR, SEISMIC.

**SEL** abbr. for Suspected Enemy Location.

**selective ordnance** euphemism for NAPALM.

**Selective Service** established in 1917 for World War I, this was the system of drafting men for war. Selective Service was made up of about 4,000 local draft boards staffed by civilian volunteers. Although there were approximately 27 million Vietnam Era draft-age men, about 16 million were deferred or disqualified from military service by going to college, marrying and having children, self-inflicted injuries, feigned homosexuality or mental illness, failure to register, leaving the country, or by joining the National Guard. Classifications of Selective Service are listed individually in this volume.

**self-help** construction work done by a unit for its own benefit. Materials to build with were issued to troops and engineering specialists supervised the work.

**seminar camp** the Laotian Communist version of the reeducation (concentration) camp for political prisoners.

**sensor** equipment which used sound to locate and indicate terrain configurations, the presence of military targets, and other natural and manmade objects. It could also detect activities by means of environmental disturbances which were converted into electrical signals.

**sensor, acoustic** U.S. listening devices used with seismic sensors to pick up the sounds of soldiers or vehicles or to confirm targets.

**sensor, seismic** U.S. sensors dropped from aircraft onto enemy trails. Their steel spikes became embedded in the earth, and they could pick up nearby vibrations and movements.

**SEP** abbr. for separate.

**separation** aerial term for the distance between the interceptor and the target aircraft. The distance could be lateral, longitudinal, or vertical.

**separation maneuver** aerial term for an energy-gaining maneuver accomplished with a low angle of attack and maximum thrust, for the purpose of increasing or decreasing the separation.

**SEPES** abbr. for Service for Social and Political Studies, a Vietnamese Civilian Intelligence agency.

**SERE** abbr. for Survival, Evasion, Resistance, and Escape.

**Sereika (Khmer Serei)** the non-Communist Cambodian resistance forces. Serei units defected to Prince Norodom Sinhanouk's army in late 1969; this was believed to be a CIA plan to weaken his government. After 1970 they were trained by U.S. Special Forces and fought as an ally, but most were killed in the war.

**serial number** before 1969, a number given to each person in the U.S. Armed Forces. In July 1969, the army changed to the use of Social Security numbers for identification. The prefix used was "U.S." for draftees and "RA" for enlistees and LIFERS.

**service medal** medal awarded for participation or service in a battle, campaign, or war. Also called campaign medal.

**Service Record Book** the file containing each marine's personal history and records.

**service ribbon** a ribbon on a uniform representing a service medal.

**service star** a small metal star worn on a service ribbon designating membership in a unit that participated in a war campaign or a battle of a campaign. When placed on a service ribbon, the stars indicate additional awards of the same decoration. Each bronze service star designated one battle or campaign. Each silver service star represented five war campaigns.

**service stripe** a stripe indicative of three years of active service. Service stripes were worn on the left sleeve of the uniform of enlisted personnel, except for naval personnel who wore them on the right sleeve. They were also called hash marks and zebras.

**set** slang for a party.

**seven and seven** one week of R & R, followed by one week of leave. This arrangement was followed in Vietnam after most of the troops had been withdrawn by 1971.

**seven-eighty-two gear** the equipment carried by marines in the field, called that because of its code number on an obsolete supply form.

**Seven Mountains** a site of two major battles in Vietnam. These battles took place near a fortified position close to the Cambodian border in IV CORPS at Nui Coto in 1969 and at Nui Khet in 1970.

**'79** slang for M–79 GRENADE LAUNCHER.

**17th parallel** the line that divided North and South Vietnam. The 17th parallel, together with a 15-mile buffer, was called the Demilitarized Zone, or DMZ.

**Seventh Fleet** the unit responsible for all U.S. Naval operations in Southeast Asia.

**SF** abbr. for U.S. Army SPECIAL FORCES, also called Green Berets.

**SFHQ** abbr. for Special Forces Headquarters in Nha Trang.

**S–5** officer in charge of the civil affairs section of a brigade or smaller unit.

**SFOB** abbr. for Special Forces Operating Base.

**S–4** officer in charge of the supply and evacuation section of a brigade or smaller unit.

**SGN** abbr. for SAIGON.

**Sgt** abbr. for Sergeant.

**Sgt. Rock** a combat-scarred World War II comic book character, referred to in Vietnam by LIFERS.

**SgtMaj** abbr. for Sergeant Major.

**Shadow** 1. C–119 aircraft carrying one search light, with STARLIGHT capabilities. They also carried four MINIGUNS, and 2,400 rounds of 7.62mm. 2. an AC–119 with MINIGUNS.

**shadow government** slang for the de facto government in rural areas in South Vietnam set up by the VIET CONG. It was also called the Government of the Night. See VCI.

**shake and bake** slang for any recent student of an NCO academy in Fort Benning in Georgia, Fort Sill in Oklahoma, or Fort Knox in Kentucky; because graduates earned their rank after a short time in uniform. Also known as Ready Whip, Nestle's Quick, and Instant NCO. See NONCOMMISSIONED OFFICER.

**sham** slang for deliberately fabricating or adding to an injury to get out of the FIELD.

**shaped charge** an explosive charge, focused in one direction.

**Sharp, U.S. Grant** commander in chief, Pacific Command (CINCPAC), 1964–1968.

**Shawnee** a transportation helicopter manufactured by Piasecki, and used by the army.

**shear load** the stresses on the wings of an aircraft.

**Shelby** a brand name of a P–38 can opener.

**shelter half** marine term for half of the two-man tent carried in the field.

**Sheridan** the M–551 armored recon assault vehicle used in armored cavalry units starting in January 1969.

**Sherwood Forest** code for an operation that set fire to large areas of land.

**shifting fire** moving artillery targets.

**Shining Brass** code name for the covert U.S. Army SPECIAL FORCES raids and RECONNAISSANCE missions into Laos, starting in 1965. Shining Brass was renamed Prairie Fire in 1968 and Phu Dung in 1971.

**shit city** slang for a bad place to be, anywhere in Vietnam.

**shit-burning detail** burning the cesspools used by GIs with diesel fuel or kerosene to sanitize them. While burning they had to be stirred constantly with a long pole. Sometimes a Vietnamese was paid to do this job, and he was nicknamed "Willie, the shit-burner."

**Shithook** slang for the CH–47 helicopter (Chinook), because of the shit that got stirred up by the large rotors. Also called Go-Go and the hook.

**shitter** slang for latrine.

**shoot an azimuth** slang expression for getting a compass reading.

**shoot and scoot** slang for an artillery technique in which a unit moves away quickly after firing to avoid receiving return fire.

**shoot me a hus** marine slang for "do me a favor." Also expressed as "cut me a hus."

**short** when a tour in Vietnam was almost over, one was considered to be short, as "I'm so short I can parachute down from a dime."

**short final**     the moment just before a helicopter touched down.

**short rounds**     1. rounds of ammunition or bombs falling short of their target. 2. the accidental delivery of ORDNANCE, resulting in injury or death to FRIENDLY forces or to rear area personnel. 3. slang for ARTILLERY rounds that accidentally fell too close to friendly positions.

**short-arm inspection**     slang leftover from earlier wars for medical checks of the genitals for signs of venereal disease.

**short-time**     slang for brief sexual intercourse.

**short-timer**     soldier with just a few weeks or days before the end of his tour.

**short-timer's calendar**     a sheet of paper about 8 × 10, numbered from one through 365 (395 for Marines), to record a tour of duty. Each number represented one day of a one-year tour in Vietnam and squares were numbered and blackened one day at a time. When one filled in number 365, the tour in Vietnam was over.

**short-timer's fever**     a common disorder toward the end of a soldier's tour of duty. Those with this disorder became less efficient and grew hostile and suspicious. The short-timer tried to keep a low profile so as to not get killed before he could board the FREEDOM BIRD home.

**short-timer's stick**     the stick a soldier marked when he had approximately two months of his tour in Vietnam remaining. He made a notch in a

long stick for each of his remaining days in-country. As each day passed he would cut another notch off the stick until on his last day, all that he had left was a small stub.

**shotgun**     1. armed guard on or in a vehicle who watched for enemy activity and returned fire if attacked. 2. a bodyguard. 3. a DOOR GUNNER on a helicopter. Also called shotgun guard and shotgunner.

**shotgunning**     slang for blowing marijuana smoke down a rifle barrel.

**Shoup, David M.**     commandant of the U.S. Marine Corps, 1960–1964.

**shrapnel**     pieces of sharp, hot metal sent flying by an explosion. Shrapnel from hand grenades, mortar rounds, and artillery shells caused many injuries and deaths in Vietnam.

**Shrike**     nickname for the AGM–45 air-to-ground radar-seeking missile.

**shrine**     slang for latrine.

**SHUFLY**     the designation for the Marine Aviation Team Unit in South Vietnam, deploying marine helicopters with the support of fixed-wing aircraft. SHUFLY began in April 1962; in January 1965 it was renamed Marine Unit, Vietnam (MUV).

**SI**     abbr. for Seriously Ill.

**Si Quan Mỹ**     Vietnamese for American officer.

**sick bay commando**     slang for a recruit who gets ill when it is time to work.

**sick call**     phrase for formation or line-up of the sick or those who needed medical attention.

**Sides, John H.**  commander in chief, Pacific Fleet, 1960–1963.

**Sidewinder**  any of several heat-seeking (infrared) missiles developed by the U.S. Navy.

**SIDS**  abbr. for SEISMIC INTRUSION DEVICES.

**sierra**  1. military phonetic for the letter S. 2. radio code for South. Sierra Echo would indicate Southeast.

**Sig**  abbr. for Signal.

**signal hill**  elevated ground on which communication antennas were mounted.

**Sihanouk, Norodom**  king of Cambodia, 1941–1955, and premier of Cambodia, 1955–1960. He was the neutral head of state from 1960 to 1970 and overthrown by Prime Minister LON NOL in 1970. After being restored as head of state in 1975 he resigned in 1976.

**Sihanouk Trail, The**  the supply route running from the coast of Cambodia to the HO CHI MINH TRAIL. This series of dirt roads connected with the Ho Chi Minh Trail at the point where Cambodia, Laos, and South Vietnam met. War supplies and rice were moved from North Vietnam to South Vietnam along the Sihanouk Trail.

**silent majority**  this term was first used by President Richard Nixon in a speech on November 3, 1969, referring to American citizens who supported his program for peace with honor in Vietnam.

**Silver Bayonet**  a mission to assist the defense of key South Vietnamese U.S. installations near PLEIKU.

**Silver Star**  the fifth highest U.S. military decoration, awarded for gallantry and bravery in action against the enemy. It ranks just below the Distinguished Service Medal.

**sin loi (xin loi)**  a Vietnamese phrase meaning "Sorry about that." The Americans used the words in fun, but the Vietnamese were very serious when they used it.

**S-ing**  aerial term for performing a series of S turns.

**single-digit midget**  slang for a SHORT-TIMER with nine days or less to serve in Vietnam. Also called single-digit fidget.

**Sioux**  an observation helicopter manufactured by Bell and used by the Army. It was nicknamed Bubble and Bubble Top.

**Sir Charles**  slang for the Viet Cong soldier.

**sit map**  the map indicating the position of allied and enemy troops.

**sit rep**  abbr. for Situation Report, a report on the condition of a unit or a command. Sit reps stated casualties, equipment broken or lost, security, and so forth.

**Sit Rep Alpha Sierra**  radio talk for Situation Report All Secure.

**six**  1. radio call sign for the unit commander or radio call for a unit commander. 2. aerial term for a six o-clock position or area, referring to the rear or the aft area of an aircraft.

**six, six, and a kick**  marine slang for a punishment of six months' confinement, six months' loss of pay, and a bad-conduct discharge. This was usually given for a serious offense such as drug use or an act of sabotage.

**six, the**   any unit commander, from the company commander upward.

**six-by**   a large flat-bed truck, usually with wooden slat sides enclosing the bed and sometimes a canvas top covering it, used for carrying men, supplies, or equipment. It was called a six-by because of its wheel layout. Sometimes spelled six-bye, it was also known as a "deuce and a half."

**sixteen**   short for M–16 RIFLE.

**six-two-six**   term for commanders speaking to each other.

**sixty-six file**   the military records of officers, the equivalent of the 201 FILE of enlisted men and women.

**skate**   slang for a task or accomplishment that required little effort or pain.

**Skid Row**   slang for a North Vietnamese punishment camp for POWs southwest of Hanoi.

**skid-lid**   slang for a parachutist's helmet.

**skinship**   see SLICK.

**skirmish**   a very minor engagement with the enemy.

**skirmish line**   a marine combat formation, where every other marine walked just a few feet behind. This formation was used for assaulting enemy positions.

**skivvy**   1. slang for prostitute. 2. slang for underwear, usually not worn by the soldiers in Vietnam.

**SKS**   Soviet semiautomatic rifle, a 7.62 bolt-action carbine.

**skunk**   radar term for an unidentified radar blip.

**sky**   slang meaning to leave or move out quickly.

**Sky Crane**   see CH–54.

**Sky Knight**   See F–3D.

**sky out**   slang meaning to flee, or to leave suddenly.

**sky pilot**   slang for a chaplain.

**Sky Six**   slang for God (a six is a unit commander).

**Sky Soldiers**   1. nickname for those of the 173d Airborne Brigade, the first major army combat unit sent into Vietnam in May 1965 because they were parachute-qualified. Also called The Herd. 2. nickname for the Hmong GUERRILLAS who fought for the CIA.

**sky trooper**   nickname for members of the First Air Cavalry Division.

**sky up**   slang for taking a trip, especially in a plane or a helicopter.

**Skyhawk**   see A–4.

**Skymaster**   the Cessna twin-engined Super Skymaster (O–2), nicknamed the Mixmaster and the Push-me Pull-you.

**Skyraider**   see A–1E.

**skyspot**   1. radar controlled bombing and radar-directed bombing missions. 2. computer-controlled airstrikes that could be called in on known coordinates during the night or during bad weather.

**Skywarrior**   see A–3.

**Slack**   the second man in a patrol, walking just behind the POINT man. He gave the point immediate support, or "took up his slack." He was also called the Slackman.

**Slackman**  the second man behind the POINT man. He was also called the Slack.

**slagging rag**  slang for a slow opening or malfunctioning parachute.

**SLAM**  1. abbr. for Seeking, Locating, Annihilating, and Monitoring operations (U.S) to coordinate RECONNAISSANCE and fire-power resources in concentrated attacks by fire. 2. abbr for Supersonic Low-Altitude Missile. 3. Seventh Air Force commander's tactic involving the coordination of heavy fire support with B–52 tactical air support and navy gunfire and artillery. 4. nickname for S.L.A. Marshall, a brigadier general during the Vietnam War and a military historian.

**Slam Zones**  abbr. for Seek, Locate, Annihilate, and Monitor Zones.

**slant**  derogatory slang for a Vietnamese.

**slapflare**  hand-held FLARE shaped like a paper towel cylinder.

**SLAR**  abbr. for Side Looking Airborne (or Aerial) Radar, a high-resolution radar imaging system for target discrimination that was used for detecting camouflaged targets.

**Slaughter Alley**  nickname for the zone extending from Yen Bai to Haiphong in northern North Vietnam to Ha Tinh in the south. It was called Slaughter Alley because of the heavy U.S. bombing raids there.

**slice**  aerial expression for a maximum performance hard descending turn with more than 90 degrees of bank.

**slick**  1. a UH–1 helicopter used as a troop carrier in tactical air assault operations, or as a light cargo carrier in logistical support operations. The helicopter did not have protruding armaments and was, therefore, "slick." Also called a skinship. 2. term usually referring to HUEYS.

**slicksleeve**  slang for a private E–1, because he had no stripes on his sleeve.

**sliding into some new arms**  slang for putting on a clean shirt.

**slope**  derogatory slang for an Oriental who was also called dink, gook, slant and other insulting terms.

**slopshoot**  marine slang for junk food. Also called geedunk.

**slow CAP**  Combat Air Patrol's slower aircraft, such as the EC–121, the B–52, or the B–66. Compare to FAST CAP.

**SLUF**  abbr. for Short Little Ugly Fellow, or Short Little Ugly Fucker, slang for the A–7 Corsair attack aircraft.

**SM**  abbr. for Sergeant Major.

**SM–54**  a CS GRENADE.

**smacker**  slang for drug user. Also called a head.

**small arms**  handguns and rifles.

**small white pill**  pill taken daily to prevent malaria. See DAPSONE.

**smart bomb**  LASER-GUIDED BOMBS (LGBs) and electro-optically guided bombs (EOGBs). Compare to DUMB BOMBS, or conventional bombs.

**smear**  slang for using napalm on a target.

**smelling apple pie**   slang phrase for getting close to a ROTATION out of Vietnam.

**Smell-O-Meter**   slang for a radar device that used body heat and smell to detect the enemy. See PEOPLE SNIFFER.

**SMG**   abbr. for submachine gun.

**Smiling Jack**   a shark alert in water operations. Also called Jack.

**Smith-Corona commandos**   slang for clerks, also frequently called clerks and jerks, Remington Rangers, and other names.

**Smitty Harris**   See SMITTY HARRIS TAP CODE.

**Smitty Harris Tap Code**   nickname for the alphabet code that POWs used to communicate with each other by tapping on prison walls. The code consisted of 25 letters (all except K) in a 5 by 5 arrangement. It was believed that Smitty Harris, who bailed out of his aircraft and spent seven years as a POW in North Vietnamese camps, devised the code.

SMITTY HARRIS TAP CODE
First digit = row
Second digit = column
Example

| | | | |
|---|---|---|---|
| V | 5 | - | 1 |
| I | 2 | - | 4 |
| E | 1 | - | 5 |
| T | 4 | - | 4 |
| N | 3 | - | 3 |
| A | 1 | - | 1 |
| M | 3 | - | 2 |

| A | B | C | D | E |
|---|---|---|---|---|
| F | G | H | I | J |
| L | M | N | O | P |
| Q | R | S | T | U |
| V | W | X | Y | Z |

(For K, use C)

For example, to tap out "Vietnam," the prisoner would signal each letter by tapping out its coordinates, first horizontal rows 1 through 5 and then in columns 1 through 5, with a brief pause in between, using this matrix. Thus each letter was represented by two series of taps.

**smoke**   slang for a colored SMOKE GRENADE.

**Smoke 'em if you got 'em**   announcement of a work break.

**smoke grenade**   the M–18 grenade that released brightly colored smoke, used for signaling. Available in four colors—violet, green, yellow, and red—the top part of the grenade matched the color of the smoke it discharged.

**smoke stack**   smoke rising from an enemy's rifle fire disclosing his position.

**smoked, getting**   pilot's term for being shot down.

**Smokey Bear or Smokey the Bear**   nickname for C–47 or UH–1 Huey aircraft used to drop illuminating FLARES or to employ a helicopter-mounted smoke generator which could lay screens of smoke during assault or recovery operations.

**smoking lamp**   marine term for permission to smoke. At boot camp, smoking was allowed only when the smoking lamp was lit.

**SM651 El**   a CS cartridge fired from a M–79 GRENADE LAUNCHER.

**Smudge pots**   slang for the flaming pots which surrounded fire support bases.

**Snack**   see MENU.

**SNAFU** abbr. for Situation Normal All Fucked Up, used facetiously.

**snake** 1. slang for COBRA attack gunship. 2. slang for taking a nap.

**Snake Eaters** slang for SPECIAL FORCES.

**snake eye** slang for the electronic heat sensor MQ74.

**snakeye bomb** the 500-pound bombs used on low-altitude missions.

**snakey-nape** slang for the combination of SNAKEYE BOMB and NAPALM.

**snap-roll** 1. an aerial maneuver in which an aircraft is made to do a fast, complete roll about its longitudinal axis. 2. the act of putting an aircraft into a snap-roll.

**snap-up** aerial term for a rapid pull-up to establish a climb and gain altitude to launch a weapon against an enemy aircraft at a higher altitude.

**SNB** abbr. for SNEEB.

**SNCC** abbr. for Student Nonviolent Coordinating Committee, a civil rights organization that brought many northern college students to the south to help register black voters during the early and mid-1960s.

**Sneaky Petes** 1. slang for U.S. SPECIAL FORCES personnel. 2. slang for LRRPs.

**Sneeb** a twin Beech plane called a C–45 by the U.S. Air Force, and used by the U.S. Navy and Marine Corps, also called SNB. It was nicknamed the Bugsmasher.

**snoop 'n' poop** slang for a Marine SEARCH AND DESTROY offensive mission or a RECON patrol.

**Snoopy's Nose** slang for the large curve in the Rach Ba Rai River in the Delta.

**snuffy** 1. slang for a soldier doing a menial or unimportant job. 2. any low-ranking Marine or an enlisted man.

**Snuol** a village in Cambodia where a large ammunition depot and enemy forces were located.

**Snuol, to** slang meaning to obliterate or destroy, taken from the successful engagement with the North Vietnamese Army in Snuol, Cambodia, in 1970.

**soap rounds** rounds of soap used by soldiers to safely kill rats in enclosed areas. Bullets were removed from the chamber of the M–16 and replaced with a piece of soap, leaving in a small quantity of powder. The M–16 could then be fired at the rats in a hootch or bunker without endangering other soldiers.

**Socialist Republic of Vietnam** in 1975, after North Vietnam defeated South Vietnam, the newly reunited country took this name.

**socks** a highly important item for grunts who needed supplies of clean socks to help keep their feet free of rashes and diseases. Often socks were also used to carry metal C-RATION cans.

**soft bomb** a fragmenting explosive bomb. Also called a CBU or funny bomb.

**soft ordnance** euphemism for NAPALM.

**soft target** military term for a person, as contrasted to a HARD TARGET such as a building or something made of stone or steel.

**SOG** abbr. for Studies and Observations Groups. This was the part of MACV that dealt with unconventional warfare and carried out highly secret missions in Southeast Asia.

**SOI** abbr. for Signal Operating Instructions. SOI was the booklet that contained the call signs and radio frequencies of the various units in Vietnam.

**SOL** abbr. for Shit Outta Luck.

**Soldier's Medal** the fifth highest award for heroism, in recognition of heroism not involving actual combat with an enemy, but involving personal hazard and voluntary risk of life. It ranks just below the DISTINGUISHED FLYING CROSS.

**Son Tay Prison** a prisoner-of-war camp about 25 miles north of Hanoi, where U.S. prisoners were believed to have been held.

**Son Tay Raid** the 1970 raid on the Son Tay prison compound north of Hanoi to rescue American prisoners of war held there. The raiders found that the prisoners had been moved to other locations, and the mission ended. The United States did learn, however, that prisoners who had been dispersed all over North Vietnam were now mainly together in the HANOI HILTON. This raised morale among the POWs.

**sông** Vietnamese for river or stream.

**SOP** abbr. for Standard Operating Practice or Procedure.

**Sopwith Camels** slang for light, fixed-wing reconnaissance aircraft.

**sorry 'bout that** a common saying in Vietnam (*sin loi* or *xin loi* in Vietnamese). When used by the Vietnamese it was meant sincerely, but American troops often used it in a sarcastic way.

**sortie** 1. one aircraft making one takeoff and landing for a scheduled mission. 2. a single aircraft flying a single mission.

**Souieee** slang for the EB–66 aircraft.

**Soul Alley** see SOUL CITY.

**soul brother** a black soldier or marine.

**Soul City** nickname for an area of Saigon's TU DO STREET that contained bars and brothels visited solely by black soldiers. This section was also called Soul Alley. Although there was voluntary segregation in recreational areas or on bases, out in the FIELD U. S. soldiers of all races fought side by side.

**Soulsville** a section of Saigon, in Khanh Hoi, with bars and brothels where black soldiers hung out.

**sound off** shouting or complaining.

**South Vietnam Civil Actions Medal/Unit Citation Badge** a medal awarded by the South Vietnamese government to U.S. individuals or units for meritorious service.

**South Vietnam Gallantry Cross/ Unit Badge** an award by the South Vietnamese government to an American unit for valorous combat action.

**South Vietnamese time** civil time in South Vietnam was one hour ahead of both GOLF TIME and North Vietnamese civil time.

**Southern Christian Leadership Conference** a group founded in 1957 and headed by Dr. Martin Luther King, Jr. It organized nonviolent campaigns for the rights and integration of blacks.

**souvenir** Vietnamese expression, distorted from the French, meaning to give without cost.

**souvenir me** phrase a Vietnamese woman would use when she wanted something from a soldier. She would say "Souvenir me," referring to money, cigarettes, stockings, perfume, a ride, or other desired objects.

**SP** 1. abbr. for Shore Patrol (or Police). 2. abbr. for Self-Propelled.

**Sp/5** abbr. for a Specialist Fifth Class, equivalent to a sergeant.

**Sp/4** abbr. for a SPECIALIST FOURTH CLASS, equivalent to a corporal.

**SP Pack** abbr. for Special Purpose Package, a box containing an assortment of candies, cigarettes, matches, toilet articles, writing papers, pens, and other sundries. These packs were issued free of charge to all combat units.

**Sp Trps** abbr. for Special Troops.

**space cadet** slang for a young pilot who shows off.

**Spad** nickname for A–1 single-engine fighter plane widely used in the Vietnam War. It was also nicknamed Sandy.

**Sparrow** nickname for the AIM–7 radar-guided missile carried by the F–4 in Vietnam. It could attack an unseen enemy aircraft.

**SPD** abbr. for Separation Program Designator. See SPN.

**Speaker** brand name of a P–38 can opener.

**Spec** abbr. for specialist.

**Spec-4** abbr. for SPECIALIST FOURTH CLASS.

**Special Feces** derogatory slang for SPECIAL FORCES.

**Special Forces** designation for U.S. soldiers trained in the techniques of guerrilla warfare. In Vietnam, Special Forces carried out many covert counterinsurgency operations. They also trained the South Vietnamese and MONTAGNARDS in counterinsurgency and antiguerrilla warfare. Special Forces soldiers were popularly known as Green Berets because they were awarded the green berets as distinctive emblems.

**Special Forces Prayer** " Y e a though I walk through the valley of the shadow of death, I will fear no evil, for I am the meanest motherfucker in the valley." (also known as Airborne Prayer, Infantryman's Prayer, Marine's Prayer, and so forth).

**Special Forces Project Delta** an elite United States and South Vietnamese long-range RECONNAISSANCE group. See PROJECT DELTA.

**Special Landing Force** a rotating marine reserve battalion serving aboard ships of the navy's Seventh Fleet. This battalion took part in operations along the Vietnamese coast.

**special operations** military operations requiring special, elite, or nonroutine forces.

**special warfare** all military maneuvers and activities as well as those activities related to unconventional warfare. All PSYCHOLOGICAL OPERA-

TIONS and COUNTERINSURGENCY operations were considered to be special warfare.

**specialist** designation indicating expertise in a particular MOS, followed by a number indicating enlisted rank, as in Spec–4.

**Specialist Fourth Class** This was an enlisted rank immediately above PRIVATE FIRST CLASS. Most enlisted men who had completed their ADVANCED INDIVIDUAL TRAINING and had been on duty for a few months were Spec–4s. This was the most common rank in the Vietnam Era army.

**Specified Strike Zone** specific unpopulated areas of heavy jungle or swampland which could be cleared for firing for a certain period if U.S. military ground clearance had been obtained. When South Vietnamese military forces had an AREA OF OPERATION in the SSZ, ARVN clearance was also required. The term was coined in 1967 to replace the term FREE FIRE ZONE which had previously been called a Free Strike Zone and Fire Bombing Zone.

**Spectre** an AC–130 with MINIGUNS, VULCAN MACHINE GUNS, and a 105mm HOWITZER.

**speedbrakes** aerial term for flaps designed for slowing down an aircraft in flight.

**sperm** nickname for the Hughes OH–6 (LOH).

**spider hole** a camouflaged one-man foxhole, usually occupied by a VIET CONG soldier and often connected to a tunnel network. From this spot the Viet Cong could shoot at U.S. troops. A spider hole was also called a SPIDER TRAP.

**spider trap** see SPIDER HOLE.

**SPIES-rig** abbr. for Suspended Personnel Insertion-Extraction System, a method of inserting and extracting troops in dangerous situations. Similar to the MCGUIRE RIG and the STABO.

**spike pit** a booby trap set by the Viet Cong in which a person stepped on a bamboo trap causing him to drop down onto spikes.

**spike team** SOG RECONNAISSANCE teams made up of 12 men: 3 Americans and 9 indigenous soldiers. For code names, these teams used states of the United States, the names of poisonous snakes, and finally, tools.

**spikebuoy** a SENSOR mounted on a metal probe driven into the ground.

**spit shine** the mirrored shine put on leather by lengthy, tedious polishing.

**splash** radio code indicating that destruction of the target has been verified by visual means or by radar.

**splib** a term originated by black marines to identify other blacks. It was thought to imply superior qualities.

**split-plane maneuvering** aerial term for aircraft maneuvering in relation to one another, but in different planes or altitudes.

**split-S** aerial term for a 180 degree rotation about an aircraft's longitudinal axis followed by a 180 degree change of heading in a vertical plane.

**SPN** (pronounced spin) abbr. for Separation Program Number, which appeared on the discharge papers (DD214) of many honorably discharged Vietnam veterans. This number was usually printed on the DD214 in the block marked "reason and authority." Sometimes it was designated as SPD for Separation Program Designation or as TIN for Transaction Identification Number. SPN codes were often negative, such as 281 meaning "unsanitary habits," 361 for "homosexual tendencies," or 388, for "sexual perversions." The codes could also be neutral or positive, such as 201 for "expiration of term of service," or 202 for "expiration of term of enlistment." The negative codes usually had no basis, and were believed to have been added carelessly or randomly by clerks. After the war, many corporate personnel offices obtained lists of the SPN codes; this made getting a job another difficulty for some veterans. Starting in 1974, it became possible to secure a new copy of the DD214 discharge paper without the SPN code on request. It is also possible to correct an erroneous code. See RE CODES.

**spoiling attack** a tactical maneuver used to weaken a hostile attack.

**Sponson Box** the tool box on a tank fender.

**spook** 1. slang for a civilian intelligence agent. 2. slang for COUNTERINTELLIGENCE personnel.

**spook drop** slang for a high-speed small-team parachute INSERT, carried out at night.

**Spooky** 1. nickname for the C–47 armed aircraft with 7.62mm. GATLING guns and illumination FLARES. Spookys were large propeller-driven aircraft capable of firing 6,000 rounds per minute. 2. GUNSHIP helicopters equipped with miniguns, which were nicknamed Puff The Magic Dragon.

**spoon** slang for an Army cook.

**spotter plane** the small aircraft which indicated with colored smoke the front lines of friendly units and enemy targets.

**spotter round** the first round of mortar or artillery fire which was then adjusted until the rounds were on target.

**spray** slang for opening fire on the enemy, especially when using automatic fire.

**spread** an air force formation involving a basic fighting course with supporting units remaining near the leader.

**SPT** abbr. for Support.

**Sqdn** abbr. for Squadron; also abbreviated Sqdron.

**squad** in the U.S. Army and Marine Corps, the basic fighting element of usually 8 to 10 men commanded by a sergeant.

**squad bay** marine term for living quarters.

**squadron** in the U.S. Army, the squadron designated a battalion-sized unit of cavalry, commanded by a lieutenant colonel.

**square away** to put things in order.

**squared away** in order, or neat.

**squash bomber** slang for the THUNDERCHIEF F–105 aircraft.

**squawk** radio code for transmitting Identification Friend or Foe, IFF signals.

**squid** marine slang for sailors.

**SRAO** abbr. for Supplemental Recreational Activities Overseas, referring to the American RED CROSS.

**SRB** abbr. for Service Record Book, the file containing each marine's personal history and records.

**SRO** abbreviation for Senior Ranking Officer.

**SR–71** Lockheed's Blackbird, the fastest and highest flying air-breather in the world until it was retired by a budget-cutting Pentagon in January 1990.

**SRV** abbr. for Socialist Republic of Vietnam, North Vietnam.

**SS** 1. naval abbr. for Submarine. 2. naval abbr. for Steamship.

**SSgt** abbr. for staff sergeant.

**SSN** naval designation for Nuclear Powered Attack Submarine.

**SSS** abbr. for SELECTIVE SERVICE SYSTEM.

**SSZ** abbr. for SPECIFIED STRIKE ZONE.

**STAB** abbr. for SEAL Team Assault Boat.

**stability operation** an internal operation to reclaim order after a period of some form of violence.

**STABO** a torso harness rig with ring clips at the shoulders, similar to the MCGUIRE RIG. This device permitted a person to be picked up by a helicopter and taken to a safer area. It was frequently used by unconventional U.S. forces.

**stack trooper** slang for a model soldier.

**Staff Sergeant** an E–6, the second-lowest noncommissioned officer rank.

**stage** processing soldiers who are traveling from one area to another.

**stand in the door** airborne slang for the moment one steps out the door of an aircraft.

**standard arm** nickname for the AGM–78 air-to-ground missile, anti-radiation type.

**standdown** 1. an infantry unit's return from the FIELD to base camp for refitting and training, with the halting of all activity except that which is absolutely necessary for security. Standdown was usually a three-day rest period for troops coming out of the field. 2. preparation for the final movement of a unit back to the United States.

**starch** slang for plastic explosives.

**Stardust** nickname for an area of cells in the Las Vegas section of the North Vietnamese Hoa Lo Prison, the HANOI HILTON.

**Starlifter** Lockheed's intercontinental medium jet transport, the C–141.

**Starlight** 1. night RECONNAISSANCE or surveillance operation using a light-intensifier scope. 2. code for the first regimental-size U.S. battle in the Vietnam War. This marine operation took place near Chu Lai in August 1965.

**Starlight scope** an image magnifier that used reflected light from the stars or moon to illuminate targets. After the explosion of rockets or other fire, it would take the operator's eye some time to adjust to the darkness to use the scope.

**Stars and Stripes** U.S. military newspaper issued at no cost to military personnel outside the United States.

**Star shell** an illumination shell for artillery pieces.

**status SOL** abbr. for the slang phrase, status Shit-Out-of-Luck.

**steam and cream** slang for the services of a prostitute that included sauna, steam bath, massage, and then intercourse and/or fellatio. This was also called steam job and blow bath.

**steam job** see STEAM AND CREAM.

**steel pot** slang for the standard U.S. Army helmet with an outer metal cover.

**steering dot** aerial term for the electronic dot appearing on a radar scope when the radar is locked on, yielding computerized directional steering information.

**sterile** anything that was unmarked. A sterile weapon had no numbers on it and was, therefore, untraceable. A sterile uniform had no insignia.

**S–3** officer in charge of the operations and training section of a brigade or smaller unit.

**stick** slang for a group of paratroopers.

**sticks** slang for pants.

**Stieng** a MONTAGNARD tribe living mainly in BINH LONG and PHUOC LONG provinces.

**stiffs** slang for dead bodies.

**Stinger** nickname for the AC–119K GUNSHIP.

**stingray** marine RECONNAISSANCE patrols inserted to use artillery and air strikes to destroy the enemy.

**stingray patrols** a marine tactic in which five-man teams went out into the field and used *guerrilla* methods to confront the enemy. These missions were often successful; in 1968 their use was expanded.

**stitched** slang for killed.

**Stone Elephant, The** slang for the Officers' Club in Da Nang.

**stoppage** the failure of a weapon to fire.

**stopper** creating a barrier of fire to prevent enemy movement across a fortified line or area.

**Stormy Weather** code for the Cambodian border.

**Strac** 1. abbr. for Strategic Army Command or Strategic Army Corps. 2. abbr. for the slang expression Soldier Trained and Ready Around the Clock. 3. slang for a good soldier who sticks exactly to regulations. It was also spelled strack.

**strack** see STRAC.

**strafe** to fire machine guns or cannons from low-flying aircraft at targets on the ground.

**straight fin** a sarcastic term for one who is not SCUBA qualified. Also called guppy or fin.

**straight leg** see STRAIGHT LEG GRUNTS.

**straight leg division** slang for non-airborne army INFANTRY.

**straight leg grunts** slang for infantry who are not AIRBORNE, AIRMOBILE, nor transported in ARMORED

PERSONNEL CARRIERS, but were on foot, thus their legs were straight.

**straitjacket duty**  slang for an individual on limited offensive activities or an especially hazardous assignment.

**strap**  See STRAPHANGER.

**straphanger**  derogatory slang for personnel in the rear areas, also called pencil pusher and paper pusher and strap.

**Strategic Air Command (SAC)** the U.S. manned bomber and land-based missile nuclear strike force, which reported to the secretary of defense.

**strategic hamlet**  a small village created to house Vietnamese peasants and isolate them from the rural VIET CONG.

**strategic hamlet program**  a controversial pacification and village self-defense program implemented by the government of NGO DINH DIEM beginning in February 1962. This program attempted to turn all 16,000 South Vietnamese HAMLETS into fortified compounds by moving peasants off their farms and into fortified stockades to protect them from the Viet Cong. It was codenamed Sunrise; earlier names for this program were New Life Program and Ap Moi Hamlet Program.

**Stratofortress**  nickname for the B–52.

**Stratotanker**  Boeing's KC–135, used by the air force for air refueling. It was nicknamed the "flying gas station" and "gas station in the sky."

**stray**  slang for a lone enemy soldier.

**streamer**  a parachute that does not open all the way, but instead, streams or drags backward.

**Street without Joy**  nickname for Highway 1, the main supply route, in Vietnam.

**Strela missile**  a Soviet-made, heat-seeking ground-to-air missile supplied to the Viet Cong. It made its first appearance in Vietnam during the 1972 offensive and proved highly effective against low-flying planes and helicopters.

**Strieng**  a MONTAGNARD tribe living mainly in KONTUM Province.

**strike**  an attack on a surface target, with the goal of inflicting damage or destroying an enemy objective.

**strike CAP**  aircraft prepared for a primary strike role with a secondary air defense role. It was allowed to jettison strike ORDNANCE and engage the enemy only if they were under direct attack.

**striker**  1. slang for a navy enlisted man studying for advancement to a new rating or specialty. 2. a member of a SPECIAL FORCEs strike force. 3. a defender of a MONTAGNARD hamlet.

**string**  a group of hand-implanted SENSORS.

**strings**  helicopter slang for ropes.

**strip alert**  1. an armed aircraft on the ground at a forward strip able to take off within five minutes. 2. a state of readiness for a REACTION FORCE usually near an aircraft.

**strobe**  a hand-held light for marking LANDING ZONES at night.

**Studies and Observation Groups** SOG teams that performed clandestine operations throughout South Vietnam.

**stuffer** nickname for a parachute rigger, also called rag stuffer and trash bagger.

**stump jumper** slang for grunt. See INFANTRYMAN.

**S-turn** aerial term for a turn to one side of a reference heading followed by a turn to the other side. These maneuvers presented a difficult tracking problem for ground radar.

**S-2** officer in charge of the military intelligence section of a brigade or smaller unit.

**sự dôt kích** Vietnamese for assault.

**sự nguy hiểm** Vietnamese for danger.

**sự phá-hoại** Vietnamese for sabotage.

**sự tàn-sát** Vietnamese for massacre.

**subdued rank and insignia** rank and insignia in less colorful tones, worn inside headgear and uniforms to make men and officers less easily seen by the enemy.

**sub-gunny** slang for a substitute doorgunner.

**sugar reports** slang for mail from home, especially from a girlfriend. Although heard during World War II and the war in Korea, this term was still used in Vietnam.

**SUM** abbr. for Surface-to-Underwater Missile.

**súng cối** Vietnamese for mortar. Also spelled súng mot ché.

**súng không giật** Vietnamese for recoilless rifle.

**súng liên-thanh** Vietnamese for machine gun.

**súng lục** Vietnamese for pistol.

**súng mọt chê** Vietnamese for mortar. Also spelled súng coî.

**súng phun lửa** Vietnamese for flamethrower.

**súng trưởng** Vietnamese for rifle.

**Sunrise** code for the 1962 STRATEGIC HAMLET PROGRAM.

**SUPCOM** abbr. for Support Command.

**super grunt** nickname for a FORCE RECON marine.

**Super Jolly Green Giant** nickname for the HH–53 rescue and recovery helicopter manufactured by Sikorsky and used by the U.S. Air Force.

**Super Sabre** North American Aviation F–100 bomber used early in the Vietnam War. It was also called lead sled.

**super teargas** nickname for CS gas.

**super-chicken** slang for specialist–5 rank or above, in the army.

**Superskymaster** Cessna's twin-engined FAC aircraft, the 0–2. It was also known as the Push-Me, Pull-You and the Mixmaster.

**super-striper** slang for E–6 or above in the army.

**Supper** see MENU.

***supporting fire*** fire provided by supporting units to assist or fortify a unit in combat.

***suppression*** see RULES OF ENGAGEMENT.

***Supreme Six*** army call sign for God, also called Sky Six (A six is a unit commander.)

***Surprise Package*** code for the larger guns first tested in a modified AC–130A, meant to destroy enemy troops and their supply lines. This resulted in U.S. gunships being able to use higher, safer altitudes. They were tested and used in 1971 and 1972. At the war's end, the remaining AC–130s were kept by the USAF.

***Surv*** abbr. for Surveillance Aircraft.

***Surv L*** abbr. for Surveillance Light Aircraft.

***survival straws*** a special drinking straw with a built-in water-purifier.

***SUU–16*** gun pod containing the M–61 VULCAN 20mm cannon used on F–4C aircraft.

***SUU–23*** gun pod containing the M–61 VULCAN 20mm cannon used on F–4D aircraft.

***Suzy*** short for Suzy Robincrotch (also called Suzy Rottencrotch). She was the girl the soldier left behind to wait.

***SV*** abbr. for Security Vehicle.

***SVC*** abbr. for Service.

***SVN*** abbr. for South Vietnam (Republic of Vietnam).

***swab*** 1. to mop. 2. the mop itself.

***swabee*** derogatory term for a sailor.

***SWAG*** abbr. for Scientific Wild Ass Guess.

***Swamp Rats*** nickname for the First Battalion, 18th Infantry.

***Swatow*** a fast gunboat. The Red Chinese converted Russian P–6 torpedo boats into Swatow gunboats and supplied a number of them to North Vietnam.

***sweat hog*** derogatory slang for an overweight soldier, serving in the rear.

***sweep*** 1. an offensive mission by several fighter aircraft to seek out and attack enemy aircraft or targets of opportunity. 2. an operation in which troops would move through a village and check it out completely, known as a village sweep. 3. an operation for checking out a stream or river, known as a blue line sweep.

***sweeping operations*** RECONNAISSANCE IN FORCE.

***swift boats*** patrol craft, fast (PCF), small modified navy patrol boats used for close-in offshore security and inland waterway patrolling. They were 50 feet in length, with aluminum hulls and armed with MACHINE GUNS and MORTARS. One officer and four enlisted men were the usual crew. Often called swifts.

***Swifts*** see SWIFT BOATS.

***swinging man trap*** slang for a particularly harsh and destructive booby trap, the MALAY WHIP.

***switchblade*** an ambush which uses the enemy's own weapons.

***syrette*** a collapsible tube of morphine attached to a hypodermic needle used by medics for treating injuries on the battlefield. The contents of the tube were injected by squeezing it like a toothpaste tube.

# T

**T & T** short for a "through and through wound," one in which a bullet or fragment has both entered and exited the body.

**TAADS** abbr. for The Army Authorization Document System, which the Army used to preserve records. This system did not work very well in that Army records were often lost or accidentally destroyed.

**TA–50** an individual soldier's standard issue of combat clothing and equipment, his field gear.

**TA–4** a two-seater aircraft used by marine FACs in surveying the HO CHI MINH TRAIL.

**TA–1** a sound-powered telephone unit used in Vietnam.

**tabasco** slang for napalm.

**tac** abbr. for tactical.

**TAC** 1. abbr. for Tactical Commander. 2. abbr. for Tactical Air Command, a branch of the USAF designed to coordinate air operations with ground forces against the enemy. Also called TACAIR.

**TAC (A)** abbr. for Tactical Air Coordinator (Airborne).

**TAC Air** 1. abbr. for Tactical Air (air force) support, the fighter-bombers and ORDNANCE dropped on enemy targets as ground forces requested it. 2. abbr. for a Tactical Air Strike of two fighter aircraft, U.S. or ARVN, jets or propeller type, controlled by a FORWARD AIR CONTROLLER.

**tác chiến** Vietnamese for combat.

**tac wire** the tactical coiled wire entanglements used in breaking enemy attack formations.

**TACA** abbr. for Tactical Air Control Airborne, an aircraft designated to control flights operating against a particular target.

**TACAIR** see TAC.

**TACAN** abbr. for Tactical Air Navigation, an active electronic navigational system which located the aircraft with respect to another installation.

**TACC** abbr. for Tactical Air Control Center, the command center for all air activity within a specified sector. The joint US–VNAF center at TAN SON NHUT was responsible for control of all operations in South Vietnam. The Seventh Air Force—headquartered there also—was responsible for operations over North Vietnam and Laos.

**TACC (NS)** abbr. for Tactical Air Control Center, North Sector.

**TACC (SS)** abbr. for Tactical Air Control Center, South Sector.

**tactical air support** the employment of air force elements in combat in conjunction with ground operations.

**tactical area of responsibility** the exact territory for which a unit was responsible.

**tactical CS** CS gas, teargas. One type of tactical CS was stored in drums, carried in CH–47 CHINOOKS, and scattered by TNT. The CH–47s each carried 30-gallon drums of what was called persistent CS. Nonpersistent CS was scattered from a dispenser by 40mm containers loaded with a gaseous form of CS.

**tadpole** slang for the OH-6 Light Observation Helicopter. Also called sperm and white bird.

**tag and bag** slang for putting a tag on a body and putting it into a BODY BAG.

**Tai** a Vietnamese ethnic group living in the mountainous regions.

**tail** slang for the last man in a patrol.

**tail rotor chain bracelet** used tail rotor chains were worn by helicopter crews as bracelets. The chains cost the government approximately $95 per inch when new.

**taildragger** an aircraft with the two main wheels in front of the center of gravity, and one wheel at the tail.

**tail-end Charlie** slang for the last man in a patrol, usually responsible for rear security. Also called TEC.

**Takhli** a U.S. air base in Thailand.

**Takua** a MONTAGNARD tribe living mainly in QUANG NAM and QUANG TIN provinces.

**talk quick** a system of secure communication.

**Tally Ho** 1. code for air reconnaissance and attack missions north of and near the Demilitarized Zone in 1966. 2. interdiction strikes into the southern portion of North Vietnam. 3. in radio communications code, a term meaning "I have the target in sight" or visual contact made with an enemy aircraft or bandit.

**Talon Vise** original code name for operation Frequent Wind, the final U.S. evacuation of U.S. embassy and military personnel in Saigon in April 1975.

**Tam An** capital of LONG AN Province.

**Tam Ky** capital of QUANG TIN Province.

**tấn công** Vietnamese for attack.

**Tan Son Nhut** the large U.S. air base on the outskirts of Saigon. The airfield was used by commercial and military aviation traffic throughout the war, making it one of the busiest airfields in the world. Tan Son Nhut was headquarters for General William Westmoreland and the MACV. It was nicknamed Pentagon East.

**tanglefoot** single strand barbed wire strung in a meshwork pattern at about ankle height. Acting as a barrier, it made crossing the obstructed area by foot difficult. It was usually placed around permanent defense positions.

**tango** military phonetic for the letter T.

**tango boat** U.S. Navy designation of a landing boat modified for waterborne operations in the MEKONG RIVER DELTA. They were armored landing craft mounted with .50-caliber machine guns, and modified to carry troops on RIVERINE operations.

**Tango Charlie** code for a request for a time check.

**tank farm** a group of storage tanks.

**tanker bar** a tool used on tanks and tracked vehicles.

**tanker's grenade**   two pounds of TNT wrapped together with barbed wire and sections of chain.

**TAOI**   abbr. for Tactical Area Of Influence, the place where enemy activity could influence operations in an area of responsibility.

**TAOR**   abbr. for Tactical Area of Operational Responsibility. A specified area of land for which responsibility is assigned to a commander who controls the forces and directs the support.

**tape and turn**   1. taping two BANANA CLIPS together, each holding 30 rounds of ammunition. 2. fastening two small-arms magazines together with tape so that when one is empty, the other can be inserted by removing and reversing them in one swift movement.

**taps**   bugle call played at lights out and at the end of certain ceremonies.

**tar**   slang for hashish.

**tar baby**   slang for soldier addicted to hashish.

**TARCAP**   abbr. for Target Combat Air Patrol. This was a section of fighters positioned near an airborne strike force for its protection to and from the target. The primary mission was to discourage rather than to destroy the threat aircraft.

**TARFU**   abbr. for Things Are Really Fucked Up.

**Tarhe**   a heavy CH–54 army transport helicopter, also known as the sky crane, manufactured by Sikorsky. (Tarhe was a Wyandot Indian chief whose name meant The Crane.)

**tarmac**   the large metal plates used as helicopter landing pads or as runways for small planes.

**Tarzan**   slang for a grunt in an infantry platoon who volunteers to be the POINTMAN.

**TAS**   abbr. for True Air Speed, in knots. This was the calibrated airspeed corrected for density and altitude factors.

**task force**   a temporary grouping of units under one commander for a specific mission.

**Task Force Alpha**   code for the infiltration surveillance center first located at TAN SON NHUT Air Base and then moved to NAKHON PHANOM RTAFB (Royal Thai Air Force Base), where IGLOO WHITE data were collected.

**Task Force 1**   see CCN.

**Task Force 75**   code for the group responsible for the evacuation of Saigon.

**Task Force 76**   this group had the responsibility for amphibious action. Many amphibious assaults were made during the Vietnam War particularly in I CORPS.

**Task Force 3**   see CCS.

**Task Force 2**   see CCC.

**taxi girl**   a prostitute who hung around bases to make money.

**Taylor, Maxwell D.**   chief of staff, U.S. Army, January–July 1959; chairman, Joint Chiefs of Staff, 1961–1964; ambassador to South Vietnam, 1964–1965. See MISSION COUNCIL.

**Tay Ninh**   one of the 44 provinces of South Vietnam, located in III CORPS.

**Tay Ninh City**   capital of TAY NINH Province.

**TB**   abbr. for tù binh, Vietnamese for prisoners of war.

**t-block**   the plastic plug put into a rifle breech to prevent it from firing accidentally.

**tbo**   aviation slang for time before overhaul.

**TBS**   abbr. for Talk Between Ships (or planes).

**TC**   1. abbr. for Tank Commander. 2. abbr. for Tactical Commander.

**teach-ins**   night-long university meetings at campuses across America regarding Vietnam issues. The first teach-in met at the University of Michigan in 1965, with faculty members discussing the war. This was followed throughout the United States by faculty members holding teach-ins for students to discuss and often oppose the escalation of the war.

**team**   1. an A detachment of 12 SPECIAL FORCES soldiers. 2. a small or temporary military unit with a specific task.

**team uniform**   the UHF radio frequency on which a team communicates. Also called company uniform. These radio frequencies were changed often to confuse any enemy surveillance.

**TEC**   abbr. for Tail-End Charlie, slang for the last person in a line of a patrol usually responsible for rear security.

**Tee-Tee (ti-ti)**   Vietnamese for very small or little.

**10**   grade for a general in the U.S. Army, Marine Corps, and Air Force

(admiral in the U.S. Navy). The symbol for this rank is four stars.

**Tên ông là gì?**   Vietnamese for What is your name?

**terminate with extreme prejudice**   a CIA term for killing people.

**Territorial Forces Evaluation System**   a companion program to the HAMLET EVALUATION SYSTEM. This was a computerized military evaluation system devised by American authorities in Saigon to assess the readiness of the militia forces. Each month, advisors at the DISTRICT level had to fill out long computer printout sheets and report on many different aspects of quantity and quality in the militia forces.

**Tet**   1. the Buddhist lunar New Year. 2. Buddha's birthday. 3. Vietnamese lunar new year festival, celebrated as a national holiday. The date fluctuates each year around late January/early February. 4. the first countrywide North Vietnamese offensive against South Vietnamese cities and towns took place between January 30, 1968, and February 29, 1968. See TET OFFENSIVE.

**Tet Counteroffensive**   campaign from January 30 to April 1, 1968. See CAMPAIGN.

**Tet Offensive**   a major uprising of VIET CONG, VC sympathizers, and the North Vietnamese Army carried out as a series of coordinated attacks against military installations and provincial capitals throughout Vietnam. It occurred during the lunar New Year at the end of January 1968 and is often referred to simply as TET. The Tet Offensive is thought to be the turning point of the war insofar as it caused the

U.S. public's support of the war to drop. President Lyndon Johnson announced soon after the Tet offensive that he would not seek reelection.

**Tet Room**  nickname for a section of the North Vietnamese Hoa Lo Prison, called HANOI HILTON.

**Tet '69 Counteroffensive**  campaign from February 28, to June 8, 1969. See CAMPAIGN.

**Tetracycline**  antibiotic widely administered in Vietnam in an attempt to prevent venereal disease.

**TF**  abbr. for TASK FORCE.

**TFES**  abbr. for TERRITORIAL FORCES EVALUATION SYSTEM.

**T–54**  a Soviet-made heavy tank supplied to the Viet Cong.

**TF–115**  Task Force 115. See MARKET TIME.

**TF–117**  Task Force 117. See MOBILE RIVERINE FORCE.

**TF–116**  Task Force 116. See GAME WARDEN.

**TFR**  abbr. for Terrain Following Radar. This was installed on some U.S. aircraft to chart the ground ahead and find obstacles.

**TFX**  see F–111.

**T.H. Agriculture and Nutrition**  one of the chemical companies that manufactured the defoliant AGENT ORANGE.

**thám-thính**  Vietnamese for reconnaissance.

**thân or thân thể²**  Vietnamese for body.

**Thanh Hoa**  a small North Vietnam port which was mined, immobilizing shipping.

**Thanh Hoa Bridge**  see BRIDGE AT THANH HOA.

**thanh-tra**  Vietnamese for surveillance.

**there it is**  an expression frequently used by grunts meaning "you're right" or "that's the way it is," to agree or confirm.

**thermite**  a mixture of finely powdered metallic aluminum and ferric oxide. When ignited, it produces very high temperatures. A brand name was Thermit.

**thermite grenade**  an incendiary grenade (AN–M14), made of metal and filled with THERMITE. It was used to set fires or to melt metal.

**Thieu, Nguyen Van**  see NGUYEN VAN THIEU.

**thiếu úy**  Vietnamese for second lieutenant.

**thing, the**  marine slang for the ONTOS, their tank-killer vehicle armed with six 106mm recoilless rifles.

**things-on-the-springs**  slang for an equipment inspection. It was also known as junk-on-the-bunk.

**third force**  generic expression used to designate, especially after the PARIS PEACE ACCORDS, all the various non-Communist organizations in opposition to the regime of South Vietnamese President Nguyen Van Theiu. The term generally referred to those who wanted peace negotiations rather than the continuation of the war.

**third hat**  slang for the assistant drill instructor in charge of discipline.

**third herd**   slang for any unit designated as the third.

**Thirty-Three**   name of a local Vietnamese beer.

**thirty-four A**   a series of covert operations in North Vietnamese waters planned by Americans and carried out in early 1964 by the South Vietnamese. Attempting to halt North Vietnamese infiltration into South Vietnam, these operations were intended to threaten North Vietnamese ports. This plan was kept secret from the American public.

**Thompson Chemical**   one of the companies that manufactured the defoliant AGENT ORANGE.

**Tho, Le Duc**   see LE DUC THO.

**Thong Nhut Blvd**   the street in Saigon where the U.S. embassy was located.

**Thot Not**   see   PROJECT DANIEL BOONE.

**thousand-yard stare**   slang for the characteristic, far-away look of the soldier who has been in combat for a long time and has seen too much.

**three**   radio call sign for the operations officer, the staff officer in charge of plans and operations. The operations officer is also known as G–3.

**III–A**   according to SELECTIVE SERVICE classification, someone registered for the draft with a child or children, or a registrant deferred by reason of extreme hardship to his dependents.

**III Corps**   the third allied MILITARY REGION extending from the Mekong Delta to the Southern Central Highlands.

**three finger fuck around**   slang for an activity with no purpose.

**three hairs**   slang for a Vietnamese female, who generally had sparse pubic hair.

**three heart rule**   a rule, not always enforced, that a soldier awarded three purple hearts for wounds received in the field, would be sent back to THE WORLD.

**III Maf**   (pronounced three maf) abbr. for Third Marine Amphibious Force, the overall marine command in Vietnam.

**Three point C and B**   slang for a bad parachute landing. The three points referred to "heels, ass, and head," while the C and B stood for "crash and burn."

**three-quarter**   short for a three-quarter-ton truck.

**three up and three down**   slang for a master sergeant, called that because of the configuration of his stripes.

**three up and two down**   slang for a sergeant first class or platoon sergeant, called that because of the configuration of his stripes.

**three-whisker mine**   slang for an M–16 mine.

**throttle jockey**   air force slang for a fighter pilot.

**Thua Thien**   one of the 44 provinces of South Vietnam, located in I CORPS.

**Thud**   1. nickname for the F–105 THUNDERCHIEF, Republic Aircraft's medium attack aircraft. Also called Squash Bomber, Ultra Hot, and Lead

Sled. 2. a plane crash or being shot down.

**Thud Ridge** 1. nickname for a mountain range beginning about 20 miles north-northwest of Hanoi and extending about 25 miles northwest, used for navigation. 2. air force slang for a hill near Hanoi, the site of a Thud aircraft attack that became a navigational landmark for F–105 pilots.

**Thue Do** Vietnamese for the mild antiseptic used by the VC.

**thump-gun** nickname for the M–79 GRENADE LAUNCHER or any 40mm grenade launcher.

**thumper** nickname for the M–79 GRENADE LAUNCHER.

**Thunderbird** nickname for a part of the North Vietnamese Hoa Lo Prison, the HANOI HILTON.

**Thunder Road** nickname for Vietnam's Highway 13. See THUNDER RUN and HIGHWAY 13.

**Thunder Run** slang for the movement of ARMORED UNITS up and down a trail or road, firing from side to side. This tactic included columns of tanks and armored personnel carriers racing along the road firing H & I fire into suspected enemy areas. This would prevent the enemy from ambushing them, or mining the area. Much of this activity took place on Highway 13, nicknamed Thunder Run or Thunder Road.

**Thunderchief** nickname for Republic aircraft's F–105.

**thuốc nổ** Vietnamese for explosives.

**Thủy Quân Lục Chiến** Vietnamese for marine corps.

**thuyền** Vietnamese for boat.

**THVN** abbr. for Tryen Hinh Vietnam, the Civil TV Network of Vietnam.

**TIC** abbr. for Target Information Center, a part of the Division Tactical Operational Center (DOTC) designed to convert source information into targeting information.

**ticket** slang for a tag filled out by a MEDIC describing a serviceman's wounds. One copy went along with the soldier to an aid station, field hospital, or home.

**ticket-punching** the policy of putting officers into the field for only a six-month period, which helped ensure their promotion but did not expose them to combat for too long a time, as in "just long enough to get his ticket punched."

**Tien Phong** a VIET CONG magazine.

**Tien Van Dung** chief of staff of the Vietnam People's Army who directed the BATTLE OF 55 DAYS.

**tiếng nổ** Vietnamese for explosion.

**tiếp-tế-phẩm** Vietnamese for supplies.

**tiểu doàn** Vietnamese for battalion.

**tiểu dôi** Vietnamese for squad.

**tieu to** Vietnamese term for the organizational cells of the Chi Bo, the lowest LAO DONG party unit, similar to a chapter.

**Tiger beer** slang for Biere La Rue, a brand of beer brewed in Saigon, with the silhouette of a tiger on the label.

Tiger beer was milder than Ba Me Ba and came in larger bottles.

**tiger cages**    the cells at the Poulo Condor Prison on an island in the South China Sea, off the Delta area of South Vietnam. At one time the South Vietnamese government used the prison for Viet Cong guerrillas and North Vietnamese prisoners of war. Poulo Condor then became known as Con Son Island, its Vietnamese name. In 1970 the small stone cells known as tiger cages were exposed by the press. In 1971 the U.S. State Department contracted for new cells for the North Vietnamese prisoners held there.

**Tiger Division**    a South Korean division that used a Tiger patch on its uniform. They fought as an ally from 1965 to the end of the war, mainly in II CORPS.

**Tiger Hound**    code name for aerial RECONNAISSANCE and bombing missions in Laos, begun in 1966 south of the 17th parallel.

**Tiger Island**    an island a few miles north of the Demilitarized Zone, just off the coast. A ROLLING THUNDER mission hit a weapons installation there in early 1965.

**tiger ladies**    slang for the Vietnamese women who worked on the runways, taxiways, aprons, and other construction at CAM RANH BAY.

**Tiger Paw Beer**    a Vietnamese beer made with formaldehyde to speed the fermentation process; nicknamed Tiger piss.

**Tiger piss**    slang for TIGER PAW BEER.

**tiger stripes**    multicolor striped camouflage jungle fatigues, or camou-flage fatigue uniforms. Not authorized for most troops these were worn mainly by SPECIAL FORCES and LRRPS. They had a tigerlike striped pattern.

**tiger suits**    slang for TIGER STRIPES.

**Tiger Tracks**    nickname for the XM–571, an experimental all-purpose, light-weight articulated tracked vehicle.

**tigers**    1. slang for battalion patrol and ambush elements. 2. native to Vietnam, tigers were occasionally sighted by troops in the field.

**tight**    being close to someone, such as a good friend.

**Tijuana East**    slang for a red-light district near the U.S. air base at Bien Hoa.

**time in the barrel**    slang for duty at CON THIEN.

**time in the meatgrinder**    slang for duty at CON THIEN.

**time on target**    an ARTILLERY term referring to the coordination of an artillery or mortar barrage from different groups aimed at a single target at the same time. The phrase refers to the exact timing required for this maneuver. Abbreviated as TOT.

**time pencil**    device attached to GRENADES or CLAYMORE mines to delay detonation for a specified amount of time.

**TIN**    abbr. for Transaction Identification Number. See SPN.

**tin pot**    slang for the helmet that GIs were issued. It was also known as a steel pot.

**tinactin** a medication used in Vietnam for athlete's foot, which was rampant.

**Tinkertoy** nickname for the Skyhawk A–4 aircraft.

**tip the scale** slang for trying a stratagem to put the enemy on the defensive.

**títi** Vietnamese slang for little or very small.

**to butterfly on** slang meaning to leave someone.

**T/O** abbr. for Table of Organization. This table displayed the number of men in a particular organization, plus the grade and assignment of each.

**T O & E** see TOE.

**TOC** abbr. for Tactical Operations Center, a command ship.

**TOE** abbr. for Table of Organization and Equipment. This is the table of organization, plus a list of weapons, equipment, and vehicles assigned to an organization. Also T O & E.

**toe popper** slang for a small plastic ANTIPERSONNEL mine set off by foot pressure and used to disable the enemy.

**TOG rule** slang expression standing for "They're Only Gooks." This fictitious rule stated that killing or injuring Vietnamese civilians did not count, because they were not actually human.

**tôi** Vietnamese for I, me, my.

**tôi dầu hang** Vietnamese for I surrender.

**tôi không biết** Vietnamese for I don't know.

**tôi không hiều** Vietnamese for I don't understand

**tôi là bác-sĩ** Vietnamese for I'm a doctor.

**tom** slang for a black LIFER who gave tough duties to black subordinates; derived from Uncle Tom.

**Tonkin** the northern section of North Vietnam.

**Tonkin Gulf** waters off the coast of South Vietnam and North Vietnam.

**Tonkin Gulf Incident** see GULF OF TONKIN INCIDENT.

**Tonkin Gulf Yacht Club** slang for the U.S. Navy's Seventh Fleet.

**Tonkin Spook** slang for a deceptive radar image, a ghost, or phantom, observed in the area of the TONKIN GULF.

**tooth to tail ratio** the combat to support troops ratio. The frontline is the tooth and the rear area is the tail. In Vietnam, the U.S. military was made up of approximately 14 percent tooth.

**Top Gun** slang for the U.S. Navy Fighter Weapons School at the Naval Air Station at Miramar, California, responsible for air combat training for fighter pilots.

**top** slang for a first sergeant of a company, the top sergeant. He is also called topper, first shirt, and top kick.

**top kick** slang for first sergeant.

**topper** slang for a first sergeant of a company, a top sergeant. Also called top, first shirt, and top kick.

**topside** naval or marine term for upstairs.

**torch** 1. slang for an expert in demolitions. 2. slang meaning to set fire to something.

**torpedo boat** a small surface vessel capable of high speed. It carried torpedoes as its main armament and light guns as additional armament.

**TOT** abbr. for TIME ON TARGET.

**tour 365** the year-long tour of duty spent in Vietnam.

**Tourane** French name for the city of DA NANG.

**TOW** abbr. for Tube-launched, Optically tracked, Wire-guided missiles. These were American air-to-surface and surface-to-surface antiarmor-guided missiles.

**tower rat** slang for tower guard.

**Tower Week** slang for the middle week of jump school training.

**tp** abbr. for Troop.

**TPQ flights** bombing runs controlled by ground radar.

**Tri-Thien Front** the North Vietnamese MILITARY REGION encompassing the two northernmost provinces of South Vietnam, Quang Tri and Thua Thien.

**tr** abbr. for Transportation.

**tracer** 1. a round of ammunition chemically treated to trail colored lights; such burning shells gave a visual track of the bullet's flight. Usually in every fifth or tenth round, a tracer assisted in locating the enemy. The U.S. troops usually used red tracers, while the North Vietnamese Army and Viet Cong used red and green tracers. 2. a bullet or shell chemically treated to leave a trail of smoke or fire.

**track** 1. any vehicle that moved on treads instead of wheels and was equipped with continuous roller belts over cogged wheels. 2. slang for an armored personnel carrier.

**Tracker** 1. the twin-engined propeller-driven antisubmarine aircraft. See TRADER. 2. A British school in Malaysia which trained U.S. personnel in jungle warfare.

**tracker team** team consisting of one scout dog, two tracker dogs and handlers, and two visual trackers who followed enemy trails.

**Trader** the C–1A, the standard COD aircraft during the Vietnam War. This aircraft was a variant of the S–2 TRACKER, twin-engine, propeller-driven and antisubmarine. The C–1 delivered mail, people, and spare parts.

**trade school** slang for West Point or Annapolis.

**trafficability** terrain having the capacity to hold up under foot or vehicle traffic.

**trail** 1. an air force formation involving aircraft in a line one behind the other. Also called trail formation. 2. short for the HO CHI MINH TRAIL.

**trajectory** the path of a projectile moving in space. This must be carefully measured when firing MORTARS and ARTILLERY at the enemy.

**Tram Chim** the village serving as the DISTRICT headquarters for the Dong Thien district.

**trạm cứu thương** Vietnamese for aid station.

**trận dánh** Vietnamese for battle.

***Tran Van Don***   minister of defense of South Vietnam from 1964 to 1975.

***Tran Van Huong***   South Vietnamese president for five days between the resignation of Nguyen Van Thieu and the appointment of General Duong Van Minh.

***Transaction Identification Number***   see SPN.

***trao dõi tù binh***   Vietnamese for exchange of prisoners.

***trap***   an arrested landing aboard a carrier.

***trash bagger***   nickname for a parachute rigger.

***trash hauler***   slang for a transport plane or its pilot.

***travel bureau***   slang for GRAVES REGISTRATION POINT.

***trfd***   abbr. for transferred.

***tree line***   a row of trees at the edge of a field or rice paddy making a natural defensive location; also called green line and wood line.

***tri-border***   the area west of Dak To, South Vietnam, where the borders of Cambodia, Laos, and South Vietnam met.

***triage***   the procedure for deciding the order in which casualties were to be treated in order to maximize the number of survivors. While the injured were labeled according to the degree of their injuries—those who needed immediate attention (priority), those who needed only minimal care (routine), and those expected to die (emergency or urgent)—it was sometimes deemed more efficient to leave the hopeless cases unattended and concentrate medical attention on those who were expected to survive.

***Triangle, The***   slang for IRON TRIANGLE, a Viet Cong stronghold near Saigon.

***trick chief***   slang for the noncommissioned officer in charge of a shift.

***trioxane***   the main ingredient in HEAT TABS, used to heat C-RATIONS and to boil water.

***trip flare***   a ground FLARE put in front of a defensive position. When the enemy tripped the wire, the trip flare signaled and lit up the area.

***trip wire***   1. thin wire stretched across trails and meant to set off booby traps, flares, or other devices. 2. various tactical operations, usually conducted at night, to detect, disrupt, and disorganize the enemy.

***triple A***   slang for AAA, Anti-Aircraft Artillery, referring to weapons used for shooting at aircraft.

***triple canopy***   very thick jungle growth, with three layers of tropical foliage. Compare with DOUBLE CANOPY.

***Triple Nickel***   nickname for the 555th Tactical Fighter Squadron.

***troll***   aerial term for flying a random pattern by ECM aircraft to detect enemy electronic signals.

***trooper***   slang for soldier.

***tropical immersion foot***   a skin condition affecting the feet, caused by walking through wet areas for long periods when soldiers' feet were not able to dry out.

***Tropic Lightning***   nickname for the U.S. 25th Infantry Division, called that because of the lightning bolt on the unit's insignia.

**Tropic Moon** A–1Es (Tropic Moon I), B–57Bs (Tropic Moon II), and B–57Gs (Tropic Moon III), aircraft fitted with Low Light Level Television (LLLTV) used for night attacks along the HO CHI MINH TRAIL.

**Truc Giang** capital of KIEN HOA Province.

**truck war, the** slang for the efforts taken against North Vietnamese Army vehicle movement on the HO CHI MINH TRAIL.

**Trung sisters** Vietnamese noblewomen who unsuccessfully rebelled against the Chinese in the first century A.D. They became the symbol of independence from foreign rule for the Vietnamese people.

**trung sĩ** Vietnamese for sergeant.

**trung doàn** Vietnamese for regiment.

**trung dôi** Vietnamese for platoon.

**trung dôi trưởng** Vietnamese for platoon leader.

**trung liên** Vietnamese for automatic rifle.

**trung úy** Vietnamese for first lieutenant.

**Truong Chinh** a close collaborator of HO CHI MINH.

**Truong Son Corridor** the supply line that paralleled the HO CHI MINH TRAIL, following along the Truong Son Mountains in South Vietnam. The route was also called Corridor 613.

**TS** abbr. for Top Secret.

**T/Sgt** abbr. for Technical Sergeant.

**TSN** abbr. for the American-built TAN SON NHUT air base near SAIGON, and the headquarters for General William WESTMORELAND.

**T–34** a Soviet light tank used by the North Vietnamese Army.

**TT–33** a pistol used by the North Vietnamese.

**tù binh** Vietnamese for prisoner.

**Tu do** Vietnamese word for freedom. Tu Do (Freedom) Street was the principal thoroughfare in SAIGON. Formerly called by its French name of Rue Catinat, it later became Dong Khoi (Uprising) Street soon after South Vietnam fell. 2. a Vietnamese cigarette.

**tu tai** Vietnamese for a high school diploma earned in Vietnam.

**tube artillery** ARTILLERY that fired projectiles from a gun barrel or tube, as opposed to ROCKET artillery.

**tube steak** slang for hot dogs.

**tuck-under** aerial term for a tendency of certain aircraft to drop their noses when flying at or near their critical MACH number.

**Tung Nghia** capital of TUYEN DUC Province.

**tunnel** the Viet Cong used tunnels for factories, hospitals, and storage. These tunnels were all over South Vietnam, especially in the IRON TRIANGLE area and in Cu Chi, 25 miles from Saigon. Tunnels were first dug by the VIET MINH during the war with the French from 1946–1954.

**tunnel flushers** portable devices for flushing tunnels of the enemy, booby traps, snakes, scorpions, and other hazards in the tunnel systems.

The commercial air blowers which had been used had many limitations. Scientists devised three new gasoline-driven air blowers, or tunnel flushers, and called them the Mars Generator, the Resojet, and the Model K Buffalo Turbine. These turned out to be heavy (the Buffalo Turbine weighed 800 pounds), used a lot of gasoline, and could not be refueled while operating. The Resojet was lighter weight but would not start reliably in the jungle climate. The Mars Generator ran at too high a temperature to be used when U.S. personnel were in the tunnels. None worked very well, and all were eventually discontinued.

***tunnel rat***   slang for U.S. personnel used to clear tunnels. U.S. soldiers, particularly those of small stature, would search enemy tunnels with a flashlight, a .45 caliber pistol, and earplugs. They also used mounted lamps, mounted microphones, and telephones with wire to communicate with those outside the tunnels. Their handguns often had silencers on them. The slogan of tunnel rats was "non gratum anus rodentum," which roughly translated means "not worth a rat's ass."

***Tunnels Mines and Booby Traps School***   training for work in tunnels, mines, and booby traps was taught at this school in CU CHI. The school had many captured VIET CONG tunnels used for training purposes.

***tu̇ớc khí giới***   Vietnamese for disarm.

***TUOC***   abbr. for Tactical Unit Operations Center.

***TURDSID***   a proposed SEISMIC INTRUSION DEVICE disguised to look like dog feces. This idea was soon abandoned, however, as there were no dogs where these were used on the HO CHI MINH TRAIL. They were then changed to resemble small pieces of wood.

***turkey jerk***   slang for a massage parlor.

***turn radius***   aerial term for the radial distance required to effect a 180 degree turn ; this distance varied with an aircraft's speed and altitude.

***turnback***   Officers Candidate School term to flag an unpromising candidate at the end of 12 weeks of training. This officer would be required to return to an earlier week of training as an alternative to elimination from the program.

***Turner Joy, C.***   See GULF OF TONKIN INCIDENT, USS C. TURNER JOY.

***turret***   1. the upper part of a tank, containing the commander, loader, gunner, weapons, and communication equipment. 2. the device on a tank that turned the guns into firing positions.

***turtle***   slang for a combat replacement, so-called because to the soldier he was replacing he always seemed to take forever to get there.

***tử trận***   Vietnamese for killed in action.

***tuần tiểu***   Vietnamese for patrol.

***Tuy Hoa***   capital of PHU YEN Province. A large U.S. air base was located here.

***Tuyen Duc***   one of the 44 provinces of South Vietnam, located in II CORPS.

***TV-Land***   slang for outlandish and far-fetched combat reasoning, usually done by those not in the FIELD.

**TWA** abbr. for slang "Teeny-Weeny-Airlines," usually referring to helicopters, an ironic twist on the name of the large commercial airlines, TWA.

**tweetybirds** slang for the A–37 aircraft.

**Twelfth General Order** The fictitious Twelfth General Order was usually recognized as "Don't get caught." General orders were permanent instructions issued as orders applying to all members of a command and usually involved policy matters or administration.

**12–7** short for the Soviet-made Degtyarev 12.7mm heavy machine gun, sometimes referred to as a .51 caliber machine gun.

**20 Mike-Mike** slang for the 20mm GATLING gun used in fighter aircraft.

**twidget** 1. a disparaging term for those who never go out into the field. 2. nickname for a specialist in electronic equipment or in various kinds of SENSORS.

**Twining, Nathan** chairman, Joint Chiefs of Staff, 1957–1960.

**twink** slang for a new guy IN-COUN-TRY. See FNG. Also used to refer to a new second lieutenant.

**twinkle** nickname for STARLIGHT SCOPE operators.

**TWIX** a military cable.

**two** refers to the radio call sign of the Intelligence Officer.

**II Corps** the second allied MILI-TARY REGION extending through the Central Highlands and through some of the Central Lowlands.

**Two Shades of Soul** nickname for the 173d Airborne Brigade, called that because of a congenial blend of black and white soldiers. The 173d was also nicknamed The Herd and Sky Soldiers.

**Two Shop** intelligence, taken from the staff or officer responsible for intelligence (G–2).

**two-step** slang for the bamboo viper, a poisonous snake found in Vietnam. It was called the two-step because of the belief that having been bitten, one would take only two steps before dying. It was also called a one-step, seven-step, and so forth.

**II–A** according to the SELECTIVE SERVICE classification, registrant deferred because of civilian occupation (except agriculture or activity in study).

**II–C** according to the SELECTIVE SERVICE classification, registrant deferred because of agricultural occupation.

**two-digit fidget** slang for having 10 to 99 days left to serve in Vietnam. Also called a double-digit fidget, double-digit midget, or two-digit midget.

**two-digit midget** see two-digit fidget.

**201 file** the military personnel file for each soldier, containing orders, citations, and personnel actions. It followed the soldier when he was assigned to a new unit. The 66 FILE is the equivalent file for officers.

**two-point-five (2.5)** a gunship rocket.

**II–S** according to the SELECTIVE SERVICE classification, a deferment due to course enrollment, usually in college.

**212** code for a general discharge issued as under honorable conditions, but unfit for military duty. It was given for minor drug use (small amounts of pot, for example) or rebellious behaviors.

**type 56–1 assault rifle** a Chinese copy of the AK–47, used by the North Vietnamese Army.

**type 68** a Chinese copy of the Soviet-made SKS rifle, used by the North Vietnamese Army.

# U

**U Minh Forest** a mangrove swamp in AN XUYEN Province in IV CORPS. The U Minh Forest was a VIET CONG base area, known by its nickname, Forest of Darkness.

**U Tapao** a U.S. air base in Thailand.

**UA** abbr. for unauthorized absence. See AWOL.

**UAM** abbr. for Underwater-to-Air Missile.

**Udorn** a U.S. air base in Thailand. See PROJECT WATER PUMP.

**UFC-10** the emergency radio beeper used by airmen.

**UH-1** Bell's Iroquois assault support helicopter used for transport, cargo, troops, MEDEVAC, or spotting. Also called Huey, Slick, Huey Slick, Huey Gunship.

**UH-1E** Bell Huey, a single-engine light helicopter used mainly for observation and COMMAND AND CONTROL.

**UH-1H** a Huey Slick.

**UH-34D** Sikorsky Sea Horse, a single-engine medium transport helicopter.

**Ultra hot** slang for the Thud, F-105 aircraft.

**UMZ** abbr. for Ultra Militarized Zone, slang which GIs gave to the Demilitarized Zone.

**unass** slang for leaving one's seat quickly.

**unbloused** pants not tucked into boot tops.

**Uncle Ho** slang for HO CHI MINH.

**Uncle Ho's Boys** slang for the enemy.

**unconventional warfare** GUERRILLA warfare conducted within hostile areas by mostly indigenous personnel.

**unfriendlies** slang for Viet Cong or North Vietnamese soldiers.

**uniform** 1. military phonetic for the letter U. 2. the UHF radio.

**Uniroyal** one of the chemical companies that manufactured the defoliant AGENT ORANGE.

**unit one** a medical bag.

**unkwn** unknown or information unavailable.

**unload** 1. aerial term meaning to reduce the angle of attack on an aircraft. The purpose of this was mainly to gain speed. 2. aerial term for placing an aircraft in zero G for maximum acceleration.

**unload ordnance** order to fire ordnance from aircraft or helicopter.

**unobserved fire** fire in which the impact cannot be seen, so that adjustments cannot be made.

**up north** slang for North Vietnam.

**urgent dustoff** a person with a sickness or injury, where loss of life or limb was imminent. Urgent dustoff operations were usually accomplished immediately when possible.

**U.S.** 1. prefix to the serial number of army draftees. After 1969, social security numbers were used instead of serial numbers. Compare with RA. 2. abbr. for United States.

**US M68**   a FRAG GRENADE.

**USA**  1. abbr. for United States of America. 2. abbr. for United States Army.

**USAF**  abbr. for United States Air Force.

**USAID**  abbr. for United States Agency for International Development. This department was responsible for giving American economic assistance to many foreign countries, including South Vietnam. The initials AID were also used.

**USARV**  abbr. for U.S. Army Republic of Vietnam. The command of operations units for all U.S. military forces in Vietnam was based in Long Binh, about 13 miles from SAIGON. During the war Long Binh became the largest military post in the free world and was the home of Long Binh jail, the military stockade also known as LBJ. The stockade served as jail for U.S. service personnel.

**USCG**  abbr. for United States Coast Guard.

**use up, to**   slang for kill.

**USMACV**  abbr. for United States Military Assistance Command, Vietnam. See MACV.

**USMC**  abbr. for United States Marine Corps.

**USMJ**  abbr. for Unified Code of Military Justice, the United States code of military law.

**USN**  abbr. for United States Navy.

**U.S. Naval Forces, Vietnam**  a new command developed in April 1966 to control the operations of naval forces inside South Vietnam and some of the coastal units, the River Patrol Force, Riverine Assault Force, Coast Guard Patrols, and Seabees. Outside the coastal waters the Seventh Fleet was, however, directed by the commander in chief of the Pacific Command in Hawaii.

**USNS**  abbr. for U.S. Naval Ship.

**USO**  abbr. for United Services Organization. The USO maintained centers at many locations in Vietnam, including Cam Ranh Bay, Da Nang, Saigon, Tan Son Nhut, Vung Tau, and elsewhere. USO personnel provided magazines, posters, milkshakes, and other items from home that the troops missed most.

**USS**  abbr. for United States Ship.

**USSAG**  abbr. for U.S. Support Activities Group. Established in Thailand after the January 1973 cease-fire, this headquarters controlled all U.S. air or naval actions in Southeast Asia. USSAG was also known as CG, Seventh Air Force.

**USSF**  abbr. for United States (Army) SPECIAL FORCES.

**utilities**   marine term for combat fatigues. In 1969, the marines' fatigues changed from olive drab uniforms to camouflaged utilities of shaded green and yellow. The traditionally buttoned fly was changed to a zipper.

**U–2** high-flying aircraft used for RE-CONNAISSANCE.

**UW** abbr. for Unconventional Warfare. This included GUERRILLA warfare, ESCAPE AND EVASION, sabotage, subversion, and covert or clandestine operations.

# V

**V device** the attachment that signifies valor, bravery, or meritorious service, to the BRONZE STAR, the AIR MEDAL, and the COMMENDATION MEDAL.

**V-A** according to the SELECTIVE SERVICE classification, registrant over the age of liability for military service.

**VA** 1. abbr. for Veterans Administration. 2. abbr. for Vice Admiral.

**Van Tien Dung** chief of staff of the North Vietnamese Army in 1953 until 1974, when he was named senior general. He was appointed commander of the Saigon Liberation Campaign Command in April 1975, and minister of national defense in 1980.

**Vandegrift** the artillery FIRE SUPPORT BASE at KHE SANH built in 1968 by U.S. Army troops and patrolled by U.S. Marines.

**Vanguard Youth** volunteer North Vietnamese youth organization mobilized into road-building brigades in the post-cease-fire period.

**Vann, John Paul** A U.S. COUNTERINSURGENCY advisor killed in a helicopter crash in June 1972. One of the United States' top Vietnam authorities Vann was attached to the U.S. Seventh Division.

**varmint special** slang for the Remington bolt-action hunting rifles that U.S. Marine Corps snipers used.

**VATLS** abbr. for the Army's Visual Airborne Target Locator System. This was a powerful telescope developed to locate ground sites for artillery or tactical air strikes, visual observation, and photography.

**VC** abbr. for VIET CONG, who were also called VICTOR CHARLIE, Charlie, or many other nicknames.

**VC National Forest** slang for an area in Vietnam controlled by the Viet Cong or by the North Vietnamese.

**VC Valley** nickname for the Dak Payou Valley in South Vietnam, southeast of Pleiku, called that because of its long-time domination by the enemy.

**VCC** abbr. for VIET CONG Captured.

**VCI** abbr. for VIET CONG Infrastructure. This was the North Vietnamese Army military term for the Viet Cong's covert government. The VC planned to have a complete government in place when their victory was finally won. When possible, Communist CADRES were secretly assigned positions as village chiefs, police officers, and postmen, as well as DISTRICT, PROVINCE, and national level officers. The VCI was also referred to as the SHADOW GOVERNMENT of the National Liberation Front, and the Government of the Night. VCI was the target of the U.S.-led PHOENIX program. Authentic VCI cadre were issued government identification cards and played an undercover role in the insurgency. Unauthorized cadre were not issued identification cards and had to hide in bunkers during the day. They operated only at night.

**VCS** abbr. for Viet Cong Suspect.

***vector*** aerial term for a command which directs an aircraft to follow a specific heading.

***vector control officer*** the person responsible for eliminating rats and disease-carrying pests, checking water supplies, and other health-related tasks.

***vertical rolling scissors*** an aerial term for a defensive rolling maneuver in the vertical plane executed in an attempt to achieve an offensive position on the attacker.

***VERTREP*** abbr. for Vertical Replenishment; being supplied or resupplied by helicopter.

***Veterans of Foreign Wars*** a U.S. national service organization open to men and women who have served on foreign soil. Abbreviated VFW.

***VFW*** abbr. for VETERANS OF FOREIGN WARS.

***VHF*** abbr. for Very High Frequency, a radio band that begins above the commercial FM frequencies.

***vị chỉ huy*** Vietnamese for commander.

***Vi Thanh*** capital of CHUONG THIEN Province.

***vic*** abbr. for Vicinity.

***victor*** military phonetic for the letter V.

***Victor, Victor Charlie*** slang for the VIET CONG.

***VID*** abbr. for Visual Identification, used when the identity of an aircraft could not be made by radar or electronic means.

***Viet Cong*** Vietnamese guerrillas at the time of the anti-American resis-

tance. The term comes from Vietnam Cong San, signifying Vietnamese Communists, and was used as a derogatory term in American usage, especially in its abbreviated form "VC." Early in the Vietnam War, both U.S. and ARVN troops attempted to restrain the Viet Cong. Later CLEAR AND HOLD tactics were used to neutralize the Viet Cong's power. The PHOENIX PROGRAM went after the VIET CONG INFRASTRUCTURE (see VCI). By that time, after TET of 1968, the Viet Cong were generally ruled by the North Vietnamese Army. Also called Charlie, Chas, Chuck, Mr. Charles, Victor Charlie, and many more names.

***Viet Cong Hunting Club*** slang for a group of grunts going out on patrol.

***Viet Cong San*** Vietnamese Communists. See VIET CONG.

***Viet Cong Secret Zone*** a well-defended enemy base in South Vietnam, unknown to the Americans.

***Viet Cong Special Forces*** the elite Vietnamese Guerrillas, known as DAC CONG.

***Viet Minh*** short form of Viet Nam Doc Lap Dong Ninh Hoi, or the Vietnamese Allied Independence League. This was the resistance front against the French colonials in 1941, and a predecessor to Viet Cong.

***Viet shits*** slang for diarrhea.

***Viet-speak*** slang for a mixture of standard English, slang, and Vietnamese or other Oriental languages, often used in Vietnam.

***Vietminh*** see VIET MINH.

***Vietnam Advisory*** first campaign of the Vietnam War, from March 15,

1962, to March 7, 1965. See CAM-PAIGN.

**Vietnam Campaign Service Medal**  this medal given by the U.S. government recognized service in Vietnam between July 3, 1965, and March 28, 1973, the official end of service for U.S. Army personnel. It was also given to those who held the Armed Forces Expeditionary Medal for service in Vietnam between July 7, 1958, and July 3, 1965. This award was given for one or more days of service in Vietnam itself aboard a navy vessel directly supporting military operations in Vietnam, or as a crew member in flights over Vietnam. Its nickname was the Been There Medal, because one had only to have been there to receive it.

**Vietnam Cease-Fire**  campaign from March 30, 1972, to January 28, 1973. See CAMPAIGN.

**Vietnam Consolidation I**  campaign from July 1 to November 30, 1971. See CAMPAIGN.

**Vietnam Consolidation II**  campaign from December 1, 1971, to March 29, 1972. See CAMPAIGN.

**Vietnam Counteroffensive**  campaign from December 25, 1965, to June 30, 1966. See CAMPAIGN.

**Vietnam Counteroffensive Phase IV**  campaign from April 2 to June 30, 1968. See CAMPAIGN.

**Vietnam Counteroffensive Phase V**  campaign from July 1, to November 1, 1968. See CAMPAIGN.

**Vietnam Counteroffensive Phase VII**  campaign from July 1, 1970, to June 30, 1971. See CAMPAIGN.

**Vietnam Counteroffensive Phase VI**  campaign from November 2, 1968, to February 22, 1969. See CAMPAIGN.

**Vietnam Counteroffensive Phase III**  campaign from July 1, 1965, to January 29, 1968. See CAMPAIGN.

**Vietnam Counteroffensive Phase II**  campaign from July 1, 1966, to May 31, 1967. See CAMPAIGN.

**Vietnam Defense**  campaign from March 8 to December 24, 1965. See CAMPAIGN.

**Vietnam flu**  euphemism for gonorrhea.

**Vietnam Moratorium Committee**  a group which sponsored anti-war demonstrations in the United States in 1969. Samuel W. Brown, a supporter of Senator Eugene McCarthy, helped organize this group in 1969. It disbanded in early 1970.

**Vietnam People's Army**  (VPA) see NVA.

**Vietnam Sanctuary Counteroffensive**  campaign from May 1, 1970, to June 30, 1970. See CAMPAIGN.

**Vietnam Service Awards**  South Vietnam awarded various decorations and medals to U.S. units and individuals. These included the Republic of Vietnam Gallantry Cross, Republic of Vietnam Civil Actions Medal, Armed Forces Honor Medal, Special Service Medal, and others.

**Vietnam-Era vet**  term usually applied to servicemen and women who served during the time of the Vietnam War in the U.S., Europe, Asia or elsewhere, but not in Vietnam.

**Vietnam Summer-Fall 1969** campaign from June 9 to October 31, 1969. See CAMPAIGN.

**Vietnam Veterans Against the War** see VVAW.

**Vietnam Veterans Agent Orange Victims, Incorporated** this organization began when Vietnam veteran Paul Reutershan died of AGENT ORANGE-related cancer in December 1978. On his deathbed, two of his Vietnam veteran friends and his sister promised to help other vets suffering from Agent Orange-related illnesses. When he became ill Paul Reutershan stated, "I died in Vietnam and didn't even know it." Ever since Reutershan's death, Vietnam Veterans Agent Orange Victims, Inc. has worked to assist Vietnam veterans and their families with Agent Orange-related and other problems.

**Vietnam Veterans of America** a service organization for Vietnam and Vietnam Era vets. It is chartered by the U.S. Congress, and has been in existence for about ten years. Its main purposes include lobbying for veterans' rights and representing veterans in hearings involving the Department of Veterans Affairs (formerly the VA).

**Vietnam Winter-Spring 1970** campaign from November 1, 1969, to April 30, 1970. See CAMPAIGN.

**Vietnamese Popular Forces** see POPULAR FORCES.

**Vietnamization** President Richard Nixon's strategy to end the war in Vietnam by gradually turning the conflict over to the South Vietnam armed forces, and withdrawing U.S. troops. This term coined by Defense Secretary Melvin Laird was a cornerstone of Nixon's 1968 campaign promise of a "peace plan" to end the war in Vietnam. The process was begun in June 1969. Vietnamization had a highly negative effect on American troops: Drug use increased as did racial incidents and tensions, and FRAGGINGS. Protests in the United States increased, some with Vietnam veterans participating. There was a general sense among the U.S. troops of uselessness and hopelessness as morale declined.

**Viggie** short for the Vigilante aircraft. See A–5.

**Vigilante** see A–5.

**village** a small group of hootches in a rural area larger than a hamlet but smaller than a town.

**village sweep** an operation in which troops would move through a VILLE and completely check it out.

**ville** Vietnamese hamlet or village, or any collection of HOOTCHES. Taken from village, ville meant anything from a small town to a few thatched huts in a clearing. SAIGON was called The Ville in the early days of the Vietnam War.

**Vinh** a small port in North Vietnam mined by U.S. forces to immobilize shipping.

**Vinh Binh** one of the 44 provinces of South Vietnam, located in IV CORPS.

**Vinh Long** one of the 44 provinces of South Vietnam, located in IV CORPS.

**Vinh Long City** capital of VINH LONG Province.

**vivax** one of the two main types of malaria troops contracted in Vietnam; the other was falciparum. See MALARIA.

**VMC** see VIETNAM MORATORIUM COMMITTEE.

**VNAF** abbr. for South Vietnamese Air Force.

**VNMC** abbr. for Vietnamese Marine Corps.

**VNN** abbr. for Vietnamese Navy.

**VNQDD** abbr. for Viet Nam Quoc Dan Dang, or Vietnamese Nationalist party, a far right South Vietnamese political party in opposition to President Nguyen Van Thieu and other leaders backed by the United States.

**VNSF** abbr. for the South Vietnamese Special Forces. See LUC LUONG DAC BIET.

**Vo Nguyen Giap** cofounder of the VIET MINH in 1941. Vo Nguyen Giap was the victor at DIEN BIEN PHU in 1954. A general, he was a master of guerrilla warfare. He was prime minister, minister of defense, and commander in chief of the DEMOCRATIC REPUBLIC OF VIETNAM (North Vietnam) until 1976. He was vice premier and minister of national defense, SOCIALIST REPUBLIC OF VIETNAM (North Vietnam) from July 1976 until his retirement in 1980. His nickname was Volcano Covered with Snow because of his moodiness.

**vô tuyến-diện** Vietnamese for radio.

**Voice of Vietnam** Hanoi's English language radio program, broadcast daily in Southeast Asia by North Vietnamese.

**void** marine term meaning to relieve a drill instructor from duty and of his D.I. MOS (8511) because of his inability to perform his job effectively or other reasons.

**void tank** naval term for a large storage area for a ship's equipment.

**Volcano Covered with Snow** nickname for VO NGUYEN GIAP, called that because of his moodiness.

**V100** the armored vehicle used by the MILITARY POLICE, with mounted machine guns attached.

**Voodoo** McDonnell Aviation's F–101.

**VPA** abbr. for Vietnam People's Army, North Vietnam's army, during the 1960s and 1970s, led by Vo Nguyen Giap. See NVA.

**VSI** Very Seriously Ill, the army designation for those servicemen who would have died without immediate and definitive medical care.

**VT** abbr. for Vertical Timed artillery rounds, which can be set to detonate a specified distance above the ground.

**Vulcan** the XM–163 fighting vehicle which mounted a 20mm six-barrel gun.

**Vulcanus** the furnace-equipped ship which incinerated the last of the defoliant AGENT ORANGE in September 1977.

**vulture's row** navy slang for the side of a flight deck where the mechanics waited for incoming planes.

**vùng** Vietnamese for zone.

**Vung Ro** a major port constructed in II CORPS.

**Vung Tau** one of the 11 AUTONOMOUS CITIES of South Vietnam.

**VVA** abbr. for VIETNAM VETERANS OF AMERICA.

**VVAW**   abbr. for Vietnam Veterans Against the War. This antiwar group begun in 1967 was made up of Vietnam veterans who threw the medals they earned in the Vietnam War onto the Capitol steps in Washington, D.C. on April 23, 1971. Their purpose was to make the United States aware of the mental suffering of the Vietnam generation.

# W

**wagon wheel** 1. the defensive maneuver used by North Vietnam to protect its MiG–17s. 2. an enemy defensive formation in which two or more aircraft circle in the horizontal plane while covering each other's rear area against attack, also called wheel or cartwheel. 3. a marine phrase for the large circle where recruits walk and cool down after physical training.

**wait a minute bushes** slang for the thorny bushes and vines which grabbed, scratched, and entangled soldiers.

**wake-up** a short-timer expression for the end of service in Vietnam. For example, "six and a wake-up" would indicate a soldier had six more days to serve and then was going home.

**walk in the sun** 1. slang for ground troop movement without risk of engagement. 2. a reference to a SEARCH AND DESTROY operation, because so often nothing happened.

**walk to the wire** marine slang meaning to put out observation or listening posts outside of the defensive perimeters.

**Walker Commission** commission which investigated the confrontation of demonstrators and police during the 1968 Democratic National Convention in Chicago. The National Commission on the Causes and Prevention of Violence ordered a study to investigate the disorder in downtown Chicago. Daniel Walker, a businessman, headed the study which concluded that what had really occurred could be described as a police riot.

**Walking Dead** nickname for the First Battalion, Ninth Marine Regiment, called that because of the casualties it took in battles near the DMZ throughout the war. Also called the Walking Death and the ghost battalion.

**Walking Death** see WALKING DEAD.

**walking on new stilts** slang phrase for wearing clean pants.

**walking slack** the man walking backup to the POINTMAN. He was nicknamed the SLACK.

**Wall, The** nickname for the national Vietnam Veterans Memorial in Washington, D.C., erected in 1982, and as of April, 1990, inscribed with the names of the 58,167 men and eight women who died in Vietnam.

**Walleye** nickname for the AGM–62 air-to-ground missile, antimateriel type.

**Walt, Lewis W.** commander of the Third Marine Division in Vietnam beginning in June 1965 and simultaneously, commander of the III Marine Amphibious Force (IIIMAF). In 1967, General Walt became assistant commandant of the U.S. Marine Corps and in February 1971 he retired from active service. Called God by his troops because he was so highly revered.

**Walter Wonderful** slang for Walter Reed Army Hospital, in Washington, D.C.

**waltz**    slang for a firefight or hand-to-hand combat.

**war belt**    the wide web belt on which marines in the field hung their ammunition pouches, canteens, and so forth.

**war of attrition**    theory of war that aims to destroy enemy troops and materiel faster than they can be replaced, thus exhausting the enemy's capacity to sustain the war. This was a theory by which the United States hoped to win the Vietnam War, but it did not work out that way.

**War Powers Act**    law passed by Congress in November 1973 that put a 90-day limit on the president's deploying of troops abroad or increasing troops abroad. This was a direct result of congressional and popular disapproval of the long, undeclared war in Vietnam.

**War Zone D**    the major Viet Cong guerrilla areas north of Saigon. War Zone D was east of WAR ZONE C, in III CORPS, and extended to the northeast II CORPS boundary. This area was also known as the IRON TRIANGLE.

**War Zone C**    the major Viet Cong guerrilla areas north of Saigon. Bordered by Cambodia to the west, it included the northern section of Tay Ninh Province. Operation JUNCTION CITY, one of the largest combat operations was carried out here in 1967. War Zone C had heavy forests; the VC and North Vietnamese Army units built base camps of bunkers with connecting tunnels.

**warm water immersion foot**    a skin problem affecting feet, caused by walking through wet areas without allowing the feet to dry.

**Warning Star**    the Lockheed EC–121 radar picket aircraft.

**Warrant Officer**    rank between a noncommissioned officer and a commissioned officer; often a person with a technical role. Many helicopter pilots in Vietnam were warrant officers.

**waste**    slang for kill.

**watch**    1. a general term for a duty or period of responsibility. 2. a naval term for the ship's crew that is on duty. Usually, about one-half of the crew is on duty at the same time. Those off duty are on call at all times, and accessible for emergencies.

**water buffalo**    1. a draft animal in Vietnam used mainly by farmers. 2. slang for a tank on wheels that contained drinking water for the troops.

**Waterboy**    code for the air traffic control center at Pleiku, South Vietnam.

**water taxi**    a small, engine-powered boat with a sheltered passenger compartment. These native craft maneuvered the major canals and rivers of Vietnam and provided a means of transportation from one village to the next.

**wax**    slang for kill.

**weapons lost/weapons captured**    used by the military command for keeping score during the war.

**weapons system**    the total combination of aircraft, crew, avionics, and ordnance.

**weave**    an aerial formation in which the two elements of a flight or the two members of an element continuously cross each other's flight path, horizontally, to increase visual coverage.

**web belt**   see WAR BELT.

**web gear**   suspenders and belt used to carry the infantryman's ammunition, canteen, first-aid pack, grenades, and other essential items needed on the battle field.

**weed**   slang for marijuana.

**weenie**   slang for a person from higher headquarters.

**weenie mobile**   slang for the double-wing CHINOOK helicopter.

**Weiner, Lee**   one of the CHICAGO SEVEN.

**Westmoreland, William C.**   chief of staff, U.S. Army, 1968–1972 and commander, U.S. MACV, 1964–1968.

**Westy**   affectionate nickname for General William Westmoreland.

**wet job**   slang for assassination.

**wetting down**   celebrating a promotion. For example, wetting down stripes for NCOs, or wetting down bars, oak leaves or eagles for officers. The person being "wet down" usually provided the beer.

**Weyand, Fred C.**   chief of staff, U.S. Army 1974–1975, and the last commander of MACV in 1972–1973. He was the third commander of the U.S. troops in South Vietnam, following General William Westmoreland and General Creighton Abrams.

**WHA**   abbr. for Wounded by Hostile Action.

**WHAM**   abbr. for Winning HEARTS AND MINDS.

**wheel**   1. an enemy defensive formation in which two or more aircraft circle in the horizontal plane while covering each other's rear area against attack. Also called wagon wheel or cartwheel. 2. term for the officer in charge of a SEAL unit.

**wheel jockeys**   slang for truck drivers on convoy, LINE-HAUL operations, or any wheeled vehicle drivers.

**Wheeler, Earle G.**   chief of staff, U.S. Army, 1962–1964, and chairman, Joint Chiefs of Staff, 1964–1970.

**whifferdill**   an aerial maneuver used to change direction 180 degrees by raising the nose 30 to 60 degrees, followed by 90 degrees of banking. This is used to reverse direction of flight and to pull the nose down below the horizon.

**whirlybird**   slang for any helicopter.

**whiskey**   1. military phonetic for the letter W. 2. a wounded FRIENDLY.

**whiskey papa**   phonetic alphabetization for WHITE PHOSPHORUS mortar or artillery rounds and grenades.

**whispering death, the**   North Vietnamese Army and Viet Cong nickname for the B–52 Stratofortress.

**whistler**   artillery fuse deliberately set to scare and confuse the enemy.

**white bird**   slang for the OH–6 Light Observation Helicopter.

**White Elephant, The**   nickname of a large military building in Da Nang.

**white envelope**   the envelope dropped by U.S. troops to the Viet Cong fighters, urging them to change sides. The envelope contained a letter asking the finder to put down his gun, as well as a safe conduct pass and a letter of amnesty. This was used in the CHIEU HOI program and was successful in recruiting KIT CARSON scouts.

**White Horse Division**   nickname for South Korea's Ninth Infantry Division, sent to Vietnam in 1965.

**White Lie Ward, The**   slang for the ward reserved for hopeless cases at the U.S. military hospital in Da Nang.

**white mice**   slang for South Vietnamese police. The nickname came from their uniform with white helmets, gloves, and shirts. They were known for their corruption and their willingness to be used by almost anyone for political purposes.

**white on rice**   slang phrase for the American point of view, or being right. See also YELLOW ON RICE.

**white phosphorus**   1. a type of explosive round in which the white phosphorus from ARTILLERY, MORTARS, or ROCKETS spread and caused serious burns. It also dispersed thick smoke. Also called WP, whiskey papa, Willie Peter, Willy Peter, willy peter, willy pete and Wilson Pickett. 2. a type of aerial bomb. The rounds explode with a huge puff of white smoke from the hotly burning phosphorus and were often used as marking rounds.

**white radio station**   a MACV and CIA established "Voice of Freedom" Studies and Observation Groups psychological radio operation that acknowledged its location in South Vietnam.

**white wall**   slang for the haircuts of most airborne troops: shaved on both sides and in the back, with about one-half inch of hair on top of the head.

**White Wing**   code for an operation of U.S. troops in Binh Dinh Province in 1966. The operation was originally called Masher, but its name was changed because of President Lyndon Johnson's dislike of the connotation of that word. This was the first large unit operation across corps boundaries. It was an attempt to banish Viet Cong and North Vietnamese Army forces from this area. In a six-week operation, the NVA gave up the region temporarily. They soon returned and the United States subsequently launched several more operations there.

**white side walls**   slang for an North Vietnamese Army haircut style where the side and back of the head are shaved with a long thatch left on top of the head.

**white team**   observation helicopters.

**White Whale, The**   slang for General William Westmoreland's personal aircraft, probably because of its color and size.

**whole world is watching, the**   expression the crowds chanted during the Democratic National Convention in Chicago in 1968 as they were being beaten by the police.

**WIA**   abbr. for Wounded In Action.

**wicker-heads**   derogatory slang for Viet Cong wearing straw hats and hiding in groups of peasants.

**widow-maker**   nickname for the M–16 rifle.

**wienie mobile**   slang for a double-wing helicopter.

**WIEU**   abbr. for Weekly Intelligence Estimate Update, also known as the MACV reports. This update included BODY COUNTS.

**wilco**   radio term meaning "will comply."

**Wild Weasel** 1. F–100F/F–105F aircraft equipped with RHAW (Radar Homing and Warning) and antiradiation missiles, which enabled them to home in on North Vietnamese Army radar guidance signals and to mark the location of missile sites. These aircraft were used to counter the NVA antiaircraft missile defense. 2. electronic jamming.

**willie fuds** nickname for the flying radar stations which did not have combat capacity, but alerted troops to imminent enemy air attacks.

**willie peter** nickname for WHITE PHOSPHORUS explosives.

**willy peter bag** nickname for the waterproof rubber-coated bag carried in an effort to keep objects dry during the rains.

**willie peter grenade** a M–15 grenade with WHITE PHOSPHORUS.

**Willie the Whale** nickname for the slow EF–10 aircraft used in Korea and at that time, the only planes equipped for electronic warfare. Early in the Vietnam war, they were used in the air war against North Vietnam, but were soon replaced by faster aircraft.

**Wilson Pickett** see WHITE PHOSPHORUS.

**wimp factor** slang for the personality characteristic of those who dodged combat duty, especially officers.

**winchester** standard radio code for "I am out of ammunition," or "all ORDNANCE has been expended."

**wing** an air force formation involving aircraft in side-by-side positions.

**wing wiper** slang for aviation marine personnel.

**wingman** pilot who flew at the side and to the rear of an element leader. In a flight of four, the pilot of number two aircraft was wingman to the lead, or number one, aircraft while number four was wingman to number three.

**Winter Soldier Investigation** the public testimony and debate about U.S. soldiers' activities in Vietnam. This was sponsored by members of the VVAW (Vietnam Veterans Against the War) who testified to make the point that U.S. soldiers had committed war crimes. Their goal was to educate the American people regarding the Vietnam War.

**Winter Soldiers, The** an antiwar group consisting of Vietnam veterans.

**wire hangers** slang for troops in the rear who could take off their clothes at night and hang them up rather than sleep in them, as those in the field did.

**wire, the** the defensive barbed wire that surrounded a "safe" area.

**Wise Old Men** slang for the Senior Advisory Board on Vietnam. Consisting of 15 diplomatic and military persons, this board was formed by President Lyndon Johnson in early 1966 to make recommendations about the conduct of the war. After the Tet Offensive (1968), the group included Clark Clifford, Averell Harriman, Henry Cabot Lodge, Omar Bradley, George Ball, Matthew Ridgway, Dean Acheson, and others. They agreed that the United States could not win the war, and soon after, President Johnson announced that he would not run for reelection.

**WO**   abbr. for WARRANT OFFICER.

**WO-1**   abbr. for WARRANT OFFICER, Grade 1, frequently the grade of a helicopter pilot.

**wood line**   a row of trees at the edge of a field or rice paddy making a natural defensive location. Also called tree line and green line.

**working hard**   slang for getting through a tough assignment.

**World, the**   slang for the United States or for anywhere except Vietnam.

**WP**   See WHITE PHOSPHORUS.

**WP rocket**   a WHITE PHOSPHORUS rocket, also called a Willie Peter rocket.

**WPB**   abbr. for Patrol Craft, an 82-foot cutter of the United States COAST GUARD.

# X

**xạ** word used in the southern part of South Vietnam for village.

**Xa Loi Pagoda** one of several Buddhist temples in Saigon which became a center of political protest in the early 1960s. This and other pagodas were attacked in early 1963, probably by Ngo Dinh Nhu, assistant to his brother Ngo Dinh Diem.

**xạ thử** Vietnamese for gunner.

**Xay Dung Nong Thon** a mid-1960s pacification plan usually translated as Rural Construction or Rural Reconstruction. Americans called it the REVOLUTIONARY DEVELOPMENT PROGRAM, or rev-dev.

**xe cam nhông** Vietnamese for truck.

**xe díp** Vietnamese for jeep.

**xenon light** a special intensely illuminating searchlight used in Vietnam at night on dark fire bases which often became the target of enemy sappers.

**xin loi** see SORRY 'BOUT THAT.

**XM177E2** a 5.56 submachine gun known as Colt Commando, or CAR–15.

**x-ray** the military phonetic for the letter X.

**XM–21** a GUNSHIP MINIGUN.

**XO** abbr. for executive officer, the second in command of a military unit.

**Xuan Loc** capital of Long Khanh Province. Xuan Loc was attacked by 40,000 NVA on April 19, 1971, and the South Vietnamese were outnumbered and defeated. On April 20, 1975, this defensive outpost of Saigon was abandoned.

**xung phong** Vietnamese for assault.

# Y

**Y-Bridge** a bridge in Saigon where a six-day battle between U.S. and Viet Cong forces took place during the Mini-Tet of May 1968. One of the branches of the Y led to Saigon's suburbs, and the other led to the MEKONG DELTA.

**ya-fi** Vietnamese for yes, surely.

**yankee** 1. military phonetic for the letter Y. 2. the north.

**Yankee Station** an area off the coast of South Vietnam in the South China Sea, about 100 miles east of Da Nang, where navy aircraft carriers were stationed. Used especially by carriers flying the ROLLING THUNDER missions against North Vietnam. Compare to DIXIE STATION.

**yards** slang for MONTAGNARDS.

**yaw** aerial term for the displacement of an aircraft about its vertical axis, with the nose either left or right.

**Yellow Brick Road** nickname for the spur of the HO CHI MINH TRAIL that led to Da Nang.

**yellow on rice** slang for the Vietnamese point of view, or being wrong. See also WHITE ON RICE.

**yellow sheet** a form filled out by returning pilots to report problems with their aircraft.

**Yen Bai** site of a MiG base in North Vietnam.

**YO–3A** a quiet RECONNAISSANCE aircraft.

**"You can tell it's Mattel, it's swell"** slogan of the Mattel Toy Company, and often repeated by GIs who struggled to use their M-16s without jamming them. Mattel was widely believed to have made some of the parts for the M-16.

**your dick falls off and you step on it** phrase for an embarrassing moment. Also phrased as "I stepped on my dick that time!"

**yo-yo** a vertical aerial combat maneuver.

**y-tá** Vietnamese for medic.

# Z

**Z-time**  Zulu time, a term for Greenwich mean time. See GOLF TIME.

**zap**  slang for to shoot and hit, wound, or kill.

**zapped**  slang for killed.

**zapper**  slang for a lethal spring-steel billy club used by unconventional warfare units.

**zebra**  slang for an NCO with multiple stripes on his sleeve.

**zero-dark-thirty**  slang for very early in the morning; from about one-half hour before the sun comes up till just after sunrise. This was also called o-dark-thirty.

**ZI**  abbr. for Zone of the Interior, term referring to the United States.

**ZIL–157**  a vehicle used to transport SAMs.

**zip**  a derogatory term for a Vietnamese. See GOOK.

**zipperhead**  derogatory term for a Vietnamese or any Oriental. See GOOK.

**zippo**  slang for any FLAME-THROWER device. Zippo was also the slang for Armored Cavalry Assault Vehicles with M10–8 flamethrowers attached.

**zippo job**  military operation which involved burning down Vietnamese villages. They were called that because often Zippo cigarette lighters were used to ignite the hootches. Also called zippo raid.

**zippo mission**  slang for a SEARCH AND DESTROY mission.

**zippo monitor**  a boat with FLAME-THROWERS.

**zippo raid**  see ZIPPO JOB.

**zippo squad**  a squad (usually the last of a tactical unit) that was designated to burn an enemy village.

**zippo squad up**  call to set fire to enemy installations.

**zippo track**  nickname for a flame-throwing tank.

**zit**  derogatory slang for Vietnamese people. See GOOK.

**ZF**  abbr. for Zone of Fire.

**Zone Time**  time according to the one-hour zone in Vietnam that corresponded to 15-degree change of longitude.

**Zoo Annex**  nickname for a section of the North Vietnamese Hoa Lo Prison, the HANOI HILTON.

**Zoo, The**  nickname for the North Vietnamese Cu Loc Prison near HANOI.

**zoom**  an aerial term for a unloaded climb, used to gain maximum altitude while using minimum energy.

**zoomies**  slang for Air Force Academy graduates or jet pilots in general.

**zot**  slang for loser, zero, nothing.

**ZPU**  (pronounced Zip-u) this was a small-caliber (14.5mm), belt-fed, rapid-firing weapon that could be lethal to low-altitude aircraft.

**zulu**   1. military phonetic for the letter Z. 2. slang for a casualty report.

**zulu time**   a term for Greenwich mean time.

**Zumwalt, Elmo R.**   chief of naval operations, 1970–1974.

**Zuni**   a five-inch air-to-ground ROCKET. Highly accurate and of high velocity, the Zuni worked best against small, hard targets.

# APPENDIX

## PROVINCES

### I Corps
Quang Nam
Quang Ngai
Quang Tin
Quang Tri
Thua Thien

### II Corps
Binh Dinh
Binh Thuan
Darlac
Khanh Hoa
Kontum
Lam Dong
Ninh Thuan
Phu Bon
Phu Yen
Pleiku
Quang Duc
Tuyen Duc

### III Corps
Bien Hoa
Binh Duong
Binh Long
Binh Tuy
Gia Dinh
Hau Nghia
Long An
Long Khanh
Phuoc Long
Phuoc Tuy
Tay Ninh

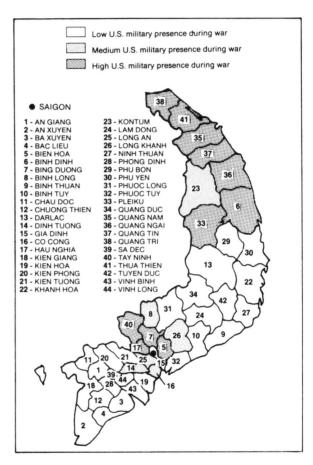

Low U.S. military presence during war
Medium U.S. military presence during war
High U.S. military presence during war

● SAIGON

| | |
|---|---|
| 1 - AN GIANG | 23 - KONTUM |
| 2 - AN XUYEN | 24 - LAM DONG |
| 3 - BA XUYEN | 25 - LONG AN |
| 4 - BAC LIEU | 26 - LONG KHANH |
| 5 - BIEN HOA | 27 - NINH THUAN |
| 6 - BINH DINH | 28 - PHONG DINH |
| 7 - BING DUONG | 29 - PHU BON |
| 8 - BINH LONG | 30 - PHU YEN |
| 9 - BINH THUAN | 31 - PHUOC LONG |
| 10 - BINH TUY | 32 - PHUOC TUY |
| 11 - CHAU DOC | 33 - PLEIKU |
| 12 - CHUONG THIEN | 34 - QUANG DUC |
| 13 - DARLAC | 35 - QUANG NAM |
| 14 - DINH TUONG | 36 - QUANG NGAI |
| 15 - GIA DINH | 37 - QUANG TIN |
| 16 - CO CONG | 38 - QUANG TRI |
| 17 - HAU NGHIA | 39 - SA DEC |
| 18 - KIEN GIANG | 40 - TAY NINH |
| 19 - KIEN HOA | 41 - THUA THIEN |
| 20 - KIEN PHONG | 42 - TUYEN DUC |
| 21 - KIEN TUONG | 43 - VINH BINH |
| 22 - KHANH HOA | 44 - VINH LONG |

### IV Corps
An Giang     Kien Giang
An Xuyen     Kien Hoa
Bac Lieu     Kien Phong
Ba Xuyen     Kien Tuong
Chau Doc     Phong Dinh
Chuong Thien     Sa Dec
Dinh Tuong     Vinh Binh
Go Cong     Vinh Long

# CHRONOLOGY

The following chronology may be useful to readers of this volume. It represents only some of the most important developments during the course of the Vietnam War. For suggestions for further reading on the history of the war, see the Bibliography.

## 1962

| | |
|---|---|
| *February* | U.S. Military Assistance Command, Vietnam (MACV) is established, headquartered in Saigon. The buildup of American advisors and other personnel begins. |
| *March* | The United States begins rural pacification with the Strategic Hamlet Program. |

## 1963

| | |
|---|---|
| *February 24* | A Senate report states that annual American aid to South Vietnam reaches $400 million and that 12,000 U.S. troops are stationed there "on dangerous assignment." |

## 1964

| | |
|---|---|
| *April 25* | President Lyndon Johnson appoints General William Westmoreland as head of MACV, beginning June 20. |
| *August 2-4* | The U.S. destroyers *Maddox* and *Turner Joy* report that they were attacked in the Tonkin Gulf by North Vietnamese patrol boats. |
| *August 7* | The U.S. Senate (82-2) and the House of Representatives (416-0) approve the Tonkin Gulf Resolution, giving President Johnson broad power to take military action in South Vietnam. |

## 1965

| | |
|---|---|
| *February 7* | U.S. military installations in South Vietnam are attacked by Viet Cong. President Johnson orders retaliatory bombing raids over North Vietnam. |
| *March 2* | Operation Rolling Thunder, the bombing of North Vietnam, begins on President Johnson's orders. |
| *March 8* | The first U.S. combat troops, a Marine regiment, arrive in Vietnam to defend the U.S. air base at Da Nang. |
| *April 6* | President Johnson authorizes U.S. ground troops to proceed with offensive action in South Vietnam. |
| *April 12* | U.S. B-52s bomb North Vietnam for the first time. |
| *May* | The first U.S. Army combat unit assigned to Vietnam, the 173rd Airborne Brigade, arrives from Okinawa. |

## 1966

| | |
|---|---|
| *January 20* | President Johnson requests from Congress $13 billion for the war in South Vietnam. A few days later, Secretary of Defense Robert McNamara recommends raising the number of U.S. troops in South Vietnam to 400,000 by December 1966. |
| *September 23* | The U.S. military command in Vietnam reports that U.S. planes are using defoliants to destroy enemy cover. |

## 1967

| | |
|---|---|
| *October 21* | 50,000 antiwar demonstrators march to the Pentagon. For the first time, it is believed, a majority of Americans oppose the war. |

## 1968

In this watershed year, U.S. troop strength reaches more than 500,000. While Johnson seeks an even greater commitment, American public opinion turns against the war, dooming Johnson's presidency.

| | |
|---|---|
| *January 31* | The Tet Offensive begins as North Vietnamese and Viet Cong forces mount major campaigns against the largest cities and provincial capitals in South Vietnam. |
| *March 16* | The My Lai incident, involving the killing of innocent civilians by U.S. troops, takes place. |
| *May 12* | Preliminary peace talks between U.S. and North Vietnamese delegates are held in Paris. |
| *October 31* | President Johnson announces a complete halt to the bombing of North Vietnam. |
| *November 6* | Richard Nixon is elected president, having promised the withdrawal of U.S. troops and a "secret plan" to end the war. |

## 1969

| | |
|---|---|
| *January 25* | Formal truce talks begin in Paris. |
| *March 18* | Nixon orders covert bombing of Cambodia. |
| *October 15* | Nationwide antiwar demonstrations take place. |
| *November 15* | 250,000 people march in an antiwar demonstration in Washington, D.C. |

## 1970

Throughout the year, many military units are withdrawn from Vietnam.

| | |
|---|---|
| *February 20* | Secret peace negotiations begin in Paris. |
| *April 30* | U.S. troops invade Cambodia. |
| *May 4* | Four students at Kent State University in Ohio are killed by National Guardsmen during an antiwar protest. On May 14, two students at Jackson State College (MI) are killed by police during a protest. |

## 1971

Throughout the year, many military units are withdrawn from Vietnam.

| | |
|---|---|
| *March 29* | Lt. William Calley is found guilty of premeditated murder for his part in the My Lai incident. |
| *June* | The U.S. Congress calls for withdrawal of U.S. troops from Vietnam by the end of 1971. |

## 1972

| | |
|---|---|
| *March 23* | The U.S. announces the indefinite suspension of the Paris peace talks. Throughout the year, the talks will proceed erratically. |
| *March 30* | The Easter Offensive begins. North Vietnam crosses the DMZ into South Vietnam. |
| *April 16* | The U.S. resumes bombing of North Vietnam after a 4-year halt. |
| *May 8* | President Nixon announces the mining of North Vietnamese harbors. |
| *August 11* | The last U.S. ground combat troops leave Vietnam, although support troops, advisors, airmen and some others remain. |
| *November 7* | Richard Nixon is re-elected president in a landslide victory. |
| *December 18* | President Nixon authorizes large bombing raids on Hanoi and Haiphong, dubbed the "Christmas bombing." |

## 1973

| | |
|---|---|
| *January 27* | A peace pact is signed by the United States, the South Vietnamese, the North Vietnamese and the National Liberation Front (Viet Cong). Secretary of Defense Melvin Laird announces the end of the military draft. The last U.S. serviceman dies in combat, hours before the truce is signed. |
| *March 29* | The last American combat troops leave Vietnam. |
| *April 1* | Hanoi releases its last acknowledged prisoners of war. |

## 1974

| | |
|---|---|
| *January* | South Vietnamese President Nguyen Van Thieu announces that the cease-fire in South Vietnam has ended and the war has resumed. |
| *August 9* | Richard Nixon resigns as president after the Watergate scandal. Vice President Gerald Ford succeeds him. |
| *September 8* | President Ford pardons Nixon. |
| *September 16* | President Ford offers clemency to draft evaders and military deserters of the Vietnam War. |

## 1975

| | |
|---|---|
| *April 13* | President Nguyen Van Thieu resigns as president of South Vietnam. On April 25, he flees Saigon. |
| *April 29-30* | All American personnel and some Vietnamese are evacuated from Vietnam during Operation Frequent Wind. |
| *April 30* | North Vietnamese troops enter and take Saigon. The South Vietnamese government surrenders unconditionally. The Vietnam War ends. |

# BIBLIOGRAPHY

This bibliography represents a selected sample of the sources used to confirm spelling, usage, and accuracy of detail. Criteria for inclusion were a combination of availability, recency, and/or richness of supply of relevant material.

## History and General Reference

Baritz, Loren. *Backfire: A History of How American Culture Led Us into Vietnam and Made Us Fight the War We Did*. New York: Morrow, 1985.

Baskir, Lawrence M., and Strauss, William A. *Chance and Circumstance: The Draft, the War, and the Vietnam Generation*. New York: Knopf, 1978.

Bonds, Ray, ed. *The Vietnam War*. New York: Crown, 1979.

——. *The Vietnam War: The Illustrated History of the Conflict in Southeast Asia*. New York: Crown, 1983.

Bonier, David E.; Champlin, Steven M.; and Kelly, Timothy S. *The Vietnam Veteran: A History of Neglect*. New York: Praeger, 1984.

Borthnick, David, and Britton, Jack. *Medals, Military and Civilian, of the United States*. Tulsa: MCN Press, 1984.

Bowman, John, ed. *The Vietnam War: An Almanac*. New York: World Almanac, 1985.

Bows, Ray A. *Vietnam Military Lore: 1959-1973*. Hanover, Massachusetts: Bows & Sons, 1988.

Britton, Jack. *United States Military Decorations and Medals*. Tulsa: MCN Press, 1979.

Burke, Tracey, and Gleason, Mimi. *The Tet Offensive*. New York: Gallery Books, 1988.

Butler, David. *The Fall of Saigon*. New York: Simon & Schuster, 1985.

Carhart, Tom. *Battles and Campaigns in Vietnam*. New York: Crown, 1984.

Cohen, Stephen. *Vietnam, Anthology and Guide to a TV History*. New York: Knopf, 1983.

Davidson, Philip B. *Vietnam at War: The History 1946-1975*. Novato, California: Presidio Press, 1988.

Department of Defense. *Dictionary of Military and Associated Terms.* Washington, D.C.: Joint Chiefs of Staff, 1974.

Dougan, Clark, and Weiss, Stephen. *The American Experience in Vietnam.* Boston: Boston Publishing Co., 1988.

Dunstan, Simon. *Vietnam Tracks: Armor in Battle 1945-1975.* Novato, California: Presidio Press, 1982.

Dupuy, Trevor N. *Dictionary of Military Terms.* New York: Wilson, 1986.

Elting, John. *Dictionary of Soldier Talk.* New York: Scribner's, 1984.

Esper, George, and The Associated Press. *The Eyewitness History of the Vietnam War.* New York: Villard Books, 1983.

Karnow, Stanley. *Vietnam: A History.* New York: Viking, 1983.

Keylin, Arleen, and Boiangiu, Suri. *Front Page Vietnam.* New York: Arco, 1979.

Kleiner, Richard. *Index of Initials and Acronyms.* New York: Auerbach, 1971.

Konerding, Erhard. *Vietnam War Facts Quiz: The Truth and Drama of American Involvement.* Middletown, Connecticut: Southfarm Press, 1986.

Krepinevich, Andrew, Jr. *The Army and Vietnam.* Baltimore: Johns Hopkins University Press, 1986.

Lawson, Don. *The United States in the Vietnam War.* New York: Crowell, 1981.

Luttwak, Edward. *A Dictionary of Modern War.* New York: Harper & Row, 1971.

Maclear, Michael. *The Ten Thousand Day War: Vietnam 1945-1975.* New York: St. Martin's Press, 1981.

Mahler, Michael. *Ringed in Steel.* Novato, California: Presidio Press, 1986.

Mangold, Tom, and Penycate, John. *The Tunnels of Cu Chi.* New York: Random House, 1985.

Mesko, Jim. *Armor in Vietnam, a Pictorial History.* Carrollton, Texas: Squadron/Signal, 1982.

Mesko, Jim, and Thompson, Leroy. *U.S. Infantry–Vietnam/U.S. Elite Forces.* Carrollton, Texas: Squadron/Signal, 1983.

Musgrave, J., and Clodfelter, M. *Vietnam Years: One Thousand Questions and Answers.* Boston: Quinlan Press, 1986.

Newcomb, Richard F. *A Pictorial History of the Vietnam War.* Garden City, N.Y.: Doubleday, 1987.

Nolan, Keith W. *Battle for Hue: Tet 1968.* Novato, California: Presidio Press, 1983.

————. *Into Laos*. Novato, California: Presidio Press, 1986.

————. *Death Valley*. Novato, California: Presidio Press, 1987.

Olson, James S. *Dictionary of the Vietnam War*. Westport, Connecticut: Greenwood Press, 1988.

Page, Tim, and Pimlott, John. *NAM: The Vietnam Experience 1965-1975*. New York: Orbis Books, 1988.

Palmer, Bruce, Jr. *The 25 Year War: America's Military Role in Vietnam*. Lexington: University of Kentucky Press, 1984.

Pettit, Clyde E., ed. *The Experts*. Secaucus, N.J.: Lyle Stuart, 1975.

Pisor, Robert. *The End of the Line: The Siege of Khe Sanh*. New York: Norton, 1982.

Pretz, Bernhard. *A Dictionary of Military and Technological Abbreviations and Acronyms*. London: Routledge & Kegan Paul, 1983.

Quick, John. *Dictionary of Weapons and Military Terms*. New York: McGraw-Hill, 1973.

Rawson, Hugh. *Dictionary of Euphemisms and Other Doubletalk*. New York: Crown, 1981.

Robinson, Anthony. *Weapons of the Vietnam War*. Greenwich, Connecticut: Bison Books, 1983.

Rosser-Owen, David. *Vietnam Weapons Handbook*. Wellingborough, U.K.: Patrick Stephens, Ltd., 1986.

Scruggs, Jan. *To Heal a Nation*. New York: Harper & Row, 1985.

Sheehan, Neil. *A Bright Shining Lie: John Paul Vann and America in Vietnam*. New York: Random House, 1988.

Smith, Richard W., and Pelz, Roy A. *Shoulder Sleeve Insignia of the U.S. Army 1946-1976*. Evansville: U. of Evansville Press, 1978.

Smyth, Cecil B. *Republic of Vietnam Territorial Forces Insignia*. Virginia Beach: Cecil B. Smyth, 1976.

Stanton, Shelby. *Vietnam Order of Battle*. Washington, D.C.: U.S. News Books, 1981.

————. *The Rise and Fall of an American Army: U.S. Ground Forces in Vietnam 1965-1973*. Novato, California: Presidio Press, 1986.

————. *Anatomy of a Division: 1st Cav in Vietnam*. Novato, California: Presidio Press, 1987.

————. *U.S. Army Uniforms of the Vietnam War*. Harrisburg, Pennsylvania: Stackpole, 1989.

Starr, Jerald M. *The Lessons of the Vietnam War: A Modular Textbook*. Pittsburgh: Center for Social Studies, 1988.

Starry, General Donn. *Armored Combat in Vietnam*. New York: Bobbs-Merrill, 1980.

Stein, Jeff. *The Vietnam Fact Book*. New York: Dell, 1987.

Summers, Harry G., Jr. *Vietnam War Almanac*. New York: Facts On File, 1985.

Thompson, Leroy. *Uniforms of the Indo-China and Vietnam Wars*. Poole, U.K.: Blandford Press, 1984.

Turley, G.H. *The Easter Offensive: Vietnam 1972*. Novato, California: Presidio Press, 1985.

———. *The Second Indochina War*. New York: New American Library, 1986.

Welsh, Douglas. *History of the Vietnam War*. New York: Galahad Books, 1982.

## Agent Orange

Buckingham, William A., Jr. *Operation Ranch Hand: The Air Force and Herbicides in Southeast Asia, 1961-1971*. Washington, D.C.: Office of Air Force History, 1982.

Dux, John, and Young, P.J. *Agent Orange, the Bitter Harvest*. Sydney, Australia: Hodder & Stoughton, 1980.

Linedecker, Clifford. *Kerry*. New York: St. Martin's Press, 1982.

Schuck, Peter H. *Agent Orange on Trial*. Cambridge: Belknap Press of Harvard University Press, 1987.

Wilcox, Fred A. *Waiting for an Army to Die: The Tragedy of Agent Orange*. New York: Random House, 1983.

## Air War

Bell, Dana. *Vietnam Warbirds in Action*. London: Arms and Armour Press, 1986.

Berent, Mark. *Rolling Thunder*. New York: Putnam, 1989.

Broughton, Jack. *Thud Ridge*. New York: Lippincott, 1969.

Cash, John, et al. *Seven Firefights in Vietnam*. New York: Bantam, 1985.

Chinnery, Phil. *Air War in Vietnam*. New York: Exeter Books, 1987.

———. *Life on the Line*. New York: St. Martin's Press, 1988.

Coleman, J.D. *Pleiku: The Dawn of Helicopter Warfare in Vietnam*. New York: St. Martin's Press, 1988.

Cunningham, Randy. *Fox Two! America's First Ace in Vietnam*. Mesa, Arizona: Champlin Museum, 1984.

Drendel, Lou. *Air War over Southeast Asia*. Carrollton, Texas: Squadron/Signal, 1984.

———. *And Kill MiGs*. Carrollton, Texas: Squadron/Signal, 1984.

———. *Huey*. Carrollton, Texas: Squadron/Signal, 1983.

Dunstan, Simon. *Vietnam Choppers*. London: Osprey, 1988.

Francillon, Rene. *Vietnam: The War in the Air*. New York: Arch Cape Press, 1987.

Grant, Zalin. *Over the Beach: The Air War in Vietnam*. New York: Norton, 1986.

Gregory, Barry. *Vietnam Helicopter Handbook*. Wellingborough: Patrick Stephens, Ltd., 1988.

Guerney, Gene. *Vietnam: The War in the Air, A Pictorial History of the U.S. Air Forces in the Vietnam War: Air Force, Army, Navy, & the Marines*. New York: Crown, 1985.

Halberstadt, H. *Airborne: Assault from the Sky*. Novato, California: Presidio Press, 1988.

Harvey, Frank. *Air War—Vietnam*. New York: Bantam, 1967.

Littauer, Raphael, and Uphoff, Norman, eds. *Air War in Indochina*. Boston: Beacon Press, 1972

Mesko, Jim. *Airmobile: The Helicopter War in Vietnam*. Carrollton, Texas: Squadron Signal, 1985.

Middleton, Drew. *Air War—Vietnam*. New York: Arno, 1978.

Nalty, Bernard C. *Air Power and the Fight for Khe Sanh*. Washington, DC: Office of Air Force History, 1973.

Nalty, Bernard C., Watson, George M., and Neufeld, Jacob. *An Illustrated Guide to the Air War Over Vietnam—Aircraft of the Southeast Asia Conflict*. New York: Arco, 1981.

Padden, Ian. *U.S. Airborne*. New York: Bantam, 1986.

Robbins, Christopher. *Air America*. New York: Putnam, 1979.

———. *The Ravens*. New York: Crown, 1987.

Trotti, John. *Marine Air: First to Fight*. Novato, California: Presidio Press, 1985.

———. *Phantom Over Vietnam*. Novato, California: Presidio Press, 1984.

## Blacks in Vietnam

Goff, Stanley, and Sandfors, Robert. *Brothers: Black Soldiers in the Nam.* Novato, California: Presidio Press, 1982.

Taylor, Clyde. *Vietnam and Black America: An Anthology of Protest and Resistance.* Garden City, N.Y.: Anchor/Doubleday, 1973.

Terry, Wallace. *Bloods: An Oral History of the Vietnam War by Black Veterans.* New York: Random House, 1984.

## Marine Corps

Bartlett, Tom, ed. *Ambassadors in Green.* Washington, D.C.: Leatherneck Association, 1971.

Ehrhart, W.D. *Vietnam-Perkasie: A Combat Marine Memoir.* Jefferson, N.C.: McFarland, 1983.

Fails, Lt. Col. William R. *Marines and Helicopters, 1962-1973.* Washington, D.C.: U.S. Marine Corps, 1978.

Hammel, Eric. *Siege in the Clouds.* New York: Crown, 1989.

Henderson, Charles. *Marine Sniper.* New York: Berkley, 1986.

Krulak, Victor H. *First to Fight: An Inside View of the U.S. Marine Corps.* Annapolis: Naval Institute Press, 1984.

Lanning, Michael L., and Stubbe, Ray William. *Inside Force Recon: Recon Marines in Vietnam.* New York: Ivy, 1989.

Lippard, Karl. *The Warriors: The United States Marines.* Lancaster, Texas: Vietnam Marine Publications, 1983.

*The Marines in Vietnam 1954-1973.* Washington, D.C.: History and Museums Division, U.S. Marine Corps, 1974.

Moskin, J. Robert. *The U.S. Marine Corps Story.* New York: McGraw-Hill, 1987.

Padden, Ian. *U.S. Marines: From Boot Camp to the Battle Zone.* New York: Bantam, 1985.

Severo, Richard, and Milford, Lewis. *The Wages of War: When America's Soldiers Came Home—From Valley Forge to Vietnam.* New York: Simon & Schuster, 1989.

Shore, Capt. Moyers. *The Battle for Khe Sanh.* Washington, D.C.: History & Museums Division, Headquarters, U.S. Marine Corps, 1969.

*U. S. Marines in Vietnam 1954-1973.* Washington, D.C.: History and Museums Division, Headquarters, U. S. Marine Corps, 1974.

## Naval War

Croziat, Victor. *The Brown Water Navy: The River and Coastal War in Indo-China and Vietnam, 1948-1972*. Poole, U.K.: Blandford Press, 1984.

———. *Vietnam Riverine Warfare*. Poole, U.K.: Blandford Press, 1986.

Cutler, Thomas J. *Brown Water, Black Berets: Coastal & Riverine Warfare in Vietnam*. Annapolis: Naval Institute Press, 1988.

Levinson, Jeffrey L. *Alpha Strike Vietnam: The Navy's Air War, 1964-1973*. Novato, California: Presidio Press, 1989.

Mersky, Peter, and Polmar, Norman. *The Naval Air War in Vietnam: 1965-1975*. Annapolis: The Nautical and Aviation Publishing Co. of America, 1981.

Mesko, Jim. *Riverine*. Carrollton, Texas: Squadron/Signal, 1985.

Moeser, Robert D. *U.S. Navy: Vietnam*. Annapolis: Naval Institute Press, 1969.

Sweetman, Jack. *American Naval History*. Annapolis: Naval Institute Press, 1984

Tillman, Barrett, and Nichols, John B. *On Yankee Station: The Naval Air War over Vietnam*. Annapolis: Naval Institute Press, 1987.

Uhlig, Frank, Jr., ed. *Vietnam: The Naval Story*. Annapolis: Naval Institute Press, 1986.

Zumwalt, Adm. Elmo. *On Watch*. New York: Quadrangle/New York Times Book Co., 1976.

## Special Forces

Bank, Col. Aaron. *From OSS to Green Beret*. New York: Pocket Books, 1986.

Berry, John Steven. *Those Gallant Men*. Novato, California: Presidio Press, 1984.

Brown, Ashley, ed. *The Green Beret*. New York: Villard Books, 1986.

Burruss, Lt. Col. L.H. *Mike Force*. New York: Pocket Books, 1989.

Griffen, W.E.B. *The Berets (Brotherhood of War Series)*. New York: Berkley, 1985.

Halberstadt, H. *Green Berets: Unconventional Warfare*. Novato, California: Presidio Press, 1988.

Padden, Ian. *U.S. Army Special Forces*. New York: Bantam, 1985.

Simpson, Charles M., III. *Inside the Green Berets: The First Thirty Years*. Novato, California: Presidio Press, 1983.

———. *Green Berets at War*. Novato, California: Presidio Press, 1985.

Stanton, Shelby. *U.S. Army Special Forces A-Team Vietnam Combat Manual.* Boulder: Paladin Press, 1988.

Thompson, Leroy. *U.S. Elite Forces in Vietnam.* Carrollton, Texas: Squadron/Signal, 1985.

## "The Vietnam Experience" Series

Casey, Michael, et al. *The Army at War.* Boston: Boston Publishing Co., 1987.

———. *Flags Into Battle.* Boston: Boston Publishing Co., 1987.

Doleman, Edgar, C., Jr. *Tools of War.* Boston: Boston Publishing Co., 1984.

Dougan, Clark, and Fulghum, David. *The Fall of the South.* Boston: Boston Publishing Co., 1985.

Dougan, Clark, and Lipsman, Samuel. *A Nation Divided.* Boston: Boston Publishing Co., 1984.

Dougan, Clark, and Weiss, Stephen. *Nineteen Sixty-Eight.* Boston: Boston Publishing Co., 1984.

Doyle, Edward, and Lipsman, Samuel. *Setting the Stage.* Boston: Boston Publishing Co., 1981.

———. *America Takes Over.* Boston: Boston Publishing Co., 1982.

Doyle, Edward; Lipsman, Samuel; and Maitland, Terrence. *The North.* Boston: Boston Publishing Company, 1986.

Doyle, Edward; Lipsman, Samuel; and Weiss, Stephen. *Passing the Torch.* Boston: Boston Publishing Co., 1986.

Doyle, Edward, and Weiss, Stephen. *A Collision of Cultures.* Boston: Boston Publishing Co., 1984.

Fischer, Julene, et al. *Images of War.* Boston: Boston Publishing Co., 1986.

Fulghum, David, and Maitland, Terrence. *South Vietnam on Trial.* Boston: Boston Publishing Co., 1984.

Hardy, Gordon, ed. *The Words of War.* Boston: Boston Publishing Co., 1988.

Isaacs, Arnold R.; Hardy, Gordon; Brown, MacAlister, et al. *Pawns of War.* Boston: Boston Publishing Co., 1987.

Lipsman, Samuel, and Weiss, Stephen. *Fighting for Time.* Boston: Boston Publishing Co., 1983.

———. *The False Peace.* Boston: Boston Publishing Co., 1985.

Maitland, Terrence, and McInerney, Peter. *A Contagion of War.* Boston: Boston Publishing Company, 1983.

Maitland, Terrence, and Weiss, Stephen. *Raising the Stakes*. Boston: Boston Publishing Co., 1982.

Manning, Robert, ed. *The Aftermath: The Legacy of War, 1975-1985*. Boston: Boston Publishing Co., 1985.

Mills, Nick. *Combat Photographer*. Boston: Boston Publishing Co., 1983.

Morrocco, John. *Thunder from Above: Air War 1941-1968*. Boston: Boston Publishing Co., 1984.

———. *Rain of Fire: Air War 1969-1973*. Boston: Boston Publishing Co., 1985.

Weiss, Stephen, et al. *A War Remembered*. Boston: Boston Publishing Co., 1986.

———. *War in the Shadows*. Boston: Boston Publishing Co., 1988.

## Fiction

Anderson, Kent. *Sympathy for the Devil*. Garden City, N.Y.: Warner, 1987.

Anderson, Robert. *Service for the Dead*. New York: Arbor House, 1986.

———. *Cooks and Bakers*. New York: Avon, 1982.

Balaban, John. *Coming Down Again*. New York: Harcourt Brace Jovanovich, 1985.

Bausch, Robert. *On the Way Home*. New York: St. Martin's Press, 1982.

Blacker, Irwin. *Search and Destroy*. New York: Dell, 1966.

Bodey, Donald. *F.N.G.* New York: Viking, 1985.

Bosse, Malcolm. *The Incident at Naha*. New York: Simon & Schuster, 1972.

Boyd, William. *On the Yankee Station*. New York: Morrow, 1984.

Boyne, Walter J. *The Wild Blue*. New York: Ballantine, 1986.

Britton, Christopher. *Paybacks*. New York: Popular Library, 1985.

Browne, Corinne. *Body Shop*. New York: Stein & Day, 1973.

Bunch, Chris, and Cole, Allan. *Reckoning of Kings*. New York: Ballantine, 1987.

Bunting, Josiah. *The Lionheads*. New York: Braziller, 1972.

Butler, Robert Olen. *Alleys of Eden*. New York: Ballantine, 1981.

———. *Sun Dogs*. New York: Ballantine, 1982.

———. *On Distant Ground*. New York: Knopf, 1985.

Butterworth, W.E. *Air Evac*. New York: Norton, 1967.

———. *Helicopter Pilot*. New York: Norton, 1967.

———. *Orders to Vietnam*. Boston: Little, Brown, 1968.

Caputo, Philip. *Delcorso's Gallery*. New York: Holt, Rinehart and Winston, 1983.

———. *Indian Country*. New York: Bantam, 1987.

Carroll, James. *Fault Lines*. Boston: Little, Brown, 1980.

———. *Prince of Peace*. Boston: Little, Brown, 1984.

Cassidy, John. *A Station in the Delta*. New York: Scribner's, 1979.

Chandler, David. *Captain Hollister*. New York: Macmillan, 1973.

Clark, Alan. *The Lion Heart*. New York: Morrow, 1969.

Clark, Johnnie M. *Semper Fidelis*. New York: Ballantine Books, 1988.
   Coleman, Charles. *Sergeant Back Again*. New York: Harper & Row, 1980.

Coonts, Stephen. *Flight of the Intruder*. Annapolis: Naval Institute Press, 1986.

Corder, E.M. *The Deer Hunter*. New York: Exeter, 1979.

Costello, Michael. *A Long Time from Home*. New York: Zebra, 1984.

Cragg, Dan. *The Soldier's Prize*. New York: Ballantine, 1986.

Crumley, James. *One to Count Cadence*. New York: Random House, 1969.

Curry, Richard. *Fatal Light*. New York: Dutton, 1988.

Dann, Jeanne Van Buren, and Dann, Jack, ed. *In the Field of Fire*. New York: Tom Doherty Associates, 1987.

Del Vecchio, John. *The Thirteenth Valley*. New York: Bantam, 1982.

DeMille, Neville. *Word of Honor*. New York: Warner, 1985.

Dodge, Ed. *Dau*. New York: Macmillan, 1984.

Duncan, Donald. *The New Legions*. New York: Random House, 1967.

Durden, Charles. *No Bugles, No Drums*. New York: Viking, 1976.

Dye, Dale. *Run Between the Raindrops*. New York: Avon, 1985.

Eastlake, William. *The Bamboo Bed*. New York: Simon & Schuster, 1969.

Ebert, Alan. *The Long Way Home*. New York: Crown, 1984.

Ely, Scott. *Starlight*. New York: Weidenfeld & Nicolson, 1987.

Ferrandino, Joseph. *Firefight*. New York: Soho Press, 1987.

Fleming, Thomas. *The Officers' Wives*. Garden City, N.Y.: Doubleday, 1981.

Flowers, A.R. *De Mojo Blues*. New York: Dutton, 1985.

Ford, Daniel. *Incident at Muc Wa*. Garden City, N.Y.: Doubleday, 1967.

Fuller, Jack. *Fragments*. New York: Morrow, 1984.

Gazzanigo, Donald A. *A Few Good Men*. New York: Signet, 1988.

Giovannitti, Len. *The Man Who Won the Medal of Honor*. New York: Random House, 1973.

Glasser, Ronald. *Another War, Another Peace*. New York: Summit, 1985.

Glick, Allen. *Winters Coming, Winters Gone*. New York: Pinnacle, 1985.

Groen, Jay. *Huey*. New York: Ballantine, 1984.

Groom, Winston. *Better Times Than These*. New York: Summit, 1978.

Haldeman, Joe. *War Year*. New York: Holt, Rinehart and Winston, 1972.

Hasford, Gustav. *Short-Timers*. New York: Harper & Row, 1979.

Hathaway, Bo. *A World of Hurt*. New York: Taplinger, 1981.

Hawkins, Evelyn. *Vietnam Nurse*. New York: Zebra, 1984.

Hawkins, Jack. *Chopper #1: Blood Trails*. New York: Ivy, 1987.

———. *Chopper #7: Kill Zone*. New York: Ivy Books, 1988.

Heineman, Larry. *Close Quarters*. New York: Farrar, Straus & Giroux, 1977.

———. *Paco's Story*. New York: Farrar, Straus & Giroux, 1979.

Helm, Eric. *Vietnam Ground Zero: The Raid*. Ontario, Canada: Worldwide, 1988.

Hempstone, Smith. *A Tract of Time*. Boston: Houghton Mifflin, 1966.

Holland, William. *Let a Soldier Die*. New York: Delacorte, 1984.

Huggett, William Turn. *Body Count*. New York: Putnam, 1973.

Hunter, Evan. *Sons*. Garden City, N.Y.: Doubleday, 1969.

Hunter, Lanny, and Hunter, Victor. *Living Dogs and Dead Lions*. New York: Viking, 1986.

James, Allston. *Attic Light*. Santa Barbara, California: Capra, 1979.

Joss, John. *Sierra Sierra*. New York: Morrow, 1978.

Just, Ward. *Stringer*. Boston: Little, Brown, 1974.

———. *American Blues*. New York: Viking, 1984.

Kalb, Bernard, and Kalb, Marvin. *The Last Ambassador*. Boston: Little, Brown, 1981.

Karlin, Wane; Paquet, Basil T.; and Rottman, Larry, eds. *Free Fire Zone: Short Stories by Vietnam Veterans*. New York: McGraw-Hill, 1973.

Kennedy, Adam. *In a Far Country*. New York: Delacorte, 1983.

Ketwig, John. *And a Hard Rain Fell*. New York: Pocket Books, 1985.

Kirk, Donald. *Tell It to the Dead*. Chicago: Nelson-Hall, 1975.

Kirkwood, James. *Some Kind of Hero*. New York: Crowell, 1975.

Klose, Kevin, and McCombs, Philip. *The Typhoon Shipments*. New York: Norton, 1974.

Kolpacoff, Victor. *The Prisoners of Quai Dong*. New York: New American Library, 1967.

Leib, Franklin Allen. *The Fire Dream*. Novato, California: Presidio Press, 1989.

Linn, Bill. *Missing in Action*. New York: Avon, 1981.

Littell, Robert. *Sweet Reason*. Boston: Houghton Mifflin, 1974.

Little, Lloyd. *Parthian Shot*. New York: Viking, 1973.

Mahoney, Tim. *Hollaran's World War*. New York: Delacorte, 1985.

Maitland, Derek. *The Only War We've Got*. New York: Morrow, 1970.

Mason, Bobbie Ann. *In Country*. New York: Harper & Row, 1985.

Maurer, David A. *The Dying Place*. New York: Dell, 1986.

McCarry, Charles. *The Tears of Autumn*. New York: Dutton, 1974.

McQuinn, Donald E. *Targets*. New York: Macmillan, 1980.

Miller, Kenn. *Tiger the Lurp Dog*. Boston: Little, Brown, 1983.

Moore, Gene. *The Killing at Ngo Tho*. New York: Norton, 1967.

Moore, Robin, and Collins, June. *The Khaki Mafia*. New York: Crown, 1971.

Morrell, David. *First Blood*. New York: M. Evans & Co., 1972.

Morris, Jim. *War Story*. Boulder: Paladin Enterprises, 1979.

Nelson, Charles. *The Boy Who Picked the Bullets Up*. New York: Morrow, 1981.

Nichols, John. *American Blood*. New York: Henry Holt, 1987.

O'Brien, Tim. *If I Die in a Combat Zone*. New York: Delacorte, 1967.

———. *Going After Cacciato*. New York: Delacorte, 1978.

Ogden, R. *Green Knight, Red Mourning*. New York: Zebra, 1985.

Parque, Richard. *Sweet Vietnam*. New York: Zebra, 1984.

Pelfrey, William. *The Big V*. New York: Liveright, 1972.

Petrakis, Harry Mark. *In the Land of Mourning*. New York: David McKay, 1973.

Pfarrer, Donald. *Neverlight*. New York: Seaview, 1982.

Porter, John B. *If I Make My Bed in Hell*. Waco, Texas: Word Books, 1969.

Pratt, John Clark. *The Laotian Fragments*. New York: Viking, 1974.

Proffitt, Nicholas. *Gardens of Stone.* New York: Carroll & Graf, 1983.

———. *The Embassy House.* New York: Bantam, 1986.

Rich, Curt. *The Advisors.* New York: Zebra, 1985.

Riggan, Rob. *Free Fire Zone.* New York: Norton, 1984.

Rivers, G., and Hudson, J. *The Five Fingers.* New York: Doubleday, 1978.

Roth, Robert. *Sand in the Wind.* Boston: Little, Brown, 1973.

Rubin, Jonathan. *The Barking Deer.* New York: Braziller, 1974.

Schaeffer, Susan Fromberg. *Buffalo Afternoon.* New York: Knopf, 1989

Scott, Leonard B. *Charlie Mike.* New York: Ballantine, 1985.

———. *The Last Run.* New York: Ballantine, 1987.

———. *The Hill.* New York: Ballantine, 1989.

Sloan, James Park. *War Games.* Boston: Houghton Mifflin, 1971.

Smith, Stephen Phillip. *American Boys.* New York: Putnam, 1974.

Stone, Robert. *Dog Soldiers.* Boston: Houghton Mifflin, 1974.

Stone, Scott. *The Coasts of War.* New York: Pyramid, 1966.

Suddick, Tom. *A Few Good Men.* New York: Avon, 1979.

Tate, Donald. *Bravo Burning.* New York: Bantam, 1986.

Tauber, Peter. *The Last Best Hope.* New York: Harcourt Brace Jovanovich, 1977.

Taylor, Thomas. *A Piece of This Country.* New York: Norton, 1970.

Tiede, Tom. *Coward.* New York: Trident Press, 1968.

Vaughn, Robert. *The Quick and the Dead.* New York: Dell, 1984.

———. *The Valkyrie Mandate.* New York: Simon & Schuster, 1974.

Vaughn, Robert, and Lynch, Monroe. *Brandywine's War.* New York: Bartholomew House, 1971.

Walsh, Patricia. *Forever Sad the Hearts.* New York: Avon, 1982.

Webb, James. *Fields of Fire.* Englewood Cliffs, N.J.: Prentice-Hall, 1978.

———. *A Sense of Honor.* Englewood Cliffs, N.J.: Prentice-Hall, 1981.

———. *A Country Such As This.* Garden City, N.Y.: Doubleday, 1983.

White, Kent, Jr. *Prairie Fire.* Canton, Ohio: Daring Press, 1983.

Williams, John. *Captain Blackman.* Garden City, N.Y.: Doubleday, 1972.

Wilson, William. *The LBJ Brigade*. New York: Pyramid Books, 1966.

Wolfe, Michael. *Chinese Fire Drill*. New York: Harper & Row, 1976.

――――. *Man on a String*. New York: Harper & Row, 1973.

Wright, Stephen. *Meditations in Green*. New York: Scribner, 1983.

## Personal Accounts

Anderson, Charles B. *The Grunts*. Novato, California: Presidio Press, 1976.

――――. *Vietnam: The Other War*. Novato, California: Presidio Press, 1982.

Anderson, William C. *Bat-21*. New York: Bantam, 1980

Bain, David Haward. *After-Shocks*. New York: Penguin, 1986.

Baker, Mark. *Nam*. New York: Morrow, 1981.

Beesley, Stanley. *The Heartland Remembers*. Norman: U. of Oklahoma Press, 1987.

Benavidez, Roy P. *The Three Wars of Roy Benavidez*. San Antonio, Texas: Corona, 1986.

Berrigan, Daniel, S.J. *Night Flight to Hanoi*. New York: Macmillan, 1968.

――――. *No Bars to Manhood*. Garden City, N.Y.: Doubleday, 1970.

Berry, John Stevens. *Those Gallant Men*. Novato, California: Presidio Press, 1984.

Block, Mickey, and Kimball, William. *Before the Dawn*. Canton, Ohio, Daring Press, 1988.

Brace, Ernest C. *A Code to Keep*. New York: St. Martin's Press, 1988.

Brandon, Heather. *Casualties*. New York: St. Martin's Press, 1984.

Branfman, F. *Voices from the Plain of Jars*. New York: Harper & Row, 1972.

Brennan, Matthew. *Brennan's War*. Novato, California: Presidio Press, 1985.

Brennan, Matthew, ed. *The Headhunters*. Novato, California: Presidio Press, 1987.

Brown, John M.G. *Rice Paddy Grunt*. New York: Regnery, 1986.

Browne, Corinne. *Body Shop*. New York: Stein & Day, 1973.

Broyles, William. *Brothers in Arms*. New York: Knopf, 1986.

Bryan, C.D.B. *Friendly Fire*. New York: Putnam, 1976.

Camper, Frank. *L.R.R.P.: The Professional*. New York: Dell, 1988.

Caputo, Philip. *A Rumor of War*. New York: Holt, Rinehart and Winston, 1977.

Carhart, Tom. *The Offering.* New York: Morrow, 1987.

Chinnery, Philip D. *Life on the Line.* New York: St. Martin's Press, 1988.

Clark, Johnnie M. *Guns Up!* New York: Ballantine, 1984.

Clodfelter, Michael. *Mad Moments and Vietnam Months: A Soldier's Memoirs.* Jefferson, N.C.: McFarland & Co., 1988.

Cook, John L. *The Advisor.* New York: Bantam, 1987.

Cortesi, Laurence. *The Magnificent Bastards of Chu Lai.* New York: Zebra, 1986.

Dengler, Dieter. *Escape from Laos.* Novato, California: Presidio Press, 1979.

Donahue, James C. *No Greater Love.* Canton, Ohio: Daring Press, 1988.

Donovan, David. *Once a Warrior King.* New York: McGraw-Hill, 1985.

Downs, Frederick. *The Killing Zone.* New York: Norton, 1978.

———. *Aftermath.* New York: Norton, 1984.

Dramesi, John A. *A Code of Honor.* New York: Norton, 1975.

Drury, Richard. *My Secret War.* New York: St. Martin's Press, 1986.

Ehrhart, W.D. *Vietnam Perkasie.* New York: Zebra, 1983.

———. *Marking Time.* New York: Avon, 1986.

Eilert, Rick. *For Self and Country.* New York: Morrow, 1983.

Emerson, Gloria. *Winners and Losers.* New York: Harcourt, Brace, 1972.

Fallaci, Oriana. *Nothing and So Be It.* Garden City, N.Y.: Doubleday, 1972.

Flesch, Ron. *Redwood Delta.* New York: Berkley, 1988

Flood, Charles Bracelen. *The War of the Innocents.* New York: McGraw-Hill, 1970.

Gadd, Charles. *Line Doggie: Foot Soldier in Vietnam.* Novato, California: Presidio Press, 1987.

Gazzaniga, Donald A. *A Few Good Men.* New York: New American Library, 1989.

Glasser, Ronald. *365 Days.* New York: Braziller, 1971.

Goldman, Peter, and Fuller, Tony. *Charlie Company: What Vietnam Did to Us.* New York: Morrow, 1983.

Grant, Zalin. *Survivors: American POWs in Vietnam.* New York: Norton, 1975.

Groom, W., and Spencer, D. *Conversations With the Enemy.* New York: Putnam, 1983.

Hackworth, Col. David, with Sherman, Julie. *About Face*. New York: Simon & Schuster, 1989.

Hamilton-Paterson, J. *The Greedy War*. New York: David McKay, 1971.

Hammer, Richard. *One Morning in the War*. New York: Coward-McCann, 1970.

Hemphill, Paul. *Too Old to Cry*. New York: Viking, 1981.

Herbert, Anthony B. *Soldier*. New York: Holt, Rinehart and Winston, 1973.

Herr, Michael. *Dispatches*. New York: Knopf, 1977.

Herrington, Maj. Stuart A. *Silence Was a Weapon: The Vietnam War in the Villages*. Novato, California: Presidio Press, 1982.

Hersh, Seymour. *My Lai 4*. New York: Random House, 1970.

Higgens, Marguerite. *Our Vietnam Nightmare*. New York: Harper & Row, 1965.

Jones, James. *Viet Journal*. New York: Delacorte, 1974.

Hughes, Larry. *You Can See a Lot Standing under a Flare in the Republic of Vietnam: My Year at War*. New York: Morrow, 1969.

Just, Ward. *Military Men*. New York: Knopf, 1970.

———. *To What End: Report from Vietnam*. Boston: Houghton Mifflin, 1968.

Ketwig, John. *And a Hard Rain Fell*. New York: Macmillan, 1985.

Kirk, Donald. *Tell It to the Dead*. Chicago: Nelson-Hall, 1975.

Klein, Joe. *Payback*. New York: Knopf, 1984.

Kovic, Ron. *Born on the Fourth of July*. New York: McGraw-Hill, 1976.

Lane, Mark. *Conversations with Americans*. New York: Simon & Schuster, 1970.

Lang, Daniel. *Casualties of War*. New York: McGraw-Hill, 1969.

Lynd, Staughton, and Hayden, Thomas. *The Other Side*. New York: New American Library, 1966.

Mason, Robert C. *Chickenhawk*. New York: Viking, 1983.

Maurer, Harry. *Strange Ground*. New York: Henry Holt, 1988

McCarthy, Mary. *Vietnam*. New York: Harcourt Brace Jovanovich, 1967.

McConnell, Malcolm. *Into the Mouth of the Cat: The Story of Lance Sijan, a Hero of Vietnam*. New York: Norton, 1984.

McDonough, James. *Platoon Leader*. New York: Bantam, 1985.

McGrady, Mike. *A Dove in Vietnam*. New York: Funk & Wagnalls, 1968.

McMullen, James P. *Cry of the Panther*. New York: McGraw-Hill, 1984.

McPherson, Myra. *Long Time Passing*. Garden City, N.Y.: Doubleday, 1984.

Meshad, Shad. *Captain for Dark Mornings*. Playa Del Rey, California: Creative Image Associates, 1982.

Morris, Jim. *War Story*. New York: Dell, 1979.

Ogden, Richard E. *Green Knight, Red Mourning*. New York: Zebra, 1985.

Parks, David. *G.I. Diary*. Washington, D.C.: Howard University Press, 1984.

Parrish, John A., M.D. *12, 20 & 5. A Doctor's Year in Vietnam*. New York: Dutton, 1972.

Pratt, John Clark. *Vietnam Voices*. New York: Penguin, 1984.

Reed, David. *Up Front in Vietnam*. New York: Funk and Wagnalls, 1967.

Risner, Gen. Robinson. *The Passing of the Night*. New York: Ballantine, 1973.

Roberts, Craig, and Sasser, Charles W. *The Walking Dead*. New York: Pocket Books, 1989.

Rowe, Maj. James N. *Five Years to Freedom*. Boston: Little, Brown, 1971.

Sack, John. *M*. New York: New American Library, 1966.

Salisbury, Harrison. *Behind the Lines—Hanoi*. New York: Harper & Row, 1967.

Santoli, Al. *Everything We Had*. New York: Random House, 1981.

Schell, Jonathan. *The Village of Ben Suc*. New York: Knopf, 1967.

———. *The Military Half*. New York: Knopf, 1968.

Schemmer, Benjamin F. *The Raid*. New York: Harper & Row, 1976.

Scutts, Jerry. *Wolfpack: Hunting MiGs Over Vietnam*. New York: Warner, 1988.

Sontag, Susan. *Trip To Hanoi*. New York: Farrar, Straus and Giroux, 1968.

Spencer, Ernest. *Welcome to Vietnam, Macho Man*. New York: Bantam, 1987.

Steinbeck, John. *In Touch*. New York: Knopf, 1969.

Stockdale, Jim, and Stockdale, Sybil. *In Love and War*. New York: Harper & Row, 1984.

Tregaskis, Richard. *Vietnam Diary*. New York: Holt, Rinehart and Winston, 1963.

Walker, Keith, ed. *A Piece of My Heart*. Novato, California: Presidio Press, 1985.

Whitmore, Terry, and Weber, Richard. *Memphis-Nam-Sweden*. Garden City, N.Y.: Doubleday, 1971.

Willson, David A. *REMF Diary*. Seattle: Black Heron Press, 1988.

Yezzo, Dominick. *A G.I.'s Vietnam Diary*. New York: Franklin Watts, 1974.

Zumbro, Ralph. *Tank Sergeant*. Novato, California: Presidio Press, 1986.

Zumwalt, Admiral Elmo, Jr., and Zumwalt, Elmo, III. *My Father, My Son*. New York: Macmillan, 1986.

## Miscellaneous

Arlen, Michael. *The Living Room War*. New York, Viking, 1969.

Bamford, James. *The Puzzle Palace*. Boston: Houghton Mifflin, 1982.

Becker, Stephen. *Dog Tags*. New York: Random House, 1973.

Berman, Larry. *Planning a Tragedy: The Americanization of the War in Vietnam*. New York: Norton, 1982.

Braestrup, Peter. *The Big Story*. New Haven, Connecticut: Yale University Press, 1977.

Browne, Malcolm. *The New Face of War*. Indianapolis: Bobbs-Merrill, 1965.

Bryan, John. *This Soldier Still at War*. New York: Harcourt, Brace, 1975.

Camper, Frank. *L.R.R.P.: The Professional*. New York: Dell, 1988.

Da Cruz, Daniel. *Boot*. New York: St. Martin's Press, 1987.

Davis, Larry. *Gunships*. Carrollton, Texas: Squadron/Signal, 1982.

Department of the Army. *Vietnam Phrase Book*. Washington, D.C.: U.S. Government Printing Office, 1962.

Department of Defense. *Pocket Guide to Vietnam, A*. Washington, D.C.: U.S. Government Printing Office, 1966.

Dickson, Paul. *The Electronic Battlefield*. Bloomington: U. of Indiana Press, 1976.

Drury, Richard S. *My Secret War*. New York: St. Martin's Press, 1979

Ethell, Jeffrey, and Price, Alfred. *One Day in a Long War*. New York: Random House, 1989.

Garland, Albert N., ed. *Infantry in Vietnam: Small Unit Actions in the Early Days 1965-1966*. Nashville: Battery Press, 1967.

———. *A Distant Challenge: The U.S. Infantryman in Vietnam 1967-1972*. Nashville: Battery Press, 1983.

Gelb, L., and Betts, R. *The Irony of Vietnam: The System Worked*. Washington, D.C.: Brookings Institute, 1979.

Generous, Kevin. *Vietnam: The Secret War*. New York: Gallery Books, 1985.

Gibson, James W. *The Perfect War: Technowar in Vietnam.* Boston: Atlantic Monthly Press, 1986.

Hendin, Herbert, and Haas, Ann P. *Wounds of War.* New York: Basic Books, 1984.

Herring, George C. *America's Longest War.* New York: Wiley, 1979.

Herrington, Stuart A. *Silence Was a Weapon: The Vietnam War in the Villages.* Novato, California: Presidio Press, 1982.

————. *Peace with Honor.* Novato, California: Presidio Press, 1983.

Hersh, Seymour. *Cover Up: The Army's Secret Investigation of the Massacre at My Lai.* New York: Random House, 1972.

Horne, A.D., ed. *The Wounded Generation: America After Vietnam.* Englewood Cliffs, N.J.: Prentice-Hall, 1981.

Hoyt, Edwin. *Airborne.* New York: Stein and Day, 1979.

Isaacs, Arnold. *Without Honor: Defeat in Vietnam and Cambodia.* Baltimore: Johns Hopkins University Press, 1983.

Jones, James. *Viet Journal.* New York: Delacorte, 1973.

Just, Ward. *Military Men.* New York: Knopf, 1970.

Kahin, George McTurnan. *Intervention: How America Became Involved in Vietnam.* New York: Knopf, 1986.

Kalb, Bernard, and Kalb, Marvin. *Kissinger.* Boston: Little, Brown, 1974.

————. *The Last Ambassador.* Boston: Little, Brown, 1981.

Klinkowitz, Jerome, and Somer, E. *Writing Under Fire.* New York: Delta, 1978.

Kubey, Craig, et al. *The Viet Vet Survival Guide.* New York: Facts On File, 1985.

Kukler, Michael. *Operation Barrooom I.* Published by the author, 1980.

————. *Operation Barrooom II.* Published by the author, 1985.

Lanning, Michael Lee. *The Only War We Had.* New York: Ivy, 1987.

————. *Vietnam 1969-1970: A Company Commander's Journal.* New York: Ivy, 1988.

————. *Inside the LRRPs: Rangers in Vietnam.* New York: Ivy, 1988.

Levy, Charles J. *Spoils of War.* Boston: Houghton Mifflin, 1974.

Lifton, Robert Jay. *Home From the War.* New York: Simon & Schuster, 1973.

Mahedy, William P. *Out of the Night.* New York: Ballantine, 1986.

Maitland, Derek. *The Only War We've Got.* New York: Morrow, 1971.

Marshall, Kathryn. *In the Combat Zone: An Oral History of American Women in Vietnam*. Boston: Little, Brown, 1987.

McDonough, James. *Platoon Leader*. New York: Bantam, 1985.

Michener, James. *Kent State*. New York: Random House, 1971.

Miller, John Grider. *The Bridge at Dong Ho*. Annapolis: Naval Institute Press, 1989.

Mole, Robert L. *The Montagnards of South Vietnam*. Rutland, Vermont: Charles Tuttle, 1970.

Moore, Gene. *The Killing at Ngo Tho*. New York: Norton, 1967.

O'Ballance, Edgar. *The Wars in Vietnam*. New York: Hippocrene, 1975.

Palmer, Dave Richard. *Summons of the Trumpet: U.S. Vietnam in Perspective*. Novato, California: Presidio Press, 1978.

Palmer, Laura. *Shrapnel in the Heart*. New York: Random House, 1985.

Patterson, James Hamilton. *The Greedy War*. New York: David McKay, 1971.

Patti, L.A. Archimedes. *Why Vietnam? Prelude to America's Albatross*. Berkeley: U. of California Press, 1980.

Peers, William. *The My Lai Inquiry*. New York: Norton, 1979.

Polner, Murray. *No Victory Parades: The Return of the Vietnam Veteran*. New York: Holt, Rinehart and Winston, 1971.

———. *When Can I Come Home?* Garden City, N.Y.: Doubleday, 1972.

Powers, Thomas. *Vietnam, The War at Home: The Antiwar Movement, 1964-1968*. Boston: G.K. Hall, 1984.

Race, Jeffrey. *War Comes to Long An*. Berkeley: U. of California Press, 1972.

Reischauer, Edwin. *Beyond Vietnam*. New York: Vintage, 1967.

Reston, James. *Sherman's March and Vietnam*. New York: Macmillan, 1984.

Rich, Curt. *The Advisors*. New York: Zebra, 1985.

Risner, Robinson. *The Passing of the Night: My Seven Years As a Prisoner of the North Vietnamese*. New York: Random House, 1974.

Roy, Jules. *Battle of Dien Bien Phu*. New York: Pyramid, 1966.

Russell, Lee E. *Armies of the Vietnam War*. London: Osprey Publishing, 1983.

Sanders, Jacquin. *The Draft and the Vietnam War*. New York: Walker, 1966.

Schoenbrun, David. *Vietnam: How We Got In, How to Get Out*. New York: Atheneum, 1968.

Shaplen, Robert. *The Road from War: Vietnam 1965-1970*. New York: Harper & Row, 1970.

Shook, John. *One Soldier*. New York: Bantam, 1986.

Snepp, Frank. *Decent Interval*. New York: Random House, 1977.

Stockwell, Dave. *Tanks in the Wire*. Canton, Ohio: Daring Press, 1989.

Summers, Harry G., Jr. *On Strategy: A Critical Analysis of the Vietnam War*. Novato, California: Presidio Press, 1982.

Thayer, Thomas C. *War Without Fronts: The American Experience in Vietnam*. Boulder: Westview, 1985.

Wagner, William. *Lightning Bugs*. Fallbrook, California: Aero, 1982.

Walt, Gen. Lewis W. *Strange War, Strange Strategy*. New York: Funk & Wagnalls, 1970.

West, Francis. *Small Unit Action in Vietnam*. New York: Arno, 1967.

Wheeler, John. *Touched with Fire: The Future of the Vietnam Generation*. New York: Franklin Watts, 1984.

Willenson, Kim. *The Bad War: An Oral History of the Vietnam Conflict*. New York: New American Library, 1987.

Zaroulis, Nancy, and Sullivan, Gerald. *Who Spoke Up? American Protest Against the War in Vietnam 1963-1975*. Garden City, N.Y.: Doubleday, 1984